WHO OWNS RELIGION?

D1570454

WHO OWNS RELIGION?

SCHOLARS AND THEIR PUBLICS IN
THE LATE TWENTIETH CENTURY

LAURIE L. PATTON

The University of Chicago Press
Chicago and London

The University of Chicago Press, Chicago 60637

The University of Chicago Press, Ltd., London

© 2019 by The University of Chicago

Published 2019

Printed in the United States of America

28 27 26 25 24 23 22 21 20 19   1 2 3 4 5

ISBN-13: 978-0-226-64934-4 (cloth)

ISBN-13: 978-0-226-67598-5 (paper)

ISBN-13: 978-0-226-67603-6 (e-book)

DOI: https://doi.org/10.7208/chicago/9780226676036.001.0001

Library of Congress Cataloging-in-Publication Data

Names: Patton, Laurie L., 1961– author.

Title: Who owns religion? : scholars and their publics in the late twentieth century / Laurie L. Patton.

Description: Chicago : University of Chicago Press, 2019. | Includes bibliographical references and index.

Identifiers: LCCN 2019024350 | ISBN 9780226649344 (cloth) | ISBN 9780226675985 (paperback) | ISBN 9780226676036 (ebook)

Subjects: LCSH: Religion—Study and teaching. | Religion and culture. | Religion and sociology.

Classification: LCC BL41 .P383 2019 | DDC 306.6—dc23

LC record available at https://lccn.loc.gov/2019024350

♾ This paper meets the requirements of ANSI/NISO Z39.48-1992 (Permanence of Paper).

For Shalom, again

CONTENTS

Introduction: Some Reasons for This Book 1

PART ONE: SCANDALS, PUBLICS, AND THE RECENT STUDY OF RELIGION

1 Scandalous Controversies and Public Spaces 19

2 Religions, Audiences, and the Idea of the Public Sphere 49

3 The 1990s: Cultural Recognition, Internet Utopias,
and Postcolonial Identities 67

4 Ancestors' Publics 85

PART TWO: CASE STUDIES

5 *Mother Earth*: The Near Impossibility of a Public 121

6 *The Construction of Religious Boundaries*:
Competing Public Histories 145

7 *Songs of Wisdom and Circles of Dance*: An Emerging
Global Public 169

8 *The Illegitimacy of Jesus*: Strong Publics in Conflict 185

9 *God's Phallus*: The Refusal of Public Engagement 201

10 *Kālī's Child*: The Challenge of Secret Publics 223

PART THREE: NEW PUBLICS, NEW POSSIBILITIES

11 Scholars, Foolish Wisdom, and Dwelling in the Space Between 245

Epilogue 265

Acknowledgments 269   Notes 271
Bibliography 303   Index 329

INTRODUCTION: SOME REASONS FOR THIS BOOK

COLLATING DEATH THREATS

During a particularly gray afternoon at my former university in 2003, I found myself collating death threats. A colleague had written a book twenty years prior that was now being reissued in India. Several members of the Hindu diaspora community objected to the psychoanalytic (and in their view obscene) content, and also to the nude cover, which was an Indian statue chosen by an Indian publisher without consultation with the author. A global petition was mounted demanding that the book be withdrawn, with room for comments by each of the signatories. Throughout the duration of the controversy, most of the critics were neighbors, friends, and interlocutors who lived elsewhere but engaged in a straightforward and civil debate about religious identity. However, at the height of its intensity, the Indian publisher received serious and credible threats from a well-known Hindu militant group. The comments were at first just vaguely threatening, before developing into explicit calls for my colleague's execution through hanging, burning, and shooting.

When the number of such threats reached twenty, the university asked me, as department chair, and the department staff to classify them in a bureaucratic fashion: "actionable" (the second-person pronoun "you" was used in the language of the threat, such as "You will soon die for your acts against us"); not actionable but still a threat (the third-person pronoun "he" was used in the language of the threat, such as "If I were sitting next to him, I would shoot him in the head"); and finally, the numerous calls for a "Hindu fatwa" mentioned on the site. (A fatwa is any legal judgment issued by Muslim religious leaders, but in this case the word was being used by Hindus as a call to action against a person who offended the religion.) All of these comments existed in between carefully thought-out critiques of the work as well as comments of appreciation.

That afternoon I sat between two extremes: the angry response to my colleague's scholarship and the banal organization of academic bureaucracy. I sat between a kind of hostility that had quickly become global and a bureaucracy that some would also call hostile, in the sense that any Western university seeking to control and repress the Other could be perceived as the neoimperialist production of knowledge. Between the death threats and the e-files, a huge, empty chasm existed—a space that used to be occupied by the humanistic study of religion and saw itself as liberal, tolerant, and appreciative. In addition, that space was occupied by engaged, impassioned conversations about the issue, where a large majority of the interlocutors remained connected and respectful, even if in deep disagreement. We were sitting in the liberal paradox: when one's tolerance and openness extend to the point where one is including those who are intolerant—and therefore, those whose values are incommensurate with one's own. In these moments, one must face intolerance in one's midst, while the challenge and paradox and, at times, impossibility become how to respond in a way that is commensurate with one's original values.

That gray afternoon was the moment I realized this book was necessary because such a space needed to be described and delineated. In the 1990s, that space was filled with controversies and scandals, or threatening situations wherein the people from communities represented by the humanistic study of religion began to speak out on their own in both political and intellectual spheres—often angrily. Authors of seemingly harmless and arcane studies on the origins of the idea of Mother Earth or the sexual dynamics of mysticism found themselves the targets of hate mail or the subjects of book-banning discussions. They were rejected by the very communities they had intellectually and emotionally embraced. The communities did not want such an embrace, and they were using their liberal democratic rights to protest what they deemed as inappropriate representation of their histories, traditions, and beliefs. Something had profoundly shifted, and scholars of religion could no longer describe their own work to themselves and to others in the same light as before.[1]

THE LANDSCAPE OF THE BOOK:
RELIGION, CONTROVERSY, AND THE PUBLIC SPHERE

Who Owns Religion? is about the cultural work of the study of religion through a discussion of extreme cases—the controversies of the late 1980s and '90s—where the work of the scholar clashed with the views of the public. In these encounters, the classically liberal cultural work of the secular study of religion was passionately refuted and refused. I did not choose the '90s because the decade provides neatly convenient boundaries of time. Rather, the decade and a half I describe (from 1987 into the early 2000s, in fact) circumscribes a set of moments in which such controversies began to emerge at a fast and furious pace. The conditions for this transformation were (1) the emergence of the multicultural politics of recognition, which changed the nature of debate in the public sphere and created the possibility for what I call in these pages "eruptive public spaces"; (2) the emergence of the internet, which changed the nature of readership for all involved in producing scholarship ("others" about whom one wrote one's "colleagues" were now readers, who could agree, disagree, praise, and condemn in public forums); and (3) in some cases, the emergence of a postcolonial global awareness on the part of transnational religious communities.

To be sure, scandal and controversy are not new to the study of religion; one can recall the audience response to the 1872 lecture of George A. Smith to the British Society of Biblical Archaeology on "the Babylonian Noah" during which his translation of the eleventh tablet of the Epic of Gilgamesh challenged the primacy of the biblical flood story. One might also recall the reaction to Friedrich Delitzsch's 1903 lectures at the German Oriental Society, "The Bible and Babel," when he similarly argued that the creation and flood stories of the book of Genesis had their sources in ancient Babylonian tales. These responses were vehement and resulted in violent outcries against the ideas and the authors who penned them. Yet the nature of the earlier controversies was about the power of science (whether linguistic, psychoanalytic, or other) to interpret the world of religious symbols. Today's controversies continue these themes, but they are also about who owns the right to interpret and the privilege to publish.

In addition, it is also essential to point out that none of the religions discussed in this book were free of controversy before the 1990s. Some controversies—say, in Sikh studies or Hindu studies—took place in colonial or recently postcolonial contexts on other continents before the religions' arrival in North America. Other controversies took place in early to mid-twentieth-century North America between Native American groups and the United States and Canadian governments. Still others took place between Jewish and Catholic seminaries and secular reading publics.

And herein lies the crucial difference. These contemporary debates may include those dimensions, but they are also about something else: the very rights of secular, Western scholars to interpret religions at all. This debate is a larger issue that has emerged in the academy. The question raised by some leading scholars of religion in response to the Danish cartoon controversy, for example, was "Is critique secular?" In a work by that same title, Talal Asad, Saba Mahmoud, Wendy Brown, and Judith Butler all question the assumption that secular critique is inherently powerful and has an unchallengeable moral force of its own.[2] To be sure, this issue has been at the front and center of the postmodern turn in literary and cultural studies. Yet these thinkers are also concerned about the issue of secular critique in the public sphere, not just the academic one. The Danish cartoon controversy raised many issues, among them: How does secular critique of religion claim a cultural space outside the walls of academic peer review? My own view is that these authors are right to query secularism's origins and point out, as many recently have, the ambiguity of the category in its relationship to religion and the state.[3] My interest is in what happens in the public sphere when secular methods are not just critiqued by intellectuals but grow entangled in debate with those whose worlds have been described by those methods.

I wonder about the space between—a place that very few scholars understood they would occupy when they were writing their PhDs. The work of this book, then, is a kind of phenomenological history of the public sphere. I use this term first because it places accounts of scandalous controversies in the study of religion in juxtaposition to key thinkers in the theory of the public sphere. Beginning with Jürgen Habermas and moving to his critics and contemporary theorists, such as Nancy Fraser and James Bohman, the book assesses the work of scholars of religion as that work has affected those outside the university's walls. It also assesses the response by the communities to the scholars and the conversation that ensues in the emergent, turbulent space—what Habermas calls the "wild sphere," and what I prefer to call an "eruptive public space."[4] As I hope readers will see in these pages, I define an eruptive public space as a sudden, rapidly emergent, and controversial public conversation about the representation of religious traditions, where offense is taken and cultural norms of open debate are violated. I distinguish it from a public sphere in that, as traditionally theorized, such a sphere usually contains either explicit or implicit norms of behavior. In addition, many of these conversations still fall within the American legal rubric of freedom of expression and freedom of academic inquiry, and legal challenges tend not to be viable. The focus of the eruptive public space, then, falls on the role of individual scholars, their respect for the traditions they study, and the privilege of the academic worlds from which they come.

I use the word "phenomenological" because I am focusing exclusively on the public sphere as it emerges in its objects that can be directly experienced—i.e., in its participants' voluntary contributions to public discourse. *Who Owns Religion?* pays primary attention to the space between scholars and their publics. In light of this emphasis, I am referring only to documents included in the public record, whether they are transcripts of the radio addresses and published journals of earlier theorists of religion, published books and book reviews of contemporary scholars involved in controversies, reports of experiences published in anthologies, or websites of resistant communities. Had I used private interviews, uncovered further secrets, and unearthed hidden documents, it would have been another kind of book indeed. Perhaps someone will write that book, too.

Who Owns Religion? is also a book that deals with the awkwardly recent period of the 1990s—a decade that is not completely archival. It is still very much within memory and yet not quite current. The decade of the '90s offers that uncomfortable perspective of what Claire Potter and Renee Romano call "recent history."[5] As they remind us, recent historians are challenged by several issues: Do they have enough of an "archive" to back up their claims? Are they writing too soon to know the full impact of certain events? Can any historian really be objective when he or she is dealing with events that still resonate in the present context? All of these are legitimate concerns; hence my term "phenomenological history of the public sphere." Fully acknowledging that the archive is still being completed, the accounts in these pages emphasize the experience and emergence of those "spaces between" as they interrupt the consciousness of both academic and religious communities.

These case studies are both comparable and incomparable. They are comparable in that they all occurred in that space in the late twentieth century when multicultural identity politics and internet readerships collided. They are also comparable in that communities that confronted scholars and universities found themselves puzzling anew over free speech and the question of religious offense. In aggregate, they comprise a "moment" in the study of religions that has shaped the twenty-first century in important ways, in that the controversies have continued and readerships have permanently shifted.

The case studies are different in that the study of every religious tradition has its own history and dynamics. Originating as they do from very different subfields in the study of religion, the case studies might seem too general for the specialist and too specialized for someone approaching the field for the first time. In addition, the scholars' identities varied in national origin, ethnicity, and position in the field. Some were outsiders to the religious traditions they studied; others were insiders; still others had been insiders and had moved away from the tradition. All of them used methods of secular history or cultural critique. Some of them understood themselves as sympathetic but critical insiders; others understood themselves as fellow-traveler outsiders; still others understood themselves as critical outsiders. Some felt their positionality changing as they experienced the controversy. And yet, in my view, these differences made the cases not incomparable but rather intriguingly different in the way that such controversies were handled and new publics erupted onto the scene.

THE PLACE FROM WHICH I WRITE

I began writing this book thirteen years ago, as a relatively young but established scholar interested in the large number of fraught interactions between academic institutions and religious communities. Thirteen years and many other projects later, my interest in the idea of the public sphere, and the intense fragility of those spaces of encounter between insiders and outsiders, has only increased. During those years I have worked as a scholar/administrator, responsible for the public sphere of the classroom and liberal arts institutions as a whole. I write now as a strong advocate for liberal learning, one who is also keenly aware of the need for change in the twenty-first century, when the definitions of readers, writers, scholars, critics, insiders, and outsiders are even more fluid than they were in the 1990s. The final chapter is influenced by this responsibility to create the conditions of a vibrant, inclusive public sphere—one where more and more voices are included and fundamental freedoms must also be preserved. Because of that experience, it is clear to me that advocacy for the study of religion to exist in the academy, no matter how broadly rooted, is not enough. Nor is the simple intellectual resistance to academic structures of power that may threaten the study of religion. Another form of activity is also necessary: reflection about, and understanding of, the forms of pluralism that constitute the worlds both within and outside the academy. Such reflection is no longer a luxury, or even an important scholarly pursuit: it is a democratic necessity. Scholars who see their roles primarily as social critics may not be comfortable with what might seem in their view overly normative suggestions about possible ways forward; scholars who are primarily looking for solutions may not be completely comfortable with the detail of the case studies—which in my view is necessary to make the case for a new relationship to the public sphere. I call this combination of approaches "high pragmatism": the merging of scholarly views focused on social critique and those favoring solutions.

To put it another way, ongoing inquiry into the nature of our publics, our scholarly contexts, and our individual positions within those contexts is necessary not only so that we might have a coherent sense of our topics of study, as scholars of the mid-twentieth century argued, or of our subjective positions, as scholars of the late twentieth century argued. Rather, such reflection is necessary because we need analyses of the "spaces between," where contact between academic institutions and the communities they study occurs in all of its richness, controversy, and eruptive power.

Moreover, in the thirteen years since I began work on this book, simply by virtue of the passing of time, what was an assessment of "our current dilemma" became an exercise in recent intellectual history. The time period figured as all the more important because it traced one small part of what Andrew Hartman called "the war for the soul of America" in the 1990s, when culture clashes emerged in the headlines as a major piece of our everyday experience in the academy. Following the work of Robert Greene and other thinkers about that decade, citizens of all kinds may have a real challenge in moving beyond such clashes and the fracturing of American culture that appeared with such frequency in that period.[6]

The major theoretical interlocutors through which I make sense of these events are Jürgen Habermas and those critics who engage his recent turn to address religion in the early twenty-first century. As I will discuss in a later chapter, Habermas's treatment of religion in the public sphere is motivated by two factors: the idea that religion could be a source for more secular ideas of human dignity, and that the resurgent fundamentalism of the late twentieth and early twenty-first century is worthy of investigation and critique. Habermas became interested in the politics of ethnic identity, which focused on culturally substantive discourse rather than procedures of common reasoning.[7] These interests led him to posit what he has called a "wild sphere" in which members of religious communities could not enter the public sphere without becoming unintelligible, and it became necessary to translate religious reasons into secular ones in order to participate fully in the democratic sphere.

If such translation is required, then how does participation in the public sphere occur for religious communities? The critiques of Habermas by Nancy Fraser, María Herrera Lima, Thomas McCarthy, and James Bohman, among others, raise questions of who belongs, who is marginalized, and whose histories are accepted in the delineation of the public sphere.[8] They also propose a stronger role for historical studies in the reading of the public square, in order "to understand the changed historical and social conditions for religious beliefs and practices in our secular age."[9] The historical studies in this book demonstrate that Habermas could benefit from what Thomas McCarthy calls "a still sharper descent from the heights of transcendental philosophy," where modern discourse is open at multiple points to contestation.[10] Moreover, they join Charles Taylor in emphasizing the fact that in its contemporary forms, religion is one factor among others in choice of identity. Thus, religious thought and practice cannot be a sole remedy, nor a sole cause, for the fracturing of the public sphere, given that it is appealed to as one cultural form of identity among many. These points of fracture in the public sphere are endless, and in my view worthy of study in their own right. They represent the failure of liberal culture to find "a third way between old antagonsms."[11]

The recent history of the case studies in this book shows that such fractures are caused by resistance to the rules of the public sphere; that resistance occurs for a variety of reasons. It might occur because a traumatic history of colonization has made it historically impossible or disadvantageous for the communities to engage until now. That same history might have made it only recently and sporadically possible to engage on equal terms. It might occur because the established norms of religious reasoning are threatened by secular norms of reasoning, whether because of sexual taboos or social-historical ones. It might occur because of a combination of these factors. The balance of power may or may not lie with academic institutions in these cases, but all of them force such institutions to reflect on their status, privilege, and ability to interpret in this new environment. Hence their eruptive, scandalous nature.

I also write having made particular hermeneutic choices. My focus is on the work of the individual scholar, and the nature of the public record surrounding that scholar's work, including public accounts of the scholar's individual experience. Readers will likely find, as I did in the writing of this book, that they identify with different communities at different moments—sometimes seeing more clearly the reasons of the academy, sometimes those of the communities. For all the reasons we know so well, I make no pretense to neutral description. I am a scholar of South Asia by training; thus, three of the case studies I encountered are informed by South Asian perspectives, as are some of the theorists I have found compelling in thinking through transnational issues raised by the case studies in this book. I am committed to and have written about academic freedom. I am also supportive of both critics and sympathizers in a broadly conceived "big tent" study of religion. Most importantly for this work, I am committed to creating an academic practice where scholars with a variety of methodological approaches and stances can regularly engage in more sustained reflection about eruptive public spaces and organized public spheres. In the contexts of these commitments, I have nonetheless tried to be as evenhanded as possible in focusing on the dialogue that occurs between religious and scholarly worlds.

My interpretive choices are also based on the idea that, while it is surely not the only category—nor even a superior one—an individual scholarly agent is a helpful category with which to think. There are several other analytical vantage points I hope can and will be pursued by others; for example, it would be important to examine the long-term institutional histories of these controversies, over decades or even centuries, whether at an individual academic establishment or within an individual religious tradition, or move into more sustained analysis of the uses and balances of power and privilege in these and other cases. An individual scholar's capacity to write in, respond to, and reflect on the public sphere is only one place from which to start. There are many perspectives with which we can, in Tom Tweed's words, "cross and dwell" into further contexts and implications of our scholarship today.

THE CHAPTERS

In chapter 1, "Scandalous Controversy and Public Spaces," I look at the words used to describe the spaces in between academic institutions and their publics in the study of religion. In my analysis of the terms "controversy" and "scandal," I argue that they are useful words to describe what happens when liberal scholars with good intent write books about religious communities that the religious communities themselves object to. I find a great deal of useful material with which to address the experiences and concerns of scholars in the twenty-first century. They are compelling, dramatic, painful, and instructive "spaces in between," and worthy of analysis in their own right.

In chapter 2, "Public Spheres/Public Spaces," I consider these cultural conflicts in light of theories of the public sphere. These moments are challenges to the Habermasian idea of the public sphere, and in my view are best analyzed in light of that tradition. In my discussion of Habermas and his critics, I pursue a theoretical assessment of the idea of the public sphere and its relevance to controversies and scandals in the study of religion. As I anticipate the analysis of the case studies to follow in part 2, I use the ways in which Habermas's critics make the public sphere a multiple and complex space. In addition, I point out the distinction between the concept of a rule-governed public "sphere" and that of a less contractual, more chaotic public "space." This is what Habermas calls, in a later essay, the "wild sphere." Because of its problematic connotations of a civilized/wild opposition, I suggest instead the idea of an eruptive public space, which I define as a form of discourse that interrupts and refuses to follow the implicit or explicit rules governing established public spheres.

I also discuss in particular the role of history and sexuality in the debates. When these debates are indeed conducted as part of a shared conversation between members of a religious community and scholars, they are to be distinguished from the new trends in public history, where rules of marking history are negotiated in a collegial and clear environment. In contrast, I argue that these histories are best understood as eruptive histories, part of an eruptive public space.

Chapter 3, "The 1990s: Cultural Recognition, Internet Utopias, and Postcolonial Identities," turns to look at these controversies in light of the multicultural politics of recognition that emerged so powerfully in the '90s. I begin by arguing that most of these episodes took place in the larger American context in which the culture wars were heating up on both sides of American public life. Then, drawing on Kwame Anthony Appiah's *Ethics of Identity* and other writings, I argue that Appiah's three categories of multicultural recognition—respect, life-script, and membership within a community—are key drivers of the dynamics of these scandalous episodes. I also argue, with James Beckford, that religion is best understood in these controversies as a "cultural resource" to be mobilized, rather than a transcendent or private personal refuge. These cases show that religious identity is also an inherently multiple and intersectional one. However, the dynamics of the controversies show that it can seldom be recognized as such in the context of eruptive public space.

In addition, I look at the dynamics of the early emergence of the internet in each of these controversies. I argue that the spontaneous forms of internet communities that emerged in the '90s in resistance to scholarship from the academy had some of the characteristics of what scholars call "religion online" or "religion through the net." In addition, much of the internet discourse and theory of the '90s had the utopian tone that viewed the internet as the best medium for democratic considered debate. However, the ultimate results of internet practices tended to be ones of attack and censorship, where "paper tigers" could engage more aggressively than they might have in person.

In chapter 4, "Ancestors' Publics," I begin to think about the idea of the public sphere within the field's own recent intellectual history—exploring the theories of W. C. Smith and Mircea Eliade. Rather than focus on the usual issues in relationship to their work—the question of tradition and faith (or the representation of Islam in the case of W. C. Smith, or the methodology of the morphology of religion and comparative work of symbols in the case of Mircea Eliade)—I take up the important but until now somewhat peripheral question of their approach to the idea of the public sphere. How did they understand the role of the scholar in relationship to the larger public? What did they understand the cultural implication of their work to be?

We see in both cases that their answers, while different from each other, still assume a straightforward liberalization of the public sphere as the number one cultural work of the scholar of religion. In W. C. Smith's case, it is the creation of a religious commons in which people of all faiths can interact. In the case of Mircea Eliade, it is the creation of a liberal perspective through interpretation of ancient texts—an interpretation that can allow for a new version of the sacred to emerge in public life, particularly through arts and literature. In neither case does the complexity of the public sphere emerge in its own right. In their view, the study of religion correctly conducted will find a way to modify and open up any lack of tolerance in culture at large.

Chapter 5, "*Mother Earth*: The Near Impossibility of a Public," inaugurates part 2, my treatment of the controversies of the 1980s and '90s. In 1987, Sam Gill wrote a book called *Mother Earth: An American Story*. In it, he argues that the basic idea of Mother Earth is just that—an idea, an adept use of metaphor that the Native Americans had to employ in their negotiations with the US government, but never an actual goddess. Gill's argument is that the concept of Mother Earth was not originally or fully indigenous to Native American peoples. A great movement resulted in which Native American scholars and activists witnessed to the contrary. The most moderate of his critics acknowledged that Gill was partly correct, and that the idea of Mother Earth has been interpreted and reinterpreted over time. Nonetheless, the charge was that Gill ignored evidence that the fundamental notion is both ancient and widespread.

However, the more strong-minded of Gill's critics argued that this kind of writing is, in effect, the inevitable racism of white people who studies the native. During the '90s, Native American leaders such as Russell Means, Ward Churchill, Deward Walker, Vine Deloria, and others became activists against Gill, speaking at several Indian conferences and pow-wows throughout the country. In one exchange, scholar/activist Deward Walker accused the study of anthropology of "gross irrelevance"—an intriguing and persistent claim that kept surfacing in my study of the definition of scandal as well as the controversies themselves.

Chapter 6, "*The Construction of Religious Boundaries*: Competing Public Histories," discusses the intriguing case of the Sikh response to Harjot Oberoi. Awarded a chair of Sikh studies at the University of British Columbia in 1987, he published his *Construction of Religious Boundaries: Culture, Identity, and Diversity in the Sikh Tradition* in 1994. The Sikh community's objections to the work came rapidly—most of it centering on his claims (characteristic of this generation of new historicist approaches) that the Sikh community constructed its identity according to specific social formations and power structures within the various, very different Sikh communities, rather than as a single, natural progression of Sikh revelation from God, beginning with Guru Nanak and elaborated more fully by Guru Gobind Singh.

Because members of the Sikh community had donated money for the chair, their objections were quite vociferous and circulated in a number of publications in Canada, the United States, and the Punjab. A panel of Sikh theologians was dispatched to examine Oberoi on specifics of Sikh doctrine, in which he was found greatly wanting. After some deliberation, Oberoi decided to leave his post, taking a year's leave. He has since found another academic position in the university. In this chapter, I examine the issue of postcolonial theological orthodoxy in a diaspora context, and its relative influence on the historian. I also discuss the Sikh community's use of "lists" of scholars who are friendly to Sikhism and those who are not, as a litmus test for appropriate and correct interpretation.

Chapter 7, "*Songs of Wisdom and Circles of Dance*: An Emerging Global Public," takes up several of the postcolonial issues raised by Oberoi's work but places them in the context of a newly conservative community of Ismaili Muslims. In 1995, Tazim Kassam published her book *Songs of Wisdom and Circles of Dance: Hymns of the Satpanth Ismāʾīlī Muslim Saint, Pīr Shams*. A thirteenth-century saint, Pir Shams was also a composer and a pivotal figure in the tradition of Ginans, daily liturgical hymns used by the Fatand Nizari Ismaili sect of Shia Muslims. Many of these Ginans represent a Hindu-Muslim synthesis of a highly creative kind. Like Oberoi with his historical study of the Sikhs, Kassam attempts a historical reconstruction of the origins of a religious group: the Sat Panths Ismailis, the Indian version of the Fatand Nizari sect.

Some members of the Ismaili community who had access to the book before it was distributed found some of the language and illustrations too graphic for a community that was becoming more "Islamic." The diaspora Ismaili community launched a crusade to prevent the book from being leaving the warehouse. Kassam received email, phone, and snail-mail messages recommending fatwa and suggesting that her fate would be the same as Salman Rushdie's if the book were to be printed.

This chapter focuses on the role of an Ismaili diaspora community in transition and the ways in which a group trying to ally itself more closely with a mainstream world religion (in this case, Islam) might find the idea of syncretic tradition threatening. A historically accurate presentation may undermine the claims of Muslim legitimacy that disallow such religious blending. In this sense, Kassam's case shows the ways that the Ismaili community would prefer to deny those aspects of its own tradition.

Chapter 8, "*The Illegitimacy of Jesus*: Strong Publics in Conflict," discusses the 1987 work of Jane Schaberg. Focusing on the Gospel of Matthew, Schaberg summarizes the arguments for the Gospel text being about an illegitimate conception rather than a miraculous Virgin Birth. Only Matthew and Luke mention it (and even there, some early manuscripts of Luke imply the Virgin Birth is an interpolation into that Gospel). Moreover, as Schaberg argues, Matthew never explicitly mentions a miraculous conception, only a providential one. Gabriel's visitation allows Joseph a righteous and legal solution to the dilemma of his betrothed's pregnancy. Moreover, there are few parallels for divine birth in pagan literature of the time. Finally, Schaberg argues that the use of the term "virgin" in the Matthean account is to stress that before she became pregnant with Jesus, Mary was a virgin. Jesus, then, was a result of adultery or rape. According to Schaberg, "Matthew's point is that his [Jesus's] existence is divinely willed; his messiahship was not negated by the way he was conceived."[12]

Schaberg was vehemently attacked by the Christian right and received threats as well as excoriations of her work on the internet and in the conservative Christian press. She was hailed as the latest icon of the triumph of ideology (in this case, feminist) over Christian belief. In the view of many of her critics, no one who questioned the Virgin Birth could possibly also be a Christian. In this chapter, I focus on the negotiations of power between the various Christian schools of interpretation. Moreover, I argue that it is not simply Schaberg's denial of the Virgin Birth but her open discussion of Mary's sexuality that is offensive to both the Catholic and the Protestant orthodoxies. Her open commitment to reading the Gospels as artistic renditions as well as guides for action also creates a space for scandal in the larger public world.

Chapter 9, "*God's Phallus*: The Refusal of Public Engagement," addresses perhaps the most unusual controversy in the group of case studies—that of Howard Schwartz (formally Howard Eilberg-Schwartz). Schwartz wrote two mildly controversial works involving Freudian analysis, although neither of them engendered the level of controversy that Jeffrey Kripal's Freudian treatment of Ramakrishna did. His first work, *The Savage in Judaism: An Anthropology of Israelite Religion and Ancient Judaism* (1990), argues that Judaism shares many more elements of earlier Middle Eastern religions than most contemporary scholars are willing to admit. His second, *God's Phallus: And Other Problems for Men and Monotheism* (1995), claims there is a homoerotic element to Hebrew Bible writings. In his view, God's male qualities create interpretive challenges for both ancient and contemporary Jews.

When Schwartz did not receive tenure at Stanford, he moved to occupy the chair of Jewish studies at San Francisco State University. During his time there, Schwartz encountered pressure from both African American and pro-Israel activists. Most decisively, he experienced pressure from the Jewish community to support the policies of the State of Israel in a far more positive way than he felt able to in good conscience. Schwartz left the academy altogether and retrained himself as an internet marketing executive. At stake for Schwartz, as for Oberoi, was whether he could fulfill his community's wishes in occupying the chair of Jewish studies. And for him, the culture wars on both sides were too great.

In chapter 10, "*Kālī's Child*: The Challenge of Secret Publics," I analyze the "sexual offenses" in Jeffrey Kripal's work. In *Kālī's Child* (1995), Kripal argues that homoerotic perspectives were influential in the Hindu saint Ramakrishna's spiritual development; this is part of a larger overall argument about the relationship between eroticism and mysticism, which he later contemplated at length in his *Roads of Excess, Palaces of Wisdom* (2001). After the publication of *Kālī's Child*, scathing attacks were published in Calcutta's *Statesman* newspaper and a number of other Indian newspapers and websites; a motion to ban the book was put before the Indian Parliament, and two very lengthy reviews by Swami Tayagananda of the Boston Vedanta society and by authors on the Hindu site Sulekha emerged on the web.

In this chapter, I focus specifically on the issue of homosexuality and eroticism in contemporary study of Hinduism. The debate about *Kālī's Child* focused on Kripal's claims that some of Ramakrishna's actions were homoerotic. Some Indian publics would not interpret the same acts in the same way. Relatedly, in the course of this scandal, the hugely vexing issue of the use of Freudian psychoanalytic categories in the interpretation of Hinduism emerged front and center. Hindu critics claim that Westerners eroticize their tradition; yet these critics must still come to terms with the presence of explicitly sexual elements in many saints' biographies and Sanskrit texts of Hindu tantra.

Chapter 11 constitutes part 3, "New Publics and Eruptive Spaces." Part 3 provides the interpretive analysis central to the close readings of the case studies that I hope to have provided in part 2. In chapter 11, "Scholars, Foolish Wisdom, and the Space in Between," I analyze the nature of these eruptive public spaces. Grounded now in the previous discussions of six case studies, I return to the phenomenology of public spheres. I show here that there are various imbalances within North American culture that create fertile ground for such spaces to erupt. These are imbalances in expectations and in relative empowerment between universities and religious institutions—between scholars and members of religious communities. I argue that there are a number of vulnerabilities both on the part of scholars and on the part of communities that make these situations particularly volatile. In addition, in the public spaces that erupt, a visible sign of fissures is almost always already present in the communities' relationship to the academy.

Also in chapter 11, I return to the question of what might be done in this new environment in which we find ourselves, and how we might dwell in the space between the university and the community. Here, I suggest that the scholar of religion has a role similar to that of the wise fool in many classical dramas, and indeed in many religious traditions. They each have multiple masters, and they must move between them while speaking a truth that some of those masters may not be interested in hearing. I also suggest ways that scholars might begin to think through a theory of religion in the context of a theory of the institution in which they work and a theory of the public sphere. The epilogue briefly chronicles the cases known to me that have occurred since the 1990s.

Acknowledging such multiplicity, scholars of religion might be more able to come to terms with the liberal paradox of tolerance—the problem of engaging those who will not engage us on our own terms of tolerance. In addition, I argue that no theory of religion in the twenty-first century should exist without an accompanying theory of the university that produces such theories. Neither should a theory of religion exist without a theory of the public sphere. I end with a call to reflection, and propose a set of questions that scholars might ask themselves as they write. These questions alone might create a space for scholars and communities to enter and exit, and to reflect, to engage, and to dwell, even if only temporarily.

PART ONE

SCANDALS, PUBLICS, AND THE RECENT STUDY OF RELIGION

1

SCANDALOUS CONTROVERSIES AND PUBLIC SPACES

THE OPPORTUNITY OF THE DOUBLE, OR MULTIPLE, BIND

Until recent decades, scholars of religion may not have engaged actual communities. These communities are plural, argumentative, constantly changing, and impossible to define, but I have been haunted by their ghosts—*simulacrae* that might have been designated by the single, all-encompassing word "community." As if there were centuries of common assent, rather than dissent, behind the ghost. The ghost tapped me on the shoulder and, in my academic imagination, made a variety of demands in the past: *Be empathic. Be one of us. Don't treat us as disembodied. Don't just study our texts. Don't just study our rituals.* They were didactic ghosts, and by their very conjuring, they pointed out moral shortcomings and my inabilities to be fully relevant to the communities that I studied. Sometimes scholars were parts of those communities, and sometimes they were not. Sometimes the ghosts existed in a gray area in between communities and academies.

Then there were the ghosts of the academy tapping me on the other shoulder, making their demands: *Be scientific. Be social scientific. Be comprehensible. Be humanist. Be socially responsible. Criticize religion as an oppressor of the people. Understand religion as a function of economics, power, and polity. Only engage in a classical discipline in the study of religion, such as that of social science or literary theory.* I was haunted by the fact that many of the arguments in the study of religion and its various subfields were also arguments between disciplines played out on the body of any given religious practice, text, ideology, or theology.

Here, too, it was not the actual academic community but its ghosts—
a single glare of scientific, social scientific, or humanistic consensus to
whom religion was a profound embarrassment, if not a violation of the
norms of reason and all reasonable people. Scholars are still arguing
whether religion belongs in our academic world, and I was arguing with
our ghosts at all levels and perspectives: institutional, intellectual, and
pedagogical.

I have often found myself thinking that these ghosts can somehow,
someday be conjured up and exorcised—reading and teaching and writing
articles as if the solution might be just around the corner. Yet I also found
myself wondering whether these ghosts may never be exorcised. As long as
religions exist, there will be a need to interpret them. And the interpreter
should demand a place in the academy, and that place must be justified and
defended in a manner comprehensible to that institution of reason.

POSITIONING THE IDEA OF RELIGION

Recent decades have seen compelling work by scholars who engage the
issues on all sides of this question of positionality. While any individual
scholar's list will inevitably be incomplete, I see, broadly speaking, three
ways of thinking about the issue: (1) the call through particular religious
traditions to note the constructedness of the idea of religion and its relationship to historical consciousness; (2) the call to see the institutional
origins and ongoing inflections of the idea of religion, and the blind spots
it engenders; and (3) the call to a moral relationship with our subjects of
study as a way through those blind spots.

There are many examples from subfields in the study of religion to
think through the question of when, and how, and whether a particular
religious tradition might have come to understand itself as a "religion,"
and the institutional and social realities that undergird that understanding. The bibliography is now voluminous. Recent work in the study of Judaism examines Judaism and the idea of historical consciousness, as well
as how Judaism became a "religion" and its relative fit with the contemporary idea of religion as an individual faith choice.[1] In the past two decades,
the study of Hinduism and other South Asian traditions has been highly
active in producing a literature on the study of the "invention" of Hinduism through a colonial and postcolonial lens.[2] The study of Buddhism
has been taken up with both institutional origins and histories, as well as

Buddhist traditions fit with contemporary science.[3] The construction of religion as a category of identity in Christianity and Islam was crystallized in a foundational essay by Talal Asad contemporaneous with the controversies in this book, with many other works about the construction of religious identity in both traditions to follow.[4]

Asad's essay was important for more general reasons in this period. In it, he argues that the idea of "religion" is a "function" as much as an academic discipline; the analytic category of religion is a product of secular modernity and its discourse, not necessarily a coherent notion in its own right. Rejecting essentialist definitions of religion, many others, such as Daniel Dubuisson, Tomoko Masuzawa, Brent Nongbri, and Timothy Fitzgerald expanded upon this insight in the next decade.[5] In his well-known *Ideology of Religious Studies*, Fitzgerald argues for the abandonment of the category of "religion" altogether, stating that use of the term should be more properly situated in liberal ecumenical theology. What is more, for Fitzgerald, the use of the term over time has been at best a kind of masked Protestant theology and at worst a weapon of power in the hands of colonial and neocolonial projects.[6]

The institutional question has been taken up by Masuzawa, who argues for the construction of world religions as a function of European identity. For her, theorists of religion have understood European history as universal history and a kind of "prototype" that can give all categories of religion both their unity and their plurality. The "world religions" list is remarkably stable, and that stability is the basis upon which Masuzawa criticizes contemporary religious studies. She argues that contemporary scholars are unwilling to see their discursive practice of "world religions" as a "category and conceptual framework initially developed in the European academy." For Masuzawa, the result of that lack of awareness is that this conceptual framework continues to be totalizing, othering, suprahistorical, and depoliticizing. Masuzawa makes a normative case for historical rigor, textual precision, and theoretical sophistication, as well as a connection to understanding the emergence of a secular university.[7]

Winnifred Sullivan has raised another question of the institutional representation of religion, particularly in relationship to the perceived "secular" focus of the United States, and the way religion is defined and practiced in legal contexts. Her view is that the separation between the religious and the secular is increasingly less tenable descriptively. Understanding Americans to be fundamentally religious is now deeply embedded in government and in our public culture. This is true not only for legal and government perspectives but also because religion and spirituality are being naturalized; the idea of "faith-based organizations" and "faith-based individuals" is increasingly the norm.[8] Even generic terms such as "spirituality" have historical and institutional roots, and such practices might be better understood if they were analyzed, as Courtney Bender does, in light of those roots and not in the ahistorical dimensions in which practitioners and scholars alike often place them.[9]

The call for institutional awareness and historical situatedness can also possess a normative, if not a moral, component. This is true for Masuzawa, as well as Fitzgerald, in calling for greater awareness of the imbrication of the category of religion in the Protestant, European, and colonial projects. With his later work on South Africa, to take another example, Chidester exposes the colonial construct in the idea of religion in South Africa, as well as the influence of African colonialism in the study of religion more generally.

Relatedly, Russ McCutcheon has argued that, in addition to understanding religion's role in the context of European and American power, scholars should take their role as critics of religion seriously. If they do not, then they, too, will only continue the conundrum, the blurring of our intellectual and doctrinal roles. McCutcheon argues that this is an obligation whether scholars are members of a religious tradition or not. As his *Discipline of Religion* summarizes:

> The invention of religion as a discipline blurs the distinction between criticism and doctrine in its assertion of the relevance of faith as a credible object of study. In the leap from disciplinary criticism to avowal of actual cosmic and moral meaning, schools of religious studies extend their powers far beyond universities and into the everyday lives of those outside, managing and curtailing specific types of speech and dissent.[10]

McCutcheon goes on to argue that the liberal paradox is very rarely acknowledged or engaged by scholars, partly because it fails to acknowledge multiple publics and, as Nancy Fraser has also suggested, multiple dimensions of public life:

> Failing to have the complexity and interconnectedness of all acts of social formation brought to their attention, along with conveniently overlooking the ever-present intolerance of all social ideologies—liberalism included—

readers of such articles are thus confirmed in their presumptions that social identity is homogenous, self-evident, and eternal, that we are good,
that they are evil, that we are innocent, that they are guilty (Burton Mack's
"myth of innocence" is alive and well), and that behaviors and interests that
diverge from our sense of the status quo are simply the result of insanity or
fanaticism.[11]

McCutcheon's call for us to acknowledge the scholar's social role is part
of the larger project we might embark on, the "complexity and intercon-
nectedness of all acts of social formation." It could involve any number of
contexts of the scholar: the town where she grew up, the school she went
to, her first intellectual influences, and so on. Those certainly are subjects
of the essays in José Cabezón and Sheila Davaney's edited volume *Identity and the Politics of Scholarship in the Study of Religion*—a work that engages, at an autobiographical level, the controversies as they are lived by
the scholar in his or her historical and institutional contexts.[12]

The call for situatedness of the category of religion, and the related
call for the scholar as critic, resulted not only in a call for the oblitera-
tion of the endeavor of criticism but also in a call for the broadening of
the category. In 2005, for example, Chidester argued for the inclusion
of popular culture and its objects with local and global contexts as part of
the study of religion.[13] This approach burgeoned in the late 1990s and the
first decade of the next century, when work by Gary Laderman and others
began to look at religious elements in a wide variety of seemingly nonreligious contexts.[14] For many of these scholars of religion and culture, the
"emic" or "insider" view of a participant in a popular cultural movement
or a new religious movement has the same effect as in a more officially
designated religious tradition. These scholars' larger focus is to include a
broader number of social phenomena within the category of religion; in
this they share the idea that certain "lesser" or "wild" traditions should be
part of religious studies' purview.

In addition to jettisoning, historicizing, or broadening the term "religion" and its attendant terminology, scholars also embarked on a different project: the moral critique of practitioners of the study of religion.
One such essay, Robert Orsi's "Snakes Alive," quickly became a classic
after it was published: he points out the hierarchical judgments inherent
in religious studies, whereby scholars implicitly embrace a pecking order
of religious idioms—some more valuable than others.[15] These judgments
are, for Orsi, forms of unacknowledged bias and include distinctions like

"local," "primitive," and "infantile," descriptors that signal lesser, or often "folk," traditions. These are opposed to the scholar's idea of universal, developed, and mature traditions. Such binaries preclude scholars' real engagement and participation with their objects of study.

Orsi advocates for an "in-between" stance, "at the intersection of self and other, at the boundary between one's own moral universe and the moral world of the other." He also names the liberal paradox, as I also have in the introduction to this book: "This space is a dangerous one because one cannot after all simply abandon one's deepest values, or tolerate the intolerable."[16] In "Belief Unbracketed," Stephen Prothero takes the moral focus one step further and asks that we tackle moral issues head on by "tearing down the barrier against our own judgments and move toward a deeper moral engagement with our subjects."[17]

The approach to the question of how the idea of religion is constructed, and in particular religious pluralism, that is most helpful for this book is not a monograph but an edited volume, whose multidisciplinary approach is compatible with the present work. In their *After Pluralism: Reimagining Religious Engagement*, editors Courtney Bender and Pamela Klassen have curated essays that range from philosophy to history to legal studies and back again. Like Masuzawa, they want to avoid taking "pluralism" per se as a cultural and philosophical given, instead arguing that pluralism, and engagements between religions, "must be understood as emerging in specific contexts and places, as a discourse of the future that cannot escape the past." In their view, the study of specific entanglements involving the idea of pluralism, such as the limits of a constitutional definition of religion and how it might be experienced in a court case, or actual encounters between religious groups, is deeply instructive for scholars of religion—whether they are philosophers, political theorists, sociologists, or historians. In their words, "The doctrines and programs of pluralism that dominate contemporary academic and public conversations do not constitute a theory of understanding religious interactions as they take place in the world."[18] An analysis of those religious interactions in terms beyond a simple pluralist doctrine is necessary. So too, I would argue, the engagements between scholars and the communities they study are part of those real-world entanglements and should be studied in a theoretically grounded way.[19] The theoretical grounding of *Who Owns Religion?* is the critical discussion of religion and the public sphere, primarily in the Habermasian tradition; the real-world entanglements are the case studies discussed in part 2.[20]

This idea brings us full circle to the question of how scholars might study themselves. In his early essay, Asad called not only for situating the origins of the idea of religion in academic practice but for a study of academic performance itself—with conversation about religion as one of its language games. As Asad states in an interview on the twentieth anniversary of *Genealogies of Religion*, he wants to place the idea of religion "as practice, language, and sensibility set in social relationships rather than as systems of meaning."[21] This present book might be seen as a partial contribution to that call—focused as it is on historical cases of arguments between scholars and practitioners, two publics with different kinds of rules, about the very idea of religion. As a way of taking up Asad's invitation, I found myself wondering, What if scholars grow comfortable with the ghosts? And the multiple nature of all the worlds they inhabit? And the insolubility of the conflict?

Institutionally speaking, I have wondered whether scholars of religion might always exist in a double, or perhaps better a multiple, bind. The worlds to which they are accountable are at permanent odds with each other. They do not have the luxury of the humanist scholar of art or literature, where deliberate artifice is the coin of the realm and the question of transcendental reality takes second place. To work with religion as deliberate artifice is to already take a stand in the field and to configure one's relationship to the ghosts of "the community" and "the academy" in a specific way. To work with religion as transcendental reality is also to already take a stand in the field and to configure one's relationship to those ghosts in another way. To work with religion as a textual, historical, anthropological, cultural, psychological, sociological, economic, or philosophical reality is to configure oneself in yet other ways. In any direction, scholars are inevitably haunted. I wondered what it might look like if scholars became comfortable with the ghosts, the multiplicity of worlds, and the insolubility of the conflict.

I also found myself wondering, What ways might we characterize this academic practice that Asad calls us to describe? In one sense, these controversies struck me as a kind of global theater, whereby positions are taken up, lines are spoken, worlds are defended. I also wondered, What figures in theater play the role of being accountable to multiple worlds, and how do they communicate? One metaphor I found myself landing on is that of the figure of the fool. Fools exist precisely in the realm of scandal where things not to be said are said, and where things to be said are not said. I am, of course, speaking of "artificial" and role-based fools—those figures that move between worlds and convey unutterable or difficult things as guests from another world. Fools have not just been the tired figures of the limen, or threshold; they are operators within a world of questioning, abuse, invective, and innuendo. Their virtues are expressed particularly when they call forth the inappropriate moment to be contemplated. They exist in, and they themselves weave, the fabric of controversy and even scandal. Fools are, in a sense, the epitome of complex entanglements that the case studies in these pages describe. While this way of describing academic practice is decidedly "light" suggestion and not a heavy category to be imposed on our realities, I found it instructive as a way of thinking about the predicament of our scholarly practices.

What is more, with these dramas played out on the global stage, such as in the contested histories of a South Asian diaspora community or the Vatican weighing in on one scholar's assessment of the legitimacy of Jesus, I wondered, How might one describe the shifting terrain upon which a humanistic scholar of religion attempts to stand? In this book, I embark upon a beginning description of that terrain: a historical phenomenology of the public spaces that have erupted when real scholars meet real communities in dissension, and where their roles and rivalries—both anticipated and unanticipated—are put into high relief. In considering six case studies, I place them in the context of the late twentieth and early twenty-first century debates of Habermas and the critique of Habermas concerning the nature of the public sphere.[22] And in so doing, I distinguish between public space and public sphere: the public space is a place where discourse has opened up, but that discourse may not necessarily be governed by rules, while the ideal public sphere is perceived as a place where rules have emerged and are generally observed. These more contentious public spaces are constantly shifting and changing. At their least volatile, utterances between self-described secular and religious actors are less comprehensible to each other. At their most volatile, each voice contemplates, and occasionally demands, the expulsion of the other.

SECULARITIES AND SCANDALS

A word is necessary about the term "secular" here. It is beyond the scope of this book to address the myriad renewed debates about the genealogy and current status of this term in the twenty-first century. However, it is worth naming some of the dynamics of secularity as they relate to the issues in this book. The authors in the case studies to follow understand themselves to be using "secular" methods—as difficult and ambiguous as that term might be. As mentioned in the introduction, these case studies show that "secular" does not have the more unified meaning that it had in the emergence of traditional social science in the mid-twentieth century. My allotted space prevents us from engaging in a thoroughgoing critique of the voluminous recent studies on secularity, but several new meanings and connotations are worth noting here. Some challenge the idea that critique is by nature secular and focus instead on the religious roots of the very idea of secularity.[23] Others have rightly pointed out that a definition of the secular implies a relationship to religion, whatever that might be.[24]

For the purposes of this book, I define "secular" as a stance of scholarship where one group's histories and traditions are described in sociohistorical terms—terms that include the constructionist perspective, the new historical perspective, feminist criticism, and Freudian and other interpretations of sexuality, to name a few. These approaches are not necessarily always unacceptable to the religious groups; in a large majority of cases, they are part of the worldview of the group. However, occasionally they violate the norms of the representation of the group to itself and to the outside world.

I further want to propose that since the late twentieth century, the role that scholars can play in public spaces is necessarily somewhat scandalous. Indeed, one could argue that the secular study of religion is also best described as scandalous. I could, of course, invoke the truism that the *state* of the field is scandalous because there is such little agreement on where and what we should be doing. But I am going to argue instead that the field itself is scandalous and should remain so. What is more, the best cultural analogy for the secular scholar of religion in the twenty-first century might well be that of the scandalous fool in Shakespeare, or the Vidushaka in Sanskrit literature: commentators who are part of many different cultural "scenes" and are at once licentious, humorous, artistic, mocked, and ignored. Scholars of religion are the scandalous figures who wear multiple masks, have ambivalent relations with their patrons, and tell the truth no one particularly wants to hear.

The fool is one kind of light metaphor for the fluidity of this work. Another powerful way to imagine this fluidity is by thinking of the constant movement of the scholar, as Tweed does in *Crossing and Dwelling*. According to Tweed, scholars, in their ethnographic, textual, and theological studies of religions located in different times and spaces than their own, do not sit in one space to create bounded analytical categories. Rather, they "cross and dwell" in various scholarly and religious worlds with ease and alacrity. For Tweed, religions are "confluences of organic-cultural flows that intensify joy and confront suffering by drawing on human and supra-human forces to make homes and cross boundaries."[25] More importantly, for the purposes of this study of scholars in relationship to their subjects, Tweed highlights movement (the dynamics of religion across time and space), relation (interactions between religions, generations, perspectives, and spheres of influence), and position (most notably, the place of theory and theorists in relation to their subjects).

This focus on the shifting positionality of the scholar is also a central assumption of the present work. However, the case studies in *Who Owns Religion?* also focus on the space *between* the two realms of crossing, where scholars temporarily dwell in very real differences with their subjects. When he discusses crossing as an essential activity of religious traditions, Tweed understands it as a change in *location* as well as a change in *position*.[26] The same could be true of the authors of the works studied here: some are diaspora scholars whose change in location has informed their work; others are shifting locations in the academy, whether that is through a change in subfield, an engagement with community members in their own city, or involvement with the members of the hierarchy of the religions they have chosen to study.

By dwelling in this difference, scholars also remain part of the in-between space about which Habermas and his critics write so compellingly.[27] This is the place where universities ply their analytical trades and where religious traditions may articulate their needs to their own publics and to secular, even willingly listening, publics. Both languages are spoken, but the two languages they speak may not be mutually comprehensible. This is what Habermas calls the "wild sphere," not fully articulated and presenting a challenge of coexistence. The characterization of "wild" itself could indeed reinforce a "civilized/wild" dichotomy, which seems to impose on the religious subject the burden to become "reasonable," and scholars of religion will have a variety of opinions as to whether that in itself is a reasonable claim. This is the reason I choose to call these phenomena "eruptive public spaces" rather than "wild spheres."

THE NATURES OF SCANDALS AND CONTROVERSIES

What would it mean to take seriously the idea that the tension is inevitable, and never fully resolvable? What would a thought experiment look

like whereby we understand the nature of such a tension and make it creative? This book is such a thought experiment. Following the dictum "If you
can't fix it, feature it," I wondered what it might look like to place controversy and scandal at the center of our field, rather than at its anxious periphery. In the pages that follow I suggest a new lens (rather than create a
new category), whereby the insolubility of the conflicts for the scholar of
religion proves constitutive of the study itself. In other words, controversy
and scandal are not just epiphenomenal to the study of religion but a basis
for the enterprise. Before turning to the question of the challenges of the public sphere that these cases represent, let me turn first, as part of this thought
experiment, to the definition of the words "scandal" and "controversy."

I find "scandal" particularly felicitous because it has both religious and
secular meanings, as well as meanings from classical mythology—all of
which have relevance to what we are asked to think about in the present
state of the study of religions. The *Oxford English Dictionary* tells us that
the word derives from the Greek meaning a "trap" or "snare"—presumably
to moral conduct as well as to the physical body. The Latin *scandalum*
means "a cause of offense or stumbling," and in IndoGermanic **skand* is
"to spring, or leap." The earlier meanings of "scandal" in English are religious and play delightfully on the various ways in which we use the word
today: "discredit to religion occasioned by the conduct of a religious person" or "conduct, on the part of a religious person, which brings discredit
on religion." And, relatedly, scandal can mean "perplexity of conscience
occasioned by the conduct of one who is looked up to as an example." The
Old English *Ancrene Riwle* uses the earlier meaning, and Wesley's diaries
use the later; both of them are concerned with the ambiguity about who
is to be looked up to as an example and why.

New Testament translators used "scandal" for the "stumbling block"
of the cross (Galatians 5:11: Greek *skandalon tou staurou*; Latin *scandalum crucis*), which is now at the center of the Christian faith. So too, later
twentieth-century theologians used "scandal" as the focus of the particularity of the cross and of its historicity. Only in sixteenth- and seventeenth-
century common parlance do we see the word "scandal" used as "damage to reputation; rumor or general comment injurious to reputation" or,
even later, as "slander, falsehood." It also has the sense of describing a
situation as such: "a grossly discreditable circumstance, event, or condition of things, and an offense to decency and moral rectitude."

Finally, the word can mean "an irrelevancy which offends the dignity
of the court." In the study of religion, our recent scandals have focused on

damage to reputation—either of the religion in question or of the scholar in question. Both claim that the work of scholarship, or the critique of the work, is an offense to decency and moral rectitude and constitutes a "grossly discreditable circumstance in the state of scholarly affairs." Even more intriguingly, as we shall see, the charge of irrelevancy is quite common in the debates between insiders and outsiders during an academic scandal in the study of religion.

All of these terms fit the uneasy perspective of the scholar of religion today. The role of the scholar who speaks and writes about a religious tradition has moved to the center of our questions about how we relate life and work. We embody a particular kind of stumbling block, in the sense that we are historical examples of engagement with tradition; at the same time, we do not, in our modes as historians of religion, represent religious authority. This should be an obvious intellectual statement, but it is not an obvious cultural one. We all know the queries silently posed by our students after a lecture or discussion: "Should *she* be the role model? Should *he* have had (more or less) empathy?" We all know that the longing of our students to know our religious identities is in part a longing to know from which religious authority we speak, so that the rest of what we say can fall easily into place as coming from *that* perspective.

Surprisingly, then, we find that we are looked up to as exemplars of a religious tradition, or at least faithful advocates, in a variety of contexts, sometimes even within the academies that we inhabit. And thus, when the communities we represent disagree with our assessments, we have fulfilled that earliest definition of "scandal"—someone whose religious authority is questioned. Indeed, what is clear to us from the beginning is that we never assumed such religious authority, and yet it is in the nature of many religious traditions to impute such authority to one who is knowledgeable about its texts. Even as secular scholars, we assume a mantle of religious authority, even if it is one step removed from the actual hierarchical authority that is given to those ordained to a priesthood, a rabbinate, or the rank of sensei. Many of us have questioned our religious authority from the beginning of our training and wish to rebel against any such mantle being bestowed upon us. Yet in many of our teaching contexts, we must still wrestle with the question as such. This is the major issue of positionality with which so many anthropologists, cultural theorists, and religionists have grappled in recent decades.

If scholars are doing their jobs, they should also fulfill that second definition of "scandal" and spark "that perplexity of conscience occasioned by a person who is looked up to as an example." For if they know something about a tradition, then, however they know it, they are an example of *engagement with a tradition*. Many would rather be engaged with a tradition in a particular kind of way—from a distance or from a perspective of intimacy. But however scholars look at such a tradition, by virtue of their training, they have also been given the power to question that tradition through the authority of secular reason and secular reason alone. Thus, the perplexity of conscience arises because we do, like it or not, embody familiarity with a tradition at the same time as we assume we must question it.

Scholars also embody the form of scandal that asks questions in both directions of all communities, not only Janus-like but also Brahma- or even Ravana-like with ten heads. Someone with ten heads might have ten things to say, and what would scholars do then with the relentless move toward singular positionality—a singularity so fundamental to scholarly life that scholars often make a singular position out of multiple positions and hope that it will suffice to take care of the scandal that is the study of religions.

It should be clear by now that for the purposes of this book, "scandal" is not a bad word. Rather, I am using "scandal" in the sense that Wendy Steiner uses it in her *Scandal of Pleasure* (1995), in which, in a series of compelling essays, she characterizes scandal as a form of behavior that clarifies, challenges, and invigorates the assumptions of the intellectual and cultural life surrounding it. In this light, the idea of scandal (and its related trope of public spectacle) is extremely useful for my generation of scholars trained in the study of religion. It is useful because it is all-pervasive. The offense of the study of religion is now a double offense: an offense both to the religious communities who are our old and new readers and to the academy that reluctantly admitted it into its halls in the early twentieth century.

Some might argue that scholars take religious traditions so seriously that they have come up with deep, passionately held conclusions that get them in trouble on both sides of the fence. The offense in the academy is the usual offense in the study of religion—that any deeply fictive enterprise such as a religious tradition could be taken seriously at all. Meanwhile, the offense in the conservative religious community is that religion has been treated only as a fictive enterprise in which Eros, history, and ingenuity all take part in religion's construction.

Whatever one's view, in responding to this double community of critics, the study of religion is forced to partake in the perennial paradox of liberalism. For the purposes of this book, I define liberalism here as the cultural perspective that promotes inclusion of different religious and cultural groups as part of its overall commitment to civil liberties and a democratic public sphere. It must insist on tolerance and inclusion of others' religious voices even as it argues with those religious voices that are not tolerant. As Steiner describes this paradox:

> In a state controlled by fundamentalist ideas, the liberal cannot speak, but in a state controlled by liberal ideas a fundamentalist cannot act. The ideas of a fundamentalist are exclusionary and performative, i.e. valid only when turned into actions; an article of faith is not a mere topic of discussion to the believer. Thus, the liberal, in insisting on tolerance, is insisting on not only his idea but his practice. In the considerable commentary about the Rushdie affair in America, the absolute value of tolerance or free speech emerges as a point of dogmatic blindness for some and a logical embarrassment for others. Leon Wieseltier states without irony, "Let us be dogmatic about tolerance," but for Norman Mailer the issue is not so easy: "We believe in freedom of expression as an absolute. How dangerous to use the word absolute."[28]

The scholar of religion insists, and has traditionally insisted, that everyone must practice tolerance even as his or her analytic categories imply judgment. And tolerance's boundaries are always shifting; hence the difficult paradox of absolute tolerance (and therefore tolerance of intolerance) and absolute freedom of expression (and therefore freedom to express oneself by censorship of others).

In my own experience, this liberal paradox is related to another feature of an odd sort of arbitrary pluralism: our zeal to "locate" ourselves in the multiple, shifting universe. In the early twenty-first century, I am coming face-to-face with my own, only partly acknowledged hope: that if we located ourselves, somehow something in the dynamics between scholars and communities would shift toward understanding. As I have lived it, naming our locatedness has not necessarily made that shift. It has occasionally contributed to further misunderstanding between scholars and those who would themselves prefer *not* to be "located" by scholarly writing at all. This is the further complexity of the liberal paradox; naming our scholarly and personal location is an important moral act of intellectual clarity, but it may not necessarily be more than that.[29]

CONTROVERSIES AND SCANDALS

The idea of controversy is central to this book. In an earlier work, I defined myth as an argument—a set of narratives that argue for a particular way of being in the world. In this work, I am pushing the perspective even further and understanding religion as controversy—by definition filled with breakages and betrayals that I will describe. The Latin term for controversy is instructive here: it is literally *contra*, meaning "against," and *versare*, meaning "to turn," and "to turn against" has an active quality. The term "controversy" does not necessarily assume, then, that a state of hostility is the status quo, and that two parties (let us take, for example, religions and universities) must be inimical to each other. Rather, "controversy" implies a "turning away," a movement out of a possibly untroubled situation into a troubled one. And the movement away involves a kind of betrayal. As I will discuss, it could involve the betrayal of a religious community by a scholar in the representation of a religious community. Or it could involve the betrayal of a scholar by a religious community in its insistence that certain kinds of historical accounts are inimical to its own narratives of itself.

For purposes of readability and common usage, I will use "controversy" throughout this book to describe the case studies in its pages. However, it is important to note the scandalous nature of many of these controversies.[30] In the field of the study of religions, scandal can serve a variety of functions. In the larger perspective, it can serve to resolidify lines of a group between the academy and the world outside. This has been the case when questions of free speech emerge within a larger religious context that has challenged such speech. The AAUP statement on freedom of speech articulates this view; Kripal articulates this view. Scholars are committed to this view as the bedrock of what they do. Thus they scandalize other social groups by seeing themselves as separate, even "privileged," without having had to justify that privilege to the outside world. Indeed, in light of the fact that they have not been trained to justify this privilege, they are often surprised when they are attacked. My hope for this book is straightforward, and perhaps even obvious to some: it should be a given that in the study of religion, scholars represent a wide range of disciplines, methodologies, and approaches to their work. However, scholars should no longer be surprised (or scandalized) if a community disagrees publicly with them. Whatever their views (and they should be multiple), scholars should be prepared to defend and discuss their perspectives because they themselves have already reflected on their relationships to those outside the academy.

In addition to these conversations with people outside the academy, scholars also scandalize from within. Indeed, the principal manner in which the academy sees itself as separate from the world of religious censure gives us a clue to understanding the scandals within the academy: scholars reveal themselves to be "sympathetic to" or "critical of" a particular act, opinion, or judgment of a religious community, and hence "come out" with an identity that is declared, fixed, and immutable; such an identity is thus frequently used as a classificatory schema by their colleagues. The cases in this book show scholars lining up on one side or the other when a particular community objects to scholarship; they reveal their relative empathy or lack thereof with "the community" in a way that declares "a stance" and even, as we shall see, puts them on a "list"—which can be either a good list or a bad list, like the shifting social and political registers on which the hero of Philip Roth's *I Married a Communist* finds himself. Roth writes about how lists change and can only be used as classificatory schema for the political moment.

Scholars in the academy, on the other hand, for all our talk of intersectionality, still occasionally struggle with the idea of a fixed identity, the bedrock of late twentieth-century identity politics. Such a fixed view of identity inevitably leads to scandalous controversies because once a scholarly identity loosens, scholars frequently try to fix it *again* in an effort to "clarify" and "stake out" their position.[31] Scandal is not as idiosyncratic as it often appears, however. Scandals invariably connect to social problems and, when they capture public attention, may influence (magnifying, concretizing, transforming, or minimizing) the development of the social problem they are said to represent. As the sociologist Gary Fine puts it, "The depiction of the scandal comes to symbolize the problem for the public, and thus the response to the scandal shapes the response to the social problem."[32]

While I will return later to the ways in which scandal functions as a kind of metonymy for larger issues in the study of religions, the point for the present is that scandal functions as an opportunity for moral entrepreneurship—the chance to capitalize (both literally and figuratively) on morality and the public disciplining of the academy. (I remain agnostic as to whether the academy should always be immune to such disciplining.) In our cases, such disciplining tends to include the moral good of "right" representation, which always allies with some ideal religious community's views of itself. "Right" representation also gets spoken of in terms of other "rights": a community's right to construct its own history; the right to speak about sexuality in its own idiom; the right to control the public's access to its teachings; the right to smooth continuity of its lineages; and the right to correct colonial misrepresentations.[33]

Sociologists of scandal have analyzed scandal in institutional terms relevant to our topic. First, in certain institutions, social strain may be present. Such strain may be understood as the impairment of relations among social actors and the resulting tensions and possible breakdown of negotiations among institutional actors. Second, the strain allows for the problem to have "rhetorical resonance" so that moral entrepreneurs—those who, for both more and less legitimate reasons, wish to capitalize on judgment—can enter the fray when the moment is right. Third, a general belief about the breakdown of relations must crystallize and be made public. Thus, in any scandalous situation, there is ambiguity of meaning; the institution is not behaving in the way people (for any number of good and bad reasons) expect it to behave. Fourth, a precipitating or triggering mechanism focuses public attention.[34] Fifth, individuals are mobilized for action, creating opinion in public venues, which in turn invites more public commentary.[35] These elements are thus the "recipe" in the creation of public attention, which can be then capitalized on by moral entrepreneurs. Penultimately, rival groups put forth explanatory claims to control the meaning of the event. And finally, after they have been attacked, institutions respond, either by reasserting their control over norms or by changing them.[36]

.The institutions in the narratives of these pages are academic ones (colleges or universities), and the publics are communities related to the academies and ones who identify as the "subjects" of a published work. What is at issue, and what causes the "breakdown," is a particular community's doubts about its own representation within the "sanctioned" halls of the classroom and the pages of the books published by prestigious presses. The understanding of the university's ability and obligation to represent a religious tradition is at harsh odds with the community's understanding. Added to that social strain are the relative privilege and position from which those in universities can speak about a tradition and the access to public venues those speakers have.

This strain creates the rhetorical resonance of the critique of the academy within a given religious community. The trigger event is usually twofold:

the publication of a work of scholarship and its entry into the wider world of readership that the scholar may or may not have taken into account. The mobilization usually occurs through the circulation of a petition about the book or the scholar, or the denial of access to a scholar within a particular religious community. Then the media take over, and in the late twentieth-century cases discussed in this book, the internet plays, for the first time, a large role. This means for organizing the public presents as a new technology that has dramatically changed all of our lives. As a result, the net is one of the major places where moral entrepreneurship can flourish, where religious communities can criticize the Western study of religion, and where they can protest their own representations.

Academic scandals have also been studied, although with fewer socio-logical perspectives, by Ron Robin in his *Scandals and Scoundrels: Seven Cases That Shook the Academy*. They included, among others, Michael Bellesiles, Joseph Ellis, Derek Freeman, the Yanomami controversy, Rigo-berta Menchú, and the Sokal hoax. More recently, the "Sokal Squared" hoax-ers had seven false papers accepted for publication in leading humanities journals.[37] Robin sees the greater prevalence of these scandalous contro-versies as being the result of an expanded public space. A parallel process has taken place within the academy whereby diversity has accelerated the splintering of the academic community into subgroups with little meaning-ful interaction or rapport between them.[38] Hyperspecialization of the dis-ciplines can prevent meaningful intellectual interactions on a daily basis.

Such conditions have induced epistemological confusion; both the technical and the philosophical extensions of scholarly communication have increased dissonance and conflict. Robin writes, "Often the only dis-cussions garnering broad attention in such crowded cacophonous condi-tions are the provocative and intensely confrontational polemics about academic crimes and misdemeanors." He argues that such an inflation in controversies is not a sign of an existential crisis but rather the result of a change in modes of scholarly mediation. Such scandals (what he calls "deviancy debates") are necessary signs of a vibrant intellectual body, de-lineating its rules and regulations through the creation of borders and margins, but the scandals are increasingly visible.[39]

Now we see a veritable cottage industry of these controversies, and the worry has been that this results in a lowering of standards, increased decadence, and a waning of professional ethics.[40] What is more, Robin states that the "linguistic left" has come under attack because of its fo-cus on performance and constructedness, which we shall also see in the case studies of this book. Such constructionist views go directly against the identity politics of the late twentieth century, with intriguing consequences for the liberal whose commitment to empathy with those who are disenfranchised is directly at odds with his or her commitment to the "constructed" nature of the history of the same disenfranchised group.[41]

This liberal paradox directly engages the question of what Michael Walzer describes as "moral limits" to tolerance. As he puts it, "In fact, there are moral limits to toleration, too, perhaps of the same sort in domestic as in international society, ruling out intolerant and oppressive practices in any of the constituent groups. But if the groups are voluntary associations, and if exit is a real possibility for their members, these limits won't usually require legal enforcement. In multi-national empires, consociations, and nation-states, the limits are historically given, which is to say, worked out over long periods of time."[42] The case studies in this work occur at a crucial historical moment when the roles these religions and these religious identities play in public life in the contemporary nation-state are being worked out.

In addition, in their working out of these questions, latter-day scandals and controversies can become media events—performances staged for mass spectatorship. The whistleblowers of the accused parties deliberately go outside academic precincts to the public arena. Such wide diffusion has already redefined participatory parity, redrawn some of the distinctions between the legitimate and aberrant, and altered the terms of the debates. And the once clear internal procedures for identifying misrepresentations are no longer so well defined in such a porous intellectual environment.[43] This results in an eruptive public space rather than a rule-governed public sphere.[44]

In an attempt to close some of this open-endedness, Robin posits several possible "meanings" of scandal: first, scandals are not scandals but rather revelations of differing modes of writing in which the writer projects his or her own reality onto the texts. All representations of the other are ideologically driven, and scandals only serve to underscore that fact. Second, such scandals indicate that the university is in ruins, affected by a particularly virulent strain of narcissism. In contrast to what Oscar Handlin calls the "glib intellectual trend-surfers," most scholars, Robin argues, will continue to pursue their research through hard work, reasoning, and the slow accumulation of facts and data.[45]

Whichever side one takes, Robin observes, both predict impending incoherence within the ordered world of the academy. But Robin's larger point is that the environment actually demonstrates a vitality in which necessary readjustment happens, a kind of border control or technical shift in response to changes in scholarly communication. He observes, ironically, that modern-day border control is decidedly averse to revisionism and intolerant of deviancy. Amateur scholars and laypersons are forbidden in academic internet forums, as are modes of scholarly discourse that seek to experiment with canon, retool scholarly guidelines, or transgress conventional rules and regulations.[46]

Robin is, I think, right in his diagnosis of the function of scandal, but the changed role of the scholar in this new environment needs more attention, as do the controversies, rivalries, and scandals in the representation of religions. What are the many ways in which we might write differently as a result of such porous borders? A scholar's awareness of audience must now be shifted in order to attend to these new publics and expanded readership. The relationship of scholar to audience has always been an important one; it defines who scholars are and gives coherence to their academic writing as they step forward into making their arguments. Indeed, part of the very postmodern milieu in which many scholars live is reader response theory—that a text's life is predominantly derived from its audience. All the more reason to think about religious studies' own shifting audiences, and pause to query whether the meaning of scholarly work, too, has shifted as a result. The answers to such questions can and should vary widely, as widely as the dispositions of religious studies scholars themselves. But the practice of reflection might be a timely collective undertaking.

THE WINK REVEALED

Most of the works discussed in these next pages understood their scholarship as decidedly, and perhaps unconsciously, "entre nous"—a kind of knowing wink (much discussed in anthropology and sociology), to those others who also know.[47] The scholarly community has had its own language and conventions, which make it a kind of "winking" language, interpretable only to those who know the code, and perhaps not even to the subjects about which the scholars are winking. But in the past two decades, the wink has indeed been perceived by outsiders to the academy and has been deemed offensive, impenetrable, irrelevant, or damaging to the community's own sense of its ability to represent itself.

I would like to suggest that the widening knowledge of the wink might change the practice of the wink, and perhaps even the ontological status of the winker. The conflicts and scandals in the study of religions are calls for readjustments, but they are more than that as well. They raise fundamental questions about what scholars should be writing about and what the role of the university is in relationship to its publics. What is more, because scandal involves "one whose religious authority is questioned" (i.e., in some views, meaning that such authority never should have been established in the first place), the study of religions pushes these controversial issues into stark relief.

Winks are, of course, also impossible to decipher even within the same community or between two people who believe they understand each other very well. Thus, in recent years, as these scandals continue and figure more and more as the norm, we see scholars arguing about the meanings of their winks. Exchanges between them as to the meanings of their intentions, and the sensibilities that their scholarship represents, are emerging frequently in academic and more "public" debates. One is reminded of the 2006 remake of *All the King's Men*, in which Willie Stark and his journalist for hire and right-hand man are discussing their first meeting. They argue about whether or not Willie winked in that meeting, and finally Willie says, "Whether I winked or not, it is up to me to decide what it meant."

THE STUDY OF RELIGIONS AND
OTHER FORMS OF SCANDAL

The scandals and controversies in this book have a place somewhere between celebrity scandal, artistic scandal, and scandal within a religious community. The question before those parties to scandal (the institutional actors, the moral entrepreneurs, and the publics involved) is *what is understood to be illusion and what is understood to be reality*. What can be held in good faith to be illusion? What can be held in good faith to be reality? It is not only an epistemological question but also a social question of the principles upon which institutions might operate in relationship to their publics. In entertainment scandals, the actors and actresses play one kind of character on the screen but are another kind of human being altogether in their real lives. The scandal lies not in the expectation that the movie is reality, but rather that the roles of the actors and actresses carry with them a set of expectations about being a role model for others. One carries the social patina of one's role, even if Hollywood is known to be a den of iniquity.

But the larger public understands the contract between creators of films and audiences: illusion is self-conscious, a play in which the members of the audience are willing participants.[48] In the case of the artistic scandal, there tends to be the sense that artists themselves have crossed the line with their subject matter. While films frequently create this problem, the more recent scandals have included religious subject matter in artistic installations, including Andres Sorrano's "Piss Christ," Norman Kleeblatt's curated exhibit Mirroring Evil, and the well-known Indian painter M. F. Husain's portraits of Hindu gods and goddesses in voluptuous details of nudity, rendering "sanctified" imagery explicitly sensual. Such scandals are clearly about moral entrepreneurship; frequently, as in Husain's case, there is very little initial uprising until a nonelite "audience" discovers the offense and both initiates and fosters the indignation. Husain had been painting for years before the first Hindu objection came floating his way.[49]

At times, the artistic production is intentionally shocking, creating a new view of the materials and jolting the viewer into new perception. Religious communities who impart meaning to such symbols, and from whom the artist has wrested them away, are not interested in such interpretations and are usually outright hostile to them. This does not mean, however, that a multiplicity of interpretations is not allowed within religious communities; indeed, it is precisely because religious communities of all kinds, including orthodox ones, tend to pride themselves on internal diversity that an "out of the bounds" interpretation registers as particularly heinous.

What is more, the artist is not licensed to interpret, except by virtue of his or her artistry, which is already understood as marginal to social norms. In these cases, where society can agree on art as illusion or as the construction of reality, it is not ready to agree about what might be accepted into that illusory framework. We might point to the abovementioned, notorious examples of "Piss Christ," which shows a cross in a jar of urine, or the exhibit Mirroring Evil: Nazi Imagery/Recent Art, where images of death camps in various media were displayed alongside contemporary fashion logos or models holding up cans of diet soda.

The final third of our triumvirate is scandal within religious communities themselves. They especially galvanize public attention since they invoke a direct violation of what is purported to be reality. A number of complaints in the Catholic Church's sex abuse scandal, for instance, spoke to the ways in which priests pretended to be one thing, spending years as upstanding leaders of the parish, when in fact they were practicing something else entirely—something hidden and violent. In a way, religious scandals are no different from those involving people in public office where some amount of public trust is necessary to have confidence that the official will be effective. But at another level, the religious scandal is even more pernicious because religious figures claim to be representing a higher level of reality altogether. They are understood to have a double claim to reality—both in the everyday world and in the transcendent world of the spirit.

Thus, the unseen reality is similar to the inspiration of the artist and is what gives the religious figures their power. But the reality a religious figure produces is not an agreed-upon, self-conscious artifice like the artist produces. The religious figure produces a direct representation and translation of the higher reality itself. Religious scandals, then, doubly betray the social norm, in that they betray the earthly role of the religious institution and the transcendent reality it is supposed to represent. Because of the nature of such betrayals in these cases, moral entrepreneurs tend to see themselves as building back up broken-down social and monetary capital. The repair work involved in the sexual abuse scandal had to do with "rebuilding the faith" in the Roman Catholic Church as well as redistributing its property as a result of the lawsuits that came its way.

The scandals involving religious communities and scholars within a university are thus a fascinating amalgam of several agreed-upon social norms, none of them actually involving the agreed-upon artifice that gives the arts both their authority and their marginality in society. The scholar's claim to a right to interpret derives from the discourse of objectivity, and when that becomes dismantled, from the discourse of the necessity of cultural critique. Religious communities have no agency in endowing scholars with the right to interpret; they can only endow members of their own community with such a right, and take it away if necessary. They can also bestow upon scholars, after the fact, a "good list" status. There is no social contract between religious communities and university communities about an agreed-upon artistic construction, as there is between artists and their audiences. Thus, the area between universities and communities is especially fraught; it has no commonly understood norms, no agreed-upon standard as to who has the "right" to interpret, and two radically different commitments to the constitution of reality. It is ambiguous to criticize scholars of religion for claiming religious authority, because their scholarly authority comes from a different source. Frequently their religious authority is questioned from the beginning. (Even if a scholar is also ordained within a tradition, one's authority in the academy comes from elsewhere.) Rather, the scandalous part of the controversies comes from two sources: either (1) the scholar *should have had another kind of authority (i.e., religious) but did not*; or (2) the scholar is treating the religion as an artist might, as a kind of fictive or simulated material *that should not be taken as truth*. In either case, the scholar is a theologian manqué or an artist manqué and ultimately unsatisfying in the cultural contracts that society is accustomed to making with those two groups.

SCANDAL AS RIVALRY FOR REPRESENTATION

Scandal is not *only* a useful way to think about secular claims to authority; it should not be assumed that scandal is only a useful secular lens. It has been a theological category in most traditions. René Girard's *I See Satan Fall like Lightning*, veering as it does between psychoanalytic and theological emphases, touches on the unique properties of Christian religious communities and scandal. Girard's work has been used to think more broadly about rivalries, and his words are helpful here. Tracing the word back through the Greek and to the Hebrew, he writes that "scandal is not one of those ordinary obstacles that we avoid easily after we run into it the first time, but a paradoxical obstacle that is almost impossible to avoid; the more this obstacle, or scandal, repels us, the more it attracts us. Those who are scandalized put all the more ardor in inuring themselves against it because they were injured there before."[50]

Combining this idea of scandal with his theory of mimetic desire, Girard thinks of scandal as the eruption of a rivalry that is almost impossible to quell. He describes the behavior of mimetic rivals who, as they "mutually prevent each other from appropriating the object they covet, reinforce more and more their double desire, their desire for both the others' object and for the desire of the other. Each consistently takes the opposite view of the other in order to escape their inexorable rivalry, but they always return to colliding with the fascinating obstacle that each one has come to be for the other."[51]

Girard is specifically writing about a Christian context, but we can easily see how this understanding of scandal—the eruption of rivalry that is almost impossible to quell—is very much in the nature of the controversies that fill these pages. These scandals create a rivalry for the claim of the moral good and, even more importantly, for the right to represent. In Girard's view, rivalry for representation is, like all other scandals, responsible for the false infinity of mimetic rivalry. "At the height of scandal," he writes, "each reprisal calls forth a new one more violent than its predecessor. If nothing stops it, the spiral has led to a series of acts of vengeance in a perfect fusion of violence and contagion."[52] So too, the scandalous controversies described in these pages might be viewed as early, milder cases; as the epilogue will show, these have intensified in the twenty-first century.

Scandals contain the seeds of violence even if they may not necessarily bear violent fruit. More importantly, they are born from permanently tension-filled relationships, such as the relationship between religious studies departments and religious communities. And they are born from the *rivalry to represent*, where each community tries to mimic the other (the scholarly communities become sympathetic, the religious communities become historical, and so on). But even if relationships between academies and religious communities are largely sympathetic, such bonhomie cannot obscure the fundamentally irreconcilable views about the right to interpret the same religious text and artifacts.

The silencing power of scandal is also relevant to this book. In each of the cases, there have been different kinds of resulting silences—scholars who have not written subsequent books or scholars who have chosen to write about other topics. So too, communities contain traces of silence, out of a sense that the academic institutions they have taken on are unwilling to change or listen. But in each case, the sense of a common ground between academies and communities is disrupted, and the silence between them is reinforced. Silencing occurs on both sides—from the communities who have attempted to silence offensive scholarly work and from the scholars who might have inadvertently silenced communities. Each case looks different, but "shapes of silence," to use the theorist Mark Jordan's words, are almost infinite in the mimetic rivalry between communities.[53]

Jordan also writes of the moment when chatter transforms to disputation.[54] Inherent in such a situation is a certain kind of hope, to which we will return at the end of the book. Disputation need not simply grow into scandal. Rather, disputation with a mediator can move from voice to voice, silencing none of them. Jordan's mediator in disputation might well be parallel to and reminiscent of the scholar in our own cases—the one who moves between and yet whose status is unsure. As I shall suggest in the final chapter, the mediator/scholar might best be represented by the figure of the fool in classical dramas around the world—figures whose identities and patrons are constantly shifting and ambiguous.

Scandal is also about the power of an institution and how it is negotiated, renegotiated, and reasserted.[55] The institution we are speaking of here is not empire but the university, a form of social practice both complicit with and resistant to empire. To take one of many possible examples, as the recent North American conversations about slavery and the university show, many American universities were built with the labor of enslaved peoples, and many universities hosted abolitionists in their fight against slavery. Any other, less complex characterization of the university is inadequate. While postcolonial realities will take shape in any number of ways throughout these next pages, the most important point for us at the outset is to assume that universities are not simply tools of empire but rather vacillate in their own histories between objecting to empire and serving its needs. Whatever excesses of privilege university faculties, administrators, and students might enjoy, they have also exercised the privilege of academic freedom as a kind of antidote to the blindness of empire. They, too, have "crossed and dwelt," and as such are also actors in these stories of scandal.

SCANDAL IN THE STUDY OF RELIGIONS
AS POLITICAL DRAMA

Many students of scandal and controversy have observed that scandal is political drama of the most compelling kind. Our controversies and scandals are dramas in which universities and religious communities can play a crucial role, taking on voices from within their communities and outside of them. And the idea of the study of religion as spectacle is not new, although perhaps only recently placed in a larger context.

There are fundamental roles dramatic aesthetics play in the study of religions. Henry Corbin, Mircea Eliade, and Gershom Scholem all associated themselves with modern art and modernist men of letters and, as Steven Wasserstrom puts it, "successfully located audiences for their peculiarly dramatistic accounts of religion."[56] Wasserstrom goes on to note that if one could point to a single work of literature as the most deeply felt shared inspiration of all three scholars, it might be Goethe's play *Faust*. He continues:

> Drama, more generally, seems to have been an aesthetic form preferred by the historians of religions. Eliade was himself a playwright. Scholem enjoyed a certain well-honed and often noted dramatic aspect to his personality. "'I [Scholem] call myself a metaphysical clown . . . a clown hides himself in theatre.' I [Cynthia Ozick] ask whether Walter Benjamin ever hid himself that way. 'Benjamin never played theater.' How much of Professor Scholem is theatre? Scholem: 'Ask Mrs. Scholem.' Mrs. Scholem: 'One hundred percent.'"[57]

Wasserstrom points out that Corbin's hero was Swedenborg, who viewed the created and uncreated worlds together as one "representative theater" of the spiritual world, "where we can see things in their beauty if we know how to see them in the state of their Heaven."[58] Corbin, too, emphasized religion as a lived adventure, substituting "a dramaturgy for a cosmology" as all Gnostics must do.

Eliade, perhaps most of all, understood the dynamics of his theory in terms of drama. In his work on shamanism, he writes, "[Every] genuinely shamanic experience ends as a spectacle unequaled in the world of everyday experience."[59] As Wasserstrom also observes, Eliade's theories on the role of the magician as stage producer, who produces spectacle by virtue of his power and will, are central. The reach of the magician and the shaman is in their imitation of the great terrible sovereign who acts by force of their words or thought. The historian of religions is similar to the universal scholar who by force of his words makes the spectacle present. In Eliade's 1978 novella *Nineteen Roses*, the protagonist shows the transformative power of the decipherment of the symbolic: "As he puts it in the novel, knowing the religious meanings of events can become an instrument of illumination, more precisely salvation, of the masses. . . . The dramatic spectacle could become, very soon, a new eschatology or soteriology, a technique of salvation."[60]

This idea of spectacle is true of many theories of religion—although perhaps to a lesser extent. To take an early example, the dying and rising god of Adolf Jensen's Hainuwele myth depends upon a primal scenario in which the ritual is meant to be understood as a reconstructed universal drama. Even in the early teaching of religion, the idea of spectacle is present. The early twentieth-century classicist Jane Harrison understood the idea of the spectacular intuitively, arriving as she did for each class at

Newnham College at Cambridge dressed as one of the gods or goddesses whose stories she would be teaching that day. As Wasserstrom puts it, the demiurgic capacities for world-creating that all these theorists shared at the Eranos conference in Ascona, Switzerland, were like those of an artist for whom the crisis of the modern world has never, in fact, proved to be practicable.[61]

The crucial point for the present project is that for Eliade, and perhaps also his counterparts at Eranos, readers, like the audiences of spectacle, are passive. If Eliade's historian of religion is a stage producer who binds his audience in a Varuna-like spell to serve as a receiver to the transformative spectacle, this means that, at a certain level, the transformative power of the work of the historian of religions is done in front of the audience and is perhaps intended to transform the audience. Yet, in fact, there is no *actual agency on the part of the audience*. The historians of religions are masters of world-making, but the audience is not meant to respond except as recipients of the spectacle.[62]

Let me state the case perhaps even more strongly. In previous perspectives on the study of religion, the silence of the audience might well have been not just a happenstance but also a requirement of the work of the historian of religions. The historian of religions is dependent upon the presence of an audience but at the same time has no blueprint for the audience to participate, respond, negotiate, or disagree. There is a kind of splendid solitude that ignores the issue of the reception of ideas. The isolation is not that of the Nowhere Man in the Yellow Submarine, who does not care about an audience in the least, or even of the creator/demiurge, who is perhaps his own audience. It is not the loneliness of the creator Prajapati in the Brahmanic myth, who creates a companion and then pursues her as a kind of interactive audience. Rather, it is more like Toad's experience in Arnold Lobel's delightful book *Frog and Toad Together*. Toad dreams he is performing in a large hall, with his friend Frog as his audience. He performs various feats brilliantly and after each success asks Frog if he could do the same. With each "no," Frog grows smaller and smaller, until he disappears and Toad panics. When he wakes up, Frog is there. "Are you your own right size?" Toad asks. Frog assures him that he is, and Toad expresses great relief.

In the earlier history of religions, the creator creates in order to be seen but does not expect to be argued with by anyone other than his or her peers. The spectacle is only effective in the passivity of many other actors outside one's realm—and the only words allowed are those of the creator himself. Indeed, the audience must consent to becoming part of the spectacle. The spectacle depends upon a large and acquiescent crowd. One can never argue in a spectacle, unless the spectacle planned is the argument itself.

FINAL THOUGHTS

In this chapter I have suggested that, far from being a dilemma that might eventually be resolved, scandal and controversy might be helpfully understood as constitutive of the study of religion. What is more, such controversies can be understood as dramas where the rivalry of representation is played out on a national and, at times, a global stage. The controversy has included new interlocutors—frequently the members of the religious communities we study.

Wasserstrom points out that what must remain after the spectacle or performance of the historian of religions must be our criticism. Perhaps there is even a step before that: the acknowledgment that the audience has become vocal, a part of the play. And some examination of what they have said might well be part of our repertoire. The study of religions must not stop when members of the religions themselves start speaking in direct response to what historians of religions have written. Rather, we should make those responses part of the process of study itself. In doing so, we might respond in part to Talal Asad's call for a study of intellectual performance. We might also incorporate ourselves, and those whom we represent, in a newly inclusive intellectual ethnography.

2

RELIGIONS, AUDIENCES, AND THE IDEA OF THE PUBLIC SPHERE

PUBLICS MATTER/PUBLIC MATTERS

In the previous chapter I focused on the ways in which certain audiences have introduced themselves and have been introduced to scholarly work. They have, in fact, always been there but are now part of a public space of debate in a way that we cannot afford to ignore. As I shall argue in chapter 3, audiences have become part of scholarship in the study of religions because of the politics of multiculturalism of the 1990s, from which we have not completely emerged and with whose legacy we are still grappling. I shall also argue in that section that audiences have altered their role because of the internet, where numbers in readership have exponentially increased and ease of access is unprecedented. And the perspectives of the audiences have not been uniformly friendly, hostile, essentialist, or historical. They have constituted multiple publics, as Nancy Fraser would put it, and the spaces of argumentation vary as much as the scholars and the communities do.[1]

The length and scope of this study do not allow us to delve into book-length detail on theories of the public sphere; however, because we are interested in the narratives of space between universities and religious communities, it is worth devoting considerable discussion to that subject here. Any discussion of the idea of "spectacle" turns us immediately to Jürgen Habermas, whose work forms a theoretical starting point for this understanding of public spaces. Inspired in part by Hannah Arendt, Habermas delineated the emergence of the public sphere in the eighteenth century as a result of capitalist production and the long-term trade networks of news and commodities. Rational, critical debate by bourgeois actors, who gathered together to exercise reason, provided a check on the illegitimate use of power by the state. Salons, coffeehouses, and similar venues allowed for these kinds of forums and discussions where the reading public could, in its response to literature and art, form a "literary public sphere." For Habermas, the public sphere was fully developed from these beginnings in eighteenth-century Britain and evolved from there into the idea of public consensus in the European constitutional states. Public consensus was by nature resistant to and a further check on the power of the state.

But the social and economic conditions necessary for the public sphere to thrive were not necessarily permanent, and in the nineteenth and twentieth centuries, Habermas argued, the public sphere underwent "the refeudalization of society." The foundational element of the public sphere, rational critical debate conducted by private property owners gathered to pursue their ends, was replaced by the private leisure of the property owner, who may or may not choose to associate with others and exercise critical capacity. In the contemporary world, the public sphere is manufactured by mass media, and consensus is constructed by the advertising industry but not truly made by the deliberative public. Politicians present themselves before the public as kings used to do, and NGOs, advertising firms, and public relations firms replace the public gathering.

Much of the critique of Habermas in the 1960s and '70s was driven by the New Left ideologies. Critique from the right came later. From the left, Oskar Negt and Alexander Kluge, for example, criticize Habermas's idealistic portrayal of the bourgeois public sphere as being itself invested with the blindness of the bourgeoisie. In particular, in their view, Habermas maintains a division between politics and art, public and private, and work and intimacy. These divisions are even reproduced in traditional labor movements, of which they are quite critical. From their Marxist perspective, the authors propose instead a "proletarian public sphere" in which such bourgeois divisions are revealed, and perhaps even redefined, in social, economic, and political confrontation.[2]

These authors also introduce the term "public spheres of production," in which everyday experience is taken up and indeed frozen into the formal characteristics of communication, such as television and mass media. Their interest is in "opening the analytical concepts of political economy downward, toward the real experiences of human beings."[3] While the terms and issues of *Who Owns Religion?* have more to do with the study of religion and less with Marxist analysis of media, the controversies and scandals described in these chapters are indeed concerned with the real experience of human beings, insofar as controversies constitute a kind of real experience. In addition, the role of the "public spheres of production," particularly that of the university and the rise of the internet, is a central topic of concern.

RELIGIONS AND PUBLICS

In the debates, these publics are also described as religions. Thus, they are subject to all the ambiguities that religions have in a democracy. While space does not allow for an extensive philosophical discussion of religion in the public sphere, it is important to note a key framework from which the analysis of this book operates. One might begin with the basic understanding that religion per se, what John Rawls calls a "comprehensive doctrine," is not incompatible with a democracy. Neither, in principle, are any of the religions described in this book. As Rawls writes:

> A religious doctrine resting on the authority of the Church of the Bible is not, of course, a liberal comprehensive doctrine: its leading religious and moral values are not those, say, of Kant or Mill. Nevertheless, it may endorse a constitutional democratic society and recognize its public reason. Here it is basic that public reason is a political idea and belongs to the category of the political. Its content is given by the family of (liberal) political conceptions of justice satisfying the criterion of reciprocity. It does not trespass upon religious beliefs and injunctions insofar as these are consistent with the essential constitutional liberties, including the freedom of religion and liberty of conscience. There is, or need be, no war between religion and democracy. In this respect political liberalism is sharply different from and rejects Enlightenment Liberalism, which historically attacked orthodox Christianity.[4]

This view describes Rawls's central idea of reconciliation by public reason.

For Rawls, such conflicts between democracy and reasonable religious doctrine are further mitigated by the idea of toleration, defined either politically, as rights and duties protecting religious liberties in accordance with a reasonable perspective of justice, or religiously, as notions of hospitality and protection of the vulnerable within the belief systems of the religions themselves.

So far, so good. But these controversies have emerged right at one of the areas that Rawls names as the limits to public reason. For Rawls, such limits are threefold: (1) those deriving from irreconcilable comprehensive doctrines; (2) those deriving from differences in status, class position, or occupation, or from differences in ethnicity, gender, or race; and (3) those deriving from the burdens of judgment. Rawls believes that political liberalism is best equipped to deal with the first type and resolves any conflict by saying that citizens who have conflicts of doctrine may share public reasons given in terms of political conceptions of justice.[5] And when such reasons are shared, and institutions put into place new policies that reflect such reasons, "the second kind of conflict need not arise."

However, many would disagree that "the second kind of conflict need not arise." The controversies in this book place themselves in the midst of these differences in status, class, position, ethnicity, gender, and race, and participants in these controversies are not necessarily able to find the Rawlsian public reason that can reconcile these differences. What is more, religious communities in this book are shifting publics. They constitute, on the one hand, a set of doctrines and practices that should be protected by public reason's "freedom of liberty and conscience," and yet, at the same time, they emerge as communities of readers constituted by race and ethnicity—and even as communities of protest to particularly scholarly conversations. They may not always have these identities, or even take on such identities as "core," but insofar as they participate in a controversy, they use these identities to achieve their ends in the public debate. In this sense, whatever "intersections" of multiple identities might be present, one primarily religious identity is strategically used in the public debates and representative rivalry.

FRASER'S COMPETING PUBLIC SPHERES

Other theorists would argue, contra Habermas and Rawls, that recourse to public reason alone does not provide a full account of the public spheres that are at work in the controversies in this book. They would even go on to argue, as William Connolly did during this period, that the institutional language of public reason itself can reify injustice and continue to marginalize certain kinds of publics, including the religious publics described in this book (regardless of how we might assess their criticisms of scholars within the Western academy).[6] What is more, in addition to Kluge's idea of a "counter" public sphere, critics of Habermas suggest that there are multiple public spheres with multiple forms of public reason, and that these spheres are usually competing. This is the kind of mimetic rivalry that constitutes scandal in Girard's thinking, discussed above.

Nancy Fraser's 1989 work is relevant here, published as it was during the historical period of the case studies in this book.[7] It is useful both as a theoretical stance in its own right and as a way to read the controversies that were occurring at the same time. Influenced by feminist perspectives, and building on the work of Joan Landes, Mary Ryan, and Geoff Eley, she argues that the Habermasian liberal public sphere (and, by my own inference, Rawlsian public reason) is idealized. For Fraser, issues of gender, property, and race automatically exclude certain groups from the bourgeois public sphere.

Fraser's focus is on the twin dimensions of "economic redistribution and cultural recognition."[8] For her, the earlier Habermasian idea of a public sphere needs to be reconstructed for what she sees as a new historical epoch in which bourgeois society has become "welfare state mass democracy." In other words, a postbourgeois theory is needed.

Four elements are essential in building this theory. First, social equality is a necessary key to the public sphere, and thus differences in social equality must be attended to. Second, any theory should take into account that there may not be a single, liberal public sphere; other "competing" public spheres can also have significant influence in public discourse. Fraser calls these subaltern "counterpublics," which stand in contestatory relationship to the state.

Third, such citizens may determine differently what counts as public and what counts as private. Indeed, with participatory parity in the public sphere, members of subaltern counterpublics might determine that their own private interests and private matters should be counted in the public sphere. For example, the rhetoric of privacy could well be used to restrict the universe of legitimate public contestation. To take a religious instance, if a religious matter is understood as "personal or "domestic" and public discourse is channeled into specialized institutions of family law or social work, then for Fraser, this categorization reproduces gender dominance and subordination. In other words, creating participatory inclusion does not solve all the issues because newly licensed participants might be hedged by conceptions of economic or domestic privacy and therefore delimit the scope of the debate.[9]

Fourth, and finally, Fraser discusses the relationship between civil society and the state. She argues that for Habermas, the public sphere is private persons who are not state officials gathering to form public opinion, which is critical commentary and a check on the state. However, by their very definition, these private members do not authorize sovereign decisions that result in the exercise of state power. Fraser makes a distinction between "strong" public spheres, where deliberative practice consists of opinion formation and decision-making, and "weak" public spheres, consisting of opinion-making alone. For Frasier, however, parliamentary sovereignty, which is a locus of public deliberation culminating in legally binding decisions, blurs this distinction between "civil society" and the state. The relationship between parliamentary bodies and the "weak publics" they are supposed to represent is central.

For Fraser, the key is how a theory should render visible the ways in which "social inequality taints deliberation within publics." It should "show how inequality affects relations among publics, and how publics are differentially empowered or segmented, and how some are involuntarily enslaved and subordinated to others." It should "expose the way in which the labeling of some issues and interest as private limits the range of problems and approaches to problems that can be widely contested." Finally, the theory should "show how the overly weak character of some public spheres" can "denude[ ] 'public opinion' of practical force."[10]

Fraser's work is descriptive of the social conditions that might push us to create a new theory of the public sphere—particularly, but not exclusively, when it comes to religious identity. Multiple publics, competing publics, strong and weak publics, and limiting denotations of "private" are all important in *Who Owns Religion?* and affect our conception of what constitutes participatory debate and its members. Her work is also prescriptive in that she argues such a new theory should expose certain elements within contemporary understandings of the public and what they make possible—degrees of inclusion and degrees of strength.

FRASER'S RELEVANCE FOR
THE CONTROVERSIES OF THIS BOOK

Fraser's understanding of competing publics is relevant to the concerns of this book. While not all readerships are "contesting publics," several forms of contestatory readership emerged with the onset of the internet. First, readers who had new access to religious texts could also create new forms of commentary about those texts. Second, readership had access to scholarship about their own religious traditions and could create new forms of commentary about that scholarship. In addition, in the new discourse of multiculturalism, they could form collective identities of their own. These could, in turn, constitute a "counterpublic" that could contest the account given by the more established public of the university.

These various kinds of counterpublics were formed in part, but only in part, in response to the scholarship they read about on their own communities. Such responses were entirely new developments unanticipated by the paradigms of earlier scholars of religion—paradigms without audiences but filled with the entre-nous "wink" of insiders. These new readers found such work "scandalous" in the sense that it was a stumbling block to their own sense of self-representation, a "trap" to their understanding of what it meant to thrive in North America. The new readers' response produced controversy in that it represented a "turning away" from the aims of scholarship—meant ideally to help their cause—in favor of their ability to tell their own history in a multicultural world. This moment also represented a turning away of the scholar, whatever the scholar's original relationship with the community might have been. Such an evolution might be understood in Nicholas Dirks's terms of the "scandal" of empire, or in this case the more established public.

Fraser's emphasis on the shifting definitions of private and public is also relevant here. At times, such controversies involved the exposure of the private in the public sphere, such as in the case of Kripal's treatment of the saint Ramakrishna, or Kassam's treatment of the Ginans of the Ismaili communities. At times as well, it was the insertion of a public process into what should have been understood in a more transcendent fashion. This proved the case with the Native American objection to Gill's overemphasis on negotiation over Mother Earth with the US government, or Oberoi's focus on negotiation and ambiguous boundaries among competing Sikh communities. These shifting definitions also led to various forms of Gary Fine's "moral entrepreneurship" mentioned above—where groups find ways to discipline the eruption of something improper into the public sphere.

In all cases, however, the counterpublics were "weak" in the sense that they held no legislative briefs and could not enforce the power of the state. To be sure, attempts were made in each case to call upon the power of the state, whether on the part of the scholars or the communities. These calls included the contemplation of lawsuits, demands to terminate employment, and so forth. However, in the end, the debates were held, and the controversies unfolded, in the realm of public opinion and its formation.

What is more, in Fraser's terms of participatory parity, these communities had different histories as participants in public debate in North America. Some, such as the Native American groups, had experienced repeated injury in such debates. Some, such as the Sikh, Ismaili, and Hindu groups, were relatively new to them on the North American scene; some, such as the Catholic and Jewish groups, had negotiated a relatively peaceful modus vivendi with such debates through successive legal cases. This history of the groups' relationship to the democratic process also colored the tone of each controversy. So too, "scandals" of empire, as Dirks argues, have the function of allowing new participants to create a stake in the larger debates.

The late twentieth-century communities in this book voiced continual frustration that they did not have participatory parity with the competing, but more powerful, public of the university. For them, the imbalance was nearly insurmountable because of the wealth of university endowments, professorial access to well-known publishing venues, and the protection of tenure. It is ironic that the two competing publics both often saw themselves as social critics of the more mainstream public spheres, whether mainstream democracy or media production. And yet, as we shall see in the pages of this book, both publics claimed marginal status and democratic protection: in the university case, the protection of free inquiry, and in the religious community case, that of freedom of religious self-representation.

In addition, several of the cases in this book are transnational in nature. As Fraser has recently argued, the transnationalization of the public sphere is a key opportunity for study and analysis.[11] In transnational cases, the regulatory norms and even nonlegal cultures of the nation-state are no longer enforceable. As Kate Nash writes, "Transnational discussions on matters which affect people beyond national borders do not take place within a bounded political space with mechanisms whereby public influence may be translated into law-making and administration."[12] And in the cultural sphere, where most of our case studies reside, the challenge of establishing common terms of debate is even more dramatically problematic.

Thus, issues of inclusion and participatory parity come even more to the fore. As Nash puts it, "In the inclusiveness condition, discussion must in principle be open to all with a stake in the outcome. In the parity condition, all interlocutors must, in principle, enjoy roughly equal chances to state their views, place issues on the agenda, question the tacit and ex-

plicit assumptions of others, switch levels as needed, and generally receive a fair hearing."[13] In those transnational moments when members
of a represented religious community are from another nation as well as
another culture, Fraser would ask, what is the participatory parity of the
interlocutors? Are scholars and community members the same kinds of
participants? And what exactly are the moral limits of tolerance, and who
is privileged enough to define them?[14] These questions are also the topic
of this book.

CHALLENGES TO THE HABERMASIAN MODEL OF RELIGION AND SECULARITY

Fraser's work focuses on the public sphere per se and is foundational for
this book. Equally foundational are critiques of Habermas's recent discussions of religion and secularity. Scholars' responses to Habermas's assertions range from a reengagement with political theology to the possibility
or impossibility of secular reason in a postsecular age to the question of
Habermas's "middle way" between modern secularists and religious re-
vivalists, discussed above. Moreoever, his critics also question how much
religious reason can and should be translated into the public sphere, as
Rawls's reasonable pluralism, also embraced by Habermas, would permit.

Particularly salient is the need for a greater role for historical studies
in these debates, for which Charles Taylor has also argued in his magis-
terial *A Secular Age*. We are facing what María Herrera Lima has called
"changed historical and social conditions for religious beliefs and practices in our secular age," whereby the interactions between sacred and
secular groups are historically contingent processes and full of local particularities. In addition, as we shall see in the next chapter, on the context
of the 1990s, religion in these historical debates has multiple meanings.
It is often understood as one among many possible choices with which
to mobilize cultural identity, while at the same time it is understood as a
transcendent referent that authorizes and legitimates actions.[15]

Relatedly, others have argued that historical instances show that a single interpretive framework, implied by Habermas's ideas, might indeed fix
the terms of interpretation. On the ground, secular and religious thinkers
approach debates in the public sphere with a near-infinite variety of interpretive frameworks. As Thomas McCarthy argues, an overdetermined
framework can cause us to draw distinctions too sharply between the

cultural and the political, the opaque core of religious faith versus its more rationalizable elements. For him, there is a false dichotomy between the idea that religious believers have primarily an authoritarian view of knowledge and the idea that secular rationalists only have a hypothesis-testing approach. These overdetermined distinctions can make the interpretive framework too regulated and the interpretive expectations too high. What we should expect instead is that "the fault lines between faith and reason cannot be bridged finally and absolutely," but rather "repeatedly and variously in a global proliferation of situated practices.[16]

The controversies of this book are part of the global proliferation of situated practices, where we need to turn our attention. Indeed, they reveal in a number of ways, contra Habermas, that religious believers are infinitely capable of secular reasoning and reflexivity about their own traditions and use those capacities as well as religious reasoning in response to academic assessments of their work. We also learn that cultural spheres constantly overlap with political ones, and believers and secularists alike have antiauthoritarian views of knowledge as well as authoritarian ones. In addition, religious spheres as well as secular ones are capable of transformation based on the deliberative mutually corrective processes that Habermas embraces.

Equally important, the introduction of historical cases such as the ones in this volume force us to come to terms with questions of the collective historical past. As we shall see in the case studies, many religious communities have, as a way of asserting themselves in the public sphere, turned to the politics of memory. Memory politics gives us an occasion to reflect on the problems of translation, from the religious into the secular sphere, what many would call "a problematic promise" at best.[17] If the collective memory of a group emerges as part of public debate, translation from religious to secular idioms is problematic: thoroughly secular reasoning cannot proceed upon grounds that the past is completely rational, and yet religious types of remembering can be equally problematic—what Richard Rorty calls "the skyhook" of theological reasoning whereby historical facts are reinterpreted as divine acts, and where collective memory itself is a form of identity inspired by a transcendent referent beyond reason.[18]

In his critics' views, Habermas is overly optimistic in his ideas of translation because religious concepts are both open and resistant to translation, and thus the act of translation always betrays and always fails. Religious studies scholars who work from text-critical, historical, or psychoanalytic perspectives are doing some form of "translation" that fails in its ability to be comprehensible or acceptable to religious readers. Many of the resistant publics in this book are doing exactly that—becoming resistant, and thus more opaque, in their focus on the cultural substance lost in the translation to reason, which academic treatments claim. Scholars can and should differ on what the price of that loss of cultural substance is, but the presence of that resistance is quite profound in these controversies.

The case studies thus pose challenges to the Habermasian model in a variety of ways. They are grounded historical examples, as Herrera Lima advises they should be. They show a need for a more expansive public square, as Fraser advocates. They are grounded in collective understandings of the past, where secular and sacred pasts can prove mutually incomprehensible, as Max Pensky notes. And in their inauguration of seemingly endless rounds of controversies, they are part of the global proliferation of situated practices.

SECULAR AND POSTSECULAR

What is more, the Habermasian understanding of "postsecular" society, discussed above, is problematic because it assumes a false equality—one whereby in the public sphere the "epistemic and attitudinal burdens" on citizens are more or less equal between religious and secular groups as they participate in the deliberative exchange in which imperfect translations occur.[19] In this overly optimistic view, a postsecular world is one where religious and secular groups can engage, religious groups can translate themselves and thereby become comprehensible in largely secular terms of public reason, and a modus vivendi might be found.

Several critiques focusing on this false equality have emerged. Most importantly for our purposes, some have argued that the idea of the postsecular is not rich enough to take up the challenges of pluralism, emerging as it does beyond the confines of the nation-state. In the case of religious conflict, with which this book is centrally occupied, a postsecular deliberative dialogue may help create communicative understanding but does not necessarily help engender what James Bohman calls communicative *power*—that is, creating groups with genuine standing who can and will effectively persuade other groups. As Bohman argues, postsecularity should be less a condition of public deliberation in democratic states and more "a critical standard for living with the permanent fact of increasing diversity of forms of life at all levels of international society."[20]

What is more, controversies show that in the 1990s, the secular began to be used in multiple ways and in multiple contexts. Two primary ways are in tension with each other. Secularity, even stripped of its pretensions to cultural neutrality, can be seen as the ground upon which varying types of the religious can meet. Secularity can be seen in its own right as a form of power that the academy wields, to tell a religious history that differs from the ones members of the community might tell. Secularity can also be used as an appeal to the capacity for scholars to exercise academic freedom, which is necessary to their vocation and often to their society. These two definitions mirror Talal Asad's description of different ideas of freedom: "one social weapon fac[ing] another, each employing a different aspect of the modern idea."[21] The secular in an academic context, then, can be a cultural instrument of power as well as of liberation from that power.

ERUPTIVE PUBLIC SPACES

The controversies of the 1990s were filled with the failed translations between secular and religious spheres. We see the beginnings of the infinite contestations that test the Habermasian paradigm. Rather than failed translation, I prefer to describe these events as "eruptive public spaces," defined as sudden, rapidly emergent, and controversial public conversations about the representation of religious traditions, where offense is taken and cultural norms of open debate are violated. Rules of debate and agreements about evidence are dissolved. The question of who has the right, obligations, and privilege to tell the histories is the focus of a discourse where almost anything goes.

What are the contours of such spaces? The pages that follow all dispute the following questions: What Sikh groups really mattered. What the Gospels were really saying. What the sexuality of Ramakrishna really was. What the Ismaili Ginans really said and accomplished. Whether Mother Earth had a ritual and theological tradition behind her. Whether Judaism could be homoerotic and the State of Israel criticized. In none of these cases is there a denial of the existence of the figure, saint, or community, but rather something far more difficult to deal with—a statement of its *different nature*, or variance with traditional doctrine or teaching. And in these cases, the norms of public engagement in traditional public spheres fail to put to rest, in any immediate way, any concerns about these variances— both in the telling of histories and in the description of sexualities.

These two issues are the sources of noncomprehension, resentment, and contention between competing public spheres as well as the public spaces that erupt between the spheres. Historically speaking, at stake is whether an account of "what happened" is adequate and faithful to the norms and needs of the religious community. In terms of sexual mores, also at stake is whether such accounts should or should not involve descriptions of sexuality outside public norms.

In terms of Habermas's critics, we might make several further points about eruptive public spaces. First, there are competing multiple publics that wish to own both discourses of history and of sexuality, or more precisely, the histories of sexualities. Second, there are questions as to who are the appropriate participants in such debates, both in the historical moments described in these works of scholarship and in the public debates about that today. Third, there are questions, particularly in terms of sexuality, as to what is appropriate or "private," in the historical moments described as well as in the public debates. Fourth, the debates proceed depending upon the relative strong or weak state of the publics engaged in them—whether they can pass their own religious laws, what their historical relationship to the state has been, and how vulnerable they experience themselves to be either in their home state or in the diaspora, or both.

HISTORIES IN ERUPTIVE PUBLIC SPACES

Let us begin with history and historiography, and how they become the focus in an eruptive public space. Frequently, the arguments about historiography are framed as an engagement between religious history on one side and secular history on the other—the simple binary discussed earlier in this chapter. Those inside the community have certain commitments to "what happened," and certain cultural and theological principles that must be adhered to in telling the story. Yet the dynamics of each of these controversies are more complex and suggest another mode altogether. In each case, there are forms of secular history that are indeed acceptable to many religious communities, as well as forms of indigenous religious history that would be acceptable to the scholar. For example, the Roman Catholic community has been grappling with the norms of text-critical biblical scholarship for a century or so, and the Hindu and scholarly communities agree on many of the basic facts of Ramakrishna's life. If we examine the nature of these contestations, there is some agreement about the evidence, and even about the basic events that have motivated these communities' histories.

Yet there are no rules of engagement about evidence in eruptive spaces.[22] In eruptive public spaces, fundamental questions of the legitimacy of the codes of evidence are raised, and the greatness of the historical works is contested because of that very debate. Sam Gill's statement that Native Americans used the figure of Mother Earth deftly in their negotiations with the American government implied that she did not play an important role in recent Native American history. Harjot Oberoi's insistence on the fluidity of early Sikh boundaries implied that the community, as a unified community, did not exist in the nineteenth century. Jane Schaberg's insistence that the textual tradition could be read to imply Jesus's illegitimacy meant that Mary was an unwed mother and Jesus an illegitimate child; Tazim Kassam's insistence that the formerly secret Ginans be open to the public meant that their interpretation of their history could no longer be controlled; Howard Schwartz's insistence on critique of the State of Israel meant that present history could be influenced only by a Jewish diaspora ready to defend Israel at all costs; and Kripal's interpretation of the homoerotic nature of the statements both by and about Ramakrishna during his lifetime meant that Ramakrishna must have *actually been* a homosexual, his desires out of control and out of sync with the sexual mores of nineteenth-century Calcutta. In each case, the disagreement between the university and the community *created* a public space, which could not be governed by the rules of the more established public spheres of a university or a religious community.

PUBLIC HISTORY AND ERUPTIVE PUBLIC SPACES

How might such eruptive public spaces take part in the recent movement toward public history—the kind of work that makes historical accounts more accessible for and to all members of the public? Public history does indeed share many features with historical debate that erupts into the public sphere, but there are important differences that affect the way we might view its role in transnational culture. The National Council on Public History writes that its purpose is to "inspire public engagement with the past and serve the needs of practitioners in putting history to work in the world by building community among historians, expanding professional skills and tools, fostering critical reflection on historical practice, and publicly advocating for history and historians."[23] Moreover, the council promotes the collaborative study and practice of history; its practitioners embrace a mission to make their special insights accessible and useful to the public. There is a lot of debate over the term, particularly as to the nature of the collaboration between historians and their publics, as well as what kinds of lines we might draw between the two. The key here, however, is a kind of shared intentionality in the act of creating history. Ludmilla Jordanova observes that the state lies at the heart of public history, and the rise of the modern nation-state enables the possibility of historical societies, public and private archive collections, historical and heritage projects, and government agencies.[24]

The 1960s and '70s gave birth to social justice movements and an interest in the histories of those beyond the victors—women, minorities, the working class, and eventually diaspora communities. Indeed, the transnational element of the public history movement is relatively recent, coming into view with the formation of the International Federation for Public History 2010. Its purpose is to foster international exchanges about the practice and teaching of public history, an interest that dovetails with digital history, with its focus on accessibility and large-scale engagement with historical and cultural knowledge. In all of these endeavors, the idea of a shared historical authority is central.

The controversies in this book, and the roles that these controversies play in cultures, share the public aspect of public history. Many of them share the digital aspect, as we shall see in the next chapter, but, tellingly, they differ in several key ways. First, the controversies tend to set the professional university historian and interpreter of texts against the various reading publics, of which many—although not all of them religious—object to the historian's position. The collaborative sensibility is nearly completely absent; there is no shared historical authority but rather the deep contestation of that authority. Second, the controversy is usually a surprise, erupting into the public sphere in a controversial and, at times, even scandalous way. To the scholar, something that has been concealed is revealed. To the protesting publics, a powerful accusation has been made against a tradition's history that violates its central doctrine, either about the actual development of the religious community or about a sanctified person within it. The progression of such controversy figures as interruptive history, divisive history, and history that temporarily stands between the university and its communities.

SEXUALITIES AND ERUPTIVE PUBLIC SPACES

The role of sexuality in telling history is as explosive as any other historical method. Use of sexual language by secular historians can be construed as an interruption of the religious narrative; indeed, as with secular history, religious critics can even view such an approach as a replacement of the religious narrative with the sexual one. These are the pornographic readings that the Western scholar is regularly accused of performing on Asian texts. Yet scholars will claim that a study of sexuality does not replace or silence any religious narrative; it is simply an integral part of it. As one exasperated scholar put it, "Give me the date—the exact date—when we became ashamed of our genitals?"[25] In addition, some sociologists such as Roger Friedland have argued that nationalism and eroticism are integrally bound up with one another.[26] According to this view, in an attempt to recover a masculine sexuality, deviant sexualities are repressed.

In public debates about religion, Freudian analysis has played the role of the fool—both in the controversies of the 1990s and even earlier. Initially, Freud's conclusions threatened to change the narrative of the death of Moses from an act of self-sacrifice (he is denied the Promised Land by God and peacefully accepts his fate) to an act of sexual aggression and repression on the part of his followers. Freudian interpretations are religious conversation-stoppers. As one scholar of Freud and religion puts it, an encounter with Freud can result in a kind of splitting, whereby one keeps an "all-bad Freud far removed from an all-good religious faith."[27] This has certainly been the case in the Hindu context and, to a milder extent, in the Jewish one.

POSTCOLONIAL CONTEXTS AND
ERUPTIVE PUBLIC SPACES

Many of these explosive questions of historical and sexual acceptability produce eruptive public spaces in postcolonial contexts involving nationalism and religion. As Rogers Brubaker argues, "nationalism and religion are often deeply intertwined; political actors may make claims both in the name of the nation and in the name of God. Nationalist politics can accommodate the claims of religion, and nationalist rhetoric often deploys religious language, imagery, and symbolism; similarly, religion can accommodate the claims of the nation-state and religious movements can deploy nationalist language."[28] Almost all the combinations Brubaker mentions are part of our case studies.

In the Sikh and Jewish cases, nationalism is in fact coterminous with members of the religion. Those arguing for a Khalistan do so with an understanding that the formation of the state is primarily for Sikhs; those arguing for the survival of the State of Israel did so with an understanding that the formation of the state was primarily for Jews. Other cases are not identical with nationalism but intertwined with it. For example, in the Hindu case, some (but not all) critics of Kripal were also proponents of Hindutva, the Hindu nationalism that argued that the secular state of India should in fact be a Hindu state.

The dynamics of postcolonial concerns in public debates about the appropriate role of the scholar of religion are equally complex. In the Muslim, Sikh, and Hindu cases discussed above, a great deal of the anger and violence of the debate concerned the correct representation of a minority community trying to establish itself in the Americas. These communities were also dealing with the aftereffects of colonization by the West. Yet this raises the questions of when and how minority status is claimed. For example, in the Hindu and Jewish cases, minority status in the United States could not be claimed on the other side of the ocean in India and Israel. Laurent Gayer calls this dynamic "extraverted integration"—that is, the use of multicultural discourse in the diasporic country to further essentialized nationalist politics and resistant movements in the "home" country.[29]

As a result of these cases, the charges of neoimperialism, cultural colonization, and recolonization by Western scholars are common in these eruptive public debates. Yet the "traces" of colonialism in interpretation take shape in very different ways.[30] In the Sikh, Hindu, and Muslim cases, sexual and historical interpretations became functions of the neocolonial interests of the West. In the example of Schwartz, the case involved an already-established American Jewish diaspora, whose anxieties about the State of Israel are shared with the Israeli government. However, in the Native American examples, the political landscape was different: the wounds of colonialism were quite near in space and time, quite close to the heart and the mind. There was no diaspora to turn to, and there is no narrative of the successful minority.[31] Thus, from some Native American perspectives, the white scholar might well be continuing the unfinished imperialist acts of US colonization.

FINAL THOUGHTS

When self-described secular historians clash with religious ways of interpreting evidence from the past, a rivalry of representation occurs, and the debates over their histories can become eruptive public spaces that challenge rule-governed spheres. The spaces contain the rhetoric of moral entrepreneurs, as well as others who gather around the scandalous. They are filled with the mimetic rivalry of representation. They involve the arguments of the religious as well as the secular, with the "voice of the folk" as well as the "magisterium" of the university. In these eruptive public spaces, mutual comprehensibility remains a profound challenge.

These publics are shifting and transnational and create a challenge for transforming oppositional networks into some kind of publics, where there is a deeper agreement about histories and sexualities. They are also "weak" in Fraserian terms, in that they occur primarily in the realm of public opinion. But such spaces are still worth studying—particularly for the dynamics of dissent that continue to constitute the space between the university and the religious community today. Most importantly, they might help us lurch, albeit unevenly and inconsistently, toward mutual comprehensibility. And that may well be one of the more significant projects of the twenty-first century.

3

THE 1990S: CULTURAL RECOGNITION, INTERNET UTOPIAS, AND POSTCOLONIAL IDENTITIES

MULTICULTURAL PUBLICS AND THE RECOGNITION OF RELIGION

Whether in competing or collaborative, strong or weak, equal or unequal, or public or private spheres, all of the works discussed herein were in some way or another cases in cultural recognition—a major issue of the 1990s and an important context for this book. The quest for cultural recognition also emerged during the rise of the internet, which lent an immediacy, speed, and global reach to public debates, including those about religion. The late twentieth century was also a period of growing awareness of postcolonial identity, whereby those from the Global South appeared as new participants in public debates. In the public square, they were now able to express their double consciousness of the worlds of the former colonizer and the formerly colonized. In this new configuration of the late twentieth century, more people read books and commented on them, and if they did not read them, they became aware of their publication. In other words, more people belonged, or asked to belong, in public debates.

Fraser's ideas about who might count in the public sphere have everything to do with who is recognized as *belonging* to that sphere in the first place. To put it another way, a secure, nonironic place in the public sphere is an often-stated desire—both for those whose religions have been described, and for those who have done the describing. While this was not a new issue for the twentieth century, in the 1990s religious actors and scholars became increasingly vocal in creating what Charles Taylor has described as a "secure cultural context." As Taylor puts it, a secure cultural context ranks among the primary goods, basic to most people's prospects for living what they can identify as a good life.[1] Indeed, many of the participants in these controversies have argued, either explicitly or implicitly, that the recognition of religious identity is a human good to be balanced with other goods in the public realm.

In the 1990s, Charles Taylor and other thinkers were putting the issue of cultural identity on the philosophical map. They argued that cultural identity, along with the ability to maintain it, should be understood as a natural right to be protected by any democratic state. This was philosophically basic and necessary work. Without it, the situation of many minority groups in the United States would not have progressed, and they would not be able to refer to concepts and laws by which they can continue to progress. Yet there was also a risk. The risk was that identity can become so completely fused with rights that one's inherited obligation is primarily to one's ethnic or religious community, and only secondarily, if at all, to the larger society from whom one receives those rights.

RELIGION AS COMPLEX CULTURAL CATEGORY

It is important, then, to explore the role of cultural recognition in these eruptive public spaces and, relatedly, insider/outsider statuses in different religions as forms of cultural power. Is religion a public cultural identity or a private set of practices and beliefs? James Beckford, writing at the start of the period of the controversies in this book, argued that in many areas of public understanding, religion came to be viewed less as a fully embedded social institution or fully transcendent set of beliefs, and more as a cultural resource to be deployed when necessary. Symbols and practices grew unmoored from ritual, institutional, and doctrinal contexts, and thus could be used for a variety of different purposes and imbued with a variety of different meanings.[2]

Indeed, in the debates discussed in this book, religion has frequently operated most effectively as a cultural identity, or as a cultural resource for claiming power. Yet religion as a cultural resource is not just a matter of rearranging personally meaningful symbols. As a cultural resource, it still lays claim to the privacy of a protected sphere at the same time as it is understood as a cultural good to be shared. Even when religion is understood as a cultural resource, it moves across definitional boundaries.

Beckford's perspective on religion can also play a powerful role in multicultural debates. How does this characterization play out in the context of these case studies? In 1995, around the time that many of these cases were erupting, David Morley and Kevin Robins argued that "until relatively recently, debates surrounding the questions of cultural identity and cultural imperialism functioned within a largely un-interrogated model of what 'cultural identities' are."[3] We might say the same of the "religious identities" discussed in this book, particularly insofar as they claim to be parts of, or inextricably linked to, shifting cultural identities.

Many of the debates emerged just as the culture wars were heating up in the larger landscape in America, with religion at the center of arguments about decency, identity, and the role of public rhetoric. This was a public sphere upon which a singular cultural identity, including religious identity, was the premise upon which groups could claim power. Like the attempts by conservative activists to shut down the National Endowment for the Arts in the late 1980s and early '90s, these debates occurred within this larger context of an ongoing public debate about the idea of culture and what it should and should not be in order for the government to fund it.

It was no accident that a particularly vehement episode in this debate was sparked by a provocative fusion of religion and culture—Serrano's "Piss Christ." Part of a touring exhibit funded by the National Endowment for the Arts (NEA) that opened at the Virginia Museum of Fine Art in Richmond, "Piss Christ" was a photo of a crucifix suspended in the artist's own urine.[4] It was used by Senators Jesse Helms and Alfonse D'Amato and others as an example of the "offensive trash" that passed for art that US citizens' tax dollars were being used to support. This was followed by debates about the NEA funding of a Robert Mapplethorpe exhibit, which included controversial images of homoeroticism, sadomasochism, and child nudity.

The arts and, relatedly, intellectuals were linked in public debates to works offensive to conservative Christian groups, on the grounds of both religious and sexual mores—two of the major themes that also run through these cases. The public debates were about offense, but they also had to do with normative models of how to be a "religion" in public. Frequently, the controversies over a public display of a religious identity involved not artistic or intellectual critique but, rather, its offensive nature alone.

This period also witnessed a general decline in decorum and an increase in personal attacks, as Frederick Lane observes in *The Decency Wars*. The last time the Federal Communications Commission (FCC) tried to fine a station for the content of a host's personal attack on someone was 1974, and two years later, that decision was overturned by the US Court of Appeals. By the 1990s, the issue of name-calling and personal attack had become a cultural one, and it was left to the individual broadcasting company to decide whether to invite the person attacked to respond. This era also gave rise to talk-radio hosts such as Rush Limbaugh, Bob Grant, and anti-abortion activist Randall Terry, all of whom branded leaders in the Clinton White House as monsters, tyrants, cowards, or murderers. So too, they branded environmental activists as "worthy of being shot."[5]

At the same time, the larger discussion about pornography and explicit sexuality on the internet developed into a major political issue in the US public sphere, with the Communications Decency Act being debated in the mid-1990s as part of a larger public anxiety about sexuality and free speech. Thus, in the public realm, there was a "perfect storm": the unbridling of religious conservatives' use of personal invective, without penalty, and the simultaneous attempt to clamp down on internet pornography in the name of decency.[6]

Both directly and indirectly, religion became a major force in these cultural wars about decency. The terms of the argument had to do with public definitions of religion's role in the public sphere. According to one side of the argument, religion should be understood as a cultural private force, without the power of shaping public policy.[7] Behind this idea is a fundamental commitment that has important cultural implications: short of hate speech, the role of the representation of religion is fundamentally a nonlegal question, outside the realm of the courts. The conflict over the representation of religion takes place in a public sphere, but it is rarely a legal one. Rather, it is predominantly one of social and cultural norms and practices. One can look at this perspective from a negative point of view: because of our commitment to the separation of church and state, religion can only be a "private" value, and its influence can only be negotiated in the lesser "cultural" spheres of intellectual projects and marketplaces of ideas. Put in a more positive light, culture still has a primary role in making new standards of discourse about religion in the public sphere. However one looks at it, for many theorists, this separation is necessary in order to achieve the Rawlsian "public reason" mentioned in chapter 2.[8]

RELIGION AS CULTURE: LIFE-SCRIPT AND THE RELATIONSHIP BETWEEN INDIVIDUAL AND COMMUNITY

The idea of religion that emerges in these controversies of the 1990s is still a matter of public identity, but nonetheless it is a nonlegal, primarily cultural discourse. During this time, "religion as culture" also tended to shift in the public sphere, variously taking on several different aspects of culture. Kwame Anthony Appiah helpfully elucidates these as the questions of respect, life-script, and the relationships between the individual and the community to which he or she belongs.

An examination of each of these aspects might be helpful here. The cultural work of respect can be viewed in a positive way in terms of the demands of identity and dignity. Appiah uses the African American tradition as an example.

> If one is to be black in a society that is racist then one has constantly to deal with assaults on one's dignity. In this context, insisting on the right to live a dignified life will not be enough. It will not even be enough to require that one be treated with equal dignity despite being black: for that would suggest that being black counts to some degree against one's dignity. And so one will end up asking to be respected as a black.[9]

So too, the controversies of this book seem to suggest, with religion. The scholarly authors have understood themselves to be respecting Native American, Sikh, Hindu, Roman Catholic, Ismaili, and Jewish identities. Similarly, the authors' critics have asked to be respected as Native American, Sikh, Hindu, Roman Catholic, Ismaili, and Jewish. Following Appiah, their critique was that the authors undermined the basic dignity of those religious identities as embraced by both individuals and groups. Recognition of each cultural context means that institutions, such as universities, that participate in the public sphere should acknowledge rather than ignore cultural particularities, at least for people whose self-understanding depends on the vitality of their culture. The question then becomes, What *is* the cultural context that gives dignity? In Habermasian terms, how does it translate, if at all, from the religious sphere into the public sphere of secular reason?

LIFE-SCRIPTS: INDIVIDUAL AND COMMUNITY

Building on the idea of the individual whose cultural context is central to his or her identity, Appiah addresses questions emerging in the late 1980s and '90s of individual versus community identity. He begins with a compelling discussion of "life-scripts." In Appiah's view, as one moves from the script of life-hatred, one begins instead to ask to be respected as black or as gay. He writes:

> It may even be historically, strategically necessary for the story to go this way. But I think we need to go on to the next step, which is to ask whether identities constructed in this way are ones we can be happy with in the longer run. Demanding respect for people as blacks and as gays can go along with notable rigid structures as to how one is to be an African American or a person with same sex desires. In a particularly fraught and empathetic way, there will be proper modes of being black and gay: there will be demands that we made; expectations to be met, bottom lines to be drawn. It is at this point that someone who takes autonomy seriously may worry whether we have replaced one kind of tyranny with another. . . . The politics of recognition, if pursued with excessive zeal, can seem to require that one's skin color, one's sexual body should be politically engaged in ways that make it hard for those who want to treat their skin and the sexual body as personal dimensions of the self.[10]

The late twentieth-century interlocutors discussed in this book struggled in their own way with Appiah's question, only in terms of religion as a cultural identity. For them, acts of recognition and acts of nonrecognition by the individual scholar of religion ran up against the scripted, social dimensions of any politics of recognition, in this case, religious belonging as a cultural force. Demands for recognition by religious groups made a major impact on the role of the individual scholar, and vice versa. Scholars were also speaking and writing from the power of the university, and debates emerged as to the extent of that power to grant or bestow recognition. Add to the mix a rivalry of representation between universities and communities, and one has a volatile situation, as has been the case since the politics of recognition entered the world of religious studies.

If, as Appiah writes, the success of our cultural projects might derive from our having a social identity, then it is clear that some individual projects in this period registered as controversial precisely because they were at odds with the norms and values surrounding that social identity. To put it another way, the private and individual life-script that a scholar may have been composing about his or her work changed dramatically when he or she entered the public realm. In private, they might have transgressed rules of identity and scripts of cultural and religious belonging in their representations of religion. They might not even have been intentional in doing so. In public, however, the very same transgressions of representation were no longer allowed without vocal and vituperative response from the communities themselves. Community members found such transgressions a problem for community cohesiveness, for capacity-building within the community, and for its larger narrative about itself, often associated with the agency of the group.

THE CONSTRAINING PUBLICS: ACADEMIES AND RELIGIOUS COMMUNITIES

The life-script imposed by any community, including a religious one, can be potentially oppressive as well as liberating. So too, the academy can figure as coercive because, despite its occasional claims to social alterity within North American society, it has its own difficult dynamics of power and can reproduce the very cultural norms it claims to criticize. The movement between the academy and the community remains different for each author in this book, depending upon which community was primary, secondary, or even tertiary for his or her identity. A word is necessary here to address the question of the institution of the academy versus the community—in many ways at the heart of the controversies in these pages. The nature of the academy, especially for religious studies scholars, will be addressed in a later chapter, but for now, it is important to note that both of these communities are not simply two competing publics, although they are also that. In many ways, they are strong publics in their own spheres, to take Fraser's terms. They can constitute coercive bodies, the kind of social formations of identity that Linda Alcoff and other theorists understand as "placing irredeemable, alienating, artificial, and oppressive constraints on the indeterminacy of the self."[11]

Given that religion is an inherently unstable cultural category in the public sphere, we see, following Appiah, the complexity of the debates between scholars and communities that arose in the 1990s. At least three forms of cultural recognition are woven into the threads of these controversies: (1) the question of respect for religion as a force of culture; (2) the question of religious and cultural belonging at both the group and the individual level; and (3) the question of academy versus community, and the shades of identity between the two.

INTERNET PUBLICS

While many of these quests for cultural recognition took place in the traditional media of print, the 1990s also witnessed the beginnings of discourse about religion online. Since these controversies took place during the emergence of the internet, they were caught up in the attendant
utopian ideals and unregulated practices that the World Wide Web in its
infancy represented. In a sense, the net also contributed in a deeply significant way to the eruptive public space. Even though it was an emergent
technology, the internet created a new public space in which religious
communities could object to the formal publications of scholars and create online communities of solidarity in opposition to the secular scholarship of the academy. While each controversy involved the internet in a
different way, most of them in some way or other engaged in the free play
of identity and, at times, of disguise that characterized the early years of
internet discourse.

INTERNET AS PUBLIC SPACE

Many recent thinkers have analyzed what kind of public space the internet is, and can become, in a world with multiple levels of democracy and
civic engagement.[12] A well-known critic of Habermas, James Bohman, has
taken up this challenge. He begins by writing about what are, in his view,
three different necessities for a vibrant public sphere, regardless of the medium. It is worth exploring those necessities here as a prelude to considering the online conversational dynamics of some of the cases in this book.

First, in Bohman's view, the public sphere must be a forum—that is,
a social space in which speakers may express their views to others, who
in turn respond to them and raise their own opinions and concerns. The
ideal view of this modality is face-to-face interaction. Second, a democratic public sphere must manifest commitments to freedom and equality
in the communicative interaction in the forum, and such interaction takes
the specific form of a conversation or dialogue in which speakers and
hearers treat each other with equal respect and freely exchange their roles
in their responses to each other.[13] Third, there needs to be a corrective to
the face-to-face interaction; communication must address an indefinite
audience. While a public statement may be addressed to a particular per-

son, it could and should be addressed to anyone. Communication is public, then, if it is directed at an indefinite audience with the expectation of a response. In this way, a public sphere constitutes a commons, an open space for such interactions that is realized in iterated responses through similar acts of communication. What is more, a public sphere depends upon the opening up of a social space for a particular kind of repeated and open-ended interaction and thus requires technologies and institutions to secure its continued existence and regular opportunities and access to it.

Bohman suggests that the internet is in fact a possible medium for creating this kind of sphere, but with several qualitative differences of degree if not in kind. He writes:

> Computer-mediated communication also extends the forum, by providing a new unbounded space for communicative interaction. But its innovative potential lies not just in its speed and scale but also within new forms of address or interaction: a many-to-many mode of communication, it has radically lowered the costs of interaction with an indefinite and potentially large audience, especially with regard to adopting the speaker role without the costs of the mass media. Moreover, such many-to-many communication with newly increased interactivity holds out the promise of capturing the features of dialogue and communication more robustly than the print medium.[14]

Bohman accepts the fact that no public sphere is univocal in nature, and many of the issues of multivocality and inclusivity that Nancy Fraser has outlined are present on the internet as well as in other public media. But at its best, internet communication could address the problem of how to extend communicative interactions across space and time. Moreover, the internet might help a more cosmopolitan public sphere emerge, one that is not subject to the specific linguistic cultural and spatial limitations of the bounded national public spheres that have up to now supported representative democratic institutions. Bohman writes, "This network-based extension of dialogue suggests the possibility of re-embedding the public sphere in a new and potentially larger set of institutions. . . . The nature of public or publics is changing."[15]

This insight helps us understand some of the dynamics of the controversies in this book; the reembedding of the public sphere in a new and potentially larger set of institutions mediated through the internet frequently begins with an eruptive public space. This is exactly the space of interaction that many of the controversies in this book are concerned with—the collisions of the public spheres of academic institutions and those of religious communities, where people abandon the rules. In the 1990s, the internet emerged as a significant facilitator of these collisions.

ON THE INTERNET AND RELIGION

With this basic idea of the changing nature of the public in mind, it is worth turning to recent work on the interactions between the internet and religion. None of the books discussed in these chapters were published as e-books; rather, they were published in hardback and paperback, but much of the discourse about and reaction to them was on the web. Not only was the discourse on the web, but it was also characterized by a quasi-utopian exuberance typically shown in the early days of a new technology—and in the community that it formed. "The public space" of the early internet had very few rules about civility, about flaming, or about the disclosure of online identities. However, it did have the immediacy of communication and the new possibility of proximity.

In the years during and immediately after our controversies, internet theorists suggested that we make a dichotomy between religious discourses *on* cyberspace and religious discourses *in* cyberspaces. As Anastasia Karaflogka puts it, this distinction serves "to differentiate between the uploaded information of religious expressions and information which is totally virtual, in the sense that it has no presence outside the domain of the web." Like Bohman, Karaflogka understands this idea of religion in cyberspace as "extended interactive communication" that can be used to analyze ritual, practical, and theological dimensions emerging on the web. Such a distinction also allows us to think through the particular role and function of websites. It allows us to monitor existing techno-religious constructions, offers a "map" for identifying new cyber-religious movements (NCRMs), and facilitates the identifications of the discourses' relationship with and the utilization of cyber-spatial technology.[16]

Religious movements through the web have altered people's perception of time and their expectations of public interactions. The writing on religion and computers in the early to mid-1990s expressed intriguing hopes for the computer as a medium for spiritual experience. Religion on the net, as well as religion through the net, introduced the possibility of an abundance of different times ready to become real: internet time could be broken into as many "instants [and] instantaneities as the technologies of communication allow." Some specifically referred to the fact that the computer embodied Mircea Eliade's idea of "real time," that sacred time which is "circular, reversed, and recoverable, a sort of 'eternal presence.'" Such computer time can be "an eternal presence of symbols reversible and recoverable, an ontological time . . . that does not participate in the profane duration."[17] Whether Eliadean or not, the networked society could overturn the idea of time as a measureable, linear, and predictable notion.[18]

This change had important implications for how publics interact with each other and how scholars of religion interact with their various publics. As Karaflogka also notes, the publics' interactions with, adaptations of, and creative titrations of the web have created new and multifaceted research areas not previously available. Because of the speed with which change occurs on the net, and the ephemerality of internet postings, such publics are even more eruptive and more momentary than ever before.

The spatial aspects of internet publics were crucial for early internet theorists of the 1990s to consider, as well as for us as we think about these controversies in the study of religion. Spatial hierarchies could be reduced on the web because hyperlink capacities and the tendency to link beyond a single hierarchical scheme "reduced" the field of rhetoric and instead focused on "the aesthetics of collage in which radically different sources are brought together within a single cultural object." Links are both condensers of space in their collating function and expanders of space in their almost infinite referential function.[19] Relatedly, the web space was emerging as deeply relational; what was published on the web was no longer simply autonomous nor self-defined discourse but was open to a variety of voices, appearing simultaneously and with different kinds of connections to each other.[20]

In the 1990s, religious discourses and public discourses about religion on the net showed this relational mentality. They also exhibited several different characteristics: they contained vast disparities in how beliefs are to be interpreted, in how conceptions or impressions are understood and disseminated, in degrees of reaction and response to social and political issues, and in degrees of interrelation between the speaker of a religious discourse and the technology.[21] In other words, disparities between so-called great and little traditions, elite and popular traditions, and the text and the commentator had the potential to collapse.[22]

This situation set the stage for the intense conflicts over the virtual world that regularly arose: Was cyberspace a public square or a carnival?

Did common decency apply, or were all rules off? Citizens and politicians contended with each other over what the internet should be. The early internet theorist Brenda Brasher argued that religion's contribution to this public sphere could be immense, and that its public preservation as part of our online future could also represent a stabilizing influence in the virtual domain. Yet she also observed that as the internet evolved, "online religious battles may erupt as established online religions attempt to create and enforce barriers against latecomers or those whose beliefs they consider heterodox."[23]

In hopes of expanding the range of voices in the debate, the anthropologist and scholar of Native American traditions Ronald Grimes started a new public internet space that engendered one of the first online discussions about white people representing Native American traditions and spiritual practices. It created alternative and resistant intellectual discourses, such as Invasion of Sikh Boundaries, in the Sikh tradition, or Sulekha, in the Hindu one. Such new internet spaces also solidified religious identities as resistant, opaque cultural forces. The world of online creativity opened an entire alternative to the academy, as demonstrated by the case of Howard Schwartz's departure from Jewish studies. In its newfound proximity and immediacy between interlocutors, it engendered anxiety, anger, and connectivity all at once. It was both welcome and unwelcome in its intensification of public debate.

POSTCOLONIAL POSITIONS

As the internet created a new kind of global public, colonial and postcolonial identities were a large part of global multicultural debates. These identities, too, became intensified in the 1990s, and their perspectives are very much present in the controversies described in these pages. All of the authors discussed in this book take a position, if not several positions, on the insider/outsider continuum. Some had to wrestle with further complexity and forms of intersectionality that postcolonial identities introduced.

Indeed, those authors in this book who were North American from birth—Sam Gill, Jeffrey Kripal, Jane Schaberg, and Howard Schwartz—did not wrestle with their American identity in explicit ways as they were writing their books. Their understanding of their work in American contexts came later. Jeffrey Kripal struggled with his Roman Catholic identity and the role of secrecy that was part of his seminary training. As the controversies emerged, however, his American identity was part of the imposition of Western values on Hindu ones. Jane Schaberg implicitly understood her American identity as part of her right to engage in the marketplace of ideas, both before and during the controversy. Howard Schwartz, too, understood his American point of view to be part of a larger spiritual search that ultimately led him away from an official role in Judaism; that same American identity led many to expect that he would be committed to a certain view of Israel.

The scholars from the Global South, however, were deeply caught up in what the philosopher Uma Narayan, writing in the same period, called the ambivalence of the anthropological perspective: the recognition that many mainstream cultures' ignorance of other cultures is not only intellectually confining but also impractical and imprudent in a complex interdependent global economy.[24] During the 1990s, it grew difficult to combat the idea that commitment to other cultures also meant refraining from moral criticism of them. Because of the recognition of colonialism and its aftermath emerging at this time, theorists became more intensely aware that cultures of the Global South had been subject to problematic representations and interpretations. Imputations of backwardness and barbarism to Global South communities function to justify their economic exploitation and political domination.[25] Scholars studying Global South cultures, such as Kripal, were, in proffering an analysis, risking the echo of colonial judgment and accusations of neocolonialism. Hence, the rivalry of representation for religions of the Global South took on an urgent and political tone.

Conversely, scholars from a Global South culture were doubly caught in terms of representation: their insistence on inclusion in the mainstream risked reaffirming the imputations of cultural inferiority from which they had just escaped. This cultural representational bind is true of all the South Asian authors in this book. Harjot Oberoi constantly questioned the representation of "the riots" in constituting India as an essentially "violent" culture. So too, Tazim Kassam was constantly aware of her status as a South Asian woman and her implied obligation, as well as her right, to represent her own culture.

Narayan posited three roles that scholars of the Global South are frequently put into: emissary, mirror, and authentic insider. These roles, she argued, were connected to strategies that facilitate the "anthropological" project of mainstream Westerners taking an interest in other cultures without engaging in negative portraits or criticism of them. The emissary from the Global South tended to focus on Global South risk while avoiding issues that constitute Global South problems. These approaches frequently focused on the texts and artifacts of "high culture," the intellectual products of those who have access to the domains of cultural achievement and also have the power to define them as emblematic. Thus, "the religious or metaphysical views of an elite social group at a particular historical moment may be taken as defining components of the 'world views' of all Hindus or Buddhists, Chinese or Indians."[26] This perspective renders the products of other less privileged domains invisible, or defines them as "craft" rather than "art."

Narayan also suggested that this approach could develop into an acontextual "celebration" of philosophical and spiritual riches. As a result, it could ignore the indigenous hierarchies in which such riches were reproduced. In some cases, as Narayan argued is the case with the Indian philosopher Ananda Coomaraswamy, such emissary positions only reproduce the Orientalist representations they were meant to replace. What is more, to pay attention to politics or social contexts risks being a "traitor" to the larger project of weakening Western presumptions of superiority that should be part of any Global South scholar's agenda. Narayan's comments were particularly apt to describe the late twentieth-century dilemma, even more so in religious contexts. I think it is no accident that she used Indian examples to demonstrate the "emissary" position. Artifacts of religion and philosophy are particularly charged representations of high culture, and they are particularly significant when they play the role of the counterweight to colonial modes of intellectual domination.

The project of answering the West is not finished, and pointing to indigenous hierarchies, or even contestations or fluidities, interferes with the project of answering back to the West. Thus, Harjot Oberoi's betrayal needed to be exposed by traditional Sikhs fighting Western domination. To them, the fluidity and contestations that he claims were part of nineteenth-century Sikh identity undermine Sikhism as a holy, numinous tradition of high culture in India. Tazim Kassam exposed the secrets of the Ginan tradition that had tried to protect itself from criticism and persecution for so long. Her book could not be a triumphant display, since the unitary identity of Ismaili tradition was just beginning to be accepted globally. Neither Oberoi nor Kassam could successfully occupy the role of the "emissary" in their respective religious traditions because those traditions felt particularly vulnerable in their diaspora identities. At the same time, both authors were clearly conscious of themselves as vehicles of high culture. Indeed, both Sikh and Ismaili traditions were also vulnerable because, as many community leaders had also stated, they were already conscious of themselves as minorities within Global South cultures, thus occupying doubly difficult status in those religious hierarchies.

Narayan defined the "mirror" position as interest in Global South countries as sites in which Western colonialism, imperialism, economic and political hegemony, and problematic representations of self and other have played out. As an example, Narayan turned to a conference paper about colonial ideas of magic as a boundary-maker between colonizing and Western powers. She argued that there is little in the paper about native representations of magic as part of native collaborations with and resistance to high culture.[27] For Narayan, this mirror approach served to reify the big bad West and to attribute all problems of South Asia to Western colonization and continued cultural hegemony. Here, too, Jeffrey Kripal could simply fulfill the role of the bad Westerner, whose moral values included ideas of homoeroticism. Harjot Oberoi was problematic in that he did not blame colonialism wholesale but actually attributed responsibility to the Sikh *sabha* for some of its present configurations. Tazim Kassam claimed clear Ismaili ownership of the Ginans, whose status in the larger world was still fragile. Indeed, all of these scholars took a nuanced stance and claimed agency within a community, while at the same time pointing out the deep complexities, even fissures, in that identity.[28]

Narayan ended her essay by describing the third possible position: the "authentic insider," a role in which, as we shall see, neither Oberoi nor Kassam could fully function. This position, involving a proprietary relationship between the scholar and the culture he or she claims to represent, emerges especially when the Global South scholar is the only one in the conversation who is not from the West. As Narayan writes, "Western perspectives on the issues under discussion emerge with polyphonous richness, with internal diversions, differences and tensions in evidence, while 'the global south perspective' appears seamless and monolithic."[29] Such a view fails to see the Global South perspectives as divided, split, and riven by debate. Indeed, the representation of such debates in the Global South risked being at odds with the project of establishing legitimacy on a new global stage.

While Western scholars rarely make the qualification that they are not speaking for the West, South Asian scholars must often say they are not speaking for all of India. Thus, Harjot Oberoi and Tazim Kassam inherently assumed multiplicity within the traditions discussed in their books.

Yet, in the end, when their projects became more publicly controversial, they risked speaking for none of the traditions, even though some members of the communities themselves had the expectation that somehow they would.

These dynamics appear particularly salient and much theorized in the case of scholars from South Asia, but they are present in other traditions as well. In the cases of Jane Schaberg and Howard Schwartz, both scholars' positions held an implied spokesmanship for the traditions that only became apparent in the breaches. Both scholars had to take up a religious identity that shaded over into a cultural one. And both scholars knew that contributing to internal pluralism was not part of the life-script of the traditions themselves. In Schaberg's case, the life-script was that of the history of the Catholic Church hierarchy, and she had institutional backing. In Schwartz's case, the life-script had the backing of the donors for the Jewish studies chair as well as support from Jewish organizations. When the issues entered the public sphere of multicultural debate, the authority of the individual scholar was questioned. Schaberg's role as a legitimate professor at a Catholic university was interrogated; so too was Schwartz's ability to act as an authoritative representative of Judaism, and by extension, Israel. The positions the Catholic and Jewish communities required of Schaberg and Schwartz did not necessarily entail all the dynamics of the "mirror" or the "authentic insider" positions. However, they did, as Narayan also pointed out, erase major differences within the traditions. Both Judaism and Catholicism understand themselves as minority traditions in North American culture and might therefore be vulnerable to attack if such fissures in their communities were exposed.

FINAL THOUGHTS

The controversies discussed in this book did not allow for the possibility of multiple identities in public. The invariably complex, intersectional identities of authors and protesters are extremely difficult to acknowledge in debating an inherently unstable cultural category such as religion, and religious identities, in an eruptive public space. Religion can be an aspect of multicultural identity, one invoked if the group's interests are best advanced in doing so. Many have pointed out the impossibility of this position, since one must privilege one identity over another in such a way as to make implicit value judgments about its merit above other identities.[30]

Thus, in American culture wars, Native American, Catholic, Sikh, Hindu, Jewish, or Ismaili identities have only a limited number of rhetorical choices in the eruptive public spaces in which they find themselves. This tension is played out in the rhetoric of each of the cases involved. Insofar as it is celebrated as part of the landscape of diversity, religion can exist in cultural spaces that are what Rico Lie calls "spaces in a state of intercultural negotiation," whereby cultural norms of practice exist in productive tension with each other.[31] However, insofar as communities understand their religion to be misrepresented, the identities anneal as an inviolable, singular attribute where the productive tension is replaced by an unproductive one. In the eruptive public space, the space of intercultural negotiation can easily become unproductive in just this way.

Most importantly, all of these public debates featured a singularity of religious identity, in which individuals or pluralisms within religious traditions could not be adequately represented. In the 1990s, we began to live in a political reality where many minority communities felt forced to declare their own interests in competition with other communities, and had to do so in a rhetorically singular and focused way. In addition, many communities claimed to be singled out, protesting in many email messages, online essays, and other venues that "other communities" are being treated more fairly and less prejudicially than the community in question. This stance was not unique to any given community; it was a rhetorical move that all participants in identity politics had to play. Moreover, in this period, the university also began to understand itself as a "community" whose interests had to be represented.

Indeed, what many cultural theorists term intersectionality[32]—the awareness and analysis of multiple identities—became impossible in the eruptive public space when communities and academic institutions felt they must defend themselves against attack. As Amartya Sen and others have pointed out, the word "community" signaled, at best, a placeholder for uncritical acceptance of a set of practices and, at worst, a form of communalism to which no democratic person should assent.[33] Its form can be populist and resistant; it can also be elitist and conservative of the status quo. In either case, its insistence on community as the uncriticized and uncriticizable good grew problematic when multiple identities could not be acknowledged.

The work of a religious studies department, among other things, is to explore and discuss pluralism, both between and within religious traditions. The work of a religious community, among other things, is to negotiate and come to terms with such pluralism, at its external boundaries as well as within its group. But in the late twentieth century, the Habermasian project of translating a complex category such as religion into the public sphere meant that religion could not signify two things at once. Thus the clash of public spheres, which intensified in the face of rival representations of sexualities and histories. Add to this volatile mixture the proximity, urgency, and possibility of the new medium of the internet, and the further pressures of postcolonial identities establishing themselves as global voices, and you have a very fragile public space indeed.

4

ANCESTORS' PUBLICS

SETTING THE SCENE

In the preceding chapters, I alluded to the ways in which some twentieth-century theorists of religion saw their work as potentially scandalous, and yet at the same time were working in the absence of a public audience—that is to say, an audience beyond the scholarly world. The present case studies suggest ways in which this sense of publishing to a circumscribed world might no longer be an adequate description of "publishing" (making public) in the study of religion. Rather, these controversies suggest that one might reimagine "publishing" in terms of political performance. Indeed, Nancy Fraser and other theorists of the public sphere have described public space as just this kind of political theater, whereby actors on behalf of competing publics express and make a case for their interests.

Some fields, like public policy or education, would be aware of and engaged with their publics as a matter of everyday scholarly work. Still other departments, such as theater and music, are partly performative in nature and therefore necessarily engaged with publics, although that is not all they do. Even though there are dramatic exceptions, the study of religion and religious studies departments have traditionally not had a built-in public function whereby such engagements with publics are part of their daily bread and butter.

Before we examine the case studies in this book, it seems worth inquiring about the recent background to those cases—what our intellectual ancestors have said and done about the question of the various publics for the study of religion. I want to tackle this question via an analysis of two recent intellectual ancestors, W. C. Smith and Mircea Eliade. Although their works were not the only paradigms in the study of religion in the 1970s and '80s, they were two of the most dominant voices, and discussion of their legacy continues today. In both of their cases, I will argue that, insofar as these two scholars dwelt at all in the public space between the university and the religious communities, they dwelt in that space very differently. W. C. Smith understood his work as motivated by a participatory ethos, whereby religious actors could have a voice in shaping their own identities in public and private. Eliade understood his work as transformative of culture, but only insofar as any culture could throw off the yoke of the terror of history and become rejuvenated by its own archaic underpinnings.

I will also argue that, even given these different projects, both of them had an understanding of the study of religion as a liberal humanist project, a straightforward liberalism that was meant to enlighten and liberate the everyday understanding of religion into a richer public consciousness about religions. While W. C. Smith wrote at the end of his career about the failure of western liberalism vis-à-vis the development of Islam in Asia and the Middle East, neither of them lived to experience fully the paradox of liberalism that faces most scholars today: the way that religious tolerance and openness toward other religious traditions must come to terms with interlocutors from their reading publics who do not share their views.

Neither scholar explicitly spoke about the idea of a "public space," much less a "public sphere." There are very few records of either scholar engaging in open disagreement with members of a religious tradition who objected to his works. However, they both wrote about several themes that are relevant to our topic of the multiple publics in the study of religion. First, some of their work was addressed to a nonuniversity public. Second, they wrote about questions of culture at large (Eliade) and the building of a shared or common world (Smith). Third, they both wrote about the role of the university and intellectuals in relationship to the larger world. Fourth, both wrote about the questions of liberal humanism and its possibilities, albeit with very different connotations to the term.

W. C. SMITH: MULTIPLE FAITHS AND THE BUILDING OF A SHARED WORLD

W. C. Smith is best known for his work *The Meaning and End of Religion*, in which he argues against "religion" as a term of art because of its Western bias and its lack of translatability within the vocabulary of most world religions themselves. As he writes:

> One's own "religion" may be piety and faith, obedience, worship, and a vision of God. An alien "religion" is a system of beliefs or rituals, an abstract and impersonal pattern of observables. A dialectic ensues, however. If one's own "religion" is attacked, by unbelievers who necessarily conceptualize it schematically, or all religion is, by the indifferent, one tends to leap to the defense of what is attacked, so that presently participants of a faith—especially those most involved in argument—are using the term in the same externalist and theoretical sense as their opponents. Religion as a systematic entity, as it emerged in the seventeenth and eighteenth centuries, is a concept of polemics and apologetics.[1]

He advocates instead for the twin terms of "faith" and "scripture," both terms that can be readily understood by the adherents of all world religions. In the construction of faith that is the right and practice of every individual, these terms would be ones around which the individual could organize both belief and practice.

W. C. Smith is also well known for his analyses of the dynamics of contemporary Islam, as well as his thinking about a broad-based "theology of religions," which might include the insight of other traditions as its subject. Indeed, it would be difficult to overemphasize the influence that his early life in Lahore had on his writing and thinking. In Lahore, he was influenced by fellow intellectuals, Marxists, the ulama, and the religiously diverse environment in which he lived before the Partition.[2] As a result, in his early work on Islam, Smith shows an integrated understanding of the relationship between religion and society, including their dynamic interaction. In his earliest publication, *Pakistan as an Islamic State* (1951), he writes about the debate between the secular modernizers and the ulama, acknowledging that no account of the construction of a state will ever portray the Islamic ideal adequately, nor ever even adequately portray the Pakistani Muslims' interpretation of it. But he also emphasizes that the interpreters of the Islamic state ideal are not the ulama but the Constituent Assembly, the government, and the administrative services, which had in turn decided that final authority shall rest with the full electorate. In a premonition of what was to come, Smith speculates that "a major crisis, both within the country and within the development of Islam as a religion, would occur if any sizable group, or any sizable portion of the educated leaders, should come to feel that the modernist programme were good but not Islamic."[3] He goes on to state that he does not think (in 1951) this will occur, although the second half of the twentieth century proved otherwise.

In *Islam in Modern History* (1957), Smith writes of his hope for movement beyond the isolationist tendency in Islam—and this is the closest he gets to actual disagreement with Muslim thinkers:

> Some have spoken as if an Islamic economic system were one that a Muslim community should or would adopt if it were isolated, were not enmeshed within the extant vortex of international commerce and world monetary exchange and dollar dominance and the like. Similar for other aspects of social living. This approach is unfruitful; it is irrelevant on a large scale as we noted on a small scale in the particular case of Islam in India. . . . A truer recognition is surely that Muslims' "independence" will mean not isolation but renewed internal strength and a growing Islamic influence on the rest of mankind, as well as vice versa.[4]

Smith concludes this thinking by emphasizing that "freedom is participation," and that "a faith that is alive is a faith for men and societies that are involved." Participation is a theme we shall return to, and relevant for our inferences about Smith's approach to the idea of the public. In the end, however, he goes beyond the critique of an isolationist Islam and argues for engagement in the opposite direction. For him, "a healthy flourishing Islam is not only important for Muslims but for all the world today." Moreover, in his view the spirituality of Islam can effectively counter an exclusively Marxist or other economic doctrines, as well as various forms of Christian doctrine. Finally, Smith argues that the proper Christian perspective on Islam is a strong advocacy for the development of a vital Islamic society itself.[5]

W. C. Smith's contributions to the public sphere beyond the university are also striking. In addition to producing scholarly work, he regularly wrote to newspapers, advised government agencies, and conducted radio broadcasts. As early as February 1956, he produced a pamphlet for the Canadian Forces, "The Muslim World," which included questions for discussion leaders and an outline of major topics. In 1959, he delivered a sermon at the Sunday morning service of the Canadian Institute of Public Affairs conference that was broadcast by the Canadian Broadcasting Company (CBC). In that address, he spoke extensively about the effect that his time in Lahore had on the development of his thinking as well as the role of religious diversity in South Asia at the time before partition. His public radio addresses in the series *The Faith of Other Men*, also sponsored by the CBC, were well known during the time of their broadcast, as well as in printed form after their delivery.[6] Even as late as 1995, Smith was writing to the newspapers to object to characterizations of religions in various general publications.

COMMON WORLD AND AN ETHOS OF PARTICIPATION

W. C. Smith also had a keen idea of what constituted a common world and spent much of his life and work arguing for such a common world in the religious sphere. In a book review for the January 1958 issue of the *Canadian Journal of Theology*, he allows for a book's value for the public knowledge of the region—acknowledging in a short sentence that public understanding of the Middle East is a desideratum.[7] More directly, in the Harvard Divinity School newsletter's September 1964 edition, the authors celebrated the growth of its ecumenical faculty, "particularly Dr. Cantwell Smith as the new director of the Center for the Study of World Religions." Smith's address in that newsletter included the observation that a transformation in religious understanding was in progress:

> I am profoundly persuaded . . . that mankind, all over the globe, is today in process of entering a significantly new phase in the religious history of the world. . . . Whether we like it or not, and as a matter of fact most of us do like it . . . religious isolationism is coming to an end.

This movement toward a common world was part of the reason for the study of comparative religions:

> What the various religious traditions have in common is the fact that each is being carried by persons who increasingly are involved in the same problems. Christians, Jews, Buddhists, Hindus, Muslims and the others are all faced today (for the first time) by a joint challenge: to collaborate in building a common world. This must be not only the kind of world in which we can all live together, but the kind also of which we can jointly approve, and to the building and sustaining of which the faith of each can effectively inspire.[8]

The public (in this case singular), or the common world, was populated by those people of faith whose common endeavors would naturally bring them together, and whose faith would inspire them to further commonality.

As his pamphlet for the Canadian Forces on Islam reveals, Smith clearly understood that a scholar must participate in historical processes. In a lecture in honor of T. Cuyler Young at Princeton, he praises Young for the role that he played in the government in Washington and in the US embassy in Tehran in the 1940s: "It was a participation that affected the total process in the direction of humanity, of humanness, of perception of, and sensitivity toward personalism and truth."[9] He discerns *tasdiq* (faith) as signifying the affirmation and even actualization of personalist truth. For Smith, any participation that "mellows and makes to any degree more humanely true the processes of international diplomacy" should make one grateful. Personalism is key to Smith's idea of common endeavor, as is the idea of participation in the commons, whether it be government, the university, or the radio.

Indeed, in 1969, Smith goes on to discuss the idea of "Participation as a Possible Concept for a Theology of the Religious History of Mankind." He begins with the same premise he began his inaugural lecture with in 1964 for the Center for the Study of World Religions (CSWR): since intellectual and social isolation is disappearing, a theology of religions that proceeds from all of the world's religions, and not just single traditions, is possible. (Smith's discussion of this idea's implications for Christian theology is key, but not necessarily relevant to his idea of the common sphere.) Participation for him began with is forming of friendships with Muslims during his time in Pakistan and learning to see the Muslim tradition as an evolving process and not a static, one-time event. As he writes, Muslims' historical awareness has grown with the establishment of Pakistan, and gave the particular group of Muslims "a cherished opportunity to guide their corporate lives in accord with Islam; which in turn made inescapable and specific and personal a grappling with the question of what Islam is, deontologically—which is an Islamic way of saying what is right and proper, cosmically what is the Good, what is Justice, what is Truth."[10]

More importantly, Smith argues, the historical sphere is the place where religious fluidity is most obvious. Because of this, Muslims in Pakistan understood themselves no longer as "bearers of a pattern," but rather realizing now that they are "participants in a process." So whether he or she is conservative or radical, critical or sympathetic, a Muslim is someone who participates in the Islamic religious stream as a member of the community at large, and "more or less closely as a member of that minority within it whose special task it is to cherish, to formulate, and to guide the evolution of its institutions and norms."[11] The quality of participation gives a Muslim's life significance, and, mutatis mutandis, that participation also shapes the Muslim worlds (and therefore publics) around him or her.

Indeed, W. C. Smith sees that this participation even extends beyond the individual community of which a person might be a part. As he puts it, each person, perhaps not deliberately and perhaps even obliquely, participates in the ongoing process of a "neighboring community."[12] More and more, at least in the suburban churches of Boston, where he was then living, people were living out their religious lives with the background of all religions in mind. They were shaping each other's traditions in both conscious and unconscious ways.

This idea of the common shaping of, and living into, a world theology also affected his ideas about secularism. In two key essays—"Secularity and the History of Religion" (1969) and "Faith as a Universal Human Quality" (1971)—he argues for three different kinds of secularism: the correlative, the exclusivist, and the inclusivist. The first, correlative secularism, allows for the appreciation and development of religious traditions. Such a secularist sees that the soundest political theory is that which recognizes society as discerning "the religious, and even the ecclesiastical, as one legitimate, respected, even perhaps necessary sector among others, in a complex organization of society."[13]

The second, exclusive secularism, arising out of the Enlightenment, contributes to a depreciation of religious traditions and finds a continuous narrative of progress beyond religion as the only acceptable narrative of humankind's progress. For Smith, this secularity "does or would, passively or actively, reject religious, Christian, spiritual, ecclesiastical or other such consideration from one's own personal life, or in a more extreme form, from society." This more exclusivist secularity, in turn, has both a positive and a negative subset. In the positive sense, secularity in its own right could be seen as a kind of positive faith, "powerful, creative, and of transcendent reference."[14] We see this in the humanist traditions going back to Greek civilization, and in many idealistic traditions, even in atheistic humanism. However, this secularism can risk a view of life as devoid of any meaning at all. In his slightly later lecture, "Faith as a Universal Human Quality," Smith makes even stronger this distinction between positive secularism versus destructive and nihilistic secularism.[15]

Finally, there is Smith's version of a more "inclusivist" secularism, an idea that influenced various movements of the 1960s. It argues that the concern of Christians (and other religious people) should be the secular world and nothing but the secular world and that the meaning of faith is relevant to those things that have been called secular in recent Western history—such as economics, sociology, and technology.[16] Thus, for example, during the 1960s, terms like "the secular meaning of the Gospel" grew popular among certain groups.

THE ROLE OF THE UNIVERSITY IN THE WORLD

Smith's ideas about the relationship between the university and the world are equally prominent in many of his writings. It is clear from his many memos about university life, such as those to Dean Krister Stendahl about the future of Memorial Church,[17] or to the Harvard Divinity Bulletin about the next phase in the CSWR, that he cared deeply about the symbolism of buildings and programs within the university as well as between the university and the larger society.

Even with his vibrant concerns about the inner workings of the university, Smith began his early career with a deep concern about the role of intellectuals more generally. In *The Modernisation of a Traditional Society* (1965), a series of lectures given in New Delhi, he devotes the entire second chapter to the role of intellectuals. His major point in this chapter is something of a shadowboxing exercise with Marxists, in that he says the process of modernization should be possible "only if it is vividly and responsibly recognized that fundamentally in this complex process intellectual and moral awareness is primary, economics and technology are secondary and subordinate." Smith does not want to argue that this theory of economics and technology is primarily a false theory; rather, he contends that it is grossly inadequate to the task at hand. The primacy of ideas over matter should be central: "Economics is a necessary condition of socio-cultural creativity, but not a sufficient condition."[18]

What were Smith's views about the positive actions of intellectuals? First, he was writing at a time when one of the leading intellectuals of India, Jawaharlal Nehru, was leading the country and thus setting the intellectual climate and the debates around ideas. For Smith, cabinet members should be intellectually engaged, if not intellectuals themselves. In a self-admittedly inexact analogy, he writes, "Except in so far as Cabinet members are themselves intellectuals, a Cabinet is the executive of a Society's intellectuals in much the same way as the Civil Service is the executive of the Cabinet."[19] Ideologists define not the action itself but the limits to action.

Through the work of intellectuals, however, ideas can reduce some of the limits on action. This can be partly done through the active work of universities. For example, universities could play a key role in negotiating the questions of language variety and linguistic difference in contemporary India. As Smith writes:

> Intellectual awareness of this problem could be vastly greater, richer, more precise than it is; and that a country like India will be modern in relation to language only when its disciplined self-consciousness in this realm has been much increased. . . . One would like to see in every major Indian university bubbling departments of linguistic science tackling with vigour, and dedication, the many problems that cluster in this realm, with research teams hard at work comprising not only linguistic scientists afire with concern for the problems involved but also young and able participants from philosophy, history, sociology, and related departments. The problem is quite serious enough to justify this kind of full-scale intellectual attack and to reward it richly.[20]

Smith sees this ideal scenario as the very essence of modernity: universities understand the key issues facing a society, and their theoretical solutions are produced in such a way that they can be translated back into practical solutions.[21] Smith argues that a society that does not understand this role of universities is not modern.

However, Smith also argues that there is a danger if universities think that this function only applies to them. In his view, universities institutionalize and catalyze the practical function but do not exhaust it. An intellectual attitude must be widely dominant in society. Modernization is only possible with the dedication of intellectuals, but it is only effective in society when those intellectuals succeed in "conveying this confidence in new ideas, this re-orientation of ideology, more and more widely in society."[22] Hence the double mission of intellectuals—solving problems and persuading members of society that problems can be rationally solved.

Smith finally blames intellectual apathy, the idea that problems can be solved only by an application of economics and technology, on the Western "expert" who has no interest in knowing the history of the civilizations in which he or she might now be involved. This trait, in turn, is the fault of the Western university, whose faculties of arts have only in the most meager way begun to understand the non-Western world. And yet the role of intellectuals from the non-Western world could have a revitalizing effect on the Western academy.[23]

Indeed, this idea influences two later essays concerning the place of oriental studies (1956) and Asian studies (1975) in the Western university. In these essays, Smith compares the upsurge of Asian civilizations and the possibility of the study of such civilizations to the introduction of science into universities during the Enlightenment. Such an introduction has meant the development of a new outlook, and that outlook must extend to every corner of the campus.[24] The prerequisite will be one of understanding but also the discovery and eliciting of new attitudes, which the university is uniquely equipped to provide. In addition to this inculcation of new attitudes, there is also a practical element to this question. As Smith writes:

> The ivory tower has gone and must stay gone. Much of the stimulus and vitality and creativity of our studies comes and must increasingly come from our close, however purely intellectual, involvement in the greatest practical issues of our age. In fact, I think it not unfair to suggest that orientalism is strikingly contributing to the revitalization humanities studies in our day— perhaps as much as the reverse for several reasons, of which one is the close tie in our work between cultural and practical: the evident utility here of pure contemplative understanding. Another reason is the closeness in our work between detailed research and broad interpretation: the patent unanswered but urgency, of great questions of significance as well as fact.[25]

For Smith, the study of Asia is, in fact, one of the best places to tackle the deep practical issues of a multicultural world.

In his 1975 lecture on the same topic, Smith goes even further, arguing that Asian studies can actually address in a deep way the ills of the American university. In his view, the modern intellect should recapture wholeness, the kind of wholeness that includes the emotions and the imagination as part of the intellect. Asian studies can help recapture the moral and the sensuous, and help its students to see with "burning clarity that what passes for rationality and truth in much of a modern university and its technicalization is not only a betrayal of the human person in his and her integrity but a betrayal of truth, of reason. . . . Dehumanizing concepts of intellect and truth, currently prevalent in the West, are irrational, and untrue. Our universities must come to see this."[26] Smith goes on in his 1983 Presidential Address to the American Academy of Religion to say that such personal secularism in Western society's "orthodoxy" is particularly regnant in the universities. It has been the academic establishment's credo.[27]

Asian studies can accomplish this in three ways. The first is to challenge the subjective/objective disjunctions whereby objectification of persons passes for adequate study; in Smith's mind, Asian religions have always been more critically self-conscious about the subjective element of rationality and, in this way, more inclusively and humanely rational. Second, Asian studies can challenge the university not to import inappropriate categories for the study of human societies—categories that are imposed from the outside and tend to make Asian "data" conform to preconceptions. Such preconceptions, in Smith's mind, tend to conform to Western secularism. Third, the same approach must especially apply for Christianity, which, in turn, must accept its episteme as only one among many forms of thinking within a faith tradition.[28]

It should also be noted here that Smith was not *only* concerned with Western universities. In a prescient paper submitted to the well-known scholar of Indian culture D. S. Kothari, he responds to three questions on secularism, on religious studies, and on the modernization process in relation to the educational system in India. In this paper, Smith makes a cogent argument for the role of the university not just in teaching "Asian studies," a hugely different proposition in India, but in teaching moral and spiritual values. He argues that, especially in India, such issues should indeed be incorporated into the "structure of academic concern."[29] As he writes:

> Accordingly, it deserves continuing and sustained confrontation. This accords with a concept of the university as a question-asking and solution-seeking institution. Here is a major social problem: therefore let it be tackled by the university, whose business it is to address itself intellectually, experimentally, analytically, responsibly, to the challenges that face the society in, by, and for which the university stands.[30]

He proposes (mentioning the Indian mountain town of Simla as a possible host for the conference) a paper on "Moral and Spiritual Values in the Educational Process: Theory and Practice" in all institutes of education.

In response to Kothari's questions about the nature of education, he also argues that when Indian universities were established by the British they were assigned a function more like that of a college:[31] the transmission of extant knowledge of culture and the training to carry out functions in society. Now, however, the production of new knowledge is central to the university, and insofar as the modern Western university should be oriented to modern Western problems, so too Indian universities should directly orient themselves to the challenges pressing on Indian life.[32] For Smith, the structure of the sciences is moving in this direction, but the faculty of arts in India still reflects a Western bias that is wholly inappropriate to the needs of Indian culture.[33] The departments remain Western ones and the relationship between them remain Western relationships, even though the links between forms of knowledge vary from culture to culture, and this would also be true in India as it would in the West.

THE QUESTION OF LATE TWENTIETH-CENTURY LIBERALISM

How does W. C. Smith come to terms with liberalism, even if he did not live into that paradox of liberalism confronting scholars today? Did he grapple with the idea that religious tolerance and openness toward other religious traditions must come to terms with interlocutors from their reading publics who do not share their views? He wrote out most of his ideas on this tension in an essay on Islamic resurgence, in which he considers Western liberalism and its effects on the Islamic world. To his mind, the views of westernizing liberals in the Islamic world lack a moral foundation for their liberalism. Secular Western liberals often forget how fundamental the West's classical tradition and its later development in the Renaissance and the Enlightenment have been. This positive secularism understands spiritual humanism as a major force. But for Smith, the liberal Western failure to understand that (and why) Muslims cannot put "religion" aside and have anything of significance or worth left has bedeviled much of Western foreign aid policy and intellectual discourse.[34]

In a major departure from his earlier writing, Smith argues that there had been, for at least fifty years, a major possibility of the next phase of Islamic history being liberal, but it would have had to be an Islamic liberalism, a liberal Islam.[35] He agrees that there are elements upon which that tradition could have been built and could have operated within Muslim society. But Western liberals took a very different line: "progress," in the liberal sense of Western liberal Muslims, was an alternative to Islam or, at best, something parallel with it; Islam should not count in these matters. Smith thus explains the failure of liberalism in the Islamic world, since, for him, the Western outlook became a sort of self-confirming prophecy: the rise of newer and antiliberal Islam is not understood not as a liberal failure but rather as corroborating the Western liberal thesis that religion and politics do not mix. Instead, one should say that in the Islamic case, religion and politics cannot be separate; if they are not mixed well, they will be mixed badly.[36]

Even as W. C. Smith shares in the liberal critique of a Falwell or Khomeini, he further argues that this critique is no reason for liberal secularists to feel smug, for their belief in the technological progress of science is far more dangerous to the world than illiberal Islam. Muslims are eager to prove that a return to Islam is better than merging with the liberal West for two reasons: the first is the moral and social decline of the West, and the second is that Westerners themselves are seeing the limits of liberalism.[37] W. C. Smith was writing before 9/11, and also before the Arab Spring. At the time, however, he did not know whether Islamic resurgence was best understood as (1) "fascist," (2) more analogous to the French Revolution, or (3) more like the Protestant Reformation.[38] Even at this late stage, however, Smith argued for what Jonathan Herman, in his compelling analysis of Smith's thinking in light of the Salman Rushdie affair, calls a "wholesale reconstruction of religious language." He wanted a world where one could "reconceive, reimagine, and redirect public discourse" so that questions about religion are more complex and the answers to them equally sophisticated—neither a simple yes or a simple no.[39]

ELIADE: RELIGIONS AND THE
TRANSFORMATIONS OF CULTURES

Like W. C. Smith's, Eliade's corpus is large, and half of a chapter cannot do justice to everything that he might have written about the idea of a "public" or even what one might infer about his engagement with what others call "the public sphere" or "public space." As Mircea Handoca and Moshe Idel have pointed out, this corpus included monographs, editions, commentaries, numerous detailed and specific studies, and a history of religious ideas, as well as an encyclopedia, novels, short stories, plays, journals, correspondence, memoirs, and lectures delivered on Romanian radio.[40]

Eliade's ideas about a scholar's relationship to his public are deeply influenced by his activities in creative writing, as well as his early formation in Romania. Eliade wrote about his public, when he wrote about it at all, in less formal ways and usually in the singular. Much has been recently written about both. It is not my intention here to go over the cases in detail for the relationship between his novels and his scholarly work, which has been written about admirably by Bryan Rennie, Mac Linscott Ricketts, and others.[41] Nor is it my intention to review the question of his relationship to the Iron Guard in Romania, which has spawned something of a scholarly industry in the last two decades.[42] My own purpose is much more limited, as it was with W. C. Smith: to trace his own sense of what constituted a "public sphere" outside the university, the role of the scholar beyond the university, and what kind of interaction he might have had with his readers, if any. Insofar as Eliade's history plays a role in his sense of a public, it will enter into the discussion.

Eliade's autobiographical writings are key for tracing this sensibility. As Ricketts writes in his introduction to the second volume of the autobiography:

> It pleased him as much or more to be invited to address audiences of persons other than historians of religions. Among such groups were the Eranos conferences . . . , Catholic monastic communities in Wisconsin and France, artists and critics in Washington, D.C., in 1963, and a conference of philosophers in Geneva (1966), the Center for Democratic Institutions (1972), and a society of Freudian analysts in Philadelphia (1974). Indeed, his audiences at university lectures typically included faculty and students from many departments and disciplines—a fact that continually gratified him because he was always seeking to reach the broader, cultured public with his "message."[43]

Eliade speaks about the possibility of creative freedom and the public sphere in his Romanian youth. He argues that in Romania, his generation only had about ten or twelve years of this freedom, since in 1938 the royal dictatorship was established, followed by the Second World War and then the Russian occupation, resulting in an atmosphere of total silence. This atmosphere was also to affect deeply his idea of a public sphere, and its possibility in Romania. Early in his life Eliade wrote often for the public sphere. In the mid-1920's he had been given a job as an editor at the journal *Cuvântul* by his mentor, the philosopher Nae Ionescu, whose right-wing politics would later influence the young historian of religion. Eliade was also a regular columnist for the magazine *Curentul*, founded in 1928.

At the end of autumn 1927, Eliade lectured in public for the first time. His lecture was part of a series on romanticism organized by Stelian Mateescu, the secretary of the Aesthetics Society, who asked him to speak on "Religious Romanticism." Eliade's thesis was that many religious rebels who opposed the state could be understood as romantic, and this was a trend that could be studied comparatively. His longing to connect with the public is powerfully captured in his journal, where he describes his own nervous preparations, followed by a feeling of excitement and euphoria as he begins to speak calmly before abandoning his notes. He then describes the chagrin he feels for forgetting to make the case on behalf of many religions that he classified as "romantic."[44] In this memoir, then, there is a sense of "a public" who listened attentively to Eliade's remarks about Taoism and other religions.

Eliade's attempts to write well-received novels also play a clear role in his early journals. As he begins his first foray into fiction, he begins to think about his reading publics—a central theme in the chapters of *Who Owns Religion?* For example, Eliade notes that his editor Meny Touneghin, chief editor at Cartea Românească, admonished him by pointing out that the public was reading foreign novels, not Romanian ones. In 1932, Eliade describes his publics with great enthusiasm. Eliade also notes the unusual audience members who came to the soiree lectures set up to pay for a new review, *Azi*, in which a number of his journals were to be printed. He writes:

> I remember Oltenița, Roșiorii de Vede, the amazing snowdrifts and the mud when the snow melted. I remember the poorly lighted auditoriums crammed with all sorts of people, from the mayor and the priest to lycee girls and boys. There were the families of the politicians and the inevitable young intellectual with the vague ambition to become a writer or scholar, who would come up after the lecture and bemoan his failure, which he blamed on his "environment."[45]

Eliade remembers with some regret his rudeness to some of these aspirants.[46] In 1935, he speaks glowingly of his fellow intellectual Petru Comarnescu, who kept himself current on social, literary, and political activities in all types of spheres.[47] With two other colleagues Comarnescu founded a movement called Criterion (not to be confused with the University of Chicago newsletter by that name) that consisted of a series of programs, as well as a journal. As Eliade wrote then, "The public discerned that this was a significant cultural experiment and one of great proportions—and they remained faithful to us until the end. Even when the subject of the lectures was not a sensational one . . . , the auditorium was full." This series of lectures was deeply influenced by a sense of responsibility toward the public. Above all, there was "a duty to lift the public, not up to our level, but beyond, to our ideals."[48] Eliade writes about Cafe Corso, where Criterion members would retire after the symposia and continue discussion until after midnight. There, one leader, Dan Botta, expressed a powerful opinion, which in turn persuaded Eliade about the scholar's relationship to the public. Botta believed that Criterion

> could effect, in the minds of the more intelligent members of the audience, an operation of Platonic anamnesis. In attending our symposia, where many points of view were presented and debated, the public was actually witness to a new type of Socratic dialogue. The goal we were pursuing was not only to inform people; above all, we were seeking to awaken the audience, to confront them with ideas and ultimately to modify their mode of being in the world.[49]

When Eliade speaks about the disintegration of Criterion, some concern about the impossibility of the public sphere emerges. As he writes, "The members of Criterion remained friends, but some of them—for instance, Polihroniade and Tell—no longer could, or no longer wished, to discuss certain problems in public with certain speakers."[50]

Eliade thought about the role of the public in the reception of his novels as well as his scholarly work. He begins by confessing that although he is by nature a very calm and quiet person, he is "seized with panic whenever I have to write something for the public or when I must speak before a certain public."[51] For Eliade, the longing for more engagement with the "public" is charged with meaning, and always has been that way throughout his writing. He mentions twice that his novel *Nuntă în cer* (*Marriage in Heaven*) was popular both with the critics and the public—an important motivator for him to keep writing creatively as well as critically.[52] Eliade also writes in his journal that the idea of yoga was becoming of interest to a larger and more varied public, which turned out to be one of the major impetuses for him to finish his early work *Yoga: Immortality and Freedom*.[53]

Indeed, on almost every occasion of the publication of his work, Eliade mentions the question of public and critical reaction as part of his assessment of the book's impact.[54] In the autumn of 1950, he writes in hopes that *La nuit bengali* would be successful, at least with the public.[55] As well, he writes of Alain Guillermou's translation of *The Forbidden Forest* as an indicator of his own interest to write for the French and foreign public.[56]

Eliade also had a political sense of the public: during World War II, he made the rounds of newspaper offices, where he had a good number of friends, trying to explain the Romanian position and assess the question of British public opinion.[57] Additionally, he mentions offices of diplomat friends set up in Europe in order to influence European public opinion. Eliade would eventually advocate for the setting up of an Eminescu foundation, named after the Romanian poet, that focused on public lectures and gave scholarships to needy students.[58] Even in the United States, Eliade was involved in starting the Society for the Arts, Religion, and Contemporary Culture, whose purpose was to "initiate and foster collaboration among the arts, religious expressions, and contemporary culture." Fellows emerged from all the world's major religions and a variety of academic disciplines and cultural professions, including physics, law psychology, philosophy, and economics.[59]

Perhaps the most influential way in which Eliade imagines a public was his push for a "new humanism," a development that David Cave, among many others, has traced. The article "History of Religions and a New Humanism" is the most influential in this regard, and the one in which Eliade makes the case. He joins W. C. Smith in arguing that Asian thought was poised to become widely influential:

> On the one hand, the peoples of Asia have recently reentered history; on the other, the so-called "primitive" people are preparing to make their appearance in the horizon of greater history (that is they are seeking to become active subjects of history instead of its passive objects, as they have been hitherto). But if the peoples of the West are no longer the only ones to "create" history, their spiritual and cultural values will no longer enjoy the privileged place, to say nothing of the unquestioned authority, which they enjoyed some generations ago. These values are now being analyzed, computed, and judged by non-Westerners. On the other side, the Westerners are being increasingly led to study, reflect on, and understand the spiritualities of Asia and the archaic world. These discoveries and contacts must be extended through dialogues. But to be genuine and fruitful, a dialogue cannot be limited to empirical and

utilitarian language. A true dialogue must deal with the central values in the cultures of the participants. Now to understand these values rightly it is necessary to know their religious sources. For, as we know, Non-European cultures, both oriental and primitive, are still nourished by a rich religious soil.[60]

Here, Eliade views the new field of the history of religions as playing a key role in contemporary cultural life. For him, such knowledge of the history of religions—he terms them "exotic and archaic" religions—will help in a cultural dialogue with the representatives of such religions. Like W. C. Smith, he imagines a dialogue, or series of "encounters," to which historians of religion might expose themselves in order to understand different human situations from those with which they are familiar.[61] Of the import of these encounters, Eliade writes:

> [A historian of religion] will become culturally creative only when the scholar will have passed beyond the stage of pure erudition—in other words, when, after having collected, described, and classified his documents, he will also make an effort to understand them on their own plane of reference. This implies no depreciation of erudition. But after all, erudition by itself cannot accomplish the whole task of the historian of religions. . . . Like every human phenomenon, the religious phenomenon is extremely complex. To grasp all its valences and all its meanings, it must be approached from several points of view.[62]

Eliade also argues for a "true cultural function" of the field:

> This, then, was the point of the new humanism—making the meanings of religious documents intelligible to the mind of modern man—that the science of religion will fulfill its true cultural function. Whatever its role has been in the past, the comparative study of religions is destined to assume a cultural role of the first importance in the near future.[63]

Note that here Eliade understands culture as a unitary phenomenon and meaning as part of that phenomenon.

There is a key feature to Eliade's cultural project that should be emphasized. Although he mentions dialogue, and the idea that "Asians" are making their own history, the real work of the historian of religions is with documents. Documents are mentioned several times in this piece for *Criterion*, as they are in the essay "A New Humanism," published in his book *The Quest*. Understanding movements tends to involve the hermeneutic deciphering and interpreting of texts, rather than necessarily speaking to members of the movement. The sphere, then, remains essentially literary, and Eliade himself argues that historians of religions need to learn more from literary scholars in precisely this regard. As he put it in one interview with *Chicago* magazine, published posthumously:

> The texts certainly present the essentials of a religion. Indian religious life is probably better expressed in the Upanishads, for instance, than in the village ritual or the temple ritual. If you read the texts—all the Vedas, the Upanishads, Brahmans—and then you went into a temple or to a ritual in a village, you would understand what was going on there. I thought from the very beginning, that at least with the "high" religions, those that have written documents, it's better to start with the essentials, with the written documents. To go out and study a tribe was probably for me more complicated, because I was always fascinated with living the life in addition to studying the life. To go out and stay in Africa, to pick out a tribe, learn the language, and then spend time there—I thought there was a danger of too much time with this kind of fieldwork, which is usually done better by the anthropologist who is prepared for that, and who knows what types of questions to ask, and so on.[64]

For Eliade, the time-intensive work of an actual relationship is not the work of a historian of religions. He does not condemn it, although he does argue that the texts are the keys to the ritual, rather than the other way around. The early texts can give us the best understanding of a village ritual in India—a statement with which most contemporary anthropologists would vehemently disagree. Oddly enough, according to Eliade's statement, someone who participates in a ritual but is not part of a "high" tradition would therefore not be able to have a history and a deep interpretation of that ritual in quite the same way. (A great number of critics have engaged Eliade's understanding of both Indian and African religions.) Africa and India, therefore, look "different" by this criterion. In either case, the actual conversation with a religious actor is not part of Eliade's public sphere of research.

Eliade writes something similar about "books" when he speaks about the work of culture more broadly in a letter to Barbu Brezianu, a historian of art, in 1979:

> Condemned as we are to decipher the "mysteries" and "to discover the way to redemption" via culture, namely through *books* (not via oral traditions transmitted from a master to disciple), we have nothing better to do than

to deepen the dialectics of the mysterious *coincidentia oppositorum*, which allows us to discover "the sacred" camouflaged in the "profane" but also to "resacralize" in a creative manner the historical moment, in other words to transfigure it, but attribute to it [*acordindu-i*] a transcendental dimension (or "an intention").[65]

Here, Eliade admits the tragic nature of the "documentary" or "book-like" work of culture—that since we cannot engage in a guru-disciple relationship, all we have left to work with is books. This idea was what Eliade left behind when he fled from his encounters in India. Had he attributed a different value to the guru-disciple relationship, his affair with the daughter of his teacher, Surendranath Dasgupta, and his forced exile from Calcutta, could have turned out very differently. Indeed, in his guru's house in Calcutta, when he had the possibility of being transformed by an encounter such that he might have become a more tight-knit member of the group he was studying, cultural norms and his own dictates suggested that he flee instead.[66]

Moshe Idel sees three major factors in Eliade's idea of culture: his Romanian experiences, his Hindu experiences, and his acquaintances with other cultures. Idel also points out the key concept of "intercultural encounter" in the Italian Renaissance, the topic of Eliade's MA thesis in 1928. Idel observes that in his writings Eliade returns many times to the paradigmatic nature of the intercultural encounters of the Florentine Renaissance and its reverberations in the European occult among people like René Guénon (to be discussed below) and Julius Evola.[67] For Eliade, this was the new expanded humanism that involved all cultures and could be even more comprehensive than the Renaissance itself.

There are other forms of public life that have been a major topic of consideration in thinking about Eliade's influences—specifically, his engagement with the Iron Guard, and his role as a diplomat in Portugal, as well as his involvement at the Eranos conference in Switzerland, discussed by Wasserstrom and mentioned in the previous chapter of this book. Each formed a particular kind of "public" in his mind. Eliade's involvement with the Iron Guard in the 1930s has been well established through his public writing, his journals, and the journals of others. Scholars have more recently tried to interpret its significance. Perhaps Florian Turcanu sums it up best when he argues that the Iron Guard was a way for Eliade to find a renewal and a place in a public that had spurned him and a role for Romania, which stood eternally, and perhaps tragically, between the

"Orient" and the "West." A westernized Romania was a cultural offense, in Eliade's mind, not only because of its hybrid nature but also because of its historicism and rejection of the Oriental side of Romania. Turcanu writes:

> Behind the intellectual renewal implied a positive evaluation of prehistory, of mythical and symbolic thought, Eliade sets as a backdrop the dynamic he salutes: modern political messianisms. . . . Eliade's position in favor of an "Orientalized" Romanian identity is synonymous with anti-liberalism. A Romanian cultural renaissance under the sign of the Orient and of a new value granted to folklore, to myth, and to symbolic thought at the expense of the historicist model goes together with the rejection of the cultural and political effects of the Westernization of Romanian Society.[68]

Turcanu argues that there might have been a homology between the marginal position of Eliade's discipline in Romania and the position of the subversive radical movement of the Iron Guard in the 1930s. Even with its nationalism and anti-Semitism, which distilled a state of mind that permeated Romanian society, the Iron Guard remained an "antisystem" movement that would ultimately clash head-on with the state and with traditional Romanian elites. Because of Eliade's own sense of being illegitimate in the eyes of the university and Romanian intellectual opinion, the rise of the Iron Guard may have been a unique opportunity to solve, in the general identity crisis, the problem of the marginality of the history of religions in the Romanian cultural landscape.[69]

This attempt at cultural legitimacy was of course radically interrupted by Communism, which had an even more negative effect on Eliade—not only because of his dislike of Marxism but because of his fear of police states. In his autobiography, the narrative of his time being detained by King Carol II as a political prisoner stands in stark contrast to the redemptive moment that a temporary reunion with many of his literary compatriots gives him.[70] Nae Ionescu and others appear as saviors who understand the true nature of Romanian intellectual work, and they alone stand as beacons of light against the Communist desecration of Romanian culture.

In this regard, Anne Mocko, in an elegant essay, shows the relationship between Eliade's hatred of Marxism and his overall hatred of police states and governments as such. In her perusal of his writings, she observes that he did not have a systematic political ideology. However, Eliade did have a political disposition:

Eliade appears to have felt a distrust, if not fear, of invasive government forms, especially those associated with police activities. Second, he seems to have particularly (though not exclusively) associated police states with Communism. Thus, his political imagination seems to have remained tied for his entire life to Romania, suggesting that his continuing interest in the dangers of Communist states was less a function of American Cold War politics than the fate of his native country.[71]

Mocko goes on to say that Eliade deplored the emptiness of Marxist ideology that led to the "terror of history." This gave rise to what some might call his most influential book, *The Myth of the Eternal Return*. Additionally, he had a loathing of the oppression of police states, articulated in the anti-Communist sentiment expressed throughout Eliade's lifetime. Mocko also observes that Eliade treats Fascism and Communism together, indicting both as suffering from the same problems, and "not infrequently evaluating Fascism more negatively than Communism." For her, this suggests that Eliade was opposed to authoritarian governments regardless of those governments' ideological predispositions.[72]

Eranos proves a very different kind of public engagement for Eliade. He writes of his own involvement:

> The Eranos group was a new and creative cultural experiment. Ten scholars from different orientations and cultures came together for ten days, discussing the same problem from their own perspective. For the European intelligentsia, it was a chance to get out at least once a year from their own specialty, visiting, putting questions to a mathematician colleague, or a Sanskritist colleague. I think that was a very important thing.[73]

Eliade went for twelve or thirteen years, starting in 1950, but lectured only once or twice. He did not have the time to have a lecture almost ready for publication, which was the requirement at Eranos, so he did not lecture further. He says of Carl Jung, whom he met in 1950, '51, and '52, and heard lecture once: "[He was] intelligent and had such a creative mind." Eliade saw his kinship with Jung through shamanism:

> He was very much fascinated with my book on shamanism. One becomes a shaman through initiation, which often includes a very difficult illness. In some cases, in Siberia, these initiates become like madmen. The existing shaman watches over this madman during this long six months, at the same time

revealing to him the mythology of the tribe, and also the meaning of his own experiences—for he is seeing things, demons and angels. It interested Jung to see that the healing of the neurotic crisis can be compared to the initiatory experience of the shaman. It was on another level, of course, on a primitive level, but he was fascinated that the illness of the shaman—and sometimes it's not only a mental illness, but a high fever is present all of the time—is an initiation, and the healing is a reparation of his own personality. After the young madman—the shaman—is healed, he is complete. Jung was very happy to see that what psychologists are doing through their treatments— discussing dreams, and trying to heal psychological problems—is somehow related to shamanistic language.[74]

Eliade acknowledged that his theories are different from those of Jung, in the sense that Eliade does not subscribe to the idea of a collective unconscious but does acknowledge the similar associations people make around the world when their experiences are similar. This idea is the foundation of what Eliade termed "transhistorical consciousness." The idea of a public at Eranos, then, is bound up with the psychological and spiritual experiences described there, and how those experiences might connect to the language of the spiritual adept.

Steven Wasserstrom, mentioned briefly in chapter 1, has another take on Eliade's idea of the public at Eranos. In his book *Religion after Religion*, he embarks on a critique of Eranos, particularly the idea that all three historians of religions—Gershom Scholem, Mircea Eliade, and Henry Corbin—have as their goal a totality of interpretation of culture. That totality is Gnostic: the sharing of secrets without sufficient attention to the social process. For Wasserstrom, the problem with the Gnostic history of religions is that it imposes patterns on the past that were never (demonstrably) there. This ahistorical recycling, an eternal return of the same, suggests a gnosis arrogated to the historian by an a priori disgust with modernity, not by research into the previous reality. The presumption that such world-rejection could stand in for history while offering insight into totality—surely this is an unacceptable assumption for a historian to claim.[75]

As Wasserstrom sees it, the three scholars at Eranos were Cold War sages par excellence and, as such, interested in the history of religions as a regulative idea in the face of Communist ideologies. The idea of direct apprehension of symbols of the divine—along with a nostalgic idea of the sacred—could combat such ideology.[76] Most importantly, though, for Wasserstrom, they all developed a theory of religion *after* religions: when institutional religion no longer holds authoritative sway with the public, the public's understanding of the "sacred" hidden in everyday reality could nevertheless retain influence. As Wasserstrom notes most relevantly for our present purposes:

> They were outstandingly authoritative in their own fields, for obviously good reasons. They were also, furthermore, the crossover success stories of their day. That is, they spoke broadly across disciplinary boundaries to a general audience. In fact their reception crossed disciplines, religions, and gender and political differences. The Archimedean point that gave them such leverage uncannily rested outside the ordinary planet of discourse. . . . Their depreciation of society, social theory, thinking on society demanded myth and symbol . . . to be the exclusive locus of real religious meaning.[77]

It is ironic that Wasserstrom places these thinkers as founders of New Age religious movements in their own right. Many so-called secular readers, especially those in arts and psychology, as well as those committed to national identity-building, have looked to "religion after religion" as a path to a position outside all oppositions, from which promontory they could bring the complexities of contemporary life into coherence. That is why the study of the New Age and of new religious movements is so necessary for the understanding of "religion after religion." Wasserstrom sees Jung, who provided much of the rhetorical strategy, as the godfather of this secular esotericism. The New Age movement, predicated on the creative imagination, draws especially on those in the arts and the helping professions to live a new religion after "traditional" or "organized" religion.

I might note here that, in terms of the concerns of the present book, the public at Eranos was a kind of subpublic, a society that engaged in an interdisciplinary reflection but pushed beyond engagement with traditional forms of history-making and traditional kinds of social formation. The Eranos professors abandoned both the primacy of conventional politics and ethics and the Durkheimian or Weberian reflection on moral development or social evolution. They concentrated their focus instead on a myth of origins and the play of impersonal ontological symbols. Most importantly, their understanding of their public sphere was partly one of exile, and thus the nostalgia for the sacred was one created by their life condition as well as by the great political disruptions of the twentieth century.[78]

CONTEMPORARY PUBLICS

Eranos may have created a new secular esotericism, but Eliade had more to say about the role of historians of religions in the mid- to late twentieth-century milieu. A key essay for Eliade's understanding of the public nature of his work, particularly in relationship to the contemporary world of the scholar, is "Cultural Fashions and the History of Religions," in 1967. There, he asks:

> What does a historian of religions have to say about his contemporary milieu? In what sense can he contribute to the understanding of its literary or philosophical movements, its recent and significant artistic orientations? Or even more, what has he to say, as a historian of religion, in regard to such manifestation of the Zeitgeist as its philosophical and literary works—its so-called cultural fashions?[79]

Eliade's answer is that the special training of such a person should enable him [*sic*] to decipher meanings and intentions less manifest to others. These would be in works of art and cultural trends, such as Ionesco's play *Le roi se meurt*, which cannot be fully understood if one does not know *The Tibetan Book of the Dead* and the Upanishads. The historian of religions should, for example, know that there is a surprising structural analogy between James Joyce's *Ulysses* and Australian myths of the totemic hero-type of endless wandering.[80] The historian of religion's job is to recognize that there are striking similarities between the Platonic and the Australian theories of reincarnation and anamnesis.

In addition, for Eliade, there is something "religious" about a cultural trend in that such a trend is impervious to criticism. Cultural trends are neither a remarkable creation nor devoid of all value. But their popularity, especially among the intelligentsia, reveals something of Western man's [*sic*] dissatisfactions, drives, and nostalgias.[81] Eliade goes on to discuss the popularity of writers like Teilhard de Chardin, Claude Lévi-Strauss, and Sigmund Freud before him. He begins with the popular New Age magazine *Planète* and argues that *Planète* did not disregard the social and political problems of the contemporary world. Rather, it propagated a "saving science"—scientific information that was at the same time soteriological. It was a direct response to existentialism, in which man was estranged and useless in an absurd world; with *Planète*, man was no longer this.[82] Eliade further argues that while the writers of *Planète* and Teilhard de Chardin are not the same, they do have several things in common: they are tired of existentialism and Marxism, tired of continual talk about history, the historical condition, the historical moment, commitment, and so on. Eliade argues that Lévi-Strauss, too, shares this disinterest in history and instead develops intense interest in the material stuff and working out of symbols. These thinkers are interested less in history than they are in *nature* and in *life*. As Eliade concludes:

> This fascination for the elementary modes of matter betrays a desire to deliver oneself from the weight of dead forms, a nostalgia to immerse oneself in an auroral world. In this way the contemporary trends share something with the fascination of the artist in that world.[83]

When Eliade does describe a contemporary movement, which could be understood as a "public," he does so in the same kinds of documentary terms. For example, in his essay "The Occult and the Modern World," published in 1976, he discusses recent contemporary scholarly interest in the occult.[84] For Eliade, occult movements have disclosed consistent religious meaning; moreover, the cultural function of a great number of occult practices has been just this, at all levels of culture, from folk rituals to exoteric speculations in yoga, tantrism, and Gnosticism to the Masonic lodges of the Enlightenment period; all of this may be connected to the "occult explosion" of the 1970s.

Relatedly, Eliade argues that we could not present a complete picture of the contemporary craze for astrology in both the United States and Europe without the history of religion's perspective; he cites Edgar Morin in interpreting the appeal of astrology among youth of the 1960s and '70s as stemming from the cultural crisis of bourgeois society. The interest is part of a new gnosis that has a revolutionary conception of a new age, the Age of Aquarius. Eliade also remarks on Morin's observation that astrology is not found in the countryside but rather in densely populated urban centers. For Eliade, these groups have a set of specific characteristics: they are secret and initiatory groups who are in revolt against the traditional Western religious establishment, particularly the Christian church. Theirs is a sweeping dissatisfaction, not a doctrinal one. They wanted other spiritual instruction besides social ethics.[85] Second, for Eliade, such astrological enthusiasts are naïvely optimistic and want to contribute to the *renovatio* of the world. Pretense and masquerade will be dispensed

with, and every new initiate in these occult groups helps with that reno-
vation. Spiritual growth is a focus of occult groups because it means freedom from a system and an optimistic evaluation of the human mode of
being.[86]

And yet for Eliade there is also a pessimism, as encapsulated in the
work of the author René Guénon, who argues in his many books and articles that only in the East are the true esoteric traditions still alive. Guénon proclaims the irremediable decadence of the Western world and an-
nounces its end in the Kali Yuga. As Eliade sees it, Aquarian Age youth
culture and the work of Guénon are radically opposed: one is of cosmic
and historic renewal, and the other is the esotericism that assumes the
catastrophic dissolution of the world.[87] Eliade does not know what the
results of either movement will be—but does want to ask the question of
who will interpret other "signs" of the age, such as the films *Rosemary's
Baby* and *2001: A Space Odyssey*. In each case here, as mentioned above,
Eliade's perspective is that there are cultural artifacts to be examined,
rather than living believers—indeed, "publics"—to be interviewed, disagreed with, and engaged.

IS THE BANAL THE PUBLIC?

Some intriguing ideas about Eliade's relationship with a public might
also be gleaned from Idel's insight that the "camouflage of the sacred" in
the world of the banal is one of the major themes of all of Eliade's work.
(Idel argues for this centrality, even though in his view Eliade never sys-
tematically treated it at full length; Idel does not credit Eliade's essay on
camouflage in art as a full-length systematic treatment.) As Idel puts it,
there is something in Eliade's work extending back into the early 1930s
that suggests that the purpose of the scholar is to discern the extraordinary in the ordinary, even the banal, and that the spiritual adept enters a
certain institution, marriage, or academy that he considers banal in order
to search there for something much more sublime.[88] This is true both of
Eliade's marriage to his first wife, Nina, and to his fascination with the
Iron Guard, and even in his choice of the academy as his profession. In
his *Portuguese Journal*, he writes that his love for Nina and his adventure in the Iron Guard were a matter of his search for the Absolute.[89]
Only the spiritual adept can see the transcendent nature of these mundane
choices.

Idel's observations are worth quoting at length here:

> Let me draw attention to what is the most interesting aspect of the preceding passage: the confidence that Eliade himself found in a privileged position of discerning the uncommon nature of his future wife, in comparison to other people's different reactions. Neither his family nor his friends—with the exception of Mihail Sebastian—are sensitive to the special character of his choice. This privileged status assumes some form of special providence that guides someone to make the right choices, which are hardly understood by others. . . . Because the "others" belong to the banal life and judge events accordingly, the inverse of their opinion "must" be true, and Eliade stands therefore on the opposite side of their understanding of the world. . . . He assumes that by understanding the ordinary attitude, someone may extrapolate the inverse and thus reach some form of special insight. The hermeneutics of a certain situation is therefore a matter of the special individual, and hardly a matter of consensus.[90]

Thus, although from even his earliest years Eliade loved the public, it was a public who received the gnosis arrived at by a particular individual, and perhaps they were inspired to pursue their own individual "gnosis" as a result.

THE UNIVERSITY

Unlike with W. C. Smith, we see a deep ambivalence for the work of the academy in Eliade's view—a kind of worry that the university stands for erudition, while the broad transformative work that he saw in his novels and plays could not really be understood through the work of the academy. Most strongly, Eliade writes:

> This vice which I satisfy beside a library full of erudite treatises, beside a table loaded with dictionaries and texts—elevates me in my own eyes. It gives me a weird sense of freedom. I say to myself that not everything is lost. . . . With this "secular reading" I satisfy all the loathing I have for erudition, and for the honest and useless work, for these cherished sciences—which, just because they are dear to me, I burn with a desire to spite, to "betray" them, to humiliate them.[91]

This early idea of the university was to be transformed, however, as he migrated from Bucharest to Europe and to America. His destiny, as he puts it in a later interview, would permit me to do what I wanted to do, what I thought I was called to do. It has worked in such a way as not to keep me a prisoner of a career at the University of Bucharest, which would have ended after the Russian occupation of Romania. Destiny arranged that I be in London, and then in Portugal, during World War Two, and then in Paris, keeping me all the time free to do what I wanted to do. I didn't accept a position as a professor in a European university because I knew that to be a professor there you are bound. But I accepted a position in an American university because, at least in my case, they gave me the freedom to do what I wanted to do.[92]

Elsewhere, Eliade writes with some scorn of turning down positions at universities in Bucharest and other European cities, as a way of saying he was finished with that Continental way of academic life and of being an intellectual.

Eliade also notes that America is one of the few Western countries where theology is not a dead science, as he feels it is in France and Germany. In Europe, only the specialists, priests, and seminarians are interested in theology. In Eliade's view, the European believers are more concerned with questions of politics. As he observes, "They would rather understand how they can help someone in South America or in Africa than to understand the way in which Thomas Aquinas was right. Here [in America] theology is taken very seriously. People fight about theology."[93]

One interview also credits Eliade with helping to change the idea that history of religions could not be taught in government-funded universities. Eliade responds to his interlocutor in the following way:

> I knew before I came here that the Constitution says that in a state university religion cannot be taught because that's a personal decision. But it became evident that presenting the history of religion was not asking people to become or not become religious. Religions should be taken seriously as an expression of human creativity. People in Washington came to understand that it is useful to Americans to know that what the Chinese, for example, are thinking, to know something about India, about Africa. The African genius is revealed in arts, which is religious arts, and in dance, which is religious ritual. So they realized that someone who had studied the history of religions— such as a diplomat—would be better at his job because of it.[94]

Eliade ends with a declaration of his love of teaching and his connection with the younger generation that a university—any university—affords him.[95]

LIBERALISM

In this last statement of Eliade's, he provides a positive narrative of the liberalization of the American curriculum—a liberalization that stands in stark contrast to Eliade's "illiberal" reactionary mode that Turcanu writes of above, whereby the only response to his marginal position in Romanian society is the illiberalism of the Iron Guard. Matei Calinescu writes that the "liberal" Eliade may well have started in post-war Paris, in his friendship with Ionesco, who had remained doggedly anti-Fascist and survived Romania during the war years by keeping an extremely low profile in the cultural services of the Romanian legation in Vichy.

Calinescu is one of the few writers who explored the question of Eliade's understanding of his own public identity. He argues that because of Eliade's success in Romania and in Paris, he continued to see himself as a Romanian writer and "wandering scholar," and his work was beginning to be translated to a wider audience and into numerous languages. He did not need to invent himself in the first years of his exile in Paris, where he arrived in 1945 from Portugal. In Paris, reporting on his allegiance to the Iron Guard, which was written about in a dozen newspaper articles between 1937 and 1938, was not available, as the articles had been stricken from Romanian public libraries. But fellow Romanians in Paris knew of his political past and tried to prevent him from lecturing on religion at the École Pratique des Hautes Études, where Georges Dumézil and Henri-Charles Puech had invited him. Early in 1946, swastikas were scratched on the posters of his seminar. Puech suggested to him that he should not give his course to avoid hostile demonstrations. Eliade was disgusted with the Romanians; he saw their motivation as envy, because no other Romanian since Nicolae Iorga had been invited to give the seminar that he had. Another demonstration occurred on March 26, 1946, to which he attributed the same motivation.[96]

Calinescu argues that, as a result of this kind of public identity in Europe, Eliade's liberalization occurred most dramatically in America, where, as Calinescu writes, "his international recognition, the success of his books, and his appointment and career at the University of Chicago, consolidated his identity as a scholar and philosopher of myth and religion, leaving his Romanian identity in a sort of public penumbra, so that many of his students ignored his ethnic origin or considered it irrelevant." Indeed, Calinescu makes a clear aside—his popularity among members of the American counterculture of the 1960s and '70s, or among the representatives of the New Age, had nothing to do with his past.[97]

Yet it is ironic that the work of Eliade, when given the opportunity in America, was to open up and create a kind of sphere for the liberal interpretation of religion in which even the state—perhaps especially the state—should acknowledge the history of religions and its role in society. Indeed, the openness of modern life that was the liberalizing project of the 1960s is also something that Eliade found most intriguing. As he put it in an interview, "Some people in modern life—probably a great number of people—are just following the old tradition. Others, who don't look religious at all, are on the track of quite a different kind of religious experience. For instance, when the hippie moment started in the sixties, very few people saw in that movement a thrust for a real religious experience, albeit a rather archaic one." But for Eliade, the nudism, the return to nature, the singing, and making love, not war, was a religious search for beatitude, "in being free—free to make love, free to sing and not go to work in an office, a nostalgia for a religious experience that became antiquated after the revelation of monotheism. It is a kind of going back to a cosmic experience."[98]

Relatedly, much of Eliade's engagement with liberal Protestant theology came after his arrival in America, where he could take on the mantle of liberalism more freely. As Doniger and Wedemeyer put it, "Eliade took full advantage of the prestige of the Chicago position and the resources given to him there to become the person he is known as today; in the process he adopted (and adapted) a new argot—the liberal Protestant, 'phenomenological' lingo derived from Otto and van der Leeuw, as well as a bibliography that was the coin of the realm in his new domicile."[99] In America, Eliade had a new public, or in our more contemporary terms a new set of publics, who understood and embraced these terms more readily.

FINAL THOUGHTS: W. C. SMITH, MIRCEA ELIADE, AND LEGACIES OF THE PUBLIC SPHERE

In these two recent intellectual ancestors, we have a variety of approaches to the public sphere. W. C. Smith's understanding of government and university participation was more consistent throughout his life, and clearly the understanding of a liberal Protestant. Despite the fact that his colleagues and work in Lahore had a huge influence on him, his time in Pakistan was one of a "visitor," and his role remained one of a Christian and a scholar of Islam. As such, he advocated for a theology of world religions that could be created only if Christians renounced their special claim to privilege in the interreligious public sphere. For W. C. Smith, engagement with and respect for religious actors in their understanding of their own faith and tradition was paramount in the study of world religions. His liberalism was an optimistic one, in which the university contributed to the public sphere in a problem-solving way.

Eliade, in contrast, was an "exile" whose public identity was constantly shifting. He was a visitor to many countries after leaving Romania, and his Romanian identity was nearly completely camouflaged after his arrival at Chicago. His past was filled with engagements with the public sphere. In his Criterion years, he felt that the role of the intellectual and the potential influence on the public sphere were possible through the heightened intellectual circles of 1920s Romania. His involvement with the Iron Guard showed yet another, more totalizing belief in a public sphere that could and should resist the westernized Romania as well as the possibilities of Communist Romania. His posting as a diplomat in Portugal showed his pragmatic understanding of the public sphere, even as he longed to return to his scholarly and literary endeavors. Only when he arrived on American soil could he claim the language of the liberal Protestant, a language that had been available to W. C. Smith since his birth. When it comes to engagement with the public sphere, there is a marked continuity in Smith and a marked discontinuity in Eliade.

Yet there are some clear common themes. In their later works, both Eliade and Smith had a vision of a common humanity where new interactions between East and West, and the possibility of Eastern actors having the chance to make their own history on the world stage, would have world-changing effects. In this sense, both Smith and Eliade advocated for a new humanism that could transcend cultural boundaries and in which a new dialogical encounter (a term used by both scholars) was possible.

Both Smith and Eliade had a deep resistance to Marxist historicism. In Smith, it was a rallying against technology and economics; in Eliade, the new historicism led to an uninspired and even dangerous view of humanity, with no possibility of genuine renewal except through the millennialism of the revolution. For Smith, Marxism was connected to a kind of secularity that was hostile to religion, and he saw no value in it. Although Eliade, too, hated this kind of secularity, he saw a kind of camouflage of the sacred in secular movements. And later, Smith, too, saw in a more positive "religious" secularity a kind of hope for humankind.

Yet in both cases, the possibility of engagement, even disagreement, with an interlocutor of a religious tradition was not part of the lexicon of the scholar. For Smith, even though the religious actors were part of the representation of the religion, the public sphere was always one of agreement with the religious person, and that was the essence of the scholarship in comparative religion. This was true for Smith in America, in Canada, and in India. The spiritual traditions of the world were always ethically formative and positive. Individual voices and movements tended to be less emphasized than the larger, more holistic views of the religious tradition.

For Eliade, the documentary textual nature of the historian of religion's work meant that the religious actor could not be part of a discussion with scholars in the public sphere in any meaningful way. Since texts, not people, were the stuff of the historian of religion, testimony from religious actors was properly in the domain of the anthropologist. More importantly, the texts and not the rituals reveal the key elements of a religious tradition. Eliade himself loved being in the public sphere, but such participation tended to be focused on a singular "public's" reception of a singular "message" from Eliade. This singularity and unidirectionality held true in his reflections on the reception of his novels and on the reception of his scholarly work.

Finally, even though their differences are compelling, both scholars worked in a kind of liberalism that had yet to confront its own paradox or its own limits. Smith worked without limits of liberalism because it could not be imagined that the good religious people of the world would disagree with a well-intentioned description of their reality that was produced in collaboration with them. (There was a shadow of acknowledgment that this resistance to scholarship might occur in his work on the Islamic resurgence, but only a slight hint of this.) Eliade worked without knowledge of limits of liberalism because the work was one of acknowledging a message of "religion after religion," of the camouflage of the sacred that could be discovered only through texts.

Both Eliade and Smith worked with an understanding of the liberalizing projects of universities that would allow both of them to do their particular work. But they did not dwell in, nor were they confronted by, the liberal paradox of the limits of tolerance and the possibility of history talking back. The public's resistance to universities as such, the public's engagement with and reassertion of their own indigenous histories, and the public's splintering into a variety of micropublics, each with their own internet voice, occurred just after their deaths. This far more fractured, multiple, and fast-moving world was the public space into which the next generation of scholars—both Eliade's and Smith's intellectual sons and daughters, and grandsons and granddaughters—were to walk. These younger scholars' "crossing and dwelling" into various publics, to take Tom Tweed's phrase in a new light, would not be so straightforward, nor so filled with harmony and renewal.

PART TWO
CASE STUDIES

5

MOTHER EARTH: THE NEAR IMPOSSIBILITY OF A PUBLIC

Sam Gill published *Mother Earth: An American Story* in 1987. His intention was to tell the story of the figure of Mother Earth among a variety of Native American peoples in North America. By the term "Mother Earth," he meant a single deity, a creator goddess named Mother Earth, with a particular theology and ritual tradition surrounding her. Following the larger historical project of J. Z. Smith, and the particular historical project of Olof Pettersson, who questioned the whole idea of a unified Mother Earth, Gill wanted to tell the story of the making of the myth of Mother Earth in terms of historical encounters and strategies.[1] He was particularly interested in the documentary evidence for the idea and in the scholars and Native Americans involved in gathering that evidence.

Beginning with his experience studying the Navajo, Gill resists the idea of a singular "religion" within which all Native Americans participate. And he goes on to examine the documentary evidence that is generally used as the basis for these applications of the Mother Earth idea—particularly the statement made by the Shawnee Leader Tecumseh in 1810 and that of the Wanapum leader Smohalla in 1885. Gill also examines the Zuni tradition of New Mexico and the Luiseño of Southern California, the two most frequently cited tribes who give "evidence" for a belief in Mother Earth. For Gill, these historical encounters were themselves kinds of public spaces, with participants, witnesses, and major and minor interlocutors. Arguments about them had great implications for how public spaces could engage with the concept of Mother Earth in the present day.

As the first case study of this book, *Mother Earth* raises questions about the very possibility of a public sphere in the face of a long history of social inequality and traumatic relationships with the state. The controversy took place in the late 1980s and '90s as Native Americans created a place for their communities in contemporary cultures, gained a growing sense of their communities as public spheres in their own right, and continued to develop a deep commitment to maintaining a sense of belonging, privacy, and ownership over cultural knowledge. For Native Americans, the case of Sam Gill's *Mother Earth* went to the heart of these issues: whether a Native American public sphere itself could be grounded in and by the figure of Mother Earth, and thereby understood as legitimate, both in the troubled history and the contemporary relationship of Native Americans with the United States government.

SAM GILL'S WORK

In *Mother Earth*'s chapters, Gill focuses on a twofold task: unmasking the distorting accounts of historians of religions and exploring the actual accounts when Mother Earth was invoked as a figure in encounters between the United States government and Native peoples. Beginning with the Tecumseh legend, Gill takes up the various reports of Tecumseh's famous conversation with General William Henry Harrison in 1810, "The Earth is my mother, and on her bosom I will repose." This was supposedly said during a meeting with Harrison in the Indiana territorial capital, Vincennes, and addressed the settlement of the lands along the Wabash River. Tecumseh was attempting to protect those lands from settlement by the United States and to revoke (by force if necessary) a treaty of "sale" meant to allow United States settlement. This was widely perceived as the "last stand" of the Indians of the Midwest. Their encounter came after a series of messages between the two leaders and attempts by Harrison to remove the Shawnee from the land.

In tracing eyewitness and journalistic reports of the encounter over time, as well as stage dramas involving Native Americans in many other encounters, Gill argues that there is little clear evidence that Tecumseh ever said this; rather, "belief that he made the statement doubtless emerged in the explosion of legend, lore, and literature that, after his death, transformed Tecumseh from an obstacle to settlement into a heroic figure."[2] He suggests that Moses Dawson, author of an early study of Harrison and

Tecumseh's relationship, cited the speech as a first step in the mythologiza-
tion of the Shawnee chief. In Gill's view, the statement's first appearance
in print was much later than the events and coincided with the American cultural idea of Native Americans as noble savages, unable to accept
civilization.

Gill argues that the Shawnee did hold a belief in a major creator deity and a female named Go-gome-tha-na, the Grandmother, also living in
heaven. The Shawnee certainly understood that the earth could be personified as a mother, a spirit being, or a deity in the pantheon of the conceptions of the earth.[3] Yet, Gill argues, there is no clear evidence that the
Shawnee held a belief in the creator goddess named Mother Earth or anything closely related to it.

Gill's methods are similar in his treatment of the statement "Shall I tear
my mother's bosom?" attributed to a Wanapum man named Smohalla
and first recorded in James Mooney's monograph on the historical prec-
edents for the Ghost Dance of 1890, "The Ghost-Dance Religion and the
Sioux Outbreak of 1890." Gill argues that the statement is taken wildly
out of context, despite the fact that the words are widely cited by historians of religions as evidence for a Mother Earth belief. He argues that the
"Dreamers" movement founded by Smohalla, who encouraged Native
Americans to return to the ways of their ancestors, "flourished during the
1870s as part of a larger resistance by Native Americans who refused to go
onto reservations. It was a period of holding out and dreaming to maintain their millennial expectations."[4] Gill argues that Smohalla's speech
has remarkable structural similarities to the one that Tecumseh report-
edly made, and might well have been influenced by it. He cites other
Native American speakers who use earth imagery in their negotiations
with the American government, trying to explain why they find it impossible to cede to the US government's demands to give up their lands.[5] In
looking at related scholarship, he argues that the evidence comes from
situations during the negotiations over land influenced by the crisis-like
developments.[6]

In some cases, Gill does acknowledge that the Mother Earth concept
was incorporated into story tradition, such as those of the Okanagon and
the Zuni Pueblo. In the Pueblo case, Gill criticizes the original teller of the
Zuni tale, Frank Cushing, for being the creator of a metamyth—a story
about a creation story and a creation of Cushing's rather than an actual
Zuni figure. Fertilization and the idea of a world parent figure do not need
to be linked, but as Earth Mother, she appears rather as one element in

a broad pattern of Zuni thought in which things both animate and inanimate are personified, sometimes loosely anthropomorphized, and addressed in kinship terms.[7]

Gill argues something similar concerning the California Luiseño stories, in which a "mother" was represented as having been raped in order for creation to come about. Gill argues that the stories describe something different than a creator Earth Mother. Rather, they describe a creation process that establishes ordering principles and the claim to power. Internal evidence suggests that a hierarchy, a system of dominance, is the ordering power of the created Luiseño world. The dominance of brother over sister, male over female, and sky (night) over earth is accomplished by an act of incestuous rape (not culturally condoned by the Luiseño), and only then did the precreation unity, characterized as emptiness and darkness, give way to the formulation of the world and all of its attributes, peoples, and powers.[8] Early twentieth-century scholars Constance Dubois, Alfred Kroeber, and Robert Heizer all create scholarship that is dependent upon each other's narrative of the female figure as a "world parent" type. Gill points out that the Swedish scholar Åke Hultkrantz actually uses the term "Mother Earth" and that his works are a major contributor to the idea of a long-term, ritually inflected theological tradition.[9]

Gill notes that scholars in a larger comparative vein have also contributed to this idea, most particularly E. B. Tylor. Although his intentions were far more global in establishing a Mother Earth typology, the effect of Tylor's work on scholars of the Native Americans was nonetheless great. Tylor read H. H. Bancroft's work in 1882, which in turn affected the early comparative theorist Andrew Lang. Written at around the same time, Albrecht Dieterich's *Mutter Erde* is a crucial sourcebook for the Mother Earth idea. Dieterich, in turn, influenced Friedrich Heiler, Joachim Wach, Gerardus van der Leeuw, E. O. James, Raffaele Pettazzoni, and Mircea Eliade. The writings of Hartley Burr Alexander and James George Frazer also contribute to this idea. And Eliade's *Patterns in Comparative Religion* and *Myths, Dreams, and Mysteries* create a larger archetype from which many students drew on during the 1950s, '60s, and '70s for their work. In the end Gill concludes that more than a dozen major scholars have depended almost entirely upon only five sources. Mother Earth has been accepted without question and has been understood as being so primordially archetypal and fundamental that she is viewed as a key element in the demonstration of a variety of theories concerning the nature and development of religion and culture.[10]

Gill also examines the ways in which Mother Earth came to be a figure for Native American thinkers. He argues that her historical origin as
a primordial goddess actually occurred within this century and that she
emerged as a major figure to the Indians as part of their self-definitional
process in interaction with the expectations and preconceived notions
of the European and American communities and governmental agencies,
while also being encouraged by the emergence of an "Indian" identity
that has supplanted individual tribal identities. Gill identifies the writer
Charles Eastman as one such key Native American figure in the early
twentieth century, Grace Black Elk and Sun Bear in the mid-twentieth,
and his own contemporary, Russell Means, in the late twentieth. In addition, the Hopi leader Thomas Banyacya's presentation of Mother Earth
is bound up with criticizing European American history and ways of life.
Gill concludes his book by arguing that while the primordial creator goddess, a pan–Native American figure of Mother Earth, cannot be found
in the traditions of these groups, a variety of female figures in specific
tribal traditions can be found. But no rich theological or ritual tradition
associated with this figure is present in any given specific tribal way of life.
While many of these individual female figures can be interrelated struc-
turally, Gill argues that it is our views that create these interrelationships,
not the specific female figures. He goes on to argue that although scholars
create quite a powerful theology and history for the idea of Mother Earth,
their arguments are based on extremely scanty evidence. He conjectures
that this figure of Mother Earth is as deeply influenced by European and
American legacies of the idea as it is by Native American ones.

Gill concludes that the primordial "myth" of Mother Earth must be
distinguished from the history in which such a figure has been attested to
and created. He further argues that "these historical factors neither dilute
nor denigrate Mother Earth and the Indians who believe in her."[11] In the
end, he rejects "top-down" scholarship, which is synthetic in nature, in
favor of a kind of "bottom-up" scholarship, which is "directed toward particular cultures and particular people." Gill was, in his own view, trying
to focus on scholarly mythmaking and the distinct yet parallel process of
the recent construction of the Earth Mother among the Native American
community. His argument for "bottom-up" scholarship was intended as
an argument for the inclusion of Native Americans as participants in the
creation of their own myths, not as artifacts that spring full-grown from a
faceless Native American "culture" as such. It was also intended as a better
account of the experiences of particular people.

From the perspective of this book, Gill's work also narrated the story of a very fraught, unjust public sphere, where the United States government determined all the rules. The encounters described in *Mother Earth* constituted Fraser's "strong" public spheres in their own right. They were not only public conversations where one side held clear legislative force, but they were also conversations that disallowed genuine equality between interlocutors and where there was no "participatory parity."

SCHOLARLY RESPONSES

After *Mother Earth*'s publication in 1987, the critique from the academic community engendered a fascinating debate on what the effect of scholars' works on communities is and what the mode of engagement should be. Some, such as Howard L. Harrod, found Gill's straightforward attack on the distorting practices of scholars a welcome invigoration of the field so that the practices of Native communities might be better represented.[12] Bruce Forbes argues that it is a case study criticizing scholarship built on repeated, interlocking references to a very limited and mistaken set of examples."[13]

Others saw an overstatement in Gill's theory of who originated the idea of Mother Earth in the first place—whites or Native Americans. For example, in *American Indian Quarterly*, Christopher Vecsey calls it a splendid, although inconclusive, bit of text-criticism but cautions that Gill is perhaps too zealous as a revisionist historian of ideas.[14] He cites various places where Gill ignores pieces of evidence from the Shawnee, Zuni, and Luiseño records that might go against his thesis of recent invention.

Vecsey acknowledges that Gill is correct in accusing scholars of saying too much based on too little evidence. However, he disagrees with Gill about the impact of such scholarship on the Native American communities. As he writes:

> If Gill is saying that traditional Indians believed in, and prayed to, female goddesses associated with the earth, whom they sometimes referred to as mothers, but that in the last century a more unified, major Mother Earth concept has coalesced as part of a pan-Indian religious culture, it is plausible. If he is saying that American Indians had no notion of an Earth Mother until Christian Anglos gave them one, it is implausible. If he has meant his revisionism to raise questions, he has met success. If he has meant to have the last word on the matter, he will fail.[15]

Here, we can see the long-standing, deeply rooted tension in the relationship between Native communities and scholarly communities, in both their past and present incarnations. The two communities are arguing still about who gave what to whom, both in the past and in the present. The scholarly community cannot be understood wholly to have given their idea of Mother Earth to the Native Americans, for this is both inaccurate and, as we shall see below, offensive to those communities. However, to discuss the consolidation of that idea in the twentieth century would not, in Vescey's mind, be offensive. In Nancy Fraser's terms, one way to pose the issue that Vescey and other scholars began to grapple with would be to ask how, if at all, scholars and Native Americans could be equal participants in the co-construction of Mother Earth in the public sphere.

Relatedly, Åke Hultkrantz at the University of Stockholm (who is criticized roundly in the book) argues that Gill's work will probably be understood as an anti-Indian book.[16] In Hultkrantz's view, Gill wants to separate Mother Earth as metaphor and Mother Earth as goddess. For Hultkrantz, if Mother Earth is to be a goddess with the shape of a distinctly personal spirit, then Mother Earth fails. But the more fluid view of Mother Earth is, Hultkrantz maintains, very much part of the Native American view, which is that the earth concept is identical with the actual earth, her substrate. What is most offensive to Hultkrantz is Gill's claim that the "scholar's interpretation of Indian metaphors has convinced Indians that they have a Mother Earth." Gill's description of the relationship between the communities gives Hultkrantz the most difficulty. He is particularly troubled by Gill's charge against his own short article, which is that it is part of a "story" that contributes to the twentieth-century spreading of the Mother Earth concept. He ends by arguing that under Gill's criteria, most American Indian religious concepts were absent before 1800. In other words, for Hultkrantz, Gill's view is that there can be no real history (and therefore attribution of ancient status) to any Native American concepts because of a lack of sources.

In the early 1990s, another important exchange occurs, this one between Gill, Lee Irwin, and Christopher Jocks on the issue of how scholars engage in stereotyping, and how such stereotyping might affect the communities that they are studying. Gill argues that in the study of American Indian religious traditions, there is "a population of the academic study of religion with scholars and teachers who know only their own specific area, and who study it primarily because it has religious and political importance to their personal religious, racial, ethnic, or gender connection with it, and whose studies are evaluated more on the authority granted by religion, race, gender, or ethnic identity than upon academic performance."[17]

Gill writes that the academic study of religion has often failed to acknowledge what it is—academic, Western, and intellectual.[18] Anticipating Russell McCutcheon's work a decade later, *Critics Not Caretakers* (2001), Gill argues that the field as a whole has not understood that this means that the study of religion is inherently reductive, insofar as it adopts a critical and specific lens through which to review data. Gill further states that scholars have also not understood that comparative work is as much concerned with differences as with similarities. In the case of Native American religions, the study has been engaging in nonproductive or obvious questions, particularly the issue of whether one can or should be Native American in order to teach the subject. As Gill writes, "Racial or cultural distinctions cannot possibly be relevant criteria by which to predetermine research or pedagogical competence in any sub-field; indeed to do so is to refute important gains that have been made this century."[19] Gill goes on to note that (as in any bad relationship) once one discusses who should and who should not go into the field, it is a sure sign of the field's irrelevance. Much of the graduate training, in his view, consists of cultural conversations and not academic ones that engage the broader study of religion.

Christopher Jocks wrote a response to Gill, which praises important developments in the field at that time: the new move toward Native language competency, and the move toward asking about indigenous structures of knowledge and whether those structures are what the English language calls "religion." The development of linguistic competence and familiarity with local communities and histories is a long-term process and, according to Jocks, not articulated in Gill's commentary. Jocks contends that the crux of the matter is hermeneutical, not racial or political as Gill believes it has been. Jocks further suggests that for such a subtle hermeneutics of indigenous categories, it is the attitude and experience that a scholar brings to the field, and not the ethnicity, that matters.[20]

More broadly, Jocks argues, we need to understand recent work in the study of religions as a conversation between rationalities. To insist that we admit that the study of religion is Western is, in Jocks's mind, to never be able to break out of the ghetto, in which the "other" culture becomes merely another "subject" for American and European intellectual frames, categories, and tools. And once again, the authority of the scholar is taken up as the central issue. As Jocks articulates it: "Ought we not to insist that scholars who claim authority in the study of any religious tradition demonstrate adequate understanding of its depth, complexity, history, language, epistemology, and ontology before constructing theory on it?" Jocks ends by merging the political and the hermeneutical domains of the issue, saying that Native American communities do not conceive of religious knowledge apart from political knowledge and economic knowledge, for "there is no knowledge other than what is lived out, and there is no living out that is not political and historical."[21] In Fraser's terms, Jocks's argument is that what is "privately" Native American is also "public," and any conduct of actors within a public sphere should include such awareness.

Lee Irwin attempts a middle path between the two positions. He writes that it is impossible to summarize the positions of these scholars as either "Native" or "Western" in their intellectual or scholarly outlook. He argues that the training within the secular academy can be as prejudicial as any form of religious belief or conviction. Irwin then goes on to make a case that "there is no privileged discourse that represents the academy at large, only the multi-vocal interchange that occurs between partisan members of various intellectual perspectives, each espousing his or her own particular concerns and issues—religious, political, academic, or just a plain struggle for survival and recognition."[22]

For Irwin, religious studies "membership" should go to the very roots of inherited epistemologies and theories that are transmitted by cultural institutions as "superior" or "correct" methodologies. Irwin ends by arguing for a creative tension between a critical approach that is not simply a reiteration of a religious system and respect for Native traditions as a new epistemology.[23] For him, holding together both critical and Native approaches is crucial as fields "at the margins," such as Native American studies, try to find their way forward.

COMMUNITIES' RESPONSES

The critique of *Mother Earth: An American Story* from the Native American community was swift. M. Annette Jaimes and George A. Noriega published a review in the *Bloomsbury Review* in 1988, in which they point out that Gill should be faulted for not soliciting or obtaining Indian feedback of any kind. Jaimes, Noriega, and Russell Means question Gill's authority to undertake this research without possessing detailed knowledge of the religious practices in question or of the languages in which they are embedded. But they also note that Gill disavows this empirical knowledge himself, and further that the brunt of their criticism is not on the empirical adequacy of his research.[24]

In an insightful summary article, "The Politics of Discursive Authority in Research on the 'Invention of Tradition,'" Charles L. Briggs notes of Noriega and Means: "They rather ask what I see as a crucial question for discussions of invention in general: If the discursive authority of this sort of scholarly writing is not predicated on truth claims regarding historical and ethnographic accuracy, on what is it based? What constitutes appropriate grounds for contesting it?"[25] The invention-of-tradition discourse Briggs refers to is the influential work of Eric Hobsbawm and T. O. Ranger in *The Invention of Tradition*.[26] In the introduction to that work, the editors make the argument that many traditions that seem to be ancient and passed down through the centuries are in fact invented more recently. These manufactured histories are particularly true in traditions involving the formation of the nation-state and the creation of nationalist memories. Briggs places the Mother Earth controversy within this larger intellectual context. Here, then, the question of competing multiple publics is relevant: Was Mother Earth "invented" in an attempt to create a tradition? Or was it a genuine memory? And who has the authority to make that claim? Who owns Mother Earth, and who owns her invention?

At this intellectual moment in the controversy, we see a basic rift between the writer's intent and the audience's understanding of his or her intent. Jaimes and Noriega charge Gill with saying that Mother Earth is "European" in origin, and that Europeans and Americans are better able to understand Indian religions than "outsiders," such as the Indians themselves. As Briggs puts it, the book extends rather than challenges Eurocentrism. Russell Means, also in this light, argues that the authority to discuss Native American religious concepts is derived not from "all the rhetoric about 'pursuit of knowledge'" but from an individual's relationship to a social community and to norms that regularize who can legitimately possess knowledge of spiritual traditions.

In a review that same year, Ward Churchill also creates a clear line in the sand.[27] He places Gill's book squarely in the tradition of Anglo-European distortion and misrepresentation, which goes back to the Europeans' first arrival and has, in his view, taken insidious new turns in the late twentieth century. For Churchill, Gill's work is part of a larger trend that involves New Age spiritualism and commercialization. In the academic version of this trend, Gill is encouraging scholars and readers to partake of the prestige of

Native American studies, but without any responsibility toward it. Much later, Barbara Alice Mann was to take Gill's approach to task for ignoring actual Native Americans' views on the topic, as well as the widespread geographical and historical place-name evidence that Native American peoples in many different areas conceived of the earth as a mother.[28]

Clearly, for Russell Means, Ward Churchill, and many others, the issue is not only Sam Gill. In one piece, "Who Gets to Tell the Stories?" by Elizabeth Cook-Lynn, Sam Gill's story is implicated in the much larger politics of representation of the Native American: as she writes, "More complex than the question 'Who gets to tell the stories?' is the question: 'What is i[t] America wants?'" For Cook-Lynn, it is a question that anyone who claims to be a writer ought to contemplate. In other words, in the terms of this book, one might ask: Which of the competing publics is allowed to tell such narratives, and has the right to represent, and on what grounds?

And Cook-Lynn responds to her own question: "In regard to the Indian stories, there is plenty of evidence that what America wants is what America gets. 'Dances with Wolves,' *The Education of Little Tree*, Sam Gill, Arthur Kopit, James Fenimore Cooper, and other assorted outrages. It is my view, that as writers and readers at the American literary table of feast or famine, we give and get what America deserves."[29] For Cook-Lynn, Gill's story distorts the Native American experience as much as James Fenimore Cooper's, even though Gill spills chapters of ink on the distortion of Mother Earth by whites in his pages. It is distorting because, for many of his readers, Gill's claim that whites invented Mother Earth is a claim to ownership of Mother Earth, not a charge of bad scholarship about Mother Earth. And a claim to ownership also reinforces greatness of a particular kind in the American story. As Cook-Lynn puts it: "There is still, among the literati, both critics and readers, a longstanding commitment to the idea that there is inner truth and greatness in America . . . the American experience notwithstanding . . . and we have only to assert it."[30] Fascinatingly, Gill was trying to point out some of that violence in American history and to understand Mother Earth as a response to that violence. But in many critiques of Gill, this issue was overlooked. What was foregrounded was Gill's seeming dismissal of the weight of the Mother Earth concept through his use of the invention-of-tradition discourse. For many members of the Native American community, Gill was arguing that Tecumseh did not possess an "adequate" notion of Mother Earth and that such a concept is "only" a recent invention.

Gill is also mentioned in Ward Churchill's review of *The Invented Indian*, a collection edited by James Clifton. Churchill highlights the paradox of liberalism, as it is experienced by the objects of the scholar's study: those people described or those people about whom one might be liberal. Clifton's work is a collection of essays whose intent is to inject a "healthy dose of realism" into popular and academic understandings of Native Americans. Churchill acknowledges "this is a noble purpose, since only through such realism can the debunking of myths and stereotypes and the correction of more 'scientifically' erroneous information, can relations between culturally distinct peoples be bettered. This is especially true in situations such as Indians and European Americans now find themselves, where one group has come to completely dominate the other." Parity of participation in the public sphere is nearly impossible. He ends with "Unfortunately, the jacket blurbs lie." Instead, *The Invented Indian* attempts to repeal any glimmer of truth that the Native Americans have been able to establish themselves and put in its place the white supremacist colonialism in which Indians are presently engulfed. Clifton's view, writes Churchill, is that "anything positive in the native past is an entirely wrongheaded proposition." Sam Gill's article in this anthology is a smaller version of the book *Mother Earth*, and Churchill duly notes both Annette Jaimes's negative assessment of the work in the *Bloomsbury Review* and Russell Means's confirmation of that assessment in a subsequent interview. In their view, the work is an example of the new racist intellectualism in which liberal scholars engage in historical revisionism "not in the admirable sense originally connoted by the work of Alice and Staughton Lynd, Howard Zinn, and others, but in the more recent and thoroughly squalid sense exemplified by those like Arthur Butz who seek to 'debunk the myth' that the Third Reich perpetrated genocide against the Jews."[31] In Churchill's view, most of the works in the volume, including Gill's smaller version of *Mother Earth*, in their resistance to the positive assessments of Indian accomplishments in history, are, in effect, denying an American holocaust.

Vine Deloria also points clearly to the issue of the intercommunity "space" of Clifton's book, which raises many of the same issues *Mother Earth* does. Deloria characterizes Clifton's introductory essay, "Memoir, Exegesis," as one that "might be better entitled 'The Academic Meets the Real World.'" In Clifton's account of his experiences with the Bureau of Indian Affairs and the Indian Claims Commission, Deloria focuses on Clifton's surprise that the members of the Menominee tribe he worked with, who were seeking restoration for their people, had a BS, an MSW, and an LtD. "Here," says Deloria, ". . . is the clash of authority. How could the educated Menominees not listen to a man with a PhD?" Clifton found that a number of Menominees, perhaps the first generation to really see what the federal government was doing to them, were his peers in educational achievement—in effect, they had stepped out of his comfortable fictions and were determined to use modern methods to restore the fortunes of their people. Deloria is more sanguine about the "invented Indian" narrative than Churchill is: "I have no quarrel with Clifton's caricature of our current version of the Indian story because I do the same thing to the anthros' [*sic*] interpretation. All of us do it, and we should simply admit it and not adopt the pious holier-than-thou pretense that we don't."[32]

In Deloria's assessment of Gill's essay, Gill suggests that Mother Earth was a white man's invention and not part of Indian traditions at all. Deloria goes on, "Many young Indians were furious because they had uncritically accepted the comfortable slogans of popular culture and felt that Gill had directly attacked their religious sensitivities. After reading Gill's essay, I was amazed that people took offense and further astounded that some of his colleagues did not quietly advise him to withdraw it for fear of embarrassing himself and the profession generally." Deloria's contention is that there are numerous references to Mother Earth in Indian transactional documents but not in the ethnographic materials. Rather, they are in minutes of councils and treaty negotiations. For instance, Cornstalk uses the idea of a "common mother" in an attempt to persuade the Mingos of Ohio to side with the Americans in the war. So too, in 1892, a Mescalero chief refers to the fact that "the earth is our mother" and "our bodies remain with our mother who bore us." Deloria's point is that there are many other quotations about Mother Earth, and yet he also expresses fear of revealing more of them for fear of being misrepresented again by Gill in a revised version of the book. Throughout his remarks, Deloria sees the issue as one of communication and representation, not only one of power. He concludes, "Certainly we will not benefit from the charges and countercharges that will be made during this year of the Quincentennial. One thing is also certain. The next generation of American Indians must finally find a way to transcend the barriers of communication and provide sufficient information on Indians so that the next generation of whites looks at us realistically and we do not have to face bitter whites who create fantasies about us and then turn against us."[33]

Ronald Grimes, in a valiant effort to engage the tendentious discussion, posted a set of questions about this issue on the internet and hosted an online discussion about it, called "This May Be a Feud, but It Is Not a War." The internet dynamics of this exchange will be discussed below. Grimes also published his proceedings in the *American Indian Quarterly* in 1996. As is typical of Grimes, the work was an open search for the larger questions and issues that seemed to have characterized the conversation. He begins by asking whether European Americans should be teaching courses on Native religions of North America.

Deloria responds to Grimes that he has no major intellectual objection to whites teaching Native American traditions, but his personal wish is that they wouldn't. As he writes, "Until religious studies . . . adopts new language and a new orientation—unless Euroamericans grow up about what it is they think they know—they will simply continue to perpetuate misconceptions and misperceptions." Deloria names several such misconceptions and misperceptions: (1) that Native teachers are political and Euro-American ones are not; (2) that the lack of a personal interest in the tradition is a value; (3) that theories derived from Near Eastern and monotheistic religions can or should be applied to study Native American ones. He also points to the "incredible smugness" with which non-Native scholars talks about "the little they do know" concerning things Native. Deloria argues that teaching Native religions in some form must be continued because that, and that alone, can counter New Age appropriation of indigenous ways. Some teaching, even while the language is inadequate, is better than no teaching at all.

In response to Grimes, Gill posted an "Open Letter," where he described himself as being dedicated to dispelling romantic images and trying to overcome the "discourse of domination." Gill believed his efforts and his intentions had been misrepresented and distorted by many intellectuals from the communities he had hoped to ally himself with. His motives were that he found the area too politicized and felt that whatever white scholars might want to say about the topic would be regarded as irrelevant. (One of the earlier salient definitions of a scandal is "a gross irrelevancy to the court.") He writes, "My decision to switch rubrics came when I found myself angered by some of my Native American colleagues, disappointed in some of my Native American students, and dismayed by the flood of action motivated by the superficial political correctness, and distracted from the study of Native American religions by the impossible attempt to justify what I was doing."[34]

Grimes comments on the irony that both Gill and Deloria have agreed that for now their personal preference is that non-Natives should not teach

Native religions in academic classrooms. As he puts it, Deloria wishes white people would not teach Indian religions, and Gill is no longer going to teach under the rubric of Native American religions. Grimes goes on, "On the surface, it appears that Gill has conceded to Deloria's wish."

However, in the final analysis, something else transpires: Deloria calls for teaching to continue because of the dangers of not doing so, and Gill still believes in "the whole humanistic enterprise" (including, one assumes, the academic study of Native American religions). In Grimes's view, Gill makes a strategic retreat and waits, so that the political agenda and climate might change as time passes. Grimes then embarks on a very helpful and telling summary of the issues at stake in the larger feud of representation of which Gill's book was a major part. Grimes summarizes it as part of the larger internet conversation that he inaugurated, in a very hopeful tone, in order to begin a democratic conversation on the issue, in effect holding an electronic colloquium. (This fact is not insignificant and is one we will return to later.) Grimes sees the issues as threefold: being taught in the academy; being taught solely or largely by outsiders—that is, people with no social or emotional commitment to the traditions; and being construed as religion rather than as spirituality (or vice versa).[35]

Grimes expands on each of these objections in very helpful ways, ones that actually epitomize the crux of issues to come in the subsequent decades. He writes that one Native participant objected to having her practices and traditions referred to as "religion," the common reason being that "religion" reclassifies a way of life into an institution, and that it segments Indian practices into a separate sphere rather than making it part of all of life. Another Native participant objected to the term "spirituality" because it sounded too New Age and did not properly connote what Native traditions really meant.

The second area has to do with what Grimes calls "control and rights." If Sacred Lore belongs to First Nations people, non-Natives have no inherent right to it, no matter how much they may desire or need such knowledge. To assume or imply "rights" to that knowledge is to continue colonialism. The debate should not be centered in the academic world, say many, because scholarly works are used in political ways no matter what scholars intend. Therefore, research on things indigenous is necessarily political, no matter how humane the intent.

Adequate qualifications for those writing about Native American traditions remain a third issue, and a powerful one. According to one view, people from non-Native traditions are not qualified because they are not connected emotionally or spiritually to those traditions, and "no elders or tribal bodies have trained or authorized most teachers." This view is, as Grimes observes, a conundrum because many of the teachers of Native American studies have no graduate training from a legitimate program in the field, and they do not consult with Native communities. They may know one indigenous tradition but not others.

Grimes also explores the opposite side of the fence, where teachers argue that non-Natives *should* be able to teach traditions. In this case, some limitations might be observed: that one teaches the encounters, and not the traditions themselves; that one focuses on the controversies and conflict; and that one focuses on specific indigenous groups and voices, such as those contained in autobiographies, rather than traffic in generalizations. Such methods are still imperfect, writes Grimes, but they might be protection against Deloria's worry about those "who will want to use the authority of the scholarship for purely political purposes." Deloria goes on to say that the Native American case is but one example of a form of scholarship that is intrusive to all religious people, and that representations of religions tend to be so distorting that we are led to believe that "people are so filled with doctrine and starved for religious experience that they can sit and watch scholars dissecting their religious lives without the slightest feeling of insult."[36] Even though theirs is a particularly fraught case, for Deloria, Native Americans can take a place in the larger subjugation of religions to the misrepresentations of scholars.

AN EARLY ATTEMPT AT ONLINE DEMOCRACY

It is worth diving further into the dynamics of Grimes's early online discussion as part of the dynamics of this period. Grimes was attempting a combination of three different concurrent discussion lists concerned with Native American spirituality. He writes that as he wrestled with the moral and pedagogical quandary of whether and how non–Native Americans should teach Native American religions, he felt that it was not appropriate to carry on the discussion only in his head. So he turned to the internet. His characterization of the internet is filled with hope for the possibility of it being a democratic, civil space:

> Churches and sweat lodges are not places for argument, and classrooms are
> too often turf dominated by the party in power. These days, a space that more

regularly tolerates ongoing debate of issues like the ones raised here—is cyberspace. Although access to it is not perfectly democratic—depending as it
does on having sufficient equipment, time, know how, and money—there is
nevertheless a strong and articulate Native presence on electronic discussion
lists. The constituency of Natchez, for instance, is extraordinarily active, as
is Native-L, its more news-oriented counterpart. Natives and non-Natives
regularly engage one another in virtual "places" like as these [*sic*]. However
disembodied the medium of Internet discourse, and whatever the pecul-
iarities of arguing without benefit of face, gesture, or tone of voice, cyberspace is a locus of cross-cultural encounter, a frontier. Engagement is possible, perhaps, because cyberspace engagement is distanced even when it is
passionate.[37]

In hopes of a moderate discussion, Grimes began by asking for responses
to the following questions:

> I am submitting this query to invite reflection on three questions:
>
> 1. Should or should not European Americans be teaching courses on Native
>   religions of North America?
> 2. If we should not, why not and what would be the results of our deferral?
> 3. If we should, how best can we proceed?

Grimes called it an "interdisciplinary discussion," which transpired simultaneously on the three lists. In a strong moderating role, he collected
the replies and reposted them to the three groups.

In Grimes's description of his own context he writes that the impetus
had been his situation as a visiting professor at the University of Colorado,
where he was asked to teach a large, publicly visible course on the religions of Native North America. The Boulder campus was the locus of a
"highly charged stand-off" about who ought to be speaking on such matters, involving such senior figures such as Vine Deloria, Ward Churchill,
Deward Walker, and Sam Gill. Churchill's 1992 critique of Gill's *Mother
Earth* and Deloria's unpublished but public stance on the work were still
very much on people's minds. For Grimes, the internet discussion was a
place where the "stand-off" could be engaged in public debate, and the
difficult questions could be honestly posed and pondered. Clearly, such
conversations were not happening within the space of the University of
Colorado at Boulder, so why not instead try cyberspace, which was a

locus of cross-cultural encounters, an open space in a way that the Boulder campus could not be.

Grimes goes on to describe why he did not choose the option that some other white male scholars chose: to leave. In recounting many uncomfortable face-to-face encounters with colleagues on the topic, he holds that to remain in the space with modesty—teaching the plurality of Native traditions—is more faithful to his Native American colleagues than to abandon the task altogether. In that event, because there are so few Native American PhDs, the subject would cease to be taught altogether.[38]

Grimes's reflections on the early internet responses reveal the ambiguities around identity online, even in its early days: "Although one is even less sure about identity in cyberspace than in geographical space, my impression was that few First Nations people and few scholarly teachers of Native American spirituality participated in the exchange. Indian participants, a few of them self-identified, appeared almost exclusively on Native-L." And Grimes himself shared in a private email exchange the remarks of Native American scholars and then funneled those responses to the list. In other words, at that time, Native voices were less a part of the internet democracy than non-Native ones, but they nonetheless were inserted when Grimes felt it was necessary and was given permission.

Grimes's characterization of the email discussion gives force to his claim that this set of arguments was a "feud but not a war." Not a single respondent argued categorically that Euro-Americans should be prohibited from teaching Native religions. In this early version of an online survey, Grimes does privilege the longer, more negative postings of Sam Gill and Vine Deloria. Much of Grimes's subsequent edited presentation is an amalgam of oral exchanges, private email exchanges, and email exchanges on the lists.

The longer notices of Gill and Deloria, discussed above, are in many ways opposite to Grimes's stance. (As a reminder, Deloria argues whites could but wishes they would not teach about Native Americans, and Gill, in an open letter, reiterates his reasons for departure from the field in 1992 because of the hyperpoliticized, racialized climate.) These are the opposing texts from which the shorter email exchanges then follow, with the smaller, more concise arguments about the teaching of Native traditions. As editor, Grimes collated the smaller doubts into concerns about whites' lack of commitment to sacred tradition, the control of rights to that tradition, and the lack of qualifications to teach that tradition.

In addition, the substantive arguments posted in favor of non-Natives

teaching Native tradition proceeded on what Grimes calls "primary European American cultural values": the premises of a common humanity;
objective knowledge, particularly as safeguarded by universities; and individual freedom, particularly academic freedom. These were qualified
yeses, insofar as Native American contexts and privacy were respected,
resistant voices were heard, and a multiplicity of points of view was
encouraged.[39]

Several times, Grimes refers to the role of the moderator in the email
list discussion. At one point, he argues that some postings were not actually good arguments but statements that could easily "function as shields
for staving off debate." He thus, as moderator, had "played philosopher
and interpolated [in square brackets] what [he] imagine[d] to be some
of the unspoken implications."[40] This kind of editorship went above and
beyond what we now know as the role of a list moderator, but it bears
many of the same hallmarks.

Via the internet debate, Grimes successfully managed a list of values
and commitments, though he wondered what "binding moral or pedagogical force" it might have and who should decide that force. He stated
his own position that non-Natives should teach Native traditions with
"humility, collegiality, and sensitivity." He did so, however, in order to
avoid being accused of "trying to keep my hands clean by merely manag-
ing this discussion."[41]

Grimes's view of the capacity of an internet discussion, then, is that
in the hands of an active moderator who is familiar with the issues in the
field, something like a common set of parameters can emerge. Grimes
calls upon the "open" nature of the internet to do so but actively manages
the discussion in several ways:

1. by adding notes from personal conversations between himself and those
   who did not post;
2. by collating all the statements and lightly editing them so that readers
   of the article can see their implications; and
3. by stating the "overall" view of most postings that non-Natives should
   teach but with a set of clear qualifications.

In his "convening" role, Grimes repeats that Natives and non-Natives are
family and that "this may be a feud, but it is not a war." At this early stage,
then, the internet stood for openness, colloquy, a strong moderator, and
ultimate synthesis in print.

FINAL THOUGHTS

I end this case study, as I will all of them, with reference to the theoretical questions raised in earlier chapters. In Habermasian terms, the idea of Mother Earth did not translate into the sphere of Gill's own historical assessment without eruption. Moreover, Gill's revision of the history of the figure of Mother Earth, partly written for his colleagues who he felt had overblown the evidence, did not translate back into the Native American communities but rather led to what they experienced as an erasure of their traditions. For the Native American groups, as well as the scholarly voices, the debate about Mother Earth focused on the question of whiteness and Native American-ness and the related issue of the ability of outsiders to understand Native American traditions. Native American scholars and writers argued back by naming their own initiatory systems, histories, and particular understandings of Mother Earth. They created their own opacity. But the engagement was, in large measure, a cultural one—the colonial and postcolonial history of Euro-Americans' treatment of Native American groups.

In terms of cultural recognition, the historical reasoning did not acknowledge or respect the complex experiences and traditions of the figure of Mother Earth in a variety of Native American communities. Gill's critics argued that even if Mother Earth was "recorded" in a smaller way than had been claimed by European and American historians of religion, as a figure she loomed large in everyday experience and ritual. This can and should be part of the public life-script, even in the midst of the history of violence that Native Americans experienced. This long and violent history has been compellingly discussed by Michael Brown in his book *Who Owns Native Culture?*[42] In that work, the question of Native American artifacts, lands, and access to Native ceremonies is paramount. In Gill's case, however, the question became: Who owns the rights to interpret history? Even more particular is the question: Who owns the power of the metaphor and symbol of Mother Earth (and metaphor and symbol in general) as it is used in historical instances of negotiations between Native American groups and the state?

At times in the debate, history was considered a cultural artifact— hence the need to reassert it and make it opaque. We might note Russell Means's diffidence at releasing other examples of Native Americans' use of Mother Earth, for fear that Euro-American scholars like Gill, and Gill

himself, would steal those examples and take them up in the study. Ethnic identity, and the race of participants, too, emerges as a commonly
invoked theme in the debate about Gill's book. Some would argue for
the right of Euro-Americans to teach Native American culture but prefer that they wouldn't. Others also wrote about the Euro-Americans and
the white man in more polarizing terms. In this debate, the ethnic and
cultural orientation of the scholars predetermines their knowledge at the
outset. Culture contains spirituality and practice. In Appiah's terms, respect was not possible if it involved the centuries-old practice of white
scholars taking Native cultural objects, including histories, out of context.

This eruptive public space lasted several years but then broke apart
completely with Gill's departure from the field of study of Native American traditions. His leaving was not explained in terms of personal choice,
but it was done in terms of a major critique of the field and the dynamics within the field. In an article describing the reasons for his move, Gill
writes that while the American Academy of Religion has recognized the
area of Native American traditions, its original strength in doctoral programs lay in Europe, and many early scholars had their training in other
religions.[43]

Equally significant for Gill, however, are the two questions having to do
with the rights and obligations of the scholar that predominate in the field:
First, should scholars know how to speak Native American languages and
have field experience? And second, should non-Native Americans study
and teach Native American traditions? For Gill, the first question for Gill is
a moot one; even to raise the question shows that the field is not academic
enough as it stands. The second question Gill views as a purely political
one. In his mind, it has failed to address any substantive academic issues.
For Gill, then, both questions seem misplaced and hopelessly sidetrack-
ing, producing studies that are personal recitations about tribal experience or one's Native American upbringing. Or the studies are part of a
scholar's secondary field, motivated by romanticism and conducted without adequate language support. What doctoral studies are done are usually about the student's own heritage, with very little connection to the
academic study of religion. Gill ends by stating that, in his view, the issues
that plague the study of Native American religions plague the study of oral-
based religious cultures as a whole, where practitioners confuse making
clear boundaries with rigidity, narrow-mindedness, and intolerance.[44]

In his own life-script, then, Gill stood apart from the Native American communities who disavowed him. To some extent, he provided his

own critique of the scholarly community from which he emerged. In Appiah's terms, Gill found a kind of tyranny in the (in Gill's view misplaced) obsessions with who belongs to Native American traditions. He argued that scholars should rather work on developing a set of agreed-upon rules that might govern scholarly discourse—the move from an eruptive public space to a public sphere.

Gill's subsequent work has moved into Indonesian artistic traditions, outlined in a 1994 essay, "The Academic Study of Religion." These are, in his mind, less fraught with ethnic identity politics, and he analyzes them as a kind of constructive indigenous theology. Since his departure from Native American studies, Gill has maintained that ethnic identity should not play a role in the critique of a work. Even though they were central in the controversies about *Mother Earth*, Gill's argument has remained that questions of ethnicity and cultural identity simply have no place in a well-constituted academic field of study. Others might put it differently: as a white person in the academy, none of Uma Narayan's roles, "emissary," "mirror," or "authentic insider," were available to him.

As noted above, Gill's commitment to academic norms was profound; in his essay on the study of religion, he writes positively about the strength of the discipline in terms of its common pursuit of analytical questions according to shared methodologies. His relationship to the Native American community is one of analysis, although I believe he would argue that the relationship was no less profound and committed for that fact. We recall that Gill wanted to undermine discourses of domination in writing the history that he did. He left the Native American community behind but remained in the academy, preferring instead to be committed to the rules of analytic study and the public sphere that they represented.

In the Native American critics' view, however, the public sphere should begin with experience and be grounded by narratives of that experience. Personal recitations create knowledge and understanding. They create the particularity—even opacity—that has been missing in dominant cultures' study of Native traditions. Within the eruptive public space where this was debated, some acknowledgment of these differing rules occurred during Grimes's online forum. In this early case of email debates, the possibility of some connection across forms of reasoning for the two communities emerged.

The controversy about Mother Earth was characterized by the near impossibility of a public sphere. No Eliadean understanding of a symbol was possible; nor was the attempt to create the common understanding which W. C. Smith so cherished. On the one hand stands the European-dominant model, which critic Arlen Speights describes as operating "on the principle that knowledge is a kind of wealth that can be uncovered, worked for, purchased, and/or accrued at will." On the other, there is Sam Gill's representation, where "any work by a white scholar becomes for some politically powerful and visible Native Americans emblematic of the enemy. It matters not about what is done, how it is done, why it is done. All that matters is the cultural identity of the doer."[45]

In these two extremes, all of Fraser's perspectives about the public sphere came into play. Competing publics had no ground upon which to temper their suspicion. The Native Americans' "private" sphere, including their religious thoughts and practices, was experienced by Native Americans as deeply vulnerable to misrepresentation and appropriation. And because of a centuries-old history of traumatic relationships with both the state and the university, these institutions were understood as more powerful publics that have only interfered with and disenfranchised the public spaces Native Americans have built for themselves. The scholar concerned was able to discern no possibility for continued work on the topic.

I write *near* impossibility because a debate about *Mother Earth* was indeed conducted, eruptive as it was. The controversy over Sam Gill's book brought to light a wide-ranging set of concerns that also played out in a number of telling ways in the other controversies discussed in this book. The discussion of *Mother Earth* was, in a way, the paradigmatic North American controversy.

6

THE CONSTRUCTION OF RELIGIOUS BOUNDARIES: COMPETING PUBLIC HISTORIES

SETTING THE SCENE

In the mid-1990s, a scholar of Sikh studies sat writing in his office while only a short distance away, a local Sikh organization met in a nearby hall to discuss and protest his recent book. The space between them was only several blocks of a university campus. However, the intellectual and social space between them was a chasm. In 1994, Harjot Oberoi published *The Construction of Religious Boundaries: Culture, Identity, and Diversity in the Sikh Tradition.* The publication of *Constructing Religious Boundaries* underscored, and even furthered, a contestation between two public spheres—one a theologically driven diaspora sphere and the other driven by the legacy of a new historicism and the mores of a university.

When the book was published, Oberoi held a community-funded chair in Sikh and Punjabi studies at the University of British Columbia's Department of Asian Studies. The book was written with an aim similar to Sam Gill's: Oberoi wanted to show the human agency behind the development of the Sikh tradition, particularly the pluralistic identities that held sway in the Punjab region before the emergence of the Tat Khalsa in the late nineteenth century.

HARJOT OBEROI'S WORK

Oberoi's argument begins with three theoretical commitments: (1) the idea of an episteme, or organizing discourse from which knowledge and power both flow, deriving from the work of Michel Foucault; (2) the idea of practice, whereby societies are not rule governed but increasingly shaped by the intervention of social practices at a daily level, found in the work of Pierre Bourdieu; and (3) the idea of praxis, a form of human action that is not rooted in either the logic of routine activity or intentional action but has the power of transforming existing social and cultural relationships, as taken from the work of Sherry Ortner.[1] In Oberoi's view, any real account of Sikh history should be involved with these three attitudes toward history, and thus take a more suspicious view of the formation of the dominant worldview of Sikh studies today. Sikh studies should not assume a homogeneity of social groups, particularly in the reform movement of the Singh Sabha of the late nineteenth century; nor should it assume that the "reform" Sabha movement possessed the correct religious doctrine. Rather, Sikh studies should look at the ways in which the reform movement drew upon particular social groups and, in order to get a full sense of the plurality of the movement, should look at the breakaway groups that differed from the dominant reformer group. In sum, Oberoi's view was that Sikh studies should not simply examine the norm that has been established, and it should not continue to view the groups who were pushed to the margins in the reform efforts as "deviant."[2]

Oberoi goes on to make his arguments in five subsequent chapters, beginning with the earliest periods of Sikh formation. He argues that at the time of the formation of the earliest Sikh movements, the religious doctrines and cultural practices that emerged among that Nanakpanthis, or followers of Nanak, were not pronounced enough to push Sikhs toward a separate religious identity.[3] But the influx of Jats, and the Islamic orientation of Mughal polity under Aurangzeb in the seventeenth century, combined with the religious initiatives of Gobind Singh, gave the Sikhs the distinctive identity we now know as the Khalsa. Khalsa Sikhs used their own code of conduct, new rites of initiation, and other rites of passage to create this distinct identity. The political ascendancy of Khalsa Sikhs in the middle of the eighteenth century made their interpretation of Sikh doctrine into an episteme—a dominant form of discourse. Yet even in this episteme, there was some fluidity; there was not only an exclusive, fixed textual authority on the Adi Guru Granth but also some emphasis on Gobind Singh's Dasam Granth. In addition, many of the established pilgrimage patterns, as well as marriage and death rituals, had not been cast in stone.[4]

From these alliances, Oberoi goes on to argue, a rich culture involving many subsets of Khalsa traditions emerged—a culture that was "equally at home with ascetics, householders, warriors and much more."[5] The emphases of these traditions involved a focus on priestly leaders, both as religious intermediaries who performed initiations and as honored religious specialists, usually broadly defined as gurus from a variety of traditions. These more inclusive perspectives evolved into the Sanatan tradition—which was in fact the religion of the Lahore elites maintained by peasant and artisan classes who had their own idea of what Sikhism was.

In contrast, Oberoi argues, Sikh popular tradition did not emphasize the official lineages of *gurus, adasis, nirmalas, bhais*, and *gianis*—the well-known intermediaries of Sanatan Sikh tradition.[6] Rather, there were the more popular intermediaries of *pirs, bharais, mirasis, ojhas*, and *sianas*. In addition, village Sikhs gravitated toward local shrines, and not so much to major centers of pilgrimage like Amritsar or Haridwar, where much of the Sanatan tradition flourished. Despite these differences, there was a reciprocal influence between the cultures of the powerful and subordinate, so that local gods and goddesses were also patronized by the elite.[7]

The overwhelming majority of Sikhs were immersed in this Sanatan Sikh tradition until well into the nineteenth century—a tradition, Oberoi argues, that is quite different from the dominant Sikh episteme today. Body modifications, life-cycle rituals, and seasonal festivals were celebrated according to regional, clan, caste, and sect customs.[8] Sanatanists recognized several traditions and accepted multiple sources of authority in order to make this happen. Even non-Sikh authors were accorded a place within Sikh cosmology. Oberoi's view is that this inherent pluralism ensured the vitality of the Panth, or "path," and reduced the possibilities of conflicts with other religious communities. In this inclusivity, there was a "sport-like" atmosphere, in which pilgrimage to major shrines also included sporting events, and the whimsies of local gods and goddesses were taken quite seriously indeed.[9] The Amritsar Sabha kept these traditions going in its early phases.

Oberoi's major argument concerns this juncture: in the 1880s, there was a major expansion of the Singh Sabhas founded by the Amritsar Sabha earlier in the century. Commercialization of the rural economy, revolution in communication, the rise of new trading networks, print culture, and a new system of education generated a new subculture that consolidated the hold of the new elites over Sikh identity.[10] This new form of Sikhism that emerged was called the Tat Khalsa, and it was unlike Sanatan leadership in that it did not rely on everyday practices and intentional action. Tat Khalsa was the transformative praxis that changed the episteme. Tat Khalsa Sikhs wanted to move away from idolatry, polytheism, Muslim pirs (or holy people), and Brahamnical presence in rituals. In addition, they introduced some distinctly Khalsa life-cycle rituals and sacred spaces, as well as an emphasis on monotheism, scripturalism, and the divine nature of Sikhism. They could then claim that Sikhs were an independent, homogenous, and separate community with no relationship to Hinduism and Islam.[11]

Yet there were plenty of arguments and forms of resistance to this new episteme. Oberoi sees one of the major contributions of *Constructing Religious Boundaries* as tracing the dynamics of this resistance, even if it was doomed at the end. For him, the Tat Khalsa challenged the pluralistic notions of the Sanatan Sikh ways. He argues that a public battle for the minds and hearts of the people emerged during this period, whereby the Tat Khalsa also appropriated everyday resources, such as publishing houses, cultural bodies, schools, colleges, orphanages, and clubs, and thus created the "social fact" of a separate Sikh identity. As Oberoi puts it, the dynamic evolved in three distinct phases, culminating in the early twentieth century. In the first phase, only the Singh Sabhas were beginning to see themselves as the Tat Khalsa. In the second phase, many Sikhs saw themselves as the Tat Khalsa, and finally the Tat Khalsa also became accepted as Sikhs. Other identities were subordinated within this singular identity, and the vestiges of pluralistic identities, such as those of the Sahajdharis, were only included for strategic reasons.[12]

This consolidation was aided by the need of the British administration to create singular generic terms, and when the administration itself classified all Sikh traditions, only the Khalsa was deemed to have an authentic source. (Thus, for state patronage, such as induction into the British army, all Sikhs had to undergo a Khalsa baptism and uphold the five symbols of the Khalsa.) Oberoi is careful to emphasize the fact that the move toward the idea of a separate Sikh identity was not totally new, as this development can be seen even in the earlier pre-British period of the Khalsa traditions. But, in effect, what the Tat Khalsa did was reject the religious diversity that had become accepted under the Sanatan Sikh tradition. This was a movement also mirrored by Hindus and Muslims as they went through similar transformations of unification and uniformity. Thus, no single reason can explain Sikh identity—not British policy nor the elite politics of competing religious groups. Rather, it was a complex evolution in which the interactions between religious, political, and economic spheres played the key roles. Therefore, Oberoi's account of Sikh history is also an account of competing publics, each of whom argues for the ascendancy of their own practices and lineages.

SCHOLARLY RESPONSES

Oberoi's book quickly provided an important model with which to tell religious history in new ways. Oberoi wanted to accomplish more than the common Marxist move of explaining religion away in purely economic or social terms, and he wanted to do something different than the simple assertion of the sui generis nature of religion. Thus, he turned to the idea of episteme to take seriously the local, regional, and colonial power equations in the development of Sikh history. As mentioned earlier, he also embraced the Bourdieuian notion of practice to account for the dynamics of nonelitist, popular forms of Sikh identity, and Sherry Ortner's notion of praxis to account for transformations among these identities over time. Oberoi's work was immediately taken up as valuable in the same way as the work of Dipesh Chakrabarty, Bernard Cohn, Ron Inden, and Edward Said, in that it showed how vague uses of words like "cult," "modernity," "tradition," and "religion" in earlier works might prove highly problematic, and specifically how it was problematic when trying to account for the Sikh tradition.[13]

Oberoi's views about the Sikh religion's relationship to the colonial state, particularly the Tat Khalsa reform movement, also became part of the burgeoning conversation in the early 1990s regarding the question of fundamentalist religious groups and their relationship to contemporary secular politics and polities.[14] Oberoi's "middle path" in this regard is taken up by many involved in the secular critique of communalism in India. In a critique of K. N. Panikkar's Damodaran Memorial Lecture, for example, M. S. S. Pandian favorably cites Oberoi's work in that it provides a way out of the elitist, antireligious rationalism of contemporary scholars such as Panikkar, who suggests that the only means of rejecting the communalism of late twentieth-century India is "a full confrontation with religion—an all-out critique of religion, with a view to its eventual negation."[15] Oberoi, on the other hand, offers a critique of this tired "tradition vs. modernity" paradigm with its "ethnocentric straight jacket, ahistorical bias, and advancement of ideological preferences in the guise of social laws."[16] Pandian praises the ways in which Oberoi explodes the tradition-versus-modernity dichotomy, not only in *Construction of Religious Boundaries* but also in his study of the Sikh Singh Sabha's protest against the worship of Pir Sakhi Sarvar in nineteenth-century Punjab. Pandian writes:

> This study showed how the elite cultures of the Singh Sabha (as well as the Hindu Arya Samaj and Brahmo Samaj who also protested) at first sight appeared to be wedded to the cause of reason, progress, and enlightenment. But a close examination of the ideologies in play shows that the cultural values sponsored by the elite cultures were not just "modern" introductions, but a complex reordering of culture idioms whereby certain segments of tradition were dismantled while others were highlighted and reasserted. Thus the "reason" and "modernity" were of a very specific nature—those values, beliefs, and rituals that helped in the establishment of elite culture were declared rational, while the rest were made to appear irrational.[17]

And these declarations were made in an emerging public sphere of colonial India.

John E. Llewellyn also welcomes Oberoi's new view, coming more from a representation-of-Sikh-traditions perspective and less from a subaltern studies perspective. Llewellyn surveys a number of basic traditional textbooks on the study of religion and finds confirmation of the kinds of inaccurate "center-oriented" histories that Oberoi describes. As Llewellyn writes, "The general pattern is that these brief chapters cover the history of the Sikh tradition only for the period of the ten gurus, from Nanak (1469–1539) to Gobind Singh (1666–1708). On the establishing of the Khalsa by the latter, the introductory student has enough background information to move on to a summary of Sikh belief and practices that takes the Khalsa as the standard without bothering about other forms of Sikhism that did and do exist."[18]

Llewellyn believes that Oberoi's emphasis on the intervening centuries, the Sanatan Sikh pluralism, and the peripheries might serve as an important corrective to mainstream histories. While Llewellyn queries whether the Foucauldian idea of episteme can really be applied to such a small minority group in the same way it can be applied to larger civilizations, he does think that Oberoi's approach has important implications for Sikh as well as Hindu understandings of modernity today. Meeta Mehrotra joins Llewellyn in a positive appraisal of the book's focus on pluralism within history, and also cites its relevance to contemporary Indian society in non-Sikh contexts.[19]

Not all, however, appreciated Oberoi's heavy emphasis on the Sikh periphery. Nikky-Guninder Kaur Singh admires Oberoi's focus on the diversity of nineteenth-century Sikh tradition but finds that his focus on destruction, dislodgement, and disenchantment of the Sikh pluralist world leaves his overall edifice shaky. She criticizes what she understands as his "utter neglect" of the core of Sikh tradition—the Guru Granth and the nine successor gurus have no place in Oberoi's study. (While the critiques are articulated from very different places, the role of the Guru Granth is central in some scholarly objections as well as community objections.) Moreover, in her view, in Oberoi's book, the Dasam Granth, the Rahitnamas, and the literary output of the Singh Sabha poets are seldom mentioned, or, if they are, they are misinterpreted. Kaur Singh's additional argument is that, unlike Oberoi's idea that Sikh identity was fluid in the early Guru period, even in its early phases, there is ample evidence for a full and established Sikh identity.[20] Her protestation that Oberoi ignored the Sikh center in his reassessment of Sikh history anticipates some of the Sikh objections, dramatically played out after the book's publication.

Later scholarly reviews also take into account the protests that had then emerged from the Sikh community itself. Hew McLeod comes to Oberoi's defense, arguing that his historiography is "wholly convincing" and "thoroughly sound," particularly its very detailed treatment of the Sikh community prior to the Singh Sabha movement, its popular religions in the eighteenth and nineteenth centuries, and the formation of the Tat Khalsa in response to the British presence as well as its challenge to the "non-conformist" practices in various parts of the Punjab. McLeod mentions the furor around Oberoi's book and deems it "predictable," saying that "obviously the book has touched a very tender chord." As McLeod puts it, "The reason why it has touched a tender chord is that it deals with a period of Sikh history which is of crucial importance to contemporary Sikh society." This period of three decades, 1880–1909, shows the deep cleavage between the conservative Sanatan Sikhs from the radical Tat Khalsa, and thus, in McLeod's view, Oberoi challenges the accepted historiography that the Khalsa Sikh was the only legitimate Sikh.[21]

In another review, Daniel Gold also writes sympathetically. For him, Oberoi presents a different trajectory from the standard history told by older Sikh scholars, particularly the idea of the Khalsa as an institution that progressed steadily since its inception. As Gold observes:

> The praxis of Sing Sabha elites interacting with their colonial milieu in which the activists fashioned an exclusive festive cycle for the community . . . present

the role of human agency in the creation of modern Sikh identity in a very vivid way. Not just an alternative historical thesis, this presentation can appear as a radical desacralization of the modern Sikh community—now no longer eternal but manmade.

Gold goes on to cite the current context as one in which it is particularly difficult to receive Oberoi's thesis, which "comes at a time when Sikh political unrest in India can, in an age of quick communications, exacerbate anxiety about continuing identity of the youth in the Sikh diaspora; and it is articulated by a young Sikh scholar with a Western education, in whom some from the community feel a collective investment."[22]

Gold is ultimately optimistic about the final outcome of the Oberoi controversy: "Oberoi's arguments cut to the quick just because they are so finely honed and backed by such weight; it is hard to see how in the present socioreligious condition he could have avoided wounding any religious sensibilities without blunting his arguments, too. In merely pointing to the ways in which religious boundaries have been constructed, Oberoi has indeed aggravated them. But that aggravation will certainly be temporary, and perhaps finally salutary too."[23] Not unrelatedly, Oberoi's more general history figured as a reference point for many subsequent works, including those of Pashaura Singh, J. S. Grewal, and Gerald Barrier.[24]

Like the background to Sam Gill's book, the background to the Oberoi controversy has centuries behind it, beginning with colonial observations and ending with the trauma of the 1984 destruction of the Golden Temple and its aftermath. J. S. Grewal, in his *Contesting Interpretations of the Sikh Tradition*, outlines much of this history, plagued as it is with investments in description that are motivated by a will to rule. A perusal of the early descriptions of scholars such as J. D. Cunningham, Ernest Trumpp, and M. A. MacAuliffe shows that each produced "opposite" descriptions of Sikh identity: Trumpp views Sikhism as a form of Hinduism, and MacAuliffe focuses on its originality. MacAuliffe actually writes blatantly of the "value" of Sikhism to the colonial enterprise: "Sikh identity was not only distinct from that of Hindus, it was more valuable—for the British, for the Sikhs, and for the world at large."[25] Even as early as the writings of Trumpp, Sikh writers disagreed with the assessment of Trumpp in seeing Sikhism as derivative. Thus the tone of the debate was established in the European-Sikh dialogue, to borrow a phrase from Pashaura Singh.

The tone of this dialogue was reinforced by Sikh responses in the twentieth century to Hew McLeod's work. Sikh critics attributed Orientalist motives to him and offered pungent critique of his ideas. The authors of Justice Gurdev Singh's edited volume *Perspectives on the Sikh Tradition* (1986) take issue with McLeod's *Evolution of the Sikh Community* (1975).[26] They focus particularly on McLeod's treatment of the faith of Guru Nanak, Sikh religious ideologies, Sikh social environments, and the character of the Sikh social order. Many of these elements are related to claims of uniqueness of the founder, Guru Nanak: McLeod connects Guru Nanak with the "Sant" tradition of early India, while one of his critics, Daljeet Singh, argues that Guru Nanak is separate from the Sikh tradition. McLeod also gives weight to the environment of Guru Nanak, and Daljeet Singh argues that the moral vision and spiritual teaching were unique to Nanak, and thus to Sikhism.[27]

Moreover, the critics also engage in an argument over terminology. McLeod's understanding of myth, demonstrated by how he describes the hagiographical *janamsakhi*, or birth testimony, is as a descriptive term for creating a powerful truth for a community. However, Gurdev Singh resents the use of the term "myth," thinking it derogatory. In addition, McLeod argues that the Sikh Panth should have a history that includes social, historical, and economic influences, and thus analytic terminology would prove appropriate.

Finally, there is argument over the level of "outside influence" in social practices. One critic, Jagjit Singh, argues that the moral force of Sikh ideology alone drives the history of the Sikh Panth. McLeod also argues that caste status has remained as a concern in the context of negotiating marriage and other marriage conventions, despite the fact that it was rejected by the Sikh community as a basis for social discrimination. In contrast, McLeod's critics argue that Sikh Panth completely rejected the idea of caste and all that it stood for.

The basic scope of this controversy that started with McLeod's work extended into the 1990s. Grewal understands the basic outlines of the controversy as the difference between the secular colonialist historian and the Sikh theologian. The moral entrepreneurs who are part of the critique include major figures of the upper middle class—"retired judges, civil servants, army officers, former ministers, chief ministers, and vice chancellors." These scholars adopt a tone of denunciation and argue that the "culprits" should be judged through extra-academic means.[28] Further, they posit that Western scholarly modes are a form of attack on the authenticity of the Adi Granth, particularly "textual analysis," as Daljeet Singh and Kharak Singh point out. The attack arrives "under the guise of Western scholarship." As Pashaura Singh puts it, "Polemics may not be the best mode of protest but polemics do represent a form of protest." Meanwhile, the larger debate struggled with the question of personal attack and attribution of motivation, sometimes "resorting to a level of insult and insinuation intended not to refute an opponent's argument so much as to destroy his personal reputation."[29] Here is an illustration of an eruptive public sphere, where the rules of public debate are unclear or even irrelevant.

But the larger controversy was also colored deeply by the trauma that took place in 1984, the destruction of the Golden Temple. The picture on the dust jacket of Grewal's book showing the destruction of the Akal Takht in 1984 by the Indian army rightly links the present controversy with the agony through which the Sikh community passed in the last two decades. Grewal hopes that "the critical scholars realize the implications of their works for the Sikh community" and that their critics "from within the faith" realize the significance of the "methodological atheism" that characterizes all rational-empirical research in the modern world.[30]

In his work *Historical Perspectives on Sikh Identity*, Grewal makes a similar attempt to drive a "middle path" on Sikh identity. Like Nikky-Gurinder Kaur Singh, Grewal argues that McLeod should not minimize the significance of the objective sociocultural realities and the subjective consciousness of distinction inspiring the Sikh.[31] Grewal further argues that critics like Daljeet Singh are not, like Oberoi and McLeod, concerned with questions of uniformity and fixity; rather, they are operating out of a different paradigm of identity. But in Grewal's view (and I think this is central), one can invoke the same empirical evidence for two different views of Sikh identity. On the one hand, a scholar can have ideas of "center and periphery," as well as "elite and masses," which are negotiated. On the other hand, a scholar can have an idea, as Oberoi does, using this same evidence, of Sikh identity as not clearly enough defined. But then one can argue, as Daljeet Singh does, that Sikh scripture itself is the most emphatic pronouncement about the distinct and independent identity of Sikhism.[32] Each participant brings this view of historical identity to the public debate and controversy.

Both Oberoi and McLeod argue that there were multiple identities in the development of Sikhism from 1699 to 1840, particularly the Khalsa-Sahajdhari divide. Against this view, Grewal argues that neither fluidity nor diversity actually can invalidate distinct identity. McLeod argues that the Tat Khalsa solidified and clarified Sikh identity, so that it was both old and new. And Grewal goes on to remark that the "relationship to the center" (as Nikky-Guninder Kaur Singh also argues) is a better way of thinking through these issues.

This critique is related to the question of "porous boundaries," and Oberoi's particular argument that Sikh identity was always fluid. Grewal argues against Oberoi's view that the Tat Khalsa's rise to predominance and its erasure of Sanatan Sikhism is a "new episteme." He takes Oberoi to task in saying that while there is no doubt that some Sikhs embraced Hindu practices, this does not mean it is necessary to project backward and assume that Sikh identity was always fluid.

In fact, Sikh identity was distinct from the period of Guru Arjan; Sikhs were encouraged to think of themselves as a Sikh community—indeed, they constituted a public. G. S. Dhillon argues that Sikh Sabha was a revival of earlier Sikh practices, and that one should rather think of Sikh identity in terms of those who were loyal to established scripture and those who departed from it. For Grewal, there is a great deal of evidence to suggest that Sikh identity developed its own sense of distinction as it changed over time, even in interaction with peripheral or nonorthodox Sikh groups. Before and after the institution of the Khalsa, the Sikhs saw themselves as a distinct community.[33]

COMMUNITIES' RESPONSES

In Grewal's account, we have already seen some of the community's concerns with Oberoi's book. Yet it is important here to note the intersection of two publics as we move to describe these concerns more fully. Oberoi's work was published in the twentieth year of the Canadian government's legislation to establish ethnic chairs to promote its national policy of multiculturalism. Simply put, the government created a practice whereby it would match any ethnic community's funds of $300,000. The matching grant from the government would establish a chair in that community's history at a Canadian university. In his account of events, Oberoi himself notes, "This would mark the beginnings of a new heritage programme that would be covered by the usual clauses of academic freedom and university autonomy."[34] Difficult as it was, the program assumed intellectual autonomy, and this was a crucial difference between a community and a university.

While the history of this program was fractious from the start, the Sikh community was nonetheless able to establish a chair in 1987, and Oberoi was its first occupant. In the previous decades, and particularly after the assassination of Indira Gandhi and the violence at the Golden Temple, Vancouver had been a center for both Sikh professionals and a those who wished to create Khalistan, the independent Sikh nation. As in the case of *Kālī's Child*, "diasporic nationalism" became a major player in the media, both Sikh and "secular" Canadian. This movement helped create the events that were to follow.

Oberoi recounts the following:

> On the morning of 7 May 1994, a Sikh crowd gathered for a public meeting in the Auditorium Building on UBC campus. This turn of the century building is barely two hundred metres from my office—my home away from home. A transnational organization, the Canadian Sikh Study and Teaching Society, had convened a large public meeting to assess my newly released book and the workings of the Sikh chair.
>
> While most of those who participated in the forum came from metropolitan Vancouver, a few of the participants had flown in from cities across North America and some had even come from as far away as India. Federal and provincial politicians brought official greetings for the delegates. The message of all those who addressed the crowd throughout the day was the same: I was guilty of blasphemy and anti-Sikh activities. Clearly, those present in the forum were not persuaded by my historicist account. When the meeting concluded in the evening several resolutions were passed by acclamation, categorically denouncing the book and asserting the supremacy of faith over historical research.[35]

Oberoi goes on to note how fortunate he was that the university and many of his colleagues supported him during this time. The local Vancouver paper also published an editorial arguing that Oberoi's work belonged to the secular historical tradition and should be understood as such. As the scholar himself writes, the newspaper stated that "the Sikh community had misunderstood my purpose. Since I was neither a functionary of the Sikh religion nor a theologian commenting on Sikh scripture, I ought to be left alone."[36] Note here, too, the doubleness of the scholar: he is expected to be an authority in Sikhism as established by the community in collaboration with the university. Yet, despite the university's commitments to academic freedom, Oberoi is therefore, by implication, expected to confirm a particular theological stance. It must be stated as such in the controversy again and again: Oberoi was not a theologian, nor did he intend to be one. He did not have a long tradition of secular Guru

Granth scholarship behind him, as Schaberg did in the case of biblical scholarship.

In the immediate wake of this activism to remove Oberoi from the chair, a long rejection of Oberoi published on the web, *Invasion of Religious Boundaries* (1995), contains the voice of the objecting community.[37] In this volume, several Sikh voices from the Punjab, Canada, and the United States are included. The sensibility in the book is that there is an anti-Sikh movement (some in the volume call it a conspiracy), of which Oberoi is a part, to erode authentic Sikhism, to mar its image, and to declare it an amalgam of religions from India without independent identity.

The introduction provides a helpful overview to the larger themes in the volume. The first theme is that of Oberoi's complicity in Western arrogance, tied to colonial and now neocolonial rule: Oberoi is understood as following the "blind Trumpp-McLeodian" school of thinking, which is also allied with European social science and "Calvinistic thought and an arrogant belief in the inferiority of Asian religions." The authors of the introduction to the volume quote Asad's well-known essay "Multiculturalism and British Identity in the Wake of the Rushdie Affair," stating that "interventionist power insists on permeability of social groups and the unboundedness of cultural entities."[38] In this view, it is in the interest of the interventionist power to do so, in order to more effectively rule and intervene. Thus, Oberoi's historical "poststructuralist" approach that insists on fluid boundaries is parallel with, if not intimately allied with, the interests of neocolonialist intervention.

Second, and relatedly, the authors argue that the very methods used to understand Sikhism are inappropriate to Sikhism itself. As they see it, Judeo-Christian methods (which would include historical, social-scientific, and poststructuralist methods) are based on the fact that both Judaism and Christianity are historically grounded traditions, and thus historical analysis is appropriate. In contrast, as S. Kaptur Singh argues, Sikhism is essentially a religion of the numinous, and not historically grounded. Thus, applying Judeo-Christian principles will lead to a wrong result. The status of the historical events in Sikhism is different, as these authors see it. Such events represent the "unfolding of philosophy preached by gurus and enshrined in the Sri Guru Granth Sahib." Earlier in *Invasion of Religious Boundaries*, the authors recommend that Oberoi and other authors of his ilk read Edmund Husserl's phenomenology to fathom the Sikh orientation more deeply, and Rudolf Otto's *The Idea of the Holy* is positively cited as a model for understanding Sikh religion.

The irony will not be lost on postcolonial readers that some of the most essentializing work in the study of religion, such as Otto's, is now being invoked against the historicizing neocolonialist work of Oberoi. (Here there is a deep similarity to the Native American response to Sam Gill's work, whose de-essentializing of Native American identity stood as a major bone of contention and source of resentment among the communities who objected to it.)

The third important theme in *Invasion of Religious Boundaries* has to do with the concerns of the community about its own sense of itself and its own continuity. Throughout the work, the authors argue that the crucial formative centuries of Sikhism (1469–1708) must be understood to constitute a separate Khalsa identity—one which, as we have seen above, Oberoi and others argue was not fully in place during those years. In the view of the community scholars, Western-trained scholars should not deny the uniqueness of early Sikh identity from the era of Guru Nanak to the year of Guru Gobind Singh's death. In other words, Khalsa identity can and should create a competing identity in critique of the university.

Relatedly, these community scholars object to the formulation by many Western-trained scholars (Pashaura Singh, Gurinder Singh Mann, and Hew McLeod, as well as Oberoi) that Guru Gobind Singh's death was a crisis in which Sikh identity had to be renegotiated and rethought. In their view, Guru Gobind Singh sanctified Adi Guru Granth as the living spiritual guru of the Sikhs, and thus there was no discontinuity of lineage or leadership, and no crisis involved.

What is more, the fluidity of boundaries that Oberoi and others describe in the nineteenth century before the formation of the now dominant Khalsa view is anathema to these critics. They argue that there was no such fluidity, no trafficking with Hindu ideas and teachers, and that Sikhism should never be described as a combination of Islam and Hinduism. It is clear that the tenth master broke with other Indian ideologies and denied the authority of the Vedas and the Upanishads as Hindu scriptures. Such a clear and radical break with other religions is essential to the Sikhs' description of their own history.

Part of the reason this radical break is so important to this version of Sikh history is that it makes more sense of the Arya Samaj's vituperative campaign against Sikhs in the nineteenth century. This was the campaign for purification called Shuddi. In these scholars' view, it was what led to communal animosity, language tensions, ethnic clashes, and, ultimately, the bloodshed of the partition. In addition, in their view, it also led to

Operation Bluestar and the Delhi riots in the early 1980s. In other words, there exists a clear chain of causation from the distinctness of Sikh identity to their persecution and the bloodshed of the early and late twentieth century. In these scholars' view, if there were no such distinct identity, there would be no need for persecution. Their particular Sikh history in India would not make sense without this distinct identity.

In sum, the various articles in the voluminous response to Oberoi's work take great pains to show that Sikh identity is a continuous (Dhillon) and independent religion, different from all denominations of Hinduism, particularly Vaishnavisms and Vedanta (Daljeet Singh). The various authors also argue that Sikhs should not be understood (and therefore dismissed) as fundamentalists (Kharak Singh, among others).

The work also contains several documents pertaining to the history of the chair that Oberoi occupied and then vacated (Singh Mann). In their view, the Sikh community approached the University of British Columbia (UBC) in good faith, hoping that the "Western university tradition would be helpful in showing an authentic image of Sikhism" and that "evidence and critical analysis would not mean hostility or insensitivity." They wrote up an agreement between the Sikh community and UBC specifying terms. However, in their view, the search was delayed for two years in order to "groom" Professor Oberoi, who fit the university's intellectual agenda. When Oberoi was appointed and the community grew familiar with his work, they soon organized against his appointment. In *Invasion of Religious Boundaries*, the community called for an investigation of the matter by UBC.

In addition, *Invasion of Religious Boundaries* reports that a team of Sikh scholars reviewed both the agreement between the Sikh community and UBC, as well as Oberoi and his publications. Their findings are included in this work, and for reasons outlined above, the team of Sikh scholars finds that his work is incompatible with the aims of the Sikh chair, an "irrelevant" exercise in historiography, and a suppression of the crucial historical record—thereby rendering it grossly unfair to the sixteen million Sikhs in the world today. Here it is worth noting again the charge of "irrelevancy," which surfaces in a number of these cases.

RESISTANT RELIGIONS ON THE WEB I

The internet played a role in Harjot Oberoi's case in a significant way—one that also has echoes in the case of Jeffrey Kripal. In each case, the communities organized themselves on the internet as communities of protest and under-stood one of their main modes of resistance as being electronic in nature. In this way, Sikhs and Hindus created resistant religions *through* the internet, not merely religious communities whose information happens to be *on* the internet. The internet was the primary site of creating opaque histories.

As mentioned above, the internet document *Invading Religious Bound-aries* was authored by many different Sikh activists and thinkers from the Sikh community, in Canada, the USA, and India. The work originally circu-lated on the web and was hosted on two different websites, each of which argued that it provided the correct interpretation of Sikh doctrine and history and encouraged scholarship within the community.

The authors of Sikh Studies (http://www.sikhstudies.com) argue that the purpose of the website is "in keeping with their selfless devotion to the cause of spreading the authentic message of the Guru Granth Sahib." It was created to meet a felt need after the death of key "crusaders"—a need "for an online forum in the electronic media to further the crusade for continuing reference and interaction on global issues in Sikh Studies and the Adi Guru Granth Sahib." Note here that reference, interaction, and crusading on behalf of global issues in Sikh studies are seen as part and parcel of the same mission.

The authors of the website also ask, "Why Global?" They answer the question in terms of an all-encompassing need to spread the message of the fifth-largest religion and to guard against misinterpretation and (pre-sumably Christian) missionary points of view:

> Now, Sikhism has become the world's fifth largest religion. Sikh studies are currently going on worldwide and there is a need to encourage the sharing of the authentic message of the Sri Guru Granth Sahib, not only to help those who are unwittingly unfortunate to miss the message themselves, but also to dissuade those who misrepresent and misinterpret Sikhism by ideological and political blinkers along with missionary paradigms.

The website goes on to describe its activist "corrective" perspective. Its us-ers are called upon to face distortion, "in spite of the gulf between the re-sources of the two sides. Moreover, the hope is that they successfully meet "this onslaught on the Sikh way of life through vast literature in the form of books, articles, reviews and by holding international Conferences."

The website sees itself as a kind of scholarly resource, parallel to con-ventional Western modes of scholarship and welcoming of all. "The Sikh

community welcomes all scholars doing genuine research and will provide them with a vast array of resources." For these protesters, without
this effort at authentic education, the effects of this scholarship will be
deleterious.

- There will be tremendous socio-psychological repercussions in the un-
  derstanding of Sikh religion by the future generations, especially those
  born outside of India.
- The Western world will have a lopsided view of Sikhism.
- There will be erosion in the Doctrinal base of Sikhism as enshrined in
  SGGS.
- It will reflect a failure of Sikh custodians and academicians to fulfill their
  moral duty.

As a way of upholding their moral duty, the authors argue that contemporary science and Sikhism should be thought of together.

> We are thankful to all the authors who joined us in this serious and gigantic
> effort to educate the world community, Students & Scholars to re-think the
> fundamentals of modern sciences within the framework of Sikhism. It is our
> hope that our effort to compile this non-profit website will help the Sikhs to
> enlighten the richness of their heritage, for outsiders it will provide a better
> understanding and will attempt to bridge all gaps.

Another scholarly organization, called the Institute for Sikh Studies,
based itself in Chandigarh. It, too, is concerned with creating a global
presence for the correct interpretation of Sikh tradition and uses the internet to meet that goal:

> The Institute of Sikh Studies (IOSS) was established and registered in 1989
> by some learned individuals who felt concerned over the large scale mis-
> representation of Sikh doctrines, misrepresentation of Gurbani [basic Sikh
> traditions] and the lack of understanding of the message of the Gurus, its im-
> port on history and its contribution towards the development of mankind.

The specific aims and objects of the institute are quite similar to those of
the Sikh Studies website discussed above. IOSS is a nonpolitical, voluntary international organization dedicated to the correct interpretation of
Gurbani and Sikh philosophy as well as the propagation of Sikh religion

and culture. In addition, this hub of activity for indigenous intellectuals offers library resources, newsletter exchanges, publications, and center exchanges, as well as conferences and seminars. IOSS's goals are stated as follows, and worth quoting in full:

- To interpret the basic philosophy/theology of Sikhism enunciated in the original writings of Guru Nanak and the succeeding Gurus.
- To study the history of development of Sikh religious thought, society, traditions, and polity, and to bring out the contribution of Sikhism towards advancement of universal religious thought and human welfare.
- To prepare and publish suitable literature on the above aspects, and to disseminate information on Sikhism through common media, meetings, seminars, talks, discussions, etc.
- To watch and to counter any attempts to misinterpret Sikhism, or any hostile propaganda against religious philosophy, doctrines, traditions and history of Sikhs or the Sikh way of life.
- To encourage establishment of centres/groups/fora of Sikhs at suitable places in India to promote the aims and objectives of the Institute.
- To maintain close liaison with affiliated centres through visits, periodical newsletter exchange, and supply of literature published by the Institute from time to time.
- To establish and maintain contact with existing religious organisations and institutions interested in the aims and objects of the Institute, and to extend co-operation to, as well as seek co-operation and assistance from them on specific projects.
- To set up a Reference Library for the benefit of members and scholars working for the Institute.
- To prepare and introduce courses of instruction on Sikhism in schools and colleges, willing to participate.
- To cater to the needs of the masses and religious groups of Sikhs in their missionary pursuits, mainly through supply of literature.
- To co-operate with non-Sikh organisations, genuinely interested in the study of Sikh religion.

In the hands of Sikh activist intellectuals, the web becomes an international space for countering the production of stereotypes, and websites a Sikh activist resource for correct interpretation. This interpretive work can be conducted through interfaith work, through libraries, and, most importantly, by countering hostile interpretations. The web is, in its own right, a form of resistance, even as it is also an open forum. Both sites provide discussion lists as well as postings that argue against particular kinds of Western scholarship and provide constant vigilance against it.

FINAL THOUGHTS

As with the case of *Mother Earth*, the Habermasian translations between religious and secular reasons were fraught in the case of *The Construction of Religious Boundaries*. The eruptive public might best be symbolized by the meeting of resisters on the same university campus as Oberoi: two parallel universes with a fragile thread of geography holding them together. The Sikh community chose opacity; they returned to and developed their own intellectual traditions, as a form of resistance.

In terms of cultural recognition, several key points are worth making. In the case of Oberoi, as well as the two other South Asian cases, there is a deep intermingling between the two questions of religious institutional affiliation and cultural identity. The protesters of Oberoi's book maintained that Sikh identity is understood, and has always been understood, as a way of life. (The same can be said, and has been said, by members of the Ismaili and Hindu communities.[39]) Many within these communities would understand themselves as organized around the householder and *gurdwara* (Sikh place of worship) practices. Hence, Oberoi's argument that their boundaries were more fluid in the nineteenth century had a culturally offensive meaning as well as a religiously offensive one.

However, since a doctrinally correct understanding of Sikh history—such as the origin, nature, and inception of the Khalsa—is part of official Sikh religious teaching, a cultural offense shades over quickly into a religious one, and vice versa. Theological inquiry teams from an official Sikh organization were dispatched to interview Oberoi not just because of his claims about God but also because of his claims about history and culture. Oberoi was part of an ethnic Asian minority trying to establish its cultural bona fides in North America; therefore, certain cultural expectations about the Sikhs' own accounts of history applied within that group.

Like Tazim Kassam in the following chapter, Harjot Oberoi understood himself as a member of his own community. Oberoi wore a turban and saw himself as a member of the international Sikh diaspora, both at the personal and at the scholarly level. Unlike Kassam (or Schaberg or Gill), he also had the initial imprimatur of both the ethnic and academic communities with which he was involved. However, after reading his work, some North American Sikhs objected to the history that he chose to tell, thus rendering him an objectionable representative of the Sikh tradition. It is ironic that Oberoi's work, like Gill's, did in effect fulfill all the scholarly criteria regnant in the 1990s: a focus on the constructedness of traditions, on their historical contingency, and on the fluidity of their boundaries. Yet this very focus was at odds with the history the Sikh community wished to tell about itself. In Uma Narayan's terms, Oberoi could not function as an emissary, since he represented realities that were not orthodox. He could not occupy the role of the mirror, as he looked at collaborations and interactions between the colonial regime and the Sikhs; he could not be the authentic insider, since according to his critics he was not fully inside his community.

One might argue, then, that Oberoi's academic life-script was the undoing of the Sikh tradition's life-script. Like Kassam, he was confronted by his own community, although he was less active in that community than Kassam was. And like Ismaili history, the history of the Sikh community also possessed a tragic element. But Oberoi's individual way of being a Sikh included being a good historian in a way that might argue with the official Sikh narrative. The expectation of the community, especially after funding a chair, was directly at odds with such intellectual autonomy. According to the many critiques, such autonomy was understood as doing damage to the identity of the community. In their view, the official history was very little understood in North America, never mind the deconstructive one. The Sikh community's own understanding of itself and the story it wished to tell to others did not include fluid boundaries between Sikh, Muslim, and Hindu identities, or previous orthodoxies that did not remain orthodoxies. Like Gill and Kripal, Oberoi no longer works in the subarea of Sikh studies but has turned instead to larger issues in the colonial history of India.

Appiah's notions of the relationship between individual and community come starkly to the fore here. Harjot Oberoi's role in the academy was far more visible insofar as his community funded a chair from which the controversy was created. In addition, like the Ismailis, the Sikh community had its own tradition of intellectual engagement, whose intersection with Western academic mores was still relatively new. Sikhs also had their own tradition of militancy, as well as a recent traumatic past with which to contend. Oberoi's identification with the community was as strong as Kassam's, but he was thrust into a position like Schwartz's, where he was asked to be a public representative of that community.

The initial sense of all parties in both Oberoi's and Schwartz's cases was that this kind of representation would not be difficult to do, even if there were disagreements. However, in North America, there was very little intellectual presence of the Sikh tradition, and the "concerned Sikhs" catalyzed over cases like Oberoi's as time wore on. The group of orthodox theologians who interviewed Oberoi about the Sikh intellectual tradition asserted the strength of that tradition. Indeed, Oberoi's very presence in the academy, and the controversy around his book, helped to foster the intellectual community that now exists.

Like Schwartz, Oberoi was caught in a large secular university's well-intentioned efforts to reach out to a minority community. The intersection between the university's and the community's intentions was powerful and perhaps more intense in its engagement because of the expectations of both sides. The university expected multicultural depth and breadth, and the Sikh community expected enlightened orthodoxy. In this case, the university got what it wanted in a scholar like Oberoi, but at its own expense—without the funding of the chair. Oberoi, meanwhile, ended up with a more secular identity, let down by the members of his own community, although protected by the university.

From this difficult interaction, we can see that the question of fluidity of identity—a seemingly harmless phrase, and one that has determined some of the rules of the academic public sphere—has had severe repercussions when juxtaposed with traditional theology. In intriguing ways, Oberoi's case is similar to the problem of the fluidity of identity of the Earth Mother, emerging in Sam Gill's case. Both Gill and Oberoi are committed to a secular history, which, in their view, is more resistant to dominant discourse. Oberoi states that the religious community's objections to this form of history create a kind of "secular alterity." He writes: "As a chair-holder I was quickly turned into a compressed sign, this time around for the purposes of Sikh nationalism in the diaspora. When my writings historicized this nationalism and addressed its origins, I quickly came to constitute the other. It is this secular alterity that accounts for what follows."[40] For Oberoi, secular alterity is that which a religious community feels should be opposed on the very grounds of its being incompatible with forms of theological discourse, which in the Sikh case are themselves deeply politically charged.

The postcolonial dynamic colors Oberoi's own analysis of the situation. Oberoi juxtaposes his account of the Vancouver events with a narration of what happened when he and his family had to flee in the middle of the night in the 1984 Delhi riots against Sikhs after the assassination of Indira Gandhi. The overarching thread of this narrative is similar in significant ways to Kassam's case. While Oberoi was in danger because of his Sikh identity in 1984, decades later he was denounced by his own orthodoxy for treating his religious tradition in inappropriate ways.

Oberoi notes:

> While there was much in this case that was dissimilar to the Delhi "riots" there was one eerie similarity. Once again there were whispers and rumours; the subject of course was different but many of the mechanisms and intent were similar. There were three key rumours that were circulated: that I was part of a worldwide Christian conspiracy to undermine Sikhism; that I was a member of the communist party; and that I was sent to Canada by the Indian government. The first of these rumours referred to the colonial past, the second spoke of opposition to radical thought, and the third expressed disgust for the Indian state.[41]

Oberoi goes on to remark that the entirety of Indian modernity, from the colonial to postcolonial eras, is summed up in these three charges. These rumors are also part of a larger eruptive public space in which engagement and debate are ungoverned by any particularly clear norms.

The public space that emerged in this controversy was one where two competing yet clear rules of engagement for two quite distinct and strong public spheres came into explosive contact. Part of the explosiveness was determined by the inability of the Sikh theological and cultural sphere to attain global respect, whether in India, Europe, or the United States. Neither Eliade's discovery of the archaic in ancient texts nor W. C. Smith's understanding of faith and tradition could have anticipated these competing claims to the idea of the holy in history. In Nancy Fraser's terms, the debates about Oberoi's book show the emergence of a Sikh public sphere on a global stage. The community was a smaller public in Vancouver, which then took shape as a global public during the introduction of the theological panel to review the book and the advent of the diaspora community's protest of its contents. In their own view, the members of the Sikh community had a responsibility in that sphere to protest the secular account of their faith as that account was supported by the university.

What is more, the creation of a counterspace, a competing public, was begun by the creation of a website with a name similar to, but undermining, Oberoi's work. This website was a statement that such a competing public can effectively counter, and possibly even replace, the university's view. The rivalrous relationship between these two spheres involved a kind of critical mimesis: what began with a donation to the university ended with a website that mirrored the university's intellectual practices, yet denounced them at the same time.

7

SONGS OF WISDOM AND CIRCLES OF DANCE: AN EMERGING GLOBAL PUBLIC

SETTING THE SCENE

In the winter of 1995, a man arrived at the offices of the State University of New York Press and offered to buy the entire stock of Tazim Kassam's recently published book, *Songs of Wisdom and Circles of Dance: Hymns of the Satpanth Ismā'īlī Muslim Saint, Pīr Shams*. He said that its publication would result in another Rushdie affair. Although he was not specific as to what that meant, to people familiar with the issue, the possibilities of censure seemed to be only the mildest of outcomes. This controversy began with an attempt to prevent discussion in the public sphere and involved a tradition that has survived for centuries by occultation—placing into intentional obscurity some significant teachings. The interlocutors in this controversy wondered what constituted "public" and what "private" as the tradition emerged into legitimacy and the more open light in the late twentieth century.

Pir Shams, born in the twelfth century, was one of the many preacher-poets who thrived in Persia, having traveled on a mission to South Asia, particularly the Sind area in what is now present-day Pakistan. Between the eleventh and the eighteenth centuries, pirs like Pir Shams composed Ginans—hymns in vernacular Indian languages, particularly Gujarati. Even today South Asian Ismailis recite Ginans as part of their ritual prayers, and a sizable number of hymns attributed to Pir Shams are used widely in this tradition. From their rich imagery and their historical and liturgical value to the community, one could see why a young scholar such as Kassam would be attracted to studying the Ginans. But she was not prepared for what occurred as a result of her study.

Kassam begins her work by outlining the basics of the Ismaili tradition. Some background about the Ismaili tradition is in order here before turning to Kassam's book and its reception. Claiming a place within the Shia tradition, Ismailis have had a strong presence in the Middle East and in South Asia for millennia. They also have strong traditional roots in Africa and now reside in over twenty-five different communities worldwide. Ismailis are united by their allegiance to the Aga Khan, understood to be a direct descendant of the Prophet Muhammad and known as the Mawlana Hazar Imam. Ismailis share an early history with the mainstream Shia tradition in that they understand the descent of the ulama, or religious authorities, to be through Muhammad's daughter Fatima. Indeed, the family of Muhammad is understood in both Shia traditions to be divinely chosen to lead the Islamic community.

As Kassam also points out, questions of lineage are at the root of Shia Islam. Briefly put, Ali, Muhammad's nephew and Fatima's husband, succeeded to the Rashidun Caliphate (formed immediately after Muhammad's death) as the last of the First Four Caliphs. As the result of a power struggle after his death, rule passed to the Umayyad clan. That Caliphate felt threatened by the presence of Ali's son Husayn; as a result, Husayn was assassinated in a brutal way. This murder was understood as the theological beginnings of Imami Shia Islam—focusing on the purity of the lineage. Responding to Husayn's murder, his grandson Muhammad al-Baqir continued to develop the idea of succession through lineage, particularly through the figure of Ali and his wife Fatima. Others dealt differently with the question of lineage. They asked, "If God's chosen were in the line, why would it be that Husayn had to suffer and be murdered in this way?" They were the Zaydi Shia, for whom purity of descent did not matter; instead, they argued that anyone could become an imam.

Muhammad al-Baqir's son Jafar al-Sadiq developed these ideas about the purity of lineage even further. He fostered an anti-Umayyad sentiment that argued the Caliphate was corrupt and only the true linage could maintain purity. Ismaili Shiism emerged in a dispute over the relative status of two of Jafar al-Sadiq's sons: Ismail ibn Jafar was understood to have received the blessing and authority of his father, but a question arose as to whether Ismail had predeceased him. If indeed Ismail did die before his father, then the authority should have gone to Ismail's half brother Musa al-Kazim. Those who believe that the authority went to Musa al-Kazim are called Twelver Shias, because they recognize a line of twelve Imams, and form the group that most refer to as Shia Islam. The Ismailis, who believe that the authority ended with Ismail, the seventh Imam, are called Seveners.

Ismailis believe Ismail ibn Jafar to have gone into occultation, or spiritual hiding, to return one day and share his teachings. In the meantime, as a result of Ismail's death, and the disagreement with the rest of the community about succession, a tradition of secret teachings and a high intellectual focus became integral to Ismaili identity. The figure of the *dai*, or teacher, was central in the ninth-century Ismaili community. Dais were sent out from the Ismaili base in Syria to teach in a variety of communities throughout the Middle East. Thus, the relationship between teacher and student, and relatedly the sacred knowledge that passed from one to the other, evolved into one of the central emphases of Ismaili Shiism.

Ismaili Islam has frequently been viewed as less legitimate by more mainstream Sunni and Shia groups. As a result, the community's history has been a troubled one. They have been perceived as one of the more powerful minority groups of Shiites, and Ismailis were certainly controversial in their early years, when much of their attempt at establishing power was squelched by both the Mongol and the Mamluk rulers. Ismailis did establish rulership over much of the Muslim world (specifically Maghreb, Egypt, Sicily, Malta, and the Levant) during the Fatimid Caliphate, from the tenth century to the twelfth. Here, we see the relationship between official political sponsorship and the possibility of a public religious discourse.

After the fall of that empire, Ismailis built a smaller but powerful empire in Alamut, within Persia. After the Alamut Empire was sacked by the Mongols, Ismailis were scattered over the various outer regions of the Muslim world—particularly Persia, and eventually into South and Central Asia. The Ismailis thrived for several centuries "under cover" (*taqiya*) and gained converts even in this time of keeping a lower profile. Much of this survival and even expansion in the margins of the Muslim world was accomplished by the dais, or teachers, as well as by the pirs, or saints. In the Ismaili view, the Imam remained in occultation in Iran during this time. However, in the middle of the nineteenth century, the Ismailis came out of their *taqiya*, reclaimed a public identity, and reunified. They gathered under the hereditary imams and tried to take a legitimate place within the Muslim community. In Nancy Fraser's terms, they reconsolidated their public sphere, even though they inherited a number of "private" forms of worship.

Scholars such as Wladimir Ivanow and Henry Corbin point to the rich intellectual tradition of the dais and pirs in the Middle Ages,[1] but a new generation of scholars like Kassam has tried to trace its roots in ways more familiar to the historian of religious movements. The early history of the development of Ismaili tradition remains obscure. For example, very little is known about how the tenth- and eleventh-century Fatimid Ismaili state might have influenced the continuation of Ismaili Islam with a movement called the Nizari mission. This Nizari mission developed after the fall of both the Fatimid Empire and the subsequent thirteenth-century Alamut Empire in Persia. The mission was started by a great pir who went by the name Nizari and was credited with keeping the Ismaili teachings alive. This mission spawned the teachings of Pir Shams and Pir Satgur Nur, both well-known teachers in South Asia about whom very little research has actually been conducted. Scholars wonder how, even after the Fatimid Empire was destroyed by Ghaznavid attacks and the Alamut Empire was destroyed by the Mongols, the Nizari mission thrived and survived.[2]

TAZIM KASSAM'S WORK

As a result of the secrecy of the tradition, the Ginans, or sacred songs, are particularly difficult to interpret and to trace. Therefore, how do we begin to study the Ginans, which have only begun to be looked at from a text-critical approach? Tazim Kassam's work attempts to answer these questions in a way that embraces the theological seriousness of the Ginan traditions as well as the historical aspects of their development. Kassam herself provides an introduction to the hymns, a translation of a select number of them, and extensive notes and appendices, including a translation of a prose hagiography of Pir Shams and explanations of the Hindu names and epithets. As she puts it:

> A heritage of devotional poetry, the *ginān* tradition is rooted in the musical and poetic matrix of the Indian culture. . . . Traditionally recited during daily ritual prayers, *gināns* have been revered for generations . . . as sacred compositions (*śāstra*). The term *ginān* itself has a double significance: on the one hand, it means religious knowledge or wisdom, analogous to the Sanskrit work Jnana, on the other hand, it means song or recitation, which suggests a link to the Arabic *ganna* and the Urdi/Hindi *gānā*, both verbs meaning to sing.[3]

In her introduction, Kassam explains that Ginans are in many ways at the center of Ismaili liturgical and political life; they tend to be sung a cappella at morning and evening services and at more occasional rituals such as holidays and funerals. Thus, they are both "private" and at the same time at the center of public discourse in the communities. In addition, they serve as a reminder of the dais and pirs, who have historically been the charismatic central teachers of the Ismaili tradition, especially in its more secretive period. But when the Ismaili community emerged from its period of secrecy in the nineteenth century, the Ginans also acted as legal guides through which communities could organize themselves under a single imam. Thus, any scholarly work on the Ginans involves questions of historiography and religious authority, as well as poetry. It also must come to terms with the difficult question of cultural identity and so-called syncretism: Were the Indian style and imageries of the Ginans integral parts of the works, or were they forms of "dissembling" so that the authentically Muslim nature of the materials would not be as accessible and clear?

Kassam provides a conjecture about how the historical development might have come about from the Persian origin of the Nizari mission to the tradition of the Ginans that developed when Ismailis were in their time of concealment. Here, too, this history has much to do with what was deemed "private" and what "public" by the sponsoring empire. There was a clear and strong Ismaili presence in South Asia, even under the Fatimid Empire, as we see from the vassal state of Multan in Sindh (which was predominantly Ismaili even before the fall of the Fatimid Empire and the subsequent Nizari mission). Kassam conjectures, partly based on the hymns themselves, that there was an initial "activist" phase of the Nizari mission that was more outward and engaged in the community of Sindh and other parts of South Asia.[4]

Kassam further argues that over time, the Nizari movement became more inward and spiritually oriented. The teachings of Pir Shams and the larger Ismaili movement in South Asia developed from this spiritual orientation. The Ginans, in her view, contained Hindu symbols as a way of engaging and integrating the Hindu populations who were becoming part of the movement. The uses of such Hindu symbols were not simply "disguises," however, nor means of converting Hindus, but authentic forms of devotion in their own right.[5]

In addition to their translation, Kassam also provides an extensive discussion of the imagery of the Ginans. As she states, their unusual imagery is a relic of the long *taqiya* period, when inner meaning (*batin*) was enwrapped in a Vaishnavite surface structure (*zahir*) for the twofold purposes of secrecy and propaganda. For example, in the Ginans, Ali, the first

Shia Imam and nephew of the Prophet, appears as the tenth avatar of the Hindu god Vishnu and is addressed as *swami raja,* or "spiritual teacher and king," in addition to his usual Persian title Shah. In the Ginans, Ali also appears on a chariot. The pir is addressed as a *guru*—the Indian term for "teacher." Ismaili women, meanwhile, are referred to as *sati;* in Jain material, a *sati* is a very pious woman, and in Hindu works, a *sati* is a self-sacrificing woman, usually a widow who follows her husband onto the funeral pyre.[6]

SCHOLARLY RESPONSES

From a scholarly perspective, the problem with the Ginans is that they were both partly neglected and partly concealed. The scholarly assessments of Kassam's book acknowledge this tension throughout their assessments. In general, reviewers applauded her for taking on the difficult topic of the history and development of Ismailism, the problems of Ismaili cultural identity, as well as the state of scholarship of the sect. Kinga Markus, in a review in *Asian Folklore Studies,* expressed the wish that Kassam had provided more context for the references to performances in the Ginans, such as the *ghatpat* ceremony of offering up the holy water. Markus also expresses a general sense that "syncretistic traditions are not faring well nowadays." In perhaps a veiled reference to the public reception of the book, Markus goes on, "Fundamentalists are more than eager to extirpate them, and even liberals have started to view them with contempt." Markus notes that it requires great moral courage and dedication for the intellectuals of a religious minority to disclose and cherish their controversial cultural heritage. She adds that there are tendencies in Ismaili officialdom to discourage research on the Ginans. Finally, she asserts faith that individual scholars will preserve them and discuss their significance.[7]

Markus's supportive assessment was shared by Zawahir Moir, who also called attention to Kassam's courage and her "interesting" and "bold" study of a substantial group of Ginans attributed to Pir Shams. In addition, he praised her skill in articulating the idea that the Satpanth was a comprehensive and coherent religious system, subtly integrating Islamic and Hindu elements, and not just a mishmash put together to make Hindu converts feel more at home in the Ismaili faith. Moir goes on to say that Kassam's hypothesis of a measure of historical continuity between the earlier Ismaili state of Multan in South Asia and the later Nizari mission of Pir Shams opens up new interpretive possibilities, even if the idea itself is not entirely new. Overall, he agrees that the empire's acknowledgment of both the private and the public sphere was key to the Ginans' survival. Moir ends by suggesting that Kassam might have also examined the contents of several other long Ginans ascribed to Shams and looked more closely at other Persian Nizari sources. He also wonders whether she might have taken into account the manuscript versions and variants of the texts, rather than the twentieth-century printed Gujarati editions that she did use.[8]

More serious is the critique of Ali Asani. In a 1999 review, Asani questions Kassam's argument that only after an initial politically activist phase did the Satpanth evolve toward a more inward, pacifist, and mystically oriented form.[9] In Asani's view, Kassam should have supported this argument by referring to sources beyond the traditional secondary ones that she uses—well-known studies by Abbas Hamdani, Derryl MacLean, Wladimir Ivanow, and Marshall Hodgson. Asani also takes issue with Kassam using the material in the Ginans themselves to argue that historical references to this political phase are preserved "dimly through sacred narrative." Rather, she should have consulted *Gulzar I abrar*, regional histories of Sind and Punjab, and the three-volume *Folklore of the Punjab*. Asani goes on to argue that Kassam should not have constructed history from the hymns themselves, given that several other scholars have pointed out the problems with this idea. In his view, reading metaphorical or symbolic references in the text to be actual persons and events leads Kassam to several "far-fetched" conclusions. Asani also joins Moir in thinking that Kassam should have paid more attention to the vicissitudes of textual transmission and referred to manuscripts and scholarly indices (including his own)[10] in order to think through certain questions of translation and avoid certain mistranslations.

COMMUNITIES' RESPONSES

Songs of Wisdom and Circles of Dance was never as "public" a controversy as the other books discussed in this volume, although the effects of the controversy were equally powerful. The discussion of the matter never reached the excoriating waves of the internet, and much of the public response had to do with attempts at suppression of her book. Thus, much of the account of this controversy comes from Kassam's own description a decade later. Her own words perhaps best describe what happened:

> Attempts were made to prevent the publication of my book. When that failed, attempts were made to prevent its distribution and sale. I received death threats that were sent to me via the publisher, State University of New York Press (SUNY Press). Even before I had laid my hands on a copy of my own book, a person who called himself "Dr." went to the main office of SUNY Press in Albany. Claiming to be an official representative of the Ismaili Muslim community, he warned that if the book was distributed and sold, it would result in a Salman Rushdie affair. The press took the threat seriously and contacted the FBI. Meanwhile, members of the executive committees of the American Academy of Religion and the Middle Eastern Studies Association, and other international Islamic scholars, were apprised of the unfolding situation, and they came to my defense and my right to academic freedom. Although the ultimate outcome was that the book was released after the "Dr." was investigated and both his academic credentials and his claims to be speaking on behalf of the Ismaili community were shown to be suspect, the episode exacted a dear price in multiple areas of my life.[11]

She writes about her personal encounter with those who protested her book in her journal in 1995:

> January 6, 1995. Vancouver. I'm shaking to my bones in fright. What exactly happened today? I'm in total shock. "Dr." picked me up and dropped me off at Mr. Z's. I walked into the living room and on the coffee table was my book. Yes, my book! Here I am, the author, I haven't yet seen my book, and he has my book on his coffee table. What is going on? How did he get it? Why is it here? Questions burn in my brain. I felt fear slowly crawl up my spine. Something was terribly wrong. He went to make tea. No one else was around. While he was in the kitchen, I picked up my book and found it all marked up. He sat down and launched into his tirade. Why had I not consulted him before getting it published? Didn't I know that he was the expert on Ginans? I was not to be allowed to have my book published and sold. It went on like this the entire day. I wanted desperately to get out of there. Where was "Dr."?? . . . Finally, around 5:00 pm, "Dr." came. . . . I am frantic. I can't think straight. What am I to do? First, how did Z get hold of my book? It can only have been directly through the publisher. How did he manage that? Obviously I can ditch my plan to write about his career as a preacher and his knowledge

of the Ginans. But I don't think he'll let go of me. And exactly what is his relationship with "Dr.?" Did "Dr." know he had my book? Did "Dr." get the book for Z? Did he know about this inquisition? O God. I come up for tenure this fall. What's this going to mean? What if these guys create enough problems so that the book gets delayed, destroyed, or even plain withdrawn from publication? There goes my career. Why? Why is this happening? I can't believe this. My very first book! I want to celebrate the occasion with my family, enjoy a few moments of pride and accomplishment, but here I am in utter despair, terrified, absolutely terrified.[12]

The aftermath of this episode was equally difficult. Kassam experienced temporary exile from the Ismaili community. Her book was not displayed in any centers of Ismaili culture in the UK, Canada, or the United States. As she herself would comment later, it was clear that her initial sense that a study of her own vibrant community would be welcomed by that community was misplaced.

After many years of deliberation, Kassam decided to make the events following the publication of her book part of the public record in an essay, "Balancing Acts: Negotiating the Ethics of Scholarship and Identity," in the edited collection *Identity and the Politics of Scholarship in the Study of Religion*. In fear of the unpredictable repercussions of going public with the treatment she received, she struggled with how to find a right balance between silence and disclosure. In the end, she concluded that the silence would not protect her, and, if not discussed openly, her experience would discourage younger talented Ismaili scholars from specializing in Ginans.[13]

Kassam opens her essay by noting that her description of the events following the publication of her book "mirrors the uncertain movement of social conditions and personal desires both obvious and hidden." Her deliberation revealed to her "why some kinds of scholarship cannot be independent of a scholar's identity, especially when multiple positions of intellectual inquiry, critical consciousness, communal identity, and religious affiliation and the myriad ethical imperatives of inherited and acquired identities compete."[14] As in the case of Harjot Oberoi in chapter 4, these were not only competing identities but also competing public spheres: the emerging global Ismaili culture and the culture of the university. Each had the challenge of understanding the rules, or emerging norms, of the other—what was appropriate to become "public" to the other and why.

Kassam begins to unravel the meaning of her experience by noting the complexity of her identity, especially as a member of a Canadian diaspora

South Asian family who started out in Kenya, close to Uganda, where General Idi Amin expelled Asians in 1972. When a South Asian Ismaili family living near her was hacked to death in a crime of hate, her family left Kenya for Canada to escape the danger. Leaving home and returning home is thus a constant motif for Kassam. In Canada, education offered her a central way of negotiating this complex identity. Gender consciousness also played a part in Kassam's early formation; her family remembered the instructions of the third Aga Khan to women to take off the veil and become educated and financially independent.[15]

Once her family was settled in Canada, Kassam's choice to study the Ginans was partly inspired by her practices in her new multicultural and multireligious home. She wanted to belong to the Ismaili community, and the Ginans in particular brought solace and inspiration amid extraordinary changes. As she put it, "Diaspora experiences make you want to find out who you are." Kassam was especially motivated by what she calls, following Charles Taylor, "misrecognition" of her tradition. As she explains, Euro-American scholars used distorted descriptions of the Ismailis taken from the writings of Muslim opponents of the Ismaili tradition. Many of these opponents called Ismailis un-Islamic or impure, partly because the Ginans were in Gujarati and maintained a variety of Sanskrit as well as Persian and Arabic ideas and concepts.[16]

For Kassam, however, to ask a question about the Hindu-Muslim "syncretism" of the Ismaili tradition, as many scholars do, was to ask a false question. Syncretism of separate traditions might be in the eye of the observer but not necessarily the practitioner, who lives and practices within a single reality. Listening to the Hindu Ramayana and reciting the daily Arabic *du'a* was simply a part of her everyday life, and there was no tension between them. Further, Ginans were part of that daily religious life and everyday ethics. In addition to being powerful expressions of devotion, the Ginans were also critical of many forms of religious pretentiousness, both Hindu and Muslim. As Kassam puts it, "Questions as to whether the Ginans were essentially Ismailism in Hindu disguise or Hinduism overlaid with Ismaili Muslim ideas were problematic because they were premised on ahistorical, essentialist, and insular conceptions of religious identity."[17]

In her essay, Kassam goes on to explore the ethical implications of studying one's own community, and the multiple positions that such an insider/outsider status entails. A legitimate "outsider" need for intellectual inquiry clashes with a legitimate "insider" need for self-protection and status within a community that might understand itself to be vulnerable. This dilemma puts the insider scholar forever in the borderlands of his or her community.[18] Kassam was, in her own words, too young and afraid and defenseless to challenge the situation of controversy surrounding her book. In addition, she was dealing with multiple hierarchies, both those of the academy and those of the Ismaili community. For these reasons, Kassam argues that it is mistaken to believe that insider scholars enjoy special privileges or immunity because of their membership in the community. It is equally mistaken, in her view, to believe that academe fully protects a scholar's right to academic freedom.

Kassam also considers the reasons for the controversy around *Songs of Wisdom and Circles of Dance* at that particular moment in Ismaili history. As she points out, the Ismailis have had to practice *taqiya*, or dissimulation and concealment, in the face of adverse circumstances. For centuries during the time of occultation, the Ginans were performed and transmitted orally within a tightly organized community. When written down, it was in a special script known only to a small group of elites. Access to them continues to be limited. In addition, because the Ismailis constitute a minority group who has suffered attack at various points in its history, Ismailis, as a general rule, have tried not to offend or provoke others. But in Kassam's situation, there is a doubly anxious subjectivity: in a culture that is already Islamophobic, the scholar by way of her study is drawing attention to the previously marginalized traditions, and in doing so, she brings the whole community under scrutiny.[19]

Kassam also notes that the global Ismaili community, having suffered displacement from India and Kenya, was trying to get through a delicate transitional phase in the new diasporic homes of Canada, the USA, and the UK. In addition, those Ismaili communities who were living in Central Asia and the former Soviet Union began to emerge from concealment as the Soviet Union collapsed. These communities, too, had their own traditions and constituted an internal challenge to Ismaili identity. As a result of this global situation, many scholars saw value in minimizing traditions such as the Ginans because of the new intra-Ismaili tensions and the diasporic status of Ismaili culture as a whole. Some Ismaili scholars actually questioned the authenticity of the Ginans, and although Kassam was interested in restoring their status, her book was lumped together with those who sought to undermine their status. Add to these historical elements the pressure to conform to a wider "global" Islamic identity, and you have the recipe for a controversy.

FINAL THOUGHTS

In terms of the impossibility of Habermasian translation between the secular and the religious, the question of memory politics comes to the fore. In public debates, there was the challenge of the recent past, the less recent past, and the story of origins, all wrapped up into one. Ismaili citizens were grappling with what they had recently suffered, and what had been allowed to happen to them. Even more, they were grappling with facts about their collective past that they could not or ought not forget.[20]

Tazim Kassam's case shares many of the same gray areas between religion and culture as Oberoi's. Both scholars are members of the communities about which they write; both communities underwent a great deal of trauma in the 1980s; both authors are South Asians; and both are interested in telling a more accurate history. Like Oberoi, Kassam was engaged in the study of a particular practice, which constituted the culture as much as the doctrine of that particular religious group.

However, in terms of the question of cultural recognition, the Ismaili case was distinct from the Sikh one in several important respects. Following Appiah, these have to do with the question of life-script and the relationship between individual and community: (1) Kassam was studying the performed texts and was not so much interested in the different description of the particular histories as Oberoi. Indeed, Kassam's history of changes and continuities in Ismailism followed along the lines of what several scholars had suggested earlier. (2) Kassam had the added burden of secrecy in regard to the cultural and religious value of Ismaili practices. To bring the Ginan tradition out of secrecy at all was of cultural and religious value to Kassam, but the value of such exposure was not shared by other individuals in the group. (3) In the Kassam case, the theological body had a different response. The office of the Aga Khan did not officially condemn her work; nor did it officially endorse it.

Yet the actions against Kassam were more individual and covert than those against Oberoi, and therefore more slippery. Kassam dealt with an individual asking to buy an entire printing of a book as well as with unidentified death threats. In contrast, Oberoi dealt with an official inquiry by a Sikh delegation and the condemnation of a loosely organized intellectual watchdog group. In her writing, Kassam is the more focused on her own South Asian identity and sees it as part of her larger challenge in the North American scholarly world. In Kassam's case, religious identity also becomes paramount, but in a less public way. Ismailis did not publicly claim rights of representation as the critics of Oberoi did. Nor did Kassam's critics enter debates more typical of open multicultural controversies.

Like Jane Schaberg's work, to be discussed in a subsequent chapter, Tazim Kassam's work identifies with a feminist perspective. She is one of the first South Asian women scholars to narrate her own life experience and what it has to do with her scholarship. Her account of her experiences in Uganda led her to identify as a South Asian woman Ismaili—and, in Appiah's terms, to ask to be recognized as holding those identities in her work. In her view, upon her arrival in Canada, none of those identities threatened her dignity and personhood, even though they had done so in the past. Rather, these elements of her identity were to be recognized and engaged as she studied the Ginans.

However, unlike Gill or Schaberg, Kassam was and is an active member of the community she studied. She knew of, and even knew personally, some of the people who protested her scholarship. This fact made her experience all the more troubling. Kassam's pride in belonging led to an expectation that people in her community would appreciate her work. She was interested in how better to support the community through scholarship as well as active participation. Yet these expectations were the ones most painful to have shattered in the controversy around her work. As a result of her work, Kassam experienced isolation within her community, but she also did not intend to leave it. In this situation, Kassam shared with Jane Schaberg the academy's initial misunderstanding of her work. The scholarly world's inability to understand the dynamics at play made it difficult for Kassam, or her college, to defend her work when the public critique emerged and she and her community members found themselves in the eruptive public sphere. For a moment in their careers, both Kassam and Schaberg stood disavowed by academics and religious communities alike.

Kassam was attacked not because she taught at a college with Ismaili commitments but rather because her own scholarly life-script as an author of books about Ginans did not fit the life-script of the Ismaili community: the Ginans either should not be written about or should not be written about as she wrote about them. Unlike Schaberg, Kassam initially did not continue to publish in the contentious area—a silence, she writes, that was a result of the initial controversy. However, that silence was not permanent: Kassam coedited an edition of the Ginans after a long period away from the topic.[21]

Kassam understood her primary identity as that of the Ismaili community. Her memory of trauma and her memory of solidarity among the group's members were both Ismaili. Her acquired identity was that of the Western academy, not the Indian academy, nor an indigenous Ismaili intellectual tradition. While the path of becoming an imam was closed to her as a woman, she was a leader in the community in other ways. As was the case with Oberoi, however, none of Uma Narayan's three roles was available to Kassam: she could not be an emissary, because she focused on history in addition to celebration; she could not be a mirror, because global realities of the Ismailis did not lend themselves easily to a "West versus Global South" opposition; and her status as an authentic insider was also a point of contention.

To put it another way, Kassam was in a historically new situation. The study of Ismailism in the Western academy is relatively new. In addition, this particular indigenous intellectual tradition is very much tied up with its leader, the Aga Khan. Thus, Kassam was a committed insider whose adopted mores of the Western academy did not have a long tradition in the study of Ismailism. As Kassam writes, Ismailism itself was going through globalization and becoming part of mainstream Islam, absorbing many of its intellectual traditions.

Kassam concludes her article about her experience by commenting that the role of the insider intellectual is fraught with danger, partly because fragile diaspora communities may understand critique, dissent, and questioning of authority to be a form of betrayal. One risks returning home as a permanent outsider who cannot push the controversial parts of one's home culture to the shadows.[22] The historical critical stance of the scholar made it difficult for her to remain uncritically faithful to the Ginans as a sacred, carefully controlled tradition. And the very fact that she was drawing attention to their existence, with all of their controversial imagery, made the "Islamic" status of Ismaili tradition vulnerable. While Kassam now thrives at a major research university, the double bind she faced was a powerful and instructive one.

Moreover, the role of secrecy in this episode is paramount, but this is not the secrecy of Eliadean gnosis. While the scholarly community took Kassam to task for some historical conjectures, they also applauded her bravery for taking on the study of the Ginans in the first place. In relationship to her own community, however, she experienced the temporary exile that Howard Schwartz experienced from the Jewish community, that Harjot Oberoi experienced from the Sikh community, and that Jane

Schaberg experienced in a slightly different way from the Catholic community. However, in each of the other cases, there is a far more public record of the community's objections, and their dissent is discussed openly. The Ismaili communities, on the other hand, attempted to stop the public's "exposure" to the book in the first place. The idea of the public was very far indeed from W. C. Smith's common good. In this way, some Ismailis' sense of their own vulnerability resulted in an attempt to silence before the fact, rather than afterward. As a whole, this episode mirrors the secret nature of the Ginans themselves.

In this case study, the nature of the eruptive public sphere is tinged with anxiety about global status in a postcolonial environment. In Nancy Fraser's terms, we might examine this case as a question of how the empire, and later the modern nation-state, from the Abbasid Caliphate to the Persian Caliphate, allowed the members of the Ismaili tradition to create a public sphere. With the dismantling of those two empires, the Ginans became private—indeed, secret—in order to survive. Any reemergence, even in a state such as British Colonial India or twentieth-century North America, was going to involve vulnerability of that formerly "private" sphere. For the Ismaili community across those centuries, privacy (in this case, really, secrecy) was not a freedom or a right but a necessity in light of a hostile public sphere around it.

In light of the 1970s expulsion of Ismailis from East Africa, the new emergence into a diaspora public space was indeed an extremely felt vulnerability. And the modern nation-states' understanding of religion *in general* as an essentially "private" affair only adds to the confusion about how "legitimate" a public discussion of the Ginans really is, and who has the authority to own them.

8

THE ILLEGITIMACY OF JESUS: STRONG PUBLICS IN CONFLICT

SETTING THE SCENE

In 1993, Jane Schaberg read the correspondence in the *Detroit Free Press* after a critic had written an article about her book *The Illegitimacy of Jesus*, published several years earlier in 1987. Schaberg's work had been engaged critically in the academy, but the Roman Catholic hierarchy had woken up. In addition to claims that her book was blasphemous, she read comments about the precarious role of academic freedom at a Roman Catholic university—especially a poor one. Such issues frequently lie at the heart of clashes of public spheres; some traditions are older and stronger than Habermas's coffee shops, and some are only decades old. While the post-Enlightenment Catholic Church hierarchy ceased to have the power of the state, it still had control over its universities, and who could maintain employment in them. The university could claim academic freedom; so too could members of the feminist community of resistant readers; and, finally, the *Detroit Free Press* and other media could claim freedom of the media and constituted a classical public sphere in Habermas's and even Fraser's sense.

JANE SCHABERG'S WORK

As many scholars acknowledged, *The Illegitimacy of Jesus* was a work firmly based in the historical-critical method of the study of the New Testament. The work was also firmly based in a feminist hermeneutics of the Bible and an understanding, as Schaberg put it, of the "double paradox" of feminists who turn to the Bible as both enemy and ally. The Bible is an ally in that Christians can find support in New Testament theology for liberational views—including the liberation of women. It is an enemy in that it acknowledges that all such liberational ideas were formulated within a patriarchal culture and thus must be read and analyzed with a hermeneutics of suspicion.

The Virgin Birth was incorporated into the teachings of the Church as early as the second century CE. The Apostles' Creed, recited by many other Christians as well as Roman Catholics, also affirms the Virgin Birth. The doctrine is based on the New Testament Gospels of Matthew 1:18–25 and Luke 1:26–38. It is not mentioned in other Gospels or the letters of Paul. Its teaching is that Jesus was not conceived in a human way but by the power of the Holy Spirit, and Mary was still a virgin when Jesus was born.

Schaberg's own hermeneutics of suspicion led her to an important hypothesis: that the stories of Jesus's Virgin Birth actually were a replacement for a much harsher story: that of Mary's rape and Jesus's birth as an illegitimate child. Schaberg bases her arguments on old-fashioned methods, particularly on the study of the Gospels of Matthew and Luke. In her view, both Matthew and Luke transmit a tradition that originated in a story that was not about a Virgin Birth but about a birth outside the bounds of acceptable society. As early as these two Gospels, argues Schaberg, we can see the beginning of the erasure of this narrative and its replacement with something far more theologically acceptable. The subtext and scandal—Schaberg herself uses the word to describe its impact in first-century Palestine—of the birth are minimized by the evangelists.

Her first chapter identifies her methodology as a "resistant reader": resistant readers look for cracks in the text, unexplained silences, and unacknowledged inconsistencies that might point to the traces of alternative perspectives. Such a view means that she will have concern about those who are not necessarily attended to in the Gospel narratives themselves. For example, both Matthew and Luke move the readers' attention away from the scandal of the conception. Matthew, in particular, is more concerned with Joseph rather than Mary, "who is spoken about but never appears." In contrast, Schaberg is concerned with Mary, "offstage," as it were.

Schaberg begins with an analysis of the Matthean narrative in the context of Deuteronomic law, as well as the Hebrew Bible genealogies with which Matthew likewise begins. In her view, the pregnancies of four women in Mary's lineage (Tamar, Ruth, Rahab, and Bathsheba) are "the

distasteful ones" among the fruitful women of the Bible.[1] Tamar is widowed, then rejected by her husband's brother, and ultimately cast out of
the family by her father-in-law. She disguises herself as a prostitute and
convinces her father-in-law to make love to her, thus continuing the line.
Ruth is the widow who follows her mother-in-law and refuses to return
to her own people; she ultimately marries the older farmer Boaz as her
redeemer. Bathsheba was impregnated by King David while she was still
married to the warrior Uriah and ultimately widowed by the machinations
of the king so she could become his wife. Rahab, finally, was the prostitute who helped the Israelites capture the city of Jericho and ensure her
people were saved and incorporated into the Israelite clan.

Tamar and Ruth are childless young widows, Rahab a prostitute, and
Bathsheba an adulteress and then a widow pregnant with her lover's child.
All are wronged in some way by the male world. And all are in some way
redeemed by the patriarchy and accepted into the fold, making their
present and future progeny legitimate. (It should be noted that not all of
these stories are from the Hebrew Bible; nor are they necessarily part of
the Davidic lineage in the Jewish tradition.) But Schaberg points out that
Matthew is placing Mary within this tradition of women. Thus he leads
the reader to expect another story of a woman who is a social misfit, who
is wronged or thwarted and is party to a sexual act that places her in great
danger, and whose story has an outcome that repairs the social fabric and
ensures the birth of a legitimate or legitimated child.[2]

In addition, Schaberg considers the question of Matthean genealogy:
there are, Matthew claims, three sets of fourteen generations. In the
third set, in which Jesus is included, only thirteen fathers are actually
named who "beget" their sons—Joseph is named but is said to beget no
son. Schaberg points out that the biological father is never named, even
though the entire lineage depends upon biological fatherhood. In her
view, this final omission of the thirteenth biological father is conscious
and intentional on the part of Matthew. Joseph is accepted as the legal
father and also of the Davidic lineage. But Matthew avoids saying, "And
Joseph begot Jesus," as he does with all the other genealogical formula-
tions. Instead, he uses the passive: Jesus "was begotten." As Schaberg puts
it, the idea of biological fatherhood is suppressed, but not completely.
There is still a trace in the form of the genealogy itself.[3]

Schaberg then goes on to consider the question of Jesus's birth from the
perspective of Jewish law at the time of first-century Palestine. There were,
in fact, two parts of the marriage contract—one that involved a period

of betrothal and the second that involved a "homecoming," which began the proper part of the marriage. Mary becomes pregnant between these two periods. Thus Joseph has a difficult question before him: Was his wife-to-be part of a seduction or victim of a rape? The Gospel of Matthew poses the question about Joseph in such a way that it reminds the reader of Deuteronomy 22:23–27, which makes the distinction between a pregnancy as a result of a seduction and one that is due to a rape. There, if the scene happens in the city, the woman would be heard and would cry out; in the country, however, she would not be heard. Schaberg argues that the instruction to Joseph to take Mary home implies that she is no longer suspected of seduction but not relieved of the suspicion of being raped. In Schaberg's view, in constructing the narrative in this way, Matthew pays homage to Deuteronomic law about legitimacy and also incorporates an illegitimacy tradition as a kind of subtext. According to Deuteronomic law, the legal father would be Joseph, and the biological father is indirectly referred to. Rather than either the legal father, who is Joseph, or the biological father, who remains unnamed, Matthew essentially argues that God himself parented Jesus.

In the Lukan narrative, there are many similarities. Luke presents the same marital and legal situation that Matthew does, and he alludes to the Deuteronomic law, as does Matthew. In addition, Luke says that Jesus was only the "supposed" son of Joseph, and thus, in Schaberg's view, Luke takes up the illegitimacy thread. Schaberg argues, however, that the theologizing of the illegitimacy theme takes a different tack in Luke. While Mary is "offstage" in Matthew, she is "front and center" in Luke in that she speaks and comments on the situation. Mary's Magnificat, modeled clearly on the song of Hannah in the Book of Samuel, is best read, in Schaberg's view, as a response to a suffered injustice. And in Luke 1:48, specifically the passage "God has regarded the 'tapeinosis' (humility) of his servant," the word *tapeinosis* is best translated not as "humility" but as "humiliation." This usage of *tapeinosis* is similar to the way in which the word is used for the sexual humiliation of a woman (the rape of Dinah) in Genesis 34:2 and at least eight other passages in the Hebrew Bible. In addition, Luke clearly placed the miraculous conception story of Jesus in such a way that it would be clear to readers familiar with the Greco-Roman trope of great people who became immortal. However, he did not adhere to the Greco-Roman theme that Jesus's origin was an actual result of intercourse between a human and a god. The Jesus birth story was familiar to those in the Mediterranean world, but also special and unique.[4]

However, Schaberg argues, in Luke, the subtext is much deeper and more difficult to find than in Matthew. Luke obscures the illegitimacy narrative in several ways. He is more interested by parallels with John the Baptist, whereas Matthew's interest is in parallels with women in the Hebrew Bible who have undergone similar issues of illegitimacy. Moreover, Luke uses the annunciation theme and blends it with a commission theme, then adds the unusual element of Mary's consent. This consent makes it hard to understand that violence might have been done to her. Overall, Luke focuses on piety and purity, which also makes it difficult to see the presence of an illegitimacy narrative. In the end, Luke's focus on casting Jesus in the light of a Greco-Roman immortal would make it difficult to perceive the inherited tradition of illegitimacy.[5]

Schaberg understands Luke's interest in Mary more as a result of restoring her as a "legitimate" mother of Jesus, rather than arriving at any understanding of her as a role model for women or for justice. She does, however, view the angel Gabriel's visit as one of the few biblical instances of a woman who conceives illegitimately, and thus in its inversion of the natural order of things this event could be understood as the Gospel in microcosm.[6]

Finally, Schaberg goes on to discuss the illegitimacy tradition in other parts of the New Testament, as well as in the Jewish tradition. In John 8:41, questions about Jesus's parentage arise in debate with other Jews, and whether he is born of fornication. In addition, Schaberg analyzes the Markan phrase "Son of Mary" and suggests that there is some reason to think that the memory of Jesus's illegitimacy "was alive and made public either during the ministry of Jesus or during the period of writing of these two gospels" (John in the 90s and Mark in the 60s). Another tradition, the Acts of Pilate, accepts that Jesus was conceived before the betrothal— but the charge is then denied. The Gospel of Thomas 105 claims not only that Jesus was illegitimate but that his mother was a harlot. In addition, Schaberg considers Origen's *Against Celsus*, the early Christian thinker's debate with the pagan thinker Celsus. Celsus claims, via the report of "the Jew," that it was Jesus himself who fabricated the story of his birth from a virgin; Mary was driven out by the carpenter, and in disgrace she gave birth to Jesus by Panthera, who had either corrupted or seduced her. Origen accepts many of the basics of the story, including that Jesus and Mary are outsiders, but says the story of Mary's adultery is a fable attempting to overturn the miraculous conception. Schaberg argues that Celsus's story and Origen's response draw on Gospel materials and perhaps pre-Gospel tradition, but it is impossible to tell whether the name of Jesus's father, Panthera (or Pantera), belonged to the earliest tradition of illegitimacy.[7]

Schaberg next considers the rabbinic tradition, both the Tannaitic period of the first and second centuries and the Amoraic period, c. 200–500 CE. In the texts from the Tannaitic period, Jesus is understood by the rabbis to be illegitimate and his father is named Pantera, as in the story of Celsus. In the later Amoraic period, rabbis characterized Jesus as Ben Pantera, the son of Pantera, or Ben Stada, Stada most likely being a Jew who had advocated worship of deities other than Yahweh. There are also traditions that refer to an illegitimate son, a *mamzer*, who is not necessarily Jesus. Schaberg concludes that the Jewish tradition involves a correct reading of some elements of the New Testament narratives and may well also be a living extension of an early stage of the pre-Gospel tradition of the illegitimacy of Jesus. Early patristic writings (Iraenaeus, Tertullian, and Justin Martyr) suggest a strong desire to maintain the biological virginity of Mary.[8]

Schaberg acknowledges in her conclusion that Jewish and Gentile Christians did not read the Gospel narratives in the way that she has done. Nor is there any direct statement of the illegitimacy tradition in any of the Gospel materials. She responds to these understandable concerns by writing that we have only a fraction of the literature of the earliest Christians. Moreover, the insistence of some Jewish Christians that Jesus was the natural son of Joseph may well not be an entirely secondary view but rather evidence of how little the doctrine of virginal conception was taken as a matter of course during the second century. In addition, she wonders whether the illegitimacy of Jesus has ever had a proper Christian hearing—citing the patristic writings as typical of the kinds of reactions to the illegitimacy hypothesis: that it must be a lie, slander, and slur, and would make, for some Christian audiences, an intolerable description of Jesus's origins, and cast doubt on, if not entirely sully, his later life and teachings. In what is now an odd foreshadowing of the troubles to come, Schaberg ends by reminding us of Raymond Brown's words from 1977, that "illegitimacy would be an offense that challenges the plausibility of the Christian mystery."[9]

Yet Schaberg does not see this illegitimacy as in and of itself a "shock" or a "scandal." Instead, because it may well be the historical underpinning of the evangelists' narratives, it is an important lens onto an alternative theology: rather than miraculously being able to give birth without carnal relations with a man, Mary, who was violated and humiliated, was cared for by divine providence. Thus, the theology implied is of God's grace within a context of disgrace.[10]

SCHOLARLY RESPONSES

In her review article, Mary H. Schertz underscores the work's importance for the larger project of feminist biblical criticism. She argues that its importance to women, especially victimized women, is great. Schertz raises concerns over issues that Schaberg herself acknowledges in the work: the problems with the arguments from silence (if one has them, Schertz asserts, they should be consistently argued); the methodological eclecticism, which Schertz acknowledges is both a strength and a weakness of the book; and Schertz's own wish that Schaberg delve more deeply into questions of how and why the Bible is both ally and adversary for women.[11]

Janice Capel Anderson sees Schaberg's work as important both for the study of infancy narratives and for challenging certain scholarly methods of textual study of the Bible. As she puts it, Schaberg's methods are critical-historical, but her conclusions are not. Her explicitly feminist stance allows for methods of reading eschewed by male scholars, and for Anderson, this is a good thing. Anderson finds her readings of the Gospel infancy narratives plausible, if not the only possibilities, given the paucity of evidence. Anderson states that her weakest arguments are in the pre- and post-Gospel narratives, as it is impossible to establish definitively what kinds of ideologies were in the minds of receivers of the tradition or readers of the Gospels. But, Anderson suggests, Schaberg is pushed to do this because of her hypothesis of an "illegitimacy tradition" to begin with.[12] Anderson nonetheless concludes that Schaberg's work is crucial, even if one disagrees with her conclusions. She suggests that socially oriented reader response theory could enhance Schaberg's explicit methods of "reading as a woman." More importantly, she ends her review with a question: "How many of us simply assume that the infancy narratives depict virgin conception? How many of us have ever entertained the possibility that Mary was raped?"[13]

In his own article on the infancy narratives, David T. Landry uses Schaberg's critique of the annunciation narratives as a starting point for his own thinking. As he puts it, two questions are crucial in the Luke narrative: What sense does it make that a woman betrothed to be married would object to an announcement that she is about to give birth? And does that reaction by Mary affect the reader's understanding of the way in which Jesus is conceived? The questions about the annunciation passage were raised by Raymond E. Brown and Joseph A. Fitzmyer in the 1970s and were resolved in such a way that the virginal conception of Jesus was preserved, but at the expense of the narrative logic of the passage. Landry goes on to write that Schaberg has "offered a sharp critique of the Brown/Fitzmyer solution and has proposed an innovative and controversial alternative of her own." Schaberg's interpretation rescues the narrative logic of the passage but suggests that Luke presents the conception of Jesus as an illegitimate one. He goes on, "Although Schaberg's interpretation has not been widely accepted, her critique of Brown and Fitzmyer appears to have some validity and suggests the need for another alternative."[14]

The question of why a betrothed virgin like Mary would object to the idea that she will become pregnant is avoided by other scholars. As Landry describes it, in their conversation in the 1970s, Brown and Fitzmyer argue for "a literary solution rather than a psychological one—that is, one which is more important to the literary intent of the text rather than an attempt to discern what Mary was thinking when she asks the question. The scene is meant to tell the reader how the child was conceived and hence to explain his identity."[15] Landry goes on:

> In other words, [for Brown and Fitzmyer], Mary as a character would have asked this question only if she already knew that a normal conception after the home-taking, with Joseph as the father, was excluded. But nothing in the text indicates that she knows that Joseph would not be the normal father. But The Gospel of Luke already knows that this normal fatherhood will not be the way in which the child is conceived, and thus Luke phrases Mary's question the way he does because he is promulgating the tradition that the divine plan excluded a human begetting of a child. In other words, Luke has Mary ask the question for no discernible reason other than to give the angel the further opportunity to speak of the child's identity.[16]

Schaberg's counterargument is that when earlier text critics shun psychological readings, they are doing so with the idea that this is the psyche of the historical Mary. But any reader will also want to know about the psychological makeup of the character Mary, and therefore the narrative logic is just as important, if not more so. Even if Mary's question is a formal part of the story required by the logic of the annunciation, that doesn't mean that formal patterns oblige authors to disrupt the narrative logic of the story. Landry argues that Schaberg is right in suggesting that earlier authors have given up too easily on thinking through the narrative logic of the story. Literary necessity is not literary nonsense.[17]

Landry is convinced by Schaberg's insistence on narrative logic and the psychology of characters, but not convinced that the narrative logic is as Schaberg suggests. Rather, he thinks that there is evidence to support the idea that Mary understood herself to be immediately about to be pregnant, which would still be a physical impossibility, and therefore certainly worthy of a clarifying question, which is what Mary does ask the angel. Schaberg, too, admits this as a possibility. And the angel's response only makes sense if Mary is querying her pregnancy vis-à-vis the physical impossibility of its occurrence in the immediate future. The angel's response doesn't make sense at all if Mary knows that she has been illegitimately with another man. Elizabeth's congratulations to her also make sense in this situation, which is that she has faith that even in the context of a marital covenant that has not yet been fulfilled by the "hometaking," she has still allowed God's will to be done.[18]

COMMUNITIES' RESPONSES

This conversation is an excellent example of civil scholarly disagreement, proceeding on the basis of a common question: Is the best interpretive framework for the New Testament birth stories narrative logic or psychological logic? But such a common question was not shared by Schaberg's interlocutors in the larger sphere of both the Roman Catholic academic hierarchy and the reading public of the *Detroit Free Press*. Here we have two public spheres that are both "weak" in relationship to the state—in that they have no power of enforcement in the secular sphere. However, while the Roman Catholic hierarchy and press were "weak" in the secular sphere, the Roman Catholic sphere in its own right was "strong" insofar as it was able to enforce its laws among its own members.

Schaberg writes of the controversy that followed the publication of her work in "Feminism Lashes Back: Responses to the Backlash" in *Bibliocon*, a journal that published only three issues but whose aim was to "explore the ways in which the Bible has been appropriated culturally, whether in revisionist feminist interpretation, artistic interpretation, or literary creation."

As the preface to the first issue states, "Too often we have neglected the impact of the Bible on the collective unconscious of Western culture. Now it is time for our scholarly lives and our cultural experiences to converge, to see how these cultural events affect our interpretation of biblical figures and tropes."[19]

Schaberg characterizes her own work as using "the standard methods of biblical criticism": close reading, comparison of versions, intertextual reading, and philological analysis. Her intent is to train the perspectives of feminist thought on the New Testament infancy narratives, the first chapters of Matthew and Luke, in order to explore the possibilities of an alternate reading: "I argued that behind these texts lies the almost erased tradition not of the virginal conception of Jesus, but of his illegitimate conception, pointing to the law in Deuteronomy concerning the rape or seduction of a betrothed virgin."[20] In other words, in the case of Mary, Schaberg wants to call attention to the earlier law whereby the possibility of a virgin being forcibly made pregnant remains.

Schaberg goes on, "Without fully knowing what I was doing, I had touched an exposed livewire (which I would have touched anyway but perhaps with more protection and preparation had that been available)." She writes that in the years after its publication, the book was dismissed, ridiculed, praised, used, and published in paperback by Crossroad. Letters were both hostile and grateful.[21] In this, its reception was probably no more troubled than any other controversial book's.

It was the characterization in the larger press that created the firestorm. *The Illegitimacy of Jesus* was featured in *Time* magazine, which generated more hostile letters. But the watershed, as Schaberg sees it, was when the *Detroit Free Press* did a profile of her.[22] Upon meeting the religion editor, David Crumm, Schaberg felt that the paper would do a balanced and careful job and give a hearing to feminist issues. Schaberg notes that in the article she was indeed accurately quoted about "feminism's intellectual and social challenges, the impact of Detroit on my work, and Catholicism's failures," and her writing was accurately excerpted. But, Schaberg goes on, "the profile was basically of an uncredentialed, loose-cannon feminist, dogmatically preaching 'the gospel according to Jane.'" An editor above David Crumm took many quotes out of context to make the piece more sensational. And the academic disagreements were represented as the University of Detroit Mercy, where she taught, undercutting her altogether. The vice president of academic affairs, Gerald Cavanagh, both defended academic freedom *and* insisted that Schaberg's "basic teaching ... really does cut to the core of our faith. Her interpretation is not the position of this university, and I would say 99 percent of the people at this university disagree with her."[23]

This piece was the one that created the maelstrom. It is helpful to hear Schaberg's own description of what happened next:

> The phones began ringing at the university, at my house, and at the Archdiocese of Detroit. The VP for public relations told me that the University had lost over $200,000 in donations, and had been written out of two substantial wills in the first week. One of my friends, an alumnus of the university, said "a poor university can't afford academic freedom."
>
> Several hundred angry phone calls were said to have come in to the administration and Board of Trustees. Many of those fielded by the secretaries and me were hostile: they expressed religious outrage at my ideas, called me a whore, feminazi, queen of crapola, pseudointellectual, delusional, butch, blasphemer, heretic, a spiritual canker, Satanic, lesbian, and sicko. They asked often about my ethnic identity, insisted that I had no place on the faculty of a Catholic university, should not be "honored" as chair of my department, called for my resignation or firing, and in a couple of cases my death.
>
> The supportive callers asked where they could find the *Illegitimacy* book. These were from abused women asking for help, gay men expressing their alienation from the church hierarchy, young fathers contemplating their daughters' fate, women who felt rage at being silenced, men and women who had hope, or no hope, for the future of Christianity, old men with shaky handwriting protesting the second-class status of women, and from other scholars. Many remarked that the article helped them to see how the tradition could function to create compassion for the most powerless members of society.[24]

Intriguingly, the Roman Catholic Church hierarchy also weighed in with a series of public statements. As in the case of Harjot Oberoi, only with centuries of such judgment behind it in Europe and America, the question of theological correctness was taken up by those empowered to judge such cases. Archbishop Adam Maida reaffirmed the magisterium of the church hierarchy, and the need for those who teach at Catholic universities to be faithful to that magisterium. Heresies, he went on to say, would be addressed. A letter from Maida was sent to all the parishes in the Detroit area. He also published an article in the parish bulletins, reaffirming the basic Catholic teaching that Mary was a virgin before, during, and after the birth of Jesus and saying that the Virgin Birth teaching had direct relevance to questions of contemporary morality, such as assisted suicide and abortion. Schaberg writes that two offers were made to pay her salary on condition that she not teach, offers that were not communicated to her at the time.[25]

Letters from the public, Schaberg reports, also showed the problem for Catholic doctrine of thinking of "rape" and "Mary" in the same breath. One letter stated, "Mary could not have been conceived by rape, or her child Jesus would have been an imperfect human and would not have been a suitable ransom to make possible the release from sin and death for us." Another wrote, "God kept Mary and Jesus pure from the revolting, shameful things that you write about." And a third: "You are associating Mary with the lowest of the low, in claiming that she was raped and had an illegitimate child." In discussing the possibility of rape in the light of Deuteronomic law, Schaberg was for many Christians challenging Mary's purity, and the purity of Catholic doctrine, as well as the basic motivation of God for giving his only son as a sacrifice.[26]

And finally, there was the vexing question of the Catholic university, where the public sphere of intellectual freedom is intertwined with the public sphere of the Roman Catholic Church offices. Two members of the board of trustees released a formal statement and were interviewed by the *Michigan Catholic*. These members affirmed the "Catholicity" of the Religious Studies Department. Schaberg notes that the members of the department at this time included two Presbyterians, a self-styled lapsed Unitarian, a Jew, two Jesuits, a lay Catholic, and herself, "hard to classify," but certainly understood as a resistant reader. Schaberg herself was a member of the Society of the Sacred Heart of Jesus but after she joined the University of Detroit renounced her vows. Her views also inspired her to sign, with other prominent feminist Catholics, a public critique of the Roman Catholic perspective on abortion, "A Catholic Statement on Pluralism and Abortion."[27]

The members of the board also affirmed that Schaberg was protected by law against discrimination for holding unpopular views, although they also added that her views only became known after she was hired. They added two more ominous statements. The first read, "Unless there was a breakdown in the professional standard of scholarship, it would not be the business of the University's sponsors to interfere." They then went on to say that Schaberg's views would "be subject to and balanced by the review and critique of her professional colleagues." One earlier draft of the statement, Schaberg reports, also included the claim that her work was not respected by her peers, a view given by an anonymous person in a telephone interview.[28]

Students wrote in to the newspaper and claimed that Schaberg's academic freedom was not respected. Many faculty members were openly supportive and admonished the administration for not supporting Schaberg more fully. Others said that they could not state their views because they were untenured. Some faculty, including untenured ones, also tried to correct the misperceptions of the *Detroit Free Press*. As a department, Religious Studies was silent. Some professors even admonished Schaberg for endangering their own jobs and hurting the university's image. During this period, Schaberg resigned her position as chair of the department.[29]

The larger academy also tried to address the issue. Professor Pamela Milne of the University of Windsor organized scholars from the Society of Biblical Literature to write to the University of Detroit Mercy president and board of trustees. Many of them did, although Schaberg writes that neither the president nor the board ever acknowledged receiving the letters. Elisabeth Schüssler Fiorenza wrote an editorial for the *New York Times*, comparing the attack on Schaberg with those on Rosemary Radford Ruether, a feminist theologian who was and continues to be an outspoken critic of the Catholic hierarchy's stance on women's ordination, abortion, and a host of other issues, and on Chung Hyun Kyung, a liberation theologian in Korea whose works were also condemned as "syncretic with other non-Christian traditions." Schaberg writes that Schüssler Fiorenza's editorial was rejected for being too controversial.[30]

Reflecting upon her experience four years later, Schaberg comments, "I got a glimpse of the fanaticism and power with which patriarchy clings to the image of women it creates, and of the uses to which the images are put. That naked face of 'the fathers' is not one I'm ever likely to forget." Schaberg saw the "fruitless litigation and unemployment that could open under my feet," as it had "under the feet of other feminist scholars."[31] She goes on to cite Annette Kolodny, who wrote that such feminist scholarship "shatters the very foundation of a full panoply of powerful cultural conventions— from class arrangements, to gender hierarchy . . .—resistance to it will be as powerful as the privileges and culture beliefs being protected."[32]

FINAL THOUGHTS

In the case of *The Illegitimacy of Jesus*, we have a strong example of unified, organized religious tradition. There is no mention of ethnicity by participants in this conflict; rather, their concern is with the various organs that represent the Catholic Church, and how they might weigh in, and with what authority. Here was the greatest possibility of the Habermasian activity of translation, given the long theological tradition of reasoning about the Bible in the Roman Catholic Church and its historical relationship to secular reasoning. Yet the strength of the two publics still made for an eruptive public space. The role of the Church was debated, the role of the religiously affiliated university was debated, and the role of the Catholic laity was debated (about which more below). In this case, Catholicism was something consciously practiced, with a particular intellectual and liturgical culture, but its status as an official, institutional religion was paramount.

In Appiah's terms of cultural recognition, Jane Schaberg's situation was differently configured in that ethnic identity did not come into play. However, her commitment as a Catholic, and as an upholder of Catholic doctrine, figured as paramount because the institution she worked for understood itself primarily as a Catholic intellectual institution. The Catholic community's attack on her was almost simultaneous with the university's disavowal of her. Intriguingly, because she was head of a pluralistic department at the time, Schaberg herself was developing the intellectual and religious diversity that the department, by its very demographic makeup, also espoused. (She reminds us, in her essay recounting the controversy, that her departmental colleagues were a Jew, a secularist, and a Buddhist, among others.[33]) However, at the next level up, the university administrative level, Schaberg felt she had very little support for her work. As she writes, the Roman Catholic Church ceased to be her community, and the secular feminist study of religion seemed to remain more steadfast as a source of intellectual support and guidance in the ensuing maelstrom.

Intriguingly, of all the communities involved in the controversies discussed in this book, the Roman Catholic Church has the longest intellectual tradition behind it. And yet the controversy about *The Illegitimacy of Jesus* was the only one that actually erupted in personal, *ad feminam* physical violence against her property, when her car was set on fire in the middle of the night. While one would not want to posit a causal relationship here, I think it is not inconsequential that Schaberg found herself caught between the intellectual traditions and fledgling feminist community of scholars within a long-standing secular academy, on the one side, and the Roman Catholic university intellectual and administrative worlds, on the other. Equally intriguing, Schaberg is one of the few scholars in this study who continued to publish in her subfield, until her untimely death in 2012. She went on to produce a study of Mary Magdalene using many of the same text-critical methods that she used for *The Illegitimacy of Jesus*. In Appiah's terms, one might argue that the politics of recognition had a longer history of being fought over in the Catholic community than in many (though not of all) of the other communities discussed in this book.

Schaberg's own life-script also is significant here. Deeply disappointed by the academy's inability to support her in a way that showed its solidarity with her commitment to feminist scholarship combined with the norms of New Testament analysis, she was even more disappointed in the Roman Catholic community's treatment of her. The pipe bombs that set her car ablaze, the letters excoriating her and calling for her resignation in local and national papers, and her university's inaction in the face of such statements all led to a different view of what the academy was and was not willing to do to protect her. Not insignificantly, the two institutions were far more connected than in any of the other cases I have examined in this book: the administration felt compelled to say that few people at the university would agree with Schaberg's conclusions—whereas they might not have felt the same compunction had Schaberg taught at a private liberal arts university. In a sense, by remaining at Mercy, Schaberg persevered, surviving in both the academy and the community, and yet advocating the mainstream positions of neither.

The nature of this eruptive public space had less to do with postcolonial status and more to do with the two opposing strengths of theological and secular reasoning of feminist Biblical hermenutics. Gender became paramount insofar as Schaberg's feminist perspectives of listening to the silences in the text led to unacceptable theological claims. In a review of the controversy, Frank Reilly sums up the situation of the several competing strong publics in the Schaberg case quite well. Roman Catholic theologians such as Raymond Brown saw themselves first and foremost as obedient Catholics and part of the magisterium, and as such, they could not countenance a normal birth of Jesus as part of historical criticism. As Reilly notes, in 1981, Brown "wrote that he 'personally' did not think the meaning intended by a biblical writer could be contradictory to that intended by the church; and [Brown thus] rejected as 'modernism in the classic sense'—as a denial of any real content to doctrine—any openness to a historical-critical judgment 'that Jesus was conceived normally.'" Reilly goes on, "For Schaberg, also a Roman Catholic, 'reading as a woman'—which a few years later she called 'reading with a feminist consciousness'—was the most important thing. This made her a 'resistant' reader of the androcentric and patriarchal text, and especially of any story that involves a woman but is told from a male perspective. She was attentive to silences in the text, listening for the voices of women, seeking out what men might miss, aiming at 'a more comprehensive perspective, a compelling reading, a human reading.' Such a reading, she insisted, required an 'acceptance of human sexuality.'"[34]

In the one public sphere, there were the magisterium of the Roman Catholic hierarchy and the rules and ideologies of public debate that such a magisterium represents. In the other public sphere, there were the emerging norms of a resistant academic movement, using tested forms of biblical criticism at the same time as the practice of listening for the voices of women in the accounts of men.

Jane Schaberg's views, then, were discussed in a variety of public spheres, all of them "strong" within their own communities but "weak" in relationship to powers of enforcement beyond their circle. The university community had a relationship to academic freedom and yet, as a Catholic university, held a relationship to the church hierarchy that could curb that freedom. W. C. Smith's "faith" and "tradition" were at war with themselves. Meanwhile, Schaberg's close textual reading was certainly a method Eliade would espouse, but such an approach had become politically explosive. What is more, the university's norms were in a murky place, whereby pressure from the Catholic Church hierarchy might have resulted in Schaberg being censured, and at worst unemployed. In contrast, pressure from the world of scholarship, the competing strong public sphere, would have upheld her employment.

Add to this mix the introduction and discussion of Schaberg's work in *Time* magazine, the *New Yorker*, and the *Detroit Free Press*; while none of those forms of coverage pushed the boundaries of journalistic norms, the public debates in the pages of the local press and in letters sent to the university were not necessarily governed by norms of civility and decorum. Rather, they erupted with calls for Schaberg's ouster. She also experienced vandalism against her property and death threats. Schaberg's work stood at a most volatile intersection indeed.

9

GOD'S PHALLUS: THE REFUSAL OF PUBLIC ENGAGEMENT

SETTING THE SCENE

In 1996, Howard Schwartz (formerly Eilberg-Schwartz) made the decision to leave the academy because he could not reconcile the competing requirements of his academic freedom and those of the community that funded his academic position. His position was similar to that of Harjot Oberoi, discussed in chapter 4, who also occupied a chair funded by a community with specific expectations. Also as with Oberoi, the expectations colored the community's and Schwartz's interactions in the public sphere. In Schwartz's case, we see an ultimate refusal of engagement on the part of the scholar.

Howard Schwartz published *God's Phallus: And Other Problems for Men and Monotheism* through Beacon Press in 1994 and *The Savage in Judaism: An Anthropology of Israelite Religion and Ancient Judaism* through Indiana University Press in 1990. Much of his work was inspired by feminist analysis, which in its early years had provided the critique that the masculine image of God was paradigmatic for gender behavior and regulation within the religious community. Simply put, according to this view, the masculine image of God justifies patriarchy in a wide number of forms.

HOWARD SCHWARTZ'S WORK

Like Jeffrey Kripal, whose case we will discuss in chapter 9, Schwartz took sexuality, femininity, and masculinity as primary categories with which to analyze sacred texts. Freudian analysis was certainly one tool in his

toolbox, although not the only one. Like Jane Schaberg, Schwartz understood his work on biblical texts to utilize a method of "reading against the
grain." Yet his focus was not on the oppression of women by men implied
by the male image of God but rather on the implications for *masculinity*
itself. In his view, the idea of Jewish masculinity has major contradictions
within it. On the one hand, Israelites were to be God's lover and think of
themselves as a bride of God. Biblical descriptions of the covenant between God and the people of Israel were replete with marital metaphors
as well as lover metaphors. This meant (as we see in the Hindu tradition)
that men must understand themselves as wives or female lovers.[1]

Schwartz points to the example of Hosea 2:18: "In that day—declares
the Lord—you will call [Me] Ishi [my husband], and no more will you call
Me Baali [my husband Baal]." He goes on to argue that there are sexual
overtones to this, citing the prophet Ezekiel: "You were still naked and
bare when I passed by you [again] and saw that your time for love had arrived. So I spread My robe over you and covered your nakedness, and I
entered into a covenant with you by oath" (Ezekiel 16:7–8).

Yet Schwartz reasons that passages in the Bible treat sexual relationships
between men as an abomination. Leviticus 18:22 and 20:13 both condemn
such relations. Nevertheless, men were also asked to honor and love a masculine God; at times, this was communicated in marital and sexual metaphors. Like Kripal, Schwartz argues that there was an implied homoeroticism in this basic state of affairs. Schwartz's solution to the dilemma? That
God's body should be invisible. God had a body, a masculine one, but it was
forbidden as a visual object. As long as God did not have a body, and did not
have a mythology of sexuality behind him, he could be the object of male
adoration, love, and covenant. Yet men had a further dilemma, he argues;
they had to attain a sexless status in order to be like God, while at the same
time fulfilling the command to procreate. Finally, Schwartz argues, the
conflict between the male covenantal relationship and heterosexual marriage necessitated the removal of women from this encounter. Thus Moses
became celibate during his encounters with God and is the one who orders
the separation of the women during the giving of the Torah on Mount Sinai.

Schwartz thus reminds his readers of lesser-known passages in biblical
texts, where God's body is indeed referred to: "And the Lord said, 'See,
there is a place near Me. Station yourself on the rock and, as My Presence
[*Kavod*] passes by, I will put you in a cleft of the rock and shield you with
My hand until I have passed by. Then I will take My hand away and you
will see My back; but My face must not be seen'" (Exodus 33:21–23). In

this passage, God has a hand, as well as a back, as well as a face. When God takes his hand away, Moses, standing in the cleft of a rock, actually can see God's back.

Schwartz sees a resemblance between this passage and the passage where Noah is left naked, and then covered, by his sons. In both cases, a son sees a "father's" nakedness:

> Noah, the tiller of soil, was the first to plant a vineyard. He drank of wine and became drunk, and he uncovered himself within his tent. Ham, the father of Canaan, saw his father's nakedness and told his two brothers outside. But Shem and Japheth took a cloth, placed it against both their backs and walking backwards, they covered their father's nakedness; their faces were turned the other way, so that they did not see their father's nakedness. (Genesis 9:20–25)

Schwartz reads both stories as myths—stories that, in Lévi-Strauss's terms, try to resolve some fundamental dilemmas in culture. The issue in Schwartz's mind is the uneasiness at the prospect of a father's nakedness—the exposure of a body. And the need to cover the body of a father is part of the power of the myths, in both cases.

Part of what was radical in Schwartz's argument was that he was proposing a different reason for the development of Jewish monotheism. His is not a philosophical interpretation but an anthropological one. In contrast, the traditional scholarly interpretation was that the pagan gods of the Mesopotamian region were replete with human attributes and human behaviors. They had human emotions such as jealousy and lust, and they were subject to injury and even death. However, Jewish separation from these ideas was also understood as a kind of superiority, the beginning of a relationship with God in which a single God was faithful to them and existed without human attributes. This was, according to the traditional story, the "breakthrough" of ethical monotheism. It had radical implications for the development of a more humane society as well as a more humane way of thinking about God. But in Schwartz's view, the invisibility of God had less to do with God's transcendence and more to do with the erasure of the body.

THE SCHOLARLY RESPONSE

Scholarly reviews of the book commend Schwartz for his boldness and his creativity, as well as for his arguments being well embedded in the appropriate sources. Esther Fuchs particularly praises Schwartz's insistence that gender is a central feature in the history of Judaism and cannot be treated "incidentally." In addition, she endorses his call for a "feminization" of the attributes of a hypermasculine and sexless God without making God into a goddess.[2]

Stanley Rosenbaum argues that the book has considerable merits for this reason, disturbing as its content might be. Rosenbaum's criticism is that it treats all biblical sources as synchronous and not as having emerged at different time periods in the history of the development of Israel. Thus, what might be true of homoeroticism in one text may not be true of all texts and all forms of Israelite literary production. Rosenbaum strikes a note that is familiar to us in this book: he can imagine the response to Schwartz's book paralleling that to Freud, or even to *Portnoy's Complaint*, in its relentless concern with a sexual and homoerotic question: "It's true, and so a scandal that will paint Jews as polymorphously perverse among the Gentiles."[3]

God's Phallus was, according to Schwartz's own account, the book that created the most concern about his scholarly focus. As in Kripal's case, the questions of Freudian analysis were helpful to some readers and suspect to others. They were helpful in their bold introduction of questions of sexuality into texts that themselves had sexual content. At the same time, they were suspect because such questions were at risk of sexualizing content that did not have such meaning to many members of the community. While the idea of homoeroticism did not garner the explosive response in the Jewish community that Kripal's use of the term did in the Hindu one, it did risk the perception that Schwartz was overstating the significance by using explicitly Freudian terms and a worldview that many members of the Jewish community did not share. To be sure, Judaism is no stranger to Freudian analysis; indeed, one might say it is the first object of such analysis, given that its narratives were the source of Freud's theories of religion. Several Freudian studies of Judaism have been conducted since then—in riposte as well as inspiration. However, the anthropological turn places Judaism in a more vulnerable light.

Additional more significant issues that prompted Schwartz to move out of the academy emerged both before and after the publication of *God's Phallus*. These issues had to do with questions of self-criticism within Judaism, and with the more extreme version of it that has been called by some "ethnic self-hate." Related to other authors discussed in this book, the question for Schwartz became how such issues are defined in contemporary Judaism and reflected in contemporary Jewish studies. His earlier book *The Savage in Judaism* raised this question in the scholarly discussion that followed its publication. Schwartz's subsequent appointment at San Francisco State raised the question again.

In *The Savage in Judaism*, Schwartz argued that there should be a renewed interested in the history of the anthropological study of Judaism. Such study enjoyed a brief heyday in the nineteenth century before declining in the twentieth. But Schwartz sees a great deal of merit in revisiting earlier, now "outdated," authors' parallels between so-called savage societies and Jewish practices and customs, such as the comparisons that James George Frazer frequently and happily made. The case studies involve the cultural metaphors the Hebrew Bible uses to gain entry into the worldviews of the group: circumcision and menstrual taboos; the problem of semen and blood perceived as "danger"; the body as metaphor and model; and the problems of classification and status. These themes are particularly important to examine afresh with these comparative anthropological insights.

Bernhard Lang argues that such creativity in using comparative anthropological insights makes for a rich, valuable, and sophisticated book that places Schwartz among the leading interpreters of ancient Judaism of his generation.[4] Don C. Benjamin notes that Schwartz has finally made the case that anthropology is crucial for understanding biblical literature and, more broadly, for understanding Jews—not just as people of the book but also as people of the body.[5] The anthropologist Gillian Feeley-Harnik praises Schwartz for the distinctions he makes between Biblical sources (such as the Yahwist and the Priestly sources) and the ways in which he accounts for classificatory schema over time—such as the change from the biblical body metaphors to the ones of the Qumranic community and the early Christians, or his contrast between the Israelite priests and the rabbis who composed the Mishnah (180 CE).[6]

Gary Anderson agrees with the basic value of the book but disagrees precisely with the treatment that Feeley-Harnik finds so laudable: the comparison between the Israelite priests and the Mishnah. Anderson argues that there is no full way of knowing whether these two systems of thought could be analogous. He also argues that Schwartz presents certain ideas about bodily fluid as central to the Bible (such as one passage on menstruation), when there is little evidence anywhere else in the Bible that these ideas are central at all. Anderson also encourages Schwartz to denigrate indigenous systems of rationality less, but rather see the ways in which both religious and nonreligious systems engage forms of rationality appropriate to their contexts.[7]

Jonathan Boyarin also regards Schwartz's work as creative in its own right but wonders whether some of the cultural comparisons might inadvertently reinforce the now-outdated evolutionist perspective that Christianity is least concerned about bodily control and most focused on individual responsibility when compared to other religions. In addition, Boyarin argues that the anthropological history of studying Judaism and the "savage" is far more complex than a straightforward history of the romance with and the disavowal of the "primitive" in Judaism might allow. Finally, Boyarin suggests that Schwartz inadvertently reinscribes the lower/higher dichotomy in the analysis of Judaism by insisting on including the "base" parts of human nature rather than changing the terms of the debate altogether.[8]

Critics of the book, such as Ayala Gabriel, who wrote a review in the *Journal of the American Academy of Religion*, share Boyarin's worry about possible evolutionism, whereby an inevitable narrative of progress emerges, purporting a movement from the "simpler primitive" to the "more sophisticated" religion. Yet such critics register a stronger concern than a simple worry. They accuse Schwartz of reintroducing the problematic issues of late nineteenth-century anthropologists in an attempt to resuscitate those outdated insights. In introducing the idea of the "gaze" once again, he reintroduces armchair anthropology, and thus deprives Judaism of an indigenous voice. Many of the insights that Schwartz might get from African taboos—such as the comparison between circumcision and pruning—have already been noticed by indigenous thinkers such as the compilers of Genesis Rabbah, a collection of legends (*midrashim*) from the sixth century CE concerning the Book of Genesis. In other words, it is not new knowledge but rather old knowledge whose discovery may not require an African parallel. In addition, writes Gabriel, Schwartz holds the erroneous assumption that the inability to apply anthropological insights to Jewish ideas is part and parcel of a psychological attitude toward Jewish identity itself. For example, Schwartz conjectures that Lévi-Strauss's reluctance to study Judaism might be part of the larger question of being a Jew facing modernity. Gabriel disagrees with this conjecture, wondering whose standards Schwartz is applying to Jewish identity and why. Finally, Gabriel takes issue with some of the anthropological assessments of material in the book, particularly the relationship with Jacob and his mother, Rebekah, which she feels is simply re-presented in a misogynistic fashion.

In Gabriel's view, these distorted readings are because Schwartz does not sufficiently take into account the feminist traditions and anthropological traditions that had already begun reassessing the Bible by the time the book was published.[9]

In his review of *The Savage in Judaism*, Raphael Patai also suggests that Schwartz pay more attention to those early anthropologists who wrote in French and German. Like others, Patai is concerned about the slippage in the use of the word "savage." If in fact, Patai asks, the savage must be restored in the study of Judaism, why must that same savage element be removed from the contexts of the study of worlds of New Guinea? Moreover, he feels that what might be read as Schwartz's play on words actually ends up creating more ambiguity regarding the meaning of "savage." For Patai, Schwartz's phrase "the anthropological study of Judaism unleashes a savage critique of Judaism itself" only obscures any attempt at a conceptual definition that the author is trying to make.[10]

In his review, Michael Fishbane takes up a similar issue. He argues that Biblical metaphors are themselves from very different contexts and times, and that the Bible comprises many genres "composed over centuries by high literate readers and authors." In his view, there is no stable "mirror into the biblical mind." The particular difficulty that both Fishbane and Gabriel have is that the prohibition against boiling a kid in its mother's milk as a parallel with the Ndembu prohibition against incest is problematic. In the end, Fishbane wonders whether "comparative inquiry can serve as a substitute for native exegesis." But he is far more persuaded by Schwartz's treatment of postbiblical materials and believes that we must be very much in debt to the author for forcing the anthropological categories back into the biblically exegetical minds.[11]

So far, an engagement of scholarly minds and scholarly categories is at work here. But the debate reaches a higher pitch. In a review article in the *Journal for the Scientific Study of Religion*, Murray Wax entertains the possibility that Schwartz might be engaging in "ethnic self-hate." He focuses on the reasons Schwartz himself gives for writing the book: frustration and puzzlement at the rage that his homiletics professor expressed at Schwartz's own wish to focus on menstrual taboos in his sermon when he was a rabbinical student at Jewish Theological Seminary. Arguing that Schwartz is being disingenuous when he locates the entire reason for writing the book in this frustrating encounter, Wax wonders whether Schwartz's motivation might be far better located in the ethnic self-hate of many post-Enlightenment Jews. Wax cannot understand in any other way what he reads as a tone of animus in the book. He goes on to critique some of the anthropological assessments of the book, such as Weber's reading of Judaism; Malinowski's view of magic, science, and religion; and the anthropological value of the distinction between "great" and "little" traditions. (Schwartz is in favor of dispensing with it; Wax wishes to assert its value in the history of anthropological description.)[12]

Schwartz himself writes a rebuttal, arguing that the previous, more fundamental question must be asked: "What kinds of criticisms count as 'ethnic self-hate' and who in the end gets to decide?" He further states that indeed he is critical of the Judaism of post-Enlightenment discourse, which privileges Judaism over so-called primitive belief systems, a distinction that reinforces the break between savage and civilized peoples. To call this critique self-hating, as Wax does, is "to rule out the possibility of there being any legitimate reasons to criticize the picture of Judaism that dominates among its interpreters." Doing away with the distinctions between great and little traditions and acknowledging that it has outlived its usefulness will, in Schwartz's mind, allow the critical discourse of anthropology to have a say in this tradition.[13]

Unlike in the other case studies in this book, neither of Schwartz's books was the *single* lightning rod for a larger controversy between the academy and the community. However, both contributed to a larger question of "critique from within" that had been raised by a number of reviewers of Schwartz's work, particularly Rosenbaum of *God's Phallus* and Wax of *The Savage in Judaism*, where he writes of his fear of the scandal that such a portrait will create. This idea states what many minority communities fear, that the internal critique will somehow leak out and confirm the worst of the stereotypes that outsiders have of them. "It would not be good for the Jews" is a common way of putting it within the Jewish community.

COMMUNITIES' RESPONSES

Schwartz sees the perceived aggressiveness of *God's Phallus*, beginning with its title, as one of the major reasons he was denied tenure at Stanford. (Since this book is about the public discourse in the study of religion and restricts itself to publicly accessible documents—and tenure cases are confidential—this chapter will not focus on that issue.) But *God's Phallus* was not the only reason, nor perhaps indeed the primary one, for his leaving the academy. If there was to be a "scandal," as Rosenbaum described, it was not only in the assertions that Schwartz made in that book or in his earlier *The Savage in Judaism*. Events of a far more local nature precipitated his move away.

In 1994, Schwartz accepted an endowed position as associate professor of Jewish studies with tenure at San Francisco State University. The expectation of the position was that in addition to heading the program and teaching, he should also raise funds from the Jewish community in order to augment the temporary investment that the university had made in Jewish studies more broadly. The administration had approved the Jewish studies program's launch with the proviso that the budget eventually be covered by donors from the community. However, Schwartz was walking into a community fraught with interethnic tensions that made his stance of "critique from within" almost impossible for him to maintain within the public sphere of Jewish studies.[14]

Starting with his orientation to the Jewish community at the university, Schwartz began to feel uncomfortable, and those who hired him began to feel the same, when he answered a series of questions about Israel in unexpected ways. Participants were asked to move to a designated area of the room in answer to specific questions, such as "How central is Israel to Judaism?" and whether they agreed that the statement "Zionism is racism" used by critics of Israel was anti-Semitic. Schwartz moved to answer "not terribly important" to the first and "no" to the second because he saw the creation of the State of Israel within the broader context of European colonialism. Afterward, people from the Jewish community present at the orientation mentioned their disappointment at his responses.

In addition, Schwartz raised questions when he sponsored Hatem Bazian, a highly vocal Palestinian activist, to speak to his class. Schwartz remembers the class as smooth and restrained. But community members felt that Bazian was more responsible than other local activists for making Jewish students feel uncomfortable on campus; to give Bazian status and a platform was a problem. Schwartz responded to this critique by inviting other, more traditional speakers such as David Biale and Steven Zipperstein, directors of Jewish studies programs at the Graduate Theological Union and at Stanford, respectively.[15] Schwartz understood himself as mending fences, and that meant asking all sides of the conflict to speak in different venues and listening to them respectfully. His critics felt that his job was to teach, and to show the other side of the story concerning Judaism and Israel, on behalf of a beleaguered Jewish student population on campus that had suffered attacks by other student groups.

While these events created tensions, other developments helped to precipitate a crisis. Earlier in the year a local artist, Senay Dennis, painted a mural of Malcolm X on an outside wall of the student union building. The Pan-Afrikan Student Union that commissioned the mural was a group of African American students who had clear Marxist commitments and who also commissioned a mural of Cesar Chavez for the walls of the union. The Malcolm X mural was there to commemorate his birthday. On the mural were painted a number of symbols that seemed to communicate the oppression of African and African American peoples: a skull and crossbones, dollar signs, an American flag, and a Star of David. Nearby was the phrase "African blood."

A number of people in the community were outraged at the symbolism, including one African American professor who spattered red paint on the mural right after it appeared. The Jewish community on campus and beyond saw a series of anti-Semitic stereotypes: the dollar signs and the Star of David formed the simple stereotype of Jews as money-grubbing. The words "African blood" nearby also seemed clearly to communicate that Jews were responsible for American slavery (a commonly circulated rumor among anti-Semitic groups).

As Schwartz narrates the story, which is confirmed by newspaper reports from the time:

> The mural incited widespread campus protests and community pressure on the administration to have the mural removed from public space. . . . The artist and the student group that commissioned it denied that the mural was intended to be anti-Semitic, and claimed that the mural only depicted Malcolm X's anti-Israel views. They claimed it was intended to depict how tax dollars were going to Israel, while blacks were suffering in this country. After a week of protests covered in local and national news, with standoffs between local Jewish students and ethnic studies supporters of the mural, San Francisco State University President Corrigan called in a swat team and sandblasted the mural off the wall. The Afrikan Student union saw this as evidence of the Jewish conspiracy and the ability of Jews to wield power.[16]

Two campus leaders, Troy Buckner-Nkrumah of the Pan-Afrikan Student Union and Hatem Bazian of the Palestinian Students Organization, reiterated that the sentiments represented on the mural were against the State of Israel and its policies, not against Jews.

This distinction is an important one that has emerged in many debates about what constitutes anti-Semitism: anti-Israel sentiment or anti-Jewish sentiment? Or are they the same thing? The mural was supposed to show Malcolm X's anti-Israel views and remind passersby that US tax dollars were being funneled to Israel when so much was needed at home. But the two student leaders also continued to denounce Zionism and Israel in ways that seemed deeply anti-Semitic to the Jewish community. As Schwartz reports, "Troy Buckner-Nkrumah was fond of claiming that 'Zionism is Racism' and that the 'only good Zionist is a dead Zionist.'" Buckner-Nkrumah also spoke about "Jewish capitalist-conspiracy" and "Jewish control of the press." While the Jewish community was most concerned by these student groups, it believed the problem emanated from the campus's Ethnic Studies Department, the oldest ethnic studies program on an American campus.

In addition, during the year that Schwartz arrived, the Jewish Community Relations Council and Student Union Hillel had written a report, "Anti-Semitism at San Francisco State University." In that report, several incidents were alleged, such as Jewish students and Jewish groups on campus being discriminated against because they were Zionist. In this document, many students reported that they felt intimidated on their own campus. At major events involving Jewish students, such as Holocaust Day memorials, there were major protests from other student groups; Jewish speakers at political events were verbally challenged while they were speaking.

Schwartz then recounts the two competing public spheres in which he was operating. He realized that the Jewish community had different expectations of him than the academic community did. As a result of interactions with leaders of the Jewish community on and off campus, he felt they wanted him to be a spokesperson for Jews on campus, particularly about three issues: Israel, the Holocaust, and anti-Semitism. As he puts it:

When I was interviewed for the position originally, no one had asked me what I thought about these topics. And, while I had specific personal and quite passionate views about each of these issues, my academic work was focused on different topics altogether. The problem was that my own views on Israel, Anti-Semitism and the Holocaust were quite different and in some important ways antithetical to those of the organized Jewish community. Indeed, my path into academia had been partly to distance myself from the standard view that had arisen in the organized American Jewish community. I had come into contact with that view in seminary, during my year in

Israel, and in my first years of teaching. Being an academic had allowed me to speak my mind, and to toe a critical distance, from what I saw as the dominant and to my mind problematic formation of ethnic Jewish identity. Now I had taken what was purportedly an academic position, but one which would compel me to speak up about these subjects that had nothing to do with my academic work.[17]

In this manner, Schwartz expressed his personal discomfort with what he called the formation of Jewish identity in the twentieth century. In his view, Jewish identity coalesced around three things, especially after the Six-Day War: the State of Israel, the Holocaust, and anti-Semitism. His own reasons for leaving the rabbinate had to do with his dissatisfaction with these three elements as the major forces for Jewish identity. For him, spirituality and a recovery of meaning in everyday life and in the world around one was more important than an exclusive focus on peoplehood to the detriment of a broader vision. He felt that the focus on the Holocaust did not reach out enough to other peoples who had experienced genocide. He also believed that the American Jewish community defended the State of Israel to the detriment of critical reflection about its government's policies, particularly toward Palestinians and to others who were not Jewish. And, finally, he thought that charges of anti-Semitism were too quickly made.

Thus, as Schwartz recounts, in Jewish community events he attended in San Francisco, he found himself speaking more critically than other members of the community did. He was also willing to listen to campus activists, such as those mentioned above, before calling them anti-Semitic. During his year at San Francisco State, he invited these activists into his classroom in order to begin a civil dialogue. In addition, he attended activities by the Pan-Afrikan Student Union and the Palestinian Students Association, among others. He cosponsored activities and panels on controversial topics, making sure both the Jewish Studies and African American Studies Departments funded the discussions.

At the end of the year, members of the Jewish community, particularly the American Jewish Committee and the Jewish Community Relations Council, were gravely concerned about Schwartz's views and his activities. They asked to meet with him to discuss the matter. They felt that he was not "righting the balance" of the skewed view of Israel that they felt was represented by some of the activists on campus, and that he was not speaking out enough against anti-Semitic activities and stereotypes of Israel and Jews. This was similar to the Sikh community's concerns about Harjot Oberoi's representation of Sikhism, and both scholars occupied chairs donated by the community. In Schwartz's view, he felt that his academic responsibility was to air all sides of the debate and to help students make up their own minds.

> At that point I knew I couldn't keep doing what I was doing. I felt caught in an impossible dilemma. If I bowed to the Jewish community's pressure, I would be sacrificing my integrity and beliefs. If I didn't, then I would be unable to fulfill my obligation to the university to raise money for the program. Since I was now tenured, the university couldn't fire me, even if I didn't raise money for Jewish Studies. But I felt this would be unconscionable since the University had specifically hired me to help fund the Jewish Studies program.[18]

Schwartz was caught in a dilemma of expectations that has only grown more difficult since he left the academy: When are scholars obliged to give both sides of a debate, and when is giving both sides of a debate giving a platform to people whose views are morally reprehensible to the other side? When is academic discussion airing all views, and when is an invitation from a university giving legitimacy to something that according to some interest groups should be condemned? These were two irreconcilable demands of two competing public spheres. As Schwartz himself puts it: "I was struggling to deal with having been thrust from a strictly academic teaching position about religion into a highly contested symbolic role in the politics of race and ethnic identity."[19] On the one hand, this difference between "strictly academic" and "political" is a distinction that Howard Schwartz clearly wanted to keep. On the other hand, such a distinction, at least in the study of religion, is practically more and more difficult to maintain. Schwartz knew that because of his political views, he would be unable to maintain credibility in the Jewish community and raise funds from its members. Yet he also felt that such views had little to do with his academic work.

THE INTERNET AS AN ALTERNATIVE WORLD

Emblematic of this period of expectations about media, Howard Schwartz had the most remarkable relationship to the internet, in that he wasn't just momentarily but permanently consumed by it. He tracked his interlocutors down after the confrontation. As he left academia, he took advantage of being in Silicon Valley during the internet boom. Of that time he writes, "I had in fact witnessed the computer revolution first-hand. I was one of the first to buy one of the early Macintosh computers when I was in graduate school at Brown University in the early 1980s. As I taught in the early '90s at Stanford, the PC explosion had begun along with networking, email, and the internet. Cisco had just started its meteoric rise. And e-Bay was not yet a household word."[20]

In the midst of this career change, Schwartz speaks of his move as a transformation of identity, with the acquisition of skills, language, and "indigenous" vocabulary. This was a difficult process that involved connecting to the culture that was all around him at Stanford and in Silicon Valley but was not influential in his own life until he made a radical decision to let himself be transformed by it.

> Changing careers is a challenging and difficult process. You have to overcome fear and you have to learn new skills and a new language. It is very much like entering a new world and in some sense "going native." I was, of course, living in Silicon Valley and most of the jobs available around me were in "high tech."

This transformation involved erasure and selective engagement with his former identity as both a rabbi and a scholar:

> I learned that the software industry was looking for talent and were open to hiring someone who was a good writer and communicator. And so I repackaged myself. I eliminated all references to my seminary degree, since no one in the business world would be interested in a rabbi. From my resume, they would picture me with fringes and a black hat. I reduced my fifteen page academic "Curriculum Vitae" to a two-page business resume. After all, they wouldn't want an academic either, for the business world has a prejudice against academics. My ten years of teaching, three books and dozens of academic articles were reduced to a couple of bullets on the bottom of the resume. I took "Ph.D." off my name and changed my degree in "Religious Studies" to "Humanities." I knew nothing about the business world at the time and therefore sought to leverage my writing skills as I made my transition.[21]

In effect, Schwartz left behind everything but the faintest traces of his former lives as a religiously committed person and academic. In addition, he anticipated the stereotype that others might have of him in the world of the internet and changed his résumé so that this stereotype would not even occur in the minds of his potential employers. "Religious Studies" was changed to "Humanities." Books became bullet points. And rabbinical degrees disappeared. The "writer and communicator" for Silicon Valley emerged. He answered an ad for a technical writer for Genesys, the "computer telephone" software company. He remarked upon the irony of the name of the company and his former engagement with the biblical text of Genesis as a scholar and a rabbi.

As he tells it, Schwartz began as a technical writer, attacking the switching systems and the coding of UNIX with all the zeal and care of the scholar of sacred texts learning the grammar of a new language. He understood that his role was that of interpretation and knew that this primary skill was one he could use in any environment, had he the will to learn it. His success at Genesys then grew to a wish to work in marketing, which would further employ his skills as a visionary, a creative personality, and an interpreter. After several unsuccessful attempts at start-ups, Schwartz joined Uniscape, a translation company that made "stock" sentences that could be used in any number of different manuals in any number of different languages. The company was eventually acquired by Trados but survived the dot.com boom and bust of the late 1990s and early 2000s.

Schwartz, too, survived, and even thrived, in this new world. He adapted his temperament to become more conservative and less emotional, as the business world required. He leaned in to more strategic thinking as a marketer and appreciated the pragmatism and total focus on the bottom line that the business world offered him. And he successfully translated the skills he brought with him into the Silicon Valley world, and specifically a software company taking on the role of translation. Yet here, too, he also began to have his doubts:

> I had gone in search of soul and I had somehow ended up as an executive in the software industry. Was this the ironic joke or punishment of a God that I didn't believe in? Thoughts like these periodically came to mind as I pondered my fate. I was now living in the heart of Silicon Valley in the late 1990s as the computer and software revolution were in the process of fundamentally transforming our lives and our economy. I imagined I felt like Adam Smith when he witnessed the emergence of the first pin factories in England and understood that nothing would remain the same after the development of these early modern factories. For my part, I was witnessing the birth of

the digital economy from the inside and getting glimpses of the sweeping changes that were brewing and the new world that we were in the process of creating. I was no longer an academic critic in the ivory tower. I was an internal participant in an industry driving change in what some economists referred to as the new "information economy." I was consulting to HP and Nokia, companies whose names had become household brands and whose products were transforming our everyday lives. And I was heavily involved in trying to run our software business and trying to figure out how to make it a successful, profitable company.[22]

The transformation for Schwartz was not only a profoundly personal one but a profoundly cultural and economic one as well. The culture of the internet became as all-consuming as the cultures of Judaism and Jewish studies were.

Yet Schwartz could never fully leave religion. He writes:

While working in Silicon Valley, I have come to think of the question of soul and capital as one of the most pressing questions of our age. It certainly had become a pressing concern for me. As I moved from the back end of the organization into the business and executive ranks of the organization, I discovered there was still a "secular rabbi" alive and well within me. Though I was no longer committed to a specific religious tradition or community, I found myself still pondering the question of soul and wondering whether my soul could thrive in a business environment.

As a business executive thinking about soul, I once again felt like a fish out of water. I was not religious enough for the religious world. Yet, ironically, I felt too spiritual for the secular one. I was caught betwixt and between. Not feeling at home in the religious traditions of my ancestors, but wanting something more than secular capitalism could offer. I didn't want Moses and Bill Gates to be separate heroes in different traditions. I wanted to find one moral hero who combined both spirituality and business acumen, who could transcend the conflicting pulls of religion and money, profit and spirit. A hero who could transcend the very fractures of modernity.[23]

Schwartz's betwixt-and-between status is, for him, a function of the fractures of modernity; theoretically, Moses and Bill Gates should exist in the same world. Yet his experience suggests that they could not.

Schwartz also sees the dark similarities between his two worlds, certainly between the rabbinical world and the world of the internet sale:

> As I participated in the selling process, I experienced just how strong is this pull to overpromise our customers what software could and would do. At times, I joked that selling software and being a rabbi were not all that different. Both involved selling the Invisible. Rabbis called it God and software representatives called it new functionality. . . . But on a more serious level, I was disturbed by how someone like myself, who cared deeply about soul and values, could be induced to fudge the facts and mislead.[24]

Schwartz completes this assessment of his journey by invoking a clearly complex identity—one that could not be fully engaged in the culture wars of the 1990s.

> I am therefore an ex-rabbi "by choice." I no longer attend synagogue or contribute funds to the preservation of the State of Israel. I no longer keep the dietary restrictions. I do celebrate Hanukah and Passover, two holidays I still enjoy. But in my house today we have a Christmas tree because my non-Jewish wife celebrates Christmas. Am I still a Jew? The answer depends on how you define what a Jew is. If you think of it as a matter of race, and genetics, then clearly I still am genetically the same person. And whatever mix of Jewish and European genes constitute my lineage, I cannot change that nor would I want to do so (although I imagine one day science will even allow people to change their race and not only our sex!). Obviously I am still a Jew in the sense that my perceptions, reactions, inclinations were shaped by my experiences growing up in a Jewish household.[25] But my identity is so much more complex than that. I have deep commitments to the enlightenment traditions that shaped my intellect and ultimately gave me a place in American society.
>
> I am also a former professor. Well not quite. I am teaching again. But I no longer have the luxury of working full time in an academic environment. This was also a choice, based on the set of the limited available options that lay before me at the time. My intellectual work was too controversial for Stanford. I chose parenting instead of leaving the Bay area in search of another academic position. I have never looked back on that decision as painful as it was and as much as I missed academic research and teaching.[26]

Schwartz claims all his roles of rabbi, Jew, Silicon Valley professional, and professor/teacher, even if not in the same configuration that he tried to construct when he was occupying an endowed chair at San Francisco State. In his departure, he is able to engage all of his voices and be more complex than was possible when he was caught between the public and the university.

FINAL THOUGHTS

Howard Schwartz's case shows connections between cultural and religious identity in a distinctive way. The eruptive space was twofold: between ethnic traditions on campus and between Jewish communities who were supportive and those who were critical of Israel's policies. The pressure on the possibility of Habermasian translation between so-called equals was doubled, as was what Habermasian critic Max Pensky described as the challenges histories of injustice bring to the possibility of dialogue between secular and religious spheres. Given this double pressure, Schwartz—like Gill, Oberoi, and Kripal—initially refused some aspects of his academic engagements. Then he rejected the academy altogether.

Howard Schwartz understood himself as a Jew, and even more as a rabbi who represented many liberal aspects of the religion. But in his case, the questions of nationalism emerged front and center. Although Schwartz's books contributed to his profile as an outspoken and risk-taking scholar, none of his books about the Jewish religion stirred the public controversy. Rather, Schwartz's stance on Israel created the problem in the community. Indeed, the reviews of *God's Phallus* and *The Savage in Judaism* did engage the question of scandal and controversy and did, like the other minority traditions, raise questions of whether it was "good for the Jews" to be represented as "savage." However, the larger academic debate about Schwartz's work was primarily conducted in an uneventful manner.

Cultural recognition, particularly respect, came to the fore for Schwartz; the San Francisco State issue emerged specifically in debate with other ethnic groups, such as African American groups. The Ethnic Studies faculty in particular was critical of the role Jews played on campus as an ethnicity supportive of Israel's policies. Yet there was a further dynamic; in his Jewish critics' views, Howard Schwartz's public questioning of the role of Israel in contemporary politics did not suit his position as a chair funded by the Jewish community—a situation very similar to Oberoi's case. In addition, Schwartz shared with Jeffrey Kripal a controversy involving the fusion of nationalism, ethnicity, and religion and the emergent intellectual support for that fusion in the late twentieth century. Intriguingly, here, and distinct from the Hindu case, the Jewish objection was not to a very assertive revision of its own history. Rather it was the challenge to Israel's policies that created the unmendable break.

Finally, in terms of life-script, Howard Schwartz's change of identity was perhaps the most unusual in the case studies of this book. He chose no longer to be an authentic insider, and then no longer to be an insider. His departure from the academy was entirely voluntary. While Schwartz could have stayed in the academy under San Francisco State's conditions, as he put it, he no longer recognized his own Jewish community as one with which he could identify. His life-script no longer included that sense of belonging. In this sense Schwartz was more like Oberoi, whose journey involved an alienation from his own religious community of birth.

But Schwartz was also alienated from the academy itself. To be sure, the academic community's initial expectations of him were not intolerable, since he landed another academic job fairly quickly after Stanford. However, the combination of community and academic politics grew too costly for him to negotiate. Like Oberoi, Schwartz occupied a chair funded by the community with the life-script expectations of that community. Unlike Oberoi, who remained within the academy and found another place for himself within the same university, Schwartz seemed to feel that his own life-script was radically different from either the Jewish or the academic one in which he had excelled in the previous decades of his life.

What is more, Schwartz's case is more like Schaberg's Roman Catholic controversy, in that the American Jewish community had a longer history of official engagement with the North American academy. He engaged with a diaspora public that was highly organized and had a number of long-standing seminaries of its own. The Jewish community had become accepted in the academy in the last half of the twentieth century, and departments of Jewish studies were far more common than departments of Sikh or Hindu studies. Thus, the Jewish community donating the chair was an older community in its relationship to the academy than the other groups discussed in this book. And while there is indeed a history of anti-Semitism in its borders, America is, relatively speaking, still a haven for Jews. But the community's expectations of a Jewish studies chair were that this scholar would remain positively focused on Israeli identity. As in the Sikh case, the expected focus on singular group identity was, in many ways, a direct result of a tragedy within living memory—that of the Holocaust in Europe. But this focus on Israel was exactly what Schwartz could not maintain. Thus, his role in the academy was ambivalent, even though he was understood as "traditionally" successful.

In the end, the internecine strife of ethnic studies at San Francisco State involved several elements: the Jewish community members, the questions of Jewish-black relations, and the role of Israel in the world as part and parcel of Jewish identity as such. The academic community at San Francisco State supported Schwartz insofar as it did not force him to leave. However, the cultural context in which he might or might not have been able to thrive was intensely contentious.

While the question of the relationship between political views and sense of belonging might have been separated for Schwartz during the controversy at San Francisco State, the theme of one's Jewish identity and one's belonging to the community comes up as part of Schwartz's academic life from the beginning. As Jonathan Mahler puts it in his assessment of the case, it was not simply a matter of campus politics. Rather, it was "a lesson in the difficulty of reconciling two often contradictory impulses within the multicultural academy: the desire to reach out to other communities while also strengthening feelings of identity among one's own people." Schwartz raises the question of Lévi-Strauss's Jewish identity in *The Savage in Judaism*, and that question is also engaged by reviewer Ayala Gabriel. The question of ethnic self-hate also emerges in Murray Wax's review of *The Savage in Judaism* and required a response from Schwartz to clarify his views. Even Jonathan Boyarin wonders whether the representation of the savage might be detrimental to the Jewish community in that it inadvertently reinscribes a kind of Christian progressivism.

The potential damaging consequences of self-critique in the public sphere come up again in Schwartz's conversations with the Jewish community leaders of San Francisco. To be sure, these issues have come up before. But now, they arise because they are newly relevant; in the donors' view, self-critique should not be part of a job description, and in Schwartz's view, it is essential to it.

What is more, in Schwartz's case, the challenges of psychoanalytic and anthropological method are merged in some important ways. Of course, psychoanalytic method does not have the sting in the Jewish case that it clearly does in the postcolonial case of Kripal, where psychoanalysis is understood as sexualized, neocolonial imposition of Western theory. However, the psychoanalytic method clearly raises important questions about how one might think about Jewish identity. There were resonances of worry in the reviews about whether Jews would really be thought of as savage once the book came out, or in fact more primitive, even as

Schwartz tried to reinvest the term with refurbished and newly significant meaning. Moreover, the body of God goes directly to the question of
Jewish identity, particularly in the idea that the contribution of Judaism
to humankind was not the philosophical triumph of ethical monotheism
but the attempt to negotiate a psychological conflict by men about loving
a male god as a bride.

Jewish identity, then, worked in different ways for Schwartz and his
understanding of his academic role than it did for the members of the
community and the donators of the chair. The requirements of the two
spheres were so irreconcilable to Schwartz that he ended up rejecting
both, leaving both the rabbinate and the academy. Hence the debate:
most job descriptions in nonaffiliated university religion departments do
not require academics to choose whether they will be part of the religious
community they study and are willing to raise funds from that community. But an increasing number of positions funded by communities or
deeply connected to local communities do indeed come with that expectation. The meeting points between the two, and the necessary rules of
engagement in public discourse, may not overlap at all.

In Fraser's terms, Schwartz saw himself as an equal participant in both
public spheres of the community and the academy—a rabbi and a secular
scholar fully empowered with tenure and hoping to empower others. The
liberal paradox meant that the Jewish community that had empowered
him felt that he had gone too far in empowering others and had become
tolerant of intolerance. Eliadean ideas of liberalization through textual
engagement could not help this situation; nor could W. C. Smith's generic
notion of a common sphere. There were too many competing interests in
Jewish relationships to other minorities to create such a dialogue.

Schwartz's next move was to embrace the world of the internet, and
to do so as a distinct world that held real alternatives to the public sphere
of the academy. As he saw it, the internet did not just provide the possibility of a democratic forum, as it did for Grimes in the case of Native and
non-Native scholars. Nor did it provide a space for an alternative history,
governed by the theologies of resistant communities, such as in the Sikh
and Hindu cases. The world of Silicon Valley provided another world altogether—another public sphere—with its own indigenous vocabularies,
rules, and requirements.

In the end, by Schwartz's own account as a self-critical Jew, he was
understood as not privileged enough to speak by some, and overly privileged to speak by others. When the eruptive public space emerged in

controversial discussions about Judaism, Israel, and its relationship to other minorities, participation in that wilder space became increasingly difficult for him. As in the stories concerning Gill, Oberoi, and Kripal, a leave-taking was necessary. But for Schwartz, it was a farewell to the academy altogether. The liberal paradox had become too paradoxical.

10

KĀLĪ'S CHILD: THE CHALLENGE OF SECRET PUBLICS

At the height of protests about his 1995 work *Kālī's Child: The Mystical and the Erotic in the Life and Teachings of Ramakrishna*, Jeffrey Kripal cited a telling moment in his conversations with some Calcutta intellectuals. They told him, "You are right. But we cannot say that here. You, however, can and should say it over there."[1] It was an important moment, and one in which there was solidarity of scholarly aims. Such interpretations could be spoken of, but differently in different contexts. Perhaps in 1995, it seemed possible.

Ramakrishna is not an easy saint to write about. He was born in 1836 in the Hooghly district of West Bengal, and his village of Kamarkpukur was at a crossroads for pilgrims traveling to the well-known site of Puri, which is holy to the Hindu god Krishna. As a result of meeting many holy men and storytellers along this route, he learned the ancient Indian epics as well as the Bhagavata Purana, a canonical sacred text that describes the devotee's love for Krishna in terms of a lover and beloved. Ramakrishna was also given to mystical experiences and suffered the loss of his father at a young age.

In 1855, Ramakrishna became the chief priest at the recently consecrated Kali Temple in Dakshineswar, near Calcutta (now Kolkata), after the death of his older brother, who had brought him there to assist him. During this early time at the temple, he began to feel intense longing for the goddess—Mother Kali—to the detriment of his priestly duties, and experienced an all-encompassing ecstatic vision of her that was to inform the rest of this life. He also placed himself under the tutelage of a female tantric teacher, who helped him achieve tantric spiritual states; these involved the ritual embrace of impure substances and practices as a "union of opposites" between the pure and the impure. Under the guidance of a wandering ascetic monk, he achieved advanced states of *samadhi*, or absorption into the divine.

Ramakrishna's devotion and teachings were geared toward the universal, and he openly embraced other religious paths. As a result, he began to attract the attention of the leaders of the nineteenth-century reform movement the Brahmo Samaj, which was universalist in its teachings. As his reputation grew, Ramakrishna taught householders and lay visitors as well as his disciples, who were celibate members of this early order. Several disciples began to form around him at Dakshineswar, including Narendra, who was later to be known as Swami Vivekananda—the great reformer, founder of the Ramakrishna mission, and missionary to the West.

After contracting throat cancer in 1885, Ramakrishna was moved to a space outside Kolkata and nursed by his disciples until he died in 1886. Ramakrishna's teachings were not written down in a book but rather took the form of simple talks in Bengali, which were later compiled in Bengali by his disciple Mahendranath Gupta—also known as "M." The work was entitled *Sri Sri Ramakrishna Kathamrita* in Bengali. Its English rendering, *The Gospel of Sri Ramakrishna*, came out in 1942.

JEFFREY KRIPAL'S WORK

Kripal begins his account of Ramakrishna in *Kālī's Child* by arguing that we must put away the boxlike structure of Vedanta Indian philosophy in which most interpreters and scholars put Ramakrishna ("boring Vedanta," as Ramakrishna himself put it). Instead, Kripal focuses on the so-called secret talk given by Ramakrishna to his disciples and found scattered throughout the five-volume biography composed by Mahendranath Gupta. Kripal contends that Gupta's arrangement of the biography was an intentional structure, which, if read carefully, would reveal the secret talk as a set of "mystico-erotic" experiences that "Ramakrishna himself neither fully accepted nor fully understood."[2] The question of Ramakrishna's own awareness of his experiences takes us right into the privileged workshop of the Freudian analyst, which is where Kripal also leads us, but with a difference.

In his introductory methodological discussions, Kripal introduces a dialectical approach to the mystical, whereby psychological and sociological contexts are seen as integral to but not reductive of apophatic language that uses sexual imagery. Kripal prefers the term "erotic," which neither reduces religion to sexuality nor reduces sexuality to religion but is, rather, "a dimension of human experience that is simultaneously related both to the physical and emotional experience of sexuality and to the deepest ontological levels of religious experience."[3]

Kripal's ontological approach also leads him to suggest that we must use Hindu imagery itself as a means of accounting for Ramakrishna's experience: the goddess is all, and Ramakrishna's experience of *shakti*, or feminine power, makes up an important interpretive frame with which to view his mystical utterances. In fact, the entire Indological debate about whether Ramakrishna was a Vedantic philosophical teacher or a bhakta (devotional) leader misses the real center of his religious life: Tantra focused on Kali, the goddess who is both mother and lover. The best lens with which to view Ramakrishna's religious teachings is neither doctrine nor devotion but desire. Kripal's subsequent chapters outline in engaging detail the symbols with which this desire was worked out, using Gananath Obeyesekere's notion of the personal symbol as the creative interface between private fantasy and public culture. For Obeyesekere, the personal symbol exists as a third category between fantasy and culture—a profound individual motivation for those who experience and teach about it but also comprehensible to a wider social group.[4]

Kripal begins by examining Ramakrishna's initial mystico-erotic crisis in response to the deaths of father figures in his life, including the saint's own father and an elder brother. Kripal then shows the ways in which Ramakrishna organized his relationships with women through the figure of the goddess, such that the public Ramakrishna worshiped the goddess as a mother, and the private Ramakrishna worshiped the goddess as a lover. Kripal goes on to demonstrate the dialectic nature of Ramakrishna's Tantric world, whereby in the struggle between Vedanta and Tantra, Tantra wins out. He describes Ramakrishna's later relationships in the human world, particularly his all-male community where the mystic took on the role of Kali herself and used his feet as a symbolic means of awakening consciousness in his disciples. In the final section, Kripal examines Ramakrishna's profound ambivalence toward his own Tantric world and his use of the imagery of the goddess's tongue to express this ambivalence. All of these chapters lend force to Kripal's ultimate argument that in his deft use of religious symbolism, "Ramakrishna was able to transform his homoerotic desires into the driving, shaping force of his mystical life."[5]

Kripal's larger argument is also that Ramakrishna's followers suppressed the Tantric element of both his work and teaching and instead focused on the Vedantic elements. This view is based on a reading of the Kathamrita, the original text of Ramakrishna's conversation with M. He focuses on the "secret talk" passages that one reviewer, Brian Hatcher, calls the hermeneutic key that unlocks the mystery of the entire Kathamrita.[6] In addition, and following the idea of the secret, many of Kripal's arguments are based on the question of gestures and sexuality. For example, for Kripal, the feet of Ramakrishna were a constant trope. Ramakrishna habitually placed his foot in the lap of a male disciple or visitor, and the lap is understood by Kripal as a sexually defiled space, a homoerotic space. It was a problem for his main disciple, Narendra, for Ramakrishna himself, and for Saradananda, another major monastic disciple. The larger point of these kinds of arguments is that the Tantric Ramakrishna had depths to his unconscious of which he himself was not even aware—a Tantric level that was secret, sexual, mystical, and homoerotic.

SCHOLARLY RESPONSES

The academic reviews of *Kālī's Child* focused on a positive assessment of his engagement with mysticism and eroticism but also expressed concern about the Bengali translations that supported his case. Jeanne Openshaw worried that he "sexualized language in a way quite inappropriate to the material." She focuses on the "foot" discussion and argues that Bengali "body" (*ga* or *an + ga*) and "lap" (*kol*) are taken by Kripal to mean "genitals" when they may not mean such a thing at all. They may simply mean "lap."

A salient point Openshaw makes is that the paths of devotion and knowledge, rather than Vedanta and Tantra, may be the right dichotomy for thinking about Ramakrishna. Moreover, Openshaw relays an argument that presages the larger world's engagement with *Kālī's Child*: What is homoerotic and what is not, and how does one think about culture when one does so?

She writes:

> In the context of devotional Bengali Vaishnavism, where femininity represents the highest attainable condition, the cultivation of femininity by men in various ways is not necessarily abnormal. Nor can it necessarily be taken as a sign of what we would call "homosexuality," that is love between men.

Many other traits that Kripal sees as indications of "homoerotic" tendencies are not uncommon in heterosexual Bengali men. Unlike our own society, male celibacy in the sense of conservation of vital seminal essence is highly prized in rural Bengal. Male fear of women, the attempt to see all women as mothers rather than as sexual partners, and in its extreme form, a cultivated sense of revulsion for the female body—all these stem precisely from the attractive power of women, rather than from "homoerotic" tendencies.[7]

André Padoux argued that Kripal did not have a fair and nuanced reading that acknowledged that religious traditions always create a linkage between sex and asceticism.[8] My own review found homoeroticism as an element of mysticism a major contribution of the book.[9]

Malcolm McLean felt that Kripal's contribution lay in the less hagiographical and more critical study of Ramakrishna's life and experiences, particularly its use of textual analysis.[10] Hugh Urban agreed with the value of *Kālī's Child* in penetrating through the layers of "reverential distortion" and in recovering the text for English readers. Urban did have a concern about Kripal's less than rigorous use of psychoanalytic categories as well as his use of Tantra as a monolithic category when Tantra itself was frequently a contested category even in the nineteenth century.

In slightly later reviews, Glen Hayes, David Haberman, and Carl Olson also each concurred in the book's value of unmasking the Tantric secret.[11] Olson, in particular, felt that *Kālī's Child* should be noted for its usefulness in showing the ways in which later devotees, such as Vivekananda, covered up this Tantric element and excised it from their accounts of Ramakrishna's life. Olson later wrote that Ramakrishna might have been a failed Tantrika in his conscious life, but he was a successful one in his unconscious life.[12]

William Parsons reviewed *Kālī's Child* in a longer essay about the psychological study of mysticism—discussing the sexual model used by Sigmund Freud, the adaptive model of Erik Erikson, and the transformative model in Helmut Kohut and Jacques Lacan. Narasingha Sil's work on Ramakrishna, published a few years earlier than Kripal's, looked at Ramakrishna's mysticism as pathological. (Sil would go on to become one of Kripal's most strident critics.) Sudhir Kakar's *The Analyst and the Mystic* understood mysticism as therapeutic, and, as Parsons notes, Kakar "demands empathic resonance with socially constructed concepts like desire," and "shows how psychological and cultural factors relativize the complex issue of saintly eroticism."[13] Parsons argues that Kakar should have paid more attention to the texts, which he accepts without criticism.

In Parsons's view, *Kālī's Child* is sophisticated and destined to become a classic. It will do so because, as Olson also believes, it has uncovered the original text of the Kathamrita and therefore provides an accurate descriptive and historical account of Ramakrishna's mystical practices.

COMMUNITIES' RESPONSES

Narasingha Sil changed the debate about *Kālī's Child* from a scholarly one to the highly charged public sphere. It is ironic that Sil himself is not an apologist for Ramakrishna but is, in fact, the opposite; his psychoanalytic assessment falls squarely in the camp of mysticism as pathology. However, Sil's outrage about *Kālī's Child* was no less vehement for its suspicion of mystical turns. In the *Statesman*, Sil excoriated Kripal's assessment of Ramakrishna as a "gay Tantric mystic," attacking his mistranslation of numerous Bengali words and terms, done "with gay [*sic*] abandon to suit his purpose." Sil also charged, as others do, that the Tantric hermeneutic is part of a circular reasoning pattern whereby "Kripal would insist on Ramakrishna's world view and would unhesitatingly adduce spurious evidence with a highly concocted interpretation of his behavior."[14] While his attack had a personal overtone to it, Sil's main concern was ignorance of Bengali language and culture.[15]

The letters to the *Statesman* that followed were as outraged with the newspaper for allowing the review of the book and giving it publicity as they were with Kripal himself. Calls for the book to be banned were also part of the outrage, on the grounds that it was a perversion and a desecration of Ramakrishna's memory and tested the limits of Hindu tolerance. Two weeks later, the *Statesman* published a statement that suggested it had made an error in editorial judgment in allowing the book to be reviewed at all.

Swami Atmajnanananda's review of Kripal's book also focused on the Bengali text and Kripal's translations of the Kathamrita, arguing, "Time and again, [Kripal's] translations of terms presuppose the very attitudes he is trying to prove, including the 'foot' reading as well as the *mag chele* being translated as 'bitch and kids.'" Atmajnanananda's argument was that this phrase was more likely a simply colloquial term for "wife and kids."

A key part of Atmajnanananda's criticism is his attempt to focus on a different view of the Bengali public sphere. He argues that Swami Nikhilananda's omissions of the text were not due to the creation of a secret, nor to fear of revealing already hidden secrets, but rather to "his sensitivity to Western decorum." As Atmajnanananda writes, "Had this been the case, he certainly would have eliminated far more of Ramakrishna's remarks than he did."[16]

Perhaps the most important debate came between Gerald Larson and Jeffrey Kripal himself in the pages of the *Journal of the American Academy of Religion*. Larson argues first and foremost that most of the "secret" material, including Ramakrishna's syncretistic Gaudiya, Vaisnava, Sakta, and Tantrika predilection, is already well known and best understood in the context of nineteenth-century Bengal. Larson contends that Kripal reduces the mysticism of Ramakrishna to homoerotic experiences, whereby "homosexual desires explain the entire life of a saint including his mystical or spiritual experience."

The biggest question for Larson is the question of community. In his review, he states, "*Kālī's Child* would have been much more balanced and would have avoided reductionism had [Kripal] taken the trouble to engage in a frank intellectual exchange about his interpretation with the community about which and in which much of his material centers." In other words, Larson wants there to have been a public sphere, with rules of engagement, between the scholarly and religious communities. Larson argues that he is not giving the Ramakrishna mission the power of censorship; rather, "relations of symmetrical reciprocity" are the way to go if our studies are to be properly nuanced and persuasive.[17]

Kripal himself responded that the "secret" that is hidden is the responsibility of the historian of religion to uncover, and that the scholar of religion is subject to hermeneutical revenge when he or she tries to expose it. Kripal further argues that he himself wanted to avoid Freudian reductionism and has insisted throughout the book on a more complex model of both mysticism and eroticism, where neither is reduced to the other. The most passionate refutation by Kripal comes when he states

> I did in fact explore, both anecdotally and historically, the limits of the tradition's willingness (if not in the way Larson proposes). One Bengali friend would only whisper to me about the censored passages. . . . Another felt uncomfortable talking about the issue in a restaurant. . . . I also spoke to Indian intellectuals in Calcutta, whose responses could be summarized as follows: "You are right, but we cannot say that here. You, however, can and should say it over there."[18]

He argues for a willed cultural distance that allowed him insight, going on to say "there is nothing particularly new" about Ramakrishna's issues;

Ramakrishna has "always been a scandal." Kripal then draws a long list of the censorship possibilities, all of which are either contested or understood as quite local in nature and not involving the Ramakrishna order as a whole. Equally important, Kripal argues that he has engaged the Hindu tradition, including Swami Atmajnanananda, which allowed him to change some of his interpretations in the second edition.

Here is the key element for Kripal's experience, particularly in relationship to the public sphere:

> Had I engaged the culture earlier in an open fashion and learned what I know now (after the hate-mail and a movement to have the book banned in India), I indeed would not, could not, have written his book. . . . I simply would have been too afraid . . . [Censorship] was an all too real possibility. I simply was not willing to take that risk. . . . I have not abandoned or rejected dialogue with the tradition . . . [but] I chose to practice my dialogue with the official tradition only after I had published my work.[19]

The second edition of Kripal's work is an intriguing moment. Unlike others discussed in this book, in his new preface, Kripal wonders whether the devotional and Indian readers have rejected a scholar "for wanting to talk openly about the homosexual roots of Ramakrishna's mysticism, only to find themselves rejecting some of their own brothers and sisters, and ironically, their own saint." The angry reaction of Hindus involved a deep cultural rejection of homosexuality and rage at exposing the secret. Moreover, Kripal saw the rage as "unable to be engaged because there are few cultural, social, psychological, and religious support structures available in such contexts to render its ideas widely thinkable." Rather, for Kripal, the book is a shared humanity that is written in a warm, liberating revelation.[20]

Kripal's introduction to the second edition also involved an apology for the emotional pain caused to readers by his errors, and the admission that one text, the *Jivanavṛttāntra*, was not suppressed by the Ramakrishna order but in fact published by it. However, Kripal remains convinced that his approach to the text should stand, given that it situates itself within a long line of scholarly consensus. In addition, Kripal finds support from within the tradition, including one monk who reread his own tradition after reading *Kālī's Child*.

Later reviews of the book also took account of the public controversy in their works. Hugh Urban views *Kālī's Child* as highly original but worries about sensationalism, and because of this, he understands why some Hindu critics saw it as yet another example of neocolonialism and the West's exploitation of the exotic Orient.[21] Steven Walker criticizes Kripal's armchair psychology, saying that his examples don't convince the reader that there is unconscious homosexuality at work. Walker sees a pronounced genuine self-image, which is very different from unconscious homosexuality.[22]

William Radice contrasts Narasingha Sil's lurid review with Kripal's more "subtle and respectful" approach, and sees the reaction as inevitable once the focus became more on the erotic aspects of Ramakrishna's visions. But he acknowledges that there is a much broader corpus of the Kathamrita that deserves equal attention, and that the "erotic-Tantric lens is not the only one through which the Kathamrita can be read."[23]

John S. Hawley's review also notes the game-changing elements of Kripal's work. Like Radice, he sees the major strength of the book as "bathing psychoanalysis in the light of Tantra" and the homoerotic secret that becomes "a searching beacon." He observes that the work has a "bombshell" quality and has been difficult to assimilate in the Ramakrishna order. Hawley makes reference to the controversy when he remarks that students of South Asian descent do not want *Kālī's Child* on the syllabus without a balancing perspective.[24]

Brian Hatcher's framing of the debate is both a review and an assessment of the possibility of a conversation about *Kālī's Child*. Hatcher examines the issues around its critical reception in Calcutta. He notes that he underestimated the hostility and found that the only people willing to speak were scholars. In addition, Hatcher argues that his experience in Calcutta showed him what it meant to have academic freedom.

Hatcher's main argument is that Kali, and Tantra more broadly, seemed banished from the clean auditoriums of the Ramakrishna mission, and he attributes this absence to a century-old institution whose origins amid the vortex of colonial power, knowledge, and nascent nationalism more than account for its curious philosophy of dogmatic toleration and inflexible apologetic." Thus, to reveal Tantra and homoerotic tendencies is to open something that has been kept guarded for a century. Kripal's focus on the secret is a function of what happened when Kripal tried to discuss things that were not openly discussed within the order.[25]

Hatcher's overall assessment is that Kripal treats Ramakrishna and his followers in a historical and political vacuum and is unconcerned with questions of colonialism and representation. Hatcher also notes that

Bengali utterances of Ramakrishna are all available and not hidden—a point made by several other reviewers as well.

As part of his response to the controversy Kripal, like all the other authors in this book, included an autobiographical essay. In two subsequent articles, Kripal also discusses the question of the politics of scholarship in the study of Hindu Tantrism.[26] There, he places his own work in the larger context of his upbringing. From an extraordinarily happy childhood in Nebraska, he entered a Benedictine seminary to embark upon the monastic life. At seminary, after realizing his excessive fasting was causing problems, he entered psychoanalysis. Through a series of dreams, he realized that he had made an equation between food, mother, and sex: the deadly symbolic logic he had succumbed to was, "You desire the mother, the mother is food. You cannot have the mother and you cannot have food." He was able to gain weight again, and this Freudian insight saved his life.

Kripal's interest in the erotic nature of religious experiences grew out of his own mystico-erotic encounters. Many of Kripal's dreams involved resolving Oedipal themes, particularly around the mother. In addition, the Roman Catholic tradition of bridal mysticism fascinated him but seemed logically impossible for a heterosexual male. The Roman Catholic tradition could not give him adequate symbolic resources to nurture and to realize the union of the mystical and sexual. He wanted to know: Can one ever approach the divinity as a female? His encounter with Tantra in the seminar library provided the answer, as did his subsequent work with Wendy Doniger at the University of Chicago. As he writes, "My methods were not simply linguistic or theoretical; they were experiential."[27]

Kripal elaborates that he underwent

> a series of highly symbolic ecstatic experiences that were unmistakably sexual and mystical and whose meanings seemed to point in powerful if still hidden ways to the ontological identity of human sexuality and the psychological realities experienced in ecstasy, vision, and mystical union. This is what I would later call "the erotic." But with the series of mystical experiences in Calcutta and my simultaneous discovery of Ramakrishna's own "secrets" in the texts, the union of the mystical and the erotic also became the central thesis of my research on Ramakrishna. The lives of the researcher and the researched had begun to mingle in strange, confusing, and wonderful ways.[28]

This intermingling and lack of intermingling mentioned in the quote above is part and parcel of the dynamic of the Kripal case more broadly.

"WE CAN'T SAY IT HERE, BUT YOU CAN SAY IT THERE"

How might we think about this integration that Kripal describes and the lack of integration that the public controversy engendered? Let us begin with the problem of fieldwork and study of texts. We began this chapter by noting that Kripal writes of his interactions with Indian intellectuals in Calcutta, whose comments on Ramakrishna's religious life he sums up in the following way: "You are right. But we cannot say that here. You, however, can and should say it over there."[29]

We now know that saying something in one place is no longer completely disconnected from saying something in another place. We know it about Kripal's book, and we know it about others as well. I believe there are several reasons for this. The first is that the inherently episodic nature of fieldwork, where a scholar stays for a while and then goes back to "produce" knowledge that is not intended for the people about whom he or she conducted research, is no longer viable. It is no longer viable because colleagues and informants in the field do read the latest research, or a translated version of it, even when the scholar does not intend the research for that audience. Now they are part of a reading public, too, even if they read fragments of fragments distorted by hostile readers on the internet. Previously, a scholar might be a graciously acknowledged guest in a fieldwork situation and perhaps welcomed as an authority. But once he or she leaves the fieldwork site, the scholar is accountable to entirely different rules of manuscript production and review, which come not from the field but from the academy. James Clifford, Lila Abu-Lughod, Katie Cannon, and many others made us aware of this fact in the 1990s;[30] other ethnographers have responded to this dilemma by "self-situating" and narrating their positionality. This is all well and good. (Although I myself have often wondered how many people "from the field" actually want to read even more pages about scholarly positionality and how much such a move actually solves the problem.)

At stake here are two competing interpretive publics: the Indian and the Euro-American (although mostly American) scholarly tradition and the interpretive tradition of the Ramakrishna order. With the publication of *Kālī's Child*, as Pravrajika Vrajaprana and Swami Tyagananda write in their thorough study of the controversy, "two independent self-sustaining communities of Ramakrishna devotees and academics—generally complacent and isolated in their respective and non-intersecting worlds—experienced a head-on collision."[31] And the situation is probably even more complex than this quite compassionate description; several South Asia scholars weighed in on the debate as to what the appropriate relationship was with the Ramakrishna order. In addition, many Ramakrishna devotees remained unaware of the controversy, as the indignation mostly affected the English-speaking Ramakrishna community.

As this chapter has demonstrated, much of the outrage focused on the question of homosexual reductionism and the question of the relationship between Tantra and psychoanalysis, as well as between the erotic and the mystic. The focus of this book is on the implicit models of the public sphere at stake in any controversy as well as the eruptive public space that emerge with its publication.

First and foremost is the idea of the secret that cannot be made public at all. Perhaps the first "public" in this case is the psychoanalytic dyad that Kripal experienced in the seminary and gradually expanded to the public sphere of graduate school, the "there" where such categories are shared and defined in a particular way. In Kolkata, for Kripal, the further mystical experiences of his own were parallel to what he experienced as a "hushed" tone toward the things he was uncovering. There was a bifurcation in the sense of "public"—even as his own dreams and experiences were coming closer and closer to his reading and interpretations of Ramakrishna's texts. The double public was further complicated by the fact that the secret was hidden not by the Bengali text but rather by the bowdlerized English text that had made sanitized hagiography out of such a colorful mystic's biography.

The publication of *Kālī's Child* itself created two reading publics. The earlier objections, including efforts to ban the book, amounted to pleas that the book cease to exist at all in the public sphere. Objectors specified that it must not exist in the Indian public sphere or in the United States. Their objection was double—both through the Rajya Sabha, the Council of States, or upper house, of the Parliament of India, and through the publisher in the United States, who was asked to withdraw the book.

Given this thoroughgoing plea, one wonders: Would it ever be possible to share such a public space? The question of sharing at all is understood one way by the scholarly community and another way by the Ramakrishna interpretive community. Kripal insists in the second edition of the work that there are very few structures to support such ideas of Ramakrishna's homoerotic visions as "widely thinkable." In other words, "widely thinkable" means a public sphere where a number of people can hold a debate about shared notions, and given the deeply divided response to *Kālī's Child*, for Kripal, this sphere was impossible.

But Tyagananda and Vrajaprana think that this is a false understanding of the Indian public. As they write, this shared humanity is still a cultural imposition,

> taking on all the characteristics of a Western humanism that speak to Western secular values—values which are not shared by the rest of the world. Again we find a universalizing Western paradigm, with a Western scholar promoting a worldview which is presumed to be universal. If the "devotional and Indian" readers do not see what he sees, then their social, cultural, psychological, and religious support structures are at fault.[32]

In other words, for Tyagananda and Vrajaprana, neither of Kripal's imagined public spheres—both the faulty Indian one and the idealized Western one—is accurate. Kripal refers in the preface of the second edition to a Ramakrishna disciple who "had learned to reread his own tradition" in the "new light" of the theses and methods of *Kālī's Child*.[33] This statement could be read as Kripal's description of the beginning of a shared public sphere, where agreed-upon rules (theses and methods) might apply. But for Tyagananda and Vrajaprana, this statement was "all too familiar"— presumably, an all too familiar imposition of Western theses and methods on Indian ones. Once again, Fraser's perspective is relevant: what might be the beginning of a public to one set of eyes is an imposition of a dominant set of rules to another set of eyes.

Just as Western scholars have imagined Indian publics in a monolithic way, so too the scholarly community has been "imagined" by some Indian critics. For some, it is a public that is self-reinforcing and beset by cronyism. While the Freud-inflected secular study of religion from which Kripal emerged is characterized in this way by many critics, it is far from monolithic in nature. As each of these case studies also shows, the scholarly public, too, is filled with debates about Freud; indeed, schools of thought constitute themselves by virtue of their disagreements and great divergences of opinion within the school.

As well, the tradition itself is understood as a particular kind of interpretive public—to be either vilified or defended in particular ways. Several of the reviewers (Radice and Urban, just to name two) praised the book for rescuing it from an overly hagiographic tradition that renders the public sphere of the Ramakrishna order antiseptic and repressive.

Brian Hatcher even described the public spaces of the order in just this way when he visited them, contrasting their clean spaces and alters with the colorful, dirty, and chaotic spaces of the Kali temple in Kolkata.[34] Tyagananda and Vrajaprana argue that these public spaces are necessary and functional, not antiseptic, and further, there is a protocol for placing Kali on the altar (i.e., making her part of the public sphere), which requires the utmost care and devotion.[35]

They see a similar trend in their discussion of John S. Hawley's article. Hawley suggests that some followers of Ramakrishna were "struggling" to assimilate Kripal's analysis. Moreover, he argues that the book "bathes psychoanalysis in the light of Tantra" and that Kripal is able to turn Ramakrishna's homoerotic secret "into a searching beacon."[36] Tyagananda and Vrajaprana read this choice of language as implicitly arguing that the tradition's own interpretative model falls short, its light being comparatively dim. The interpretive tradition, the public sphere *within* the Ramakrishna tradition, is thereby understood by Western scholars to be impoverished.

They further argue, turning that understanding on its head, that the Ramakrishna interpretive tradition is anything but impoverished. The Bengali text was known and available to everyone. Everyone could read it, and its translation was possible. The Ramakrishna order as a whole is a robust and free public sphere, open to Westerners and yet still respectful of the power of Kali. Moreover, given this robustness, any individual Ramakrishna community should stand for the whole in Western eyes.[37]

"KĀLĪ'S CHILD:" RESISTANT RELIGIONS ON THE WEB II

In the case of *Kālī's Child*, writing on the web provides the same function as the resistance to Harjot Oberoi but has an even more marked feature of long-term institutional critique. At the time of the original Kripal controversy in the mid- to late 1990s, the internet played a role similar to the one it had in the Oberoi case; immediately after the book's publication, there were online versions of editorials and emails whose hostility seemed more difficult for the author to accept because of their immediacy and felt proximity. The e-forums in which the controversy was played out were not necessarily organized solely for the protest of *Kālī's Child* but were more sporadic in nature.

Internet critiques of *Kālī's Child* gained a second life, however, with the birth of the website Sulekha, which, like the Sikh Studies site, was devoted to the propagation and correct interpretation of Hindu ideas and principles. It was funded and populated in no small measure by diaspora Hindu communities. Originally a business and trading venture that connected Indians worldwide with classified advertisements and information about events and services including job training, immigration and green card assistance, tutoring, and many others, it also became the organ for the Hindu communities to share ideas and engagements, including concerns about misinterpretations of their beliefs.

In 2002 the article "Wendy's Child Syndrome" appeared on Sulekha, protesting a series of American scholars who, in the eyes of some Hindus, took psychoanalytic, hypersexualized, and therefore offensive approaches to Hindu thought and practice.[38] Kripal's book was thus subject to renewed critique. Only this time, Kripal was understood and portrayed as part of a larger problem with entrenched interests in and prejudices against Hinduism in the university system of the United States. From this perspective, the system regularly disregarded the work of Hindu scholars, regularly supported distorted views of Hindu communities, distorted the meanings of words in Indian vernacular languages (such as Bengali), and represented the history of Hinduism as one of caste, sex, and mindless ritualism.

As a result of the piece and the discussion around it, Kripal and his work were seen as part of a larger neocolonial academic system that should be dismantled by new generations of Hindu American university students. Those students should be Hindus themselves, and they should take back their own traditions, including reasserting the value of Hindu monotheism, the depth and subtlety of their sacred texts, and the negative influence of the West on Indian—and now global—culture. While much of the critique involved attacks on the language skills (poor or careless) and intentions (mischievous or devious) of each Western scholar involved, the larger question of the academic system was at stake in this internet critique, dubbed "anti-Hinduism studies."

Kripal responded to this renewed attack with a further essay on Sulekha, restating the validity of his interpretation of certain Bengali words, resisting the charge that he called Ramakrishna a pedophile, and arguing that Christianity was subject to the same critique as any other tradition. Here, the critique focused on the inadequately acknowledged power dynamics between the study of Christianity and the stuy of Hinduism. In the critics' eyes, it is more dangerous for Hinduism to be studied because so little is known about it and what is known is distorted. Christianity, in contrast, has divinity schools and seminars with accredited degree programs, centuries of uninterrupted self-rule by insider scholars, a biblical text unquestionably at the root of Western culture, and massive wealth and power. Scholars who are critical of Christianity do not essentially redefine it, whereas scholars who are critical of Hinduism or distort it, because of the power asymmetry, *do* redefine it. In the representation of a lesser-known tradition, a single book can stand for the whole and can have a disproportionate effect both on the undergraduate population and on the public at large.

Put into a nutshell, the church has wealth, entrenched interests, and a millennia-old hierarchy to help it survive and even combat the misrepresentation of its religion. As a global religion, Hinduism, meanwhile, has Sulekha—and thus the internet became the best vehicle for protesting. Swami Tyagananda first posted his response to Kripal on the internet and then circulated it in hard copy. This response created a larger impact by landing on the internet than it would have had by circulating first in print. In Kripal's case, then, the online community thus came to represent both religion *on* the internet and a form of resistance *through* the internet. It reinforced social bonds, as Sulekha is meant to do—not only through trade, advertisements, and so on but also through common critique and complaint.

In addition, as in Oberoi's case, this second wave of critique of Kripal's book conducted largely on and through the internet evolved into an institutional critique, not only a series of attacks on individual scholars. The internet facilitated a community-to-community argument, and the responses on the internet could, in effect, stand in for the Hindu community who claimed to be offended by Kripal's writing. The particularly contentious personalized tone of the debate became a major place where their strength of identity could be felt. As a Hindu member of the American diaspora told me, "There is no other place where they can flex their muscles. They are paper tigers."

FINAL THOUGHTS

Paper tigers or not, the Kripal case erupted onto the global stage in a collision of three public spheres with three very different sets of rules: (1) the world of scholars, with its acceptance of Freudian methods; (2) the world of gay and lesbian activists, both in India and in the United States;

and (3) the world of the Hindu nationalists, newly aware of what Western scholars were writing in a way that they had not been in previous decades. From the Habermasian perspective, Hindu religious reasons could not be translated into the gay and lesbian community; nor did the protesting Hindus understand themselves as equal partners with what was to them a hegemonic Western academy.

In terms of cultural recognition, the actors in the case of *Kālī's Child* also frequently understood cultural and ethnic identity as mixed. In the debates that followed the publication of *Kālī's Child*, protesters frequently used the terms "South Asian" and "Hindu" as if they were synonymous. Those who objected to the representations of homoeroticism frequently did so on behalf of Indian culture as well as Hindu culture. This fusion would not be surprising, given how much of the debate about India has to do with whether it is predominantly a secular nation or a Hindu nation. Hinduism, too, has claimed to be not a religion as such but a way of life, and a way of life that would not openly embrace homoeroticism (even correctly understood) in its saints.

Like Kassam, Kripal was dealing with a legacy of secrecy, yet he occupied the role differently. Kassam was viewed as the insider who should not have dared depict the Ginans in the manner she did. In contrast, Kripal played the role of the outsider who could not now, or perhaps ever, understand the secret in the first place—whether that secret was the Bengali language or the true meaning of Ramakrishna's words. Kripal's ethnicity as well as his religion proved factors in his outsider status.

Moreover, the aura of secrecy that surrounds Ramakrishna did not develop in order for the religion to survive in a repressive political region, as it did in the Ismaili case. Exposing the details of that secrecy was offensive for very different reasons, having to do with disrupting the nature of communication between a Hindu mystic and his disciples. Finally, Hinduism is not a minority tradition everywhere, as Sikhs or Ismailis are, but a majority tradition in one place—its homeland of India. Hinduism's secrets are differently understood in the politics of India than they are in the United States. This was part of the dynamic of "extraverted integration" of which Laurent Gayer writes (discussed in chapter 2), where self-perceptions and self-censorship of a minority religious community in one country look different in the place where that community is a majority.

In some ways, Jeffrey Kripal's case resembles Sam Gill's more than Harjot Oberoi's or Tazim Kassam's. Kripal's individuality emerges as part of his privilege as a Western scholar, and since he was never a part of the

Hindu community that he studied, the rejection from the indigenous intellectual community was far more binary in nature, fraught with charges of colonialism and neocolonialism. Despite Kripal's access to privileged discourse, he could not ever occupy the emissary, mirror, or authentic insider positions of which Uma Narayan writes. Kripal himself has argued strongly for intellectual autonomy in the face of protests or attempts to have his book banned. Yet intriguingly, there was a new community who did embrace him—the LGBT community in India as well as in the United States.

Beyond being an element of his own life-script, Kripal's *Kālī's Child* was itself about a life-script in Appiah's sense—the narrative of Ramakrishna's relationships to his own family and disciples. Kripal's engagement with an alternative narrative of a particular person appeared to be a stand-in for what was tolerable or intolerable about the life-script of Hinduism itself. Kripal has continued to write books, but none in the study of Hinduism. Rather, his works have focused on the life histories of scholars of religion, as well as a history of the American community of Esalen. Forms of solidarity are a good that identity creates, as Appiah reminds us.[39] But the ones that Kripal was attempting to build were as an outsider trying to connect to scholars—as well as insiders. Thus, these forms were different than they were for Kassam, Oberoi, or Schwartz, and more like Gill. Also, as in Gill's case, the breaking of solidarity involved not only costs for the scholar himself but a different (though not less difficult) kind of cost for community members.

Kripal shares with Gill an outsider status in a postcolonial study of religion. In both places where he held positions, the conditions of his employment never changed; nor was his position ever threatened. In addition, as with Oberoi and Kassam, there was a robust intellectual tradition behind the interpretation of Ramakrishna, a tradition whose mores and historical understandings Kripal had violated. Thus, Kripal's critics included members of the Ramakrishna community in India and Vedanta centers in the United States.

In addition—catalyzed by Sulekha, a website that styled itself as the intellectual center of Hindu diaspora voices—connections between Hindu activism in India and the United States were strengthened by a common critique of Kripal. Like the academic study of Sikhism, the academic study of Hinduism in the Western academy was still relatively new. Kripal's work was a catalyst for calls to train in indigenous, seminary-like institutions of Hindu learning in the United States and Europe. Those would be the places where religious arguments could be translated in a slower, less confrontational fashion than the eruptive public space of a controversial encounter. Although the landscape is changing, in the 1990s, these kinds of institutions were distinctly absent in the Hindu, Sikh, and Ismaili cases.

The case of *Kālī's Child* demonstrates how the larger issue of belonging remains; unless the scholar lives in the community that he or she studies, and is subject to its rules in some way or other, it is difficult indeed for the community and the scholar to convert a public space into a public sphere, where some common rules might be built. Thus, when disagreement about interpretation arises, and the scholar is far away or no longer present, it is even more difficult to prevent estrangement and anger from setting in, and controversy from erupting. The new public space is very much with us, where readers and authors collide and intersect, across cultures and continents, across religious and secular norms of interpretation.

Jeffrey Kripal's colleagues were thus partly wrong when they said to him, "We can't say it here, but you can and should say it there." They were wrong if they meant that a scholar could write with minimal public response because no one "there" would be watching or reading or engaging. They were describing another era, without the internet, and without more widespread Indian readership of and vigilance about works from the Western academy, and without the public anxiety about hurt sentiments of groups. It is no longer possible for any of us—American, European, or Indian—to "say it there," at least not without consequence. This idea of harmonious but ultimately separate spheres of discourse about a saint's religious identity was part of the liberal and liberalizing view of an earlier era—that of Eliade's cultural progress through textual study, or W. C. Smith's common ground empty of any notable conflict.

The Kripal case reveals that, even in the case of a "secret," we cannot say one thing in a scholarly venue and another in a fieldwork venue. The liberal paradox will not allow it. Neither venue is "privileged." The "wink" mentioned in chapter 1 of this book, where scholarly spheres can remain protected, is now seen by a multitude. Indeed, some scholars' "asides," written as an "in-joke" from one scholar to another, have been the very thing to enrage some readers, who are neither familiar with nor persuaded by such scholarly norms. And then the larger issue must be the consequences of the wink and the rules with which one deals with them. In Kripal's case, there were no rules for dealing with those consequences because there was no sense of a common space, much less a shared secret about which colleagues could whisper freely.

PART THREE
NEW PUBLICS, NEW POSSIBILITIES

11

SCHOLARS, FOOLISH WISDOM, AND DWELLING IN THE SPACE BETWEEN

In the case studies I have presented here, a variety of scandalous controversies have led to eruptive public spaces. In the case of *Mother Earth*, there was the near impossibility of two spheres coming together. The case of *The Construction of Religious Boundaries* showed us interlocutors who had created an alternative opaque history that resisted new historical methods. The case involving *Songs of Wisdom and Circles of Dance* demonstrated competing authorities in an emergent, globalizing tradition. In the case of *The Illegitimacy of Jesus*, two strong traditions of public reason exploded over the question of the sexuality of Mary. During the case of Howard Schwartz, African American critiques of Israel combined with Jewish commitment to Israel and created an eruption—one that resulted in an abandoning of the public sphere altogether. In the case of *Kālī's Child*, secrecy, postcolonial identities, and sexualities exploded to create a global drama.

All of these cases marked failures of the Habermasian project of translation from religious reasons to secular ones. They were, in some ways, demands for the more inclusive public sphere Nancy Fraser has described, as well as examples of "the global proliferation of situated practices" about which Habermas's critics on the topic of religion have written so eloquently. They embody a certain form of pos-secularity, insofar as such a condition comprises "a critical standard for living with the permanent fact of increasing diversity of forms of life at all levels of international society."[1]

A PARTING METAPHOR: FOOLISH WISDOM

In light of these chapters, one wonders what to do after reading them. Tom Tweed argues that the interpreter of religion never stays in one place and understands him or herself as constantly crossing and dwelling in different spheres. This mobility of the scholar of religion means that he or she is also a moving target in the public sphere, one that constantly shifts between multiple publics.

As I suggested in chapter 1, in light of this mobility evident in the cases and my analysis of them, one suggestive metaphor for the scholar of religion's role in public space is that of the fool.[2] Such an image might be an acknowledgment of the constantly shifting ground and the constant ambiguity that new readerships represent in the world of the scholar of religion. The fool is a recognizable figure to religious traditions and to the academy. Christianity possesses the Holy Fool; Judaism and Islam share the fool Juha; Hinduism has the *vidushaka* of classical Sanskrit drama; and the university world has the medieval scholar/jester. Like scholars of religion, all of these fools engage in debate and wordplay in the interpretation of sacred scripture and undermine the authority of the clerical class. In *Twelfth Night*, Shakespeare's Feste, too, thumbs his nose at scripture even as he is quoting it.

Fools openly exhibit traits of irony: Lear's fool frequently disguises his thoughts in ironic quotations of old songs, and it is not clear whose quotations they are. Fools openly name and enact religious vices; indeed, the precursor of the fool in England was named Vice and had various other names descended from the Seven Deadly Sins. Like Touchstone in *As You Like It*, the fool exercises his wit through ironic parody, what Robert Goldsmith calls "the sworn enemy of the didactic."[3] So too scholars of religion regularly contravene the didactic norms of the orthodoxies of the religious traditions they study. There was also a double function of the fool—both to entertain his master and to minister to the master's sense of self-importance, a role that at the same time allowed the fool relative license to criticize.

So too the scholar of religion serves many masters simultaneously and wears masks of advocacy and criticism depending on the context. As the *vidushaka* states in Bhasa's *Avimaraka*:

He is comic at parties,
and yet ferocious in war;

He is a guru when there is sorrow,
and yet rowdy at other times;
He makes for a festival within my heart. . . .
Ah but why all this babbling?
He is my flesh indeed
split, it seems, in two![4]

The trope of the fool in classical drama and royal court underscores the performative function of the scholar of religion in culture. So many of these controversies and scandals are literally "enacted" on the internet and at conferences and, as I suggest in chapter 3, follow similar performative patterns.

Moreover, the fool—and not the trickster, not the jester—is an apt metaphor for another reason: while "the comic" certainly plays a part in these controversies, the work of scholarship nonetheless partakes of classical patterns of patronage and classical patterns of dialogue similar to the more classical patterns of court dramas in different religious traditions. Their controversial histories are frequently the unmasking of an ideal, which proves more fragile and delicate than meets the eye.

Like the anti-brahminical *vidushaka* and Lear's fool, who constantly reminds Lear of his past and the injustices the mad king has committed against Cordelia, the historian's reminder of things forgotten is hardly ever welcome in the religious sphere. The function of the fool and the historian of religion is not simply to correct the narrative with facts, however; rather, in public debate, such a figure threatens *to replace one narrative entirely with another.* Despite both scholars and critics pointing to the subtleties and complexities of the issues, notice the totalizing language in the course of public debate: the Native American narrative of Mother Earth is reduced to an intentional manipulation of a symbol; human motivations replace divine ones in the construction of the Sikh canon; homosexuality becomes the defining characteristic of Ramakrishna. Here, the fool's and the scholar's jesting is harmful; Lear's fool pushes Lear into madness with his constant questioning and joking, his hammering with the alternative narrative that causes the erstwhile ruler to realize the depth of his folly.

Thus, the scholar's foolish role is not simply to engage in competing ideas about historiography and the uses of evidence but rather to become involved with the performance of history as a rhetorical exchange.[5] Moreover, with the scholar/fool's performance of the historical reminder, the stability of the religious group and coherence of its religious claim are often threatened. To put it simply, while many religious communities thought the fool was there to be their advocate and support, they have discovered that with the fool present, they can no longer tell their stories in the same way. So too the fool discovers that the telling of his or her history is very different when the communities become active readers.

Like the various stances of the fool (at times elite, at times suppressed and censored), the different positions of the scholar expose the power dynamics perceived in any given interaction between the academy and the public. Because the fool has many masters, and is alternatively resistant to or loyal to the court, the fool can become a litmus test for the perception of power imbalances in these controversial encounters. Moreover, the degree of offense taken by the communities can also be a litmus test for the vulnerability such postcolonial communities still feel.

The extreme cases discussed in this book were only the first of several cases that have opened up new fissures in the cultural roles of scholars; it is now scholars' jobs to reimagine how they might wend their way through them. To elaborate a little more: scholars might maintain the best perspectives in the study of religion by acknowledging the multiple patrons they serve, the inherent contradictoriness of their position, and their mobility between those spheres.

Acknowledging movement between multiple spheres could help make the inevitable liberal paradox of the totalitarian view of tolerance a more creative paradox. As observed earlier, the totalitarian view of tolerance produces its own conundrum: the idea that one must be tolerant is de facto an intolerant statement. Unless tolerance functions until it is threatened in deed, its sphere is purely verbal. As Wendy Steiner writes, "Tolerance applies when people do not care enough about a point of view to fight over it; once they do, the game is up."[6] Scholars' writings about religious traditions frequently come from this absolutism of tolerance, in which they can say what they want to say and insist that others from those traditions acknowledge the validity of what they say, even while they preserve the right to dismiss the claims of those same adherents to the tradition in question. I am not arguing here that scholars do not have a right to dismiss those claims. They do. I am arguing that they should be prepared to do so grounded in a thoughtful understanding of what their own theories of participation in the public sphere, or even an eruptive public space, ought to look like.

This older model presumes a lack of engagement between scholar and community. And if the scandalous controversies of the 1980s and '90s have shown us anything, it is that such complete disengagement is no longer possible. The internet and the diaspora communities in the West have rendered such a disengaged situation null and void. Like it or not, scholars now work at close proximity with "others," who watch and monitor. At the same time, this situation may not necessarily result in an exclusively sympathetic engagement as a form of response. For such a solution renders scholars ultimately susceptible to the extremism against which the field of religious studies can and must argue. In contrast to the consistently sympathetic insider scholar, the wise fool is always wondering whether he must die with his master and yet usually survives, all the wiser, to tell the tale. Fools, however, tend to perform the function of loyal opposition to their various masters. So too might scholars fulfill just such a role, loyally opposing both the academy that remains suspicious of their work and the religious communities they represent in their writings. This might look like a kind of parliamentary party system, where the power struggle is acknowledged and the necessity of debate and controversy is real.

In light of these ideas, might religious studies move into a different kind of imagining about religion? As wise fools, scholars would also be honest about the nature and extent of their own intolerance of intolerance: they could honestly critique intolerance and yet, if they chose to (and they may not), also find ways to remain connected to communities in some long-term, correctable way. Scholars' perspectives on these issues would vary widely, but the issues themselves would be present and a powerful part of everyday scholarly discourse.

In his book *We Scholars*, David Damrosch argues for a new dynamism between the scholar and society, in which the relevance of knowledge production is assumed by multiple publics and advocated for in a comprehensible way by the scholar.[7] Such a new scholarly imagination might look something like the partnerships of fools and protagonists—one where the relationship would occasionally be ruptured and stymied by bickering, occasionally exuberant in a moment of collusion and collaboration. But the conversation would retain the structure of a play, in which opposition and argument was a form of enacting a fractious relationship that lasts over time. As Shakespeare's Feste puts it, we must be "wise enough to play the fool, and to do that well craves a kind of wit" (*Twelfth Night* 3.1.66).

This will also require a different kind of understanding on the part of communities. First, most communities might move beyond demands for censorship of scholarship and acknowledge that academic institutions will continue to produce interpretations that exist on a larger spectrum of acceptability and nonacceptability to members of those communities. Scholars will also continue to self-correct, in the forms of reviews and peer review and of generational change in a field's paradigms.

Moreover, communities will need to be skilled in which register of response to adopt, and when to use it, in the event of controversy. As mentioned earlier, the secular language of scholarship will be comprehensible in a public sphere regulated by secular reason. And communities will therefore on occasion need to know how to translate their religious reasons into secular ones. As well, they will need to become literate in the language of offense—what is legally actionable and what is, in effect, calling for a form of censorship. There may, too, be times when the academic institutions should be asked to listen to, if not to act on, religious reasons issued on religious grounds alone.

THEORIES OF RELIGION,
THEORIES OF INSTITUTIONS

As discussed in chapter 1, two of the largest debates in the field of the study of religion over the past two decades have concerned (1) the role of context in the manufacture of the category of religion, and other categories like it, and (2) the position scholars take relative to their subjects—whether they are, in Russell McCutcheon's terms, "critics" or "caretakers." In light of this recent intellectual history in the study of religion, I suggest here that no theory of religion is complete without concomitant theories of the institutions that support it—including but not limited to universities, colleges, and seminaries.

With regard to the location of the scholar, there are several key elements inthe twenty-first-century study of religion that should be named. In my introduction, I mentioned that positionality had become for me an unacknowledged romantic ideal of the move to historicize and contextualize terms in the study of religion; I thought that if we only positioned ourselves more eloquently, we would be all right with other scholars and all right with the world. The cases in this book suggest otherwise. All of the scholars discussed in this book named their positions in one way or another, and such naming did not result in communities that uniformly accepted their work simply because they also wrote about their intellectual backgrounds and orientations.

Such positionality has not proved to be felicitous, unless we, as Tom Tweed suggests, understand such positionality as fluid, mobile, and constantly changing. And perhaps not even then. Scholars can do two things in response, theoretically: (1) abandon the project of positionality, understanding it as a kind of rhetorical move whose results have proven less positive than we had hoped, or (2) make such positionality even more radical. They can reflect on the nature of their theorizing at the same moment that it is being theorized, not afterward, but without the expectation that it will have any particular results. Rather, they will radicalize positionality to include the nature of the institution in which they are theorizing as well as the nature of the various publics that they understand to constitute their readerships.

Let me be even more specific. We might think of a continuum that exists in the nature of how scholars might relate to the communities about which they are writing—all the choices along the range of that continuum being viable. On the one side would be the idea that a scholar's public obligation is to redescribe religion, as Russ McCutcheon puts it, and not simply "re-present" it. That means one thinks and writes about religious claims in frameworks other than the ones that are argued for by the religions themselves; scholars think about them in forthrightly explanatory frameworks that make secular, and not religious, sense of their scholarly activity. As McCutcheon argues, and as discussed in chapter 1, this role might be part of the public obligation of the scholar so that religious communities read as intelligible to people other than themselves.

Hence, my proposition that in studying religion, we also must develop a theory of what institutions—including but not limited to universities, colleges, and seminaries—are there to do and what they are not there to do. McCutcheon is right in pointing out the critical role of the scholar in society and to remind us of his or her public role; the case studies in this book alone show that this role is central. However, his is also a normative claim about what scholars ought to argue about religion once they are in public. In my view, it is better to be agnostic about the role of the scholar, given that there may be crucial roles other than critic that are more socially necessary at particular times and places.

In other words, McCutcheon might be even more contextualized in his call for scholars to engage their social context. Let me give some examples: the re-presentation of religion might be absolutely necessary in a social world where the first step is acknowledging the existence of that religion at all. Think, for example, of David Chidester's move to include

South African tribal practices as part of the religions protected under the new South African constitution. This was a re-presentation first before it was an analytical and critical redescription. What is more, a critical stance on a particular religion in a public context where the public is already disposed to be critical of the religion for other, less legitimate reasons could be quite detrimental to a fair understanding of that tradition. One might think, for example, of the publication of a critique of Judaism in an academic institution in an area of the United States where recent anti-Semitic incidents had occurred. It is important to be clear here: the larger good can and should be publication and free exchange of ideas. The next good, however, would be reflection about and preparation for the responses that may occur.

More broadly, and central to our argument, scholars' positions have everything to do with how they understand the institutions in which they work and their public engagements. I am catholic on approaches to the study of religion and think it is important to include as many of them as possible. In doing so, we should commit to making the inevitable tension this "big tent" produces creative and not destructive. Scholars have the right to be exclusively critical or adamantly sympathetic, and everything in between. But we no longer have the right to be surprised when communities make, and publish, their own opinions about our scholarship. Because in 2018 not all scholars work in academic institutions, nor will a substantial percentage of scholars in our field necessarily do so in the future, I make the case here for reflection in many different kinds of places.

Let me begin with academic institutions. These case studies, and the eruptive public spaces they generated, demonstrate that we need sustained reflection about the nature of the academic community in which the individual scholar operates and about its relationship to the public sphere. Such a reflection is part of what many recent writers have demanded of us in making a more ethical university.[8] As we have seen, academic claims to secularity are increasingly as diverse as religious ones. The secular feminism of Jane Schaberg was different than the secular commitments of Kripal's and Schwartz' Freudian psychoanalysis, and different again from the secular historical analysis of Oberoi or Gill, or the textual criticism of the Ginans by Kassam.

For all the reasons I have suggested in earlier chapters, secularity itself is a fluid category. However, it is also true in the university. Jon Roberts and James Turner's *The Sacred and the Secular University* shows the historical dynamics of this instability. In the latter part of the nineteenth century, religion lost its power as an organizer of knowledge in American universities and was replaced by research, professionalization, and specialization. The idea of liberal education took the place of theology as a unifier of knowledge—particularly humanities as a study of the moral essence of Western civilization in literature and art.[9]

Building on this work, Talal Asad has observed that liberal universities were the birthplace of "freedom of speech" as a form of public critique, and it has since been asserted widely as an absolute value. So too has professional critique, according to the norms of the guild. Asad puts it the following way: "While the freedom to criticize is presented at once as being a right and a duty of the modern individual, its truth-producing capacity remains subject to disciplinary criteria and its material conditions of existence (laboratories, building, research funds, publishing houses, computers, tenure . . .)."[10] Thus, for Asad, while the secular is part of the contemporary American university, its structures are still part of a larger matrix of institutions (state, corporate, philanthropic) that can affect those conditions, and thus no structure is ever fully guaranteed in the way that a university's theological grounding once was understood to be.

These are the various patrons with which the scholar (as fool) is also engaged, in addition to departments and religious communities. In this newly complex and deceptively unstable world, the case studies presented here suggest that a scholar of religion, and perhaps departments as well, should think in an explicit way throughout their careers about what academic institutions are for. The great question for liberal learning today is: Are academic institutions there primarily for the creation of knowledge? Or are they there to make the world a better place (which includes vocational training as well as social activism)? While the obvious answer to this is "both," the current arguments about liberal learning turn on which of these purposes is to take primacy, and how we might characterize the goals of research, teaching, and service.

If scholars are ultimately convinced that institutions of higher learning are there for the creation of new knowledge, then the connections to the various publics will have one particular kind of coloring. The sharing of research with the communities they study may not be their primary goal, and the audience may remain the academy and the academy alone. Some researchers might even think that they should conduct normative research that might be universally applicable but also argue that their work should be read only by their students and colleagues.

However, since now a scholar's readership will likely never reside in the academy alone, such scholars should have a philosophy about how, when, and why to interact with the inevitable interlocutors from the community concerned. Indeed, some scholars could be quite eager to share research with different kinds of communities but have a clear philosophy that the normative implications of the work are not his or her concern. Some might remain at a distance and even be critical of community concerns; nonetheless, they need a clear method of engagement once it is asked for.

If scholars are ultimately convinced that institutions of higher learning are there to make the world a better place, then their perspective on community engagement will take on a different hue. It might well be that reaching out to the communities before, during, and after the publication of their research would be the norm for such scholars. They may invite readership from a wide variety of circles and welcome comments from community members who are not inducted into the academic guild. They may feel that they also have an obligation to translate their more obscure research into broader language—not just when the community demands it. Moreover, they might also be aware of the fact that some communities may not want to engage with scholars, whether those scholars be insiders, outsiders, or in between.

At a most general level, then, scholars' theories of religion should engage their theories of their publics. If scholars understand universities as places of knowledge, with little obligation to publics at large, then they will write in one particular way. If they understand universities as being accountable to multiple readerships, then they will write about religions in another way. It is primarily a matter of whose voices they wish to include in the larger conversation their work introduces. A scholar who argues that a university should manufacture knowledge for knowledge's sake may well write work that include statements about a religious tradition that are irrelevant for or even scandalous to the community. He or she may also include statements that the community agrees with. But any given community's disagreement or agreement is irrelevant to that scholar's larger work. A scholar who believes that a university should engage with its various publics may well include these same statements but will do so prepared to discuss them and to defend them, and most of all will not be surprised if and when communities wish to engage with the work. And there are, of course, various stages in between.

In each case, however, scholars should also be aware of their own relative power within the academy and beyond. How does tenure create a kind of privilege, which might allow public engagement or the refusal of public engagement to be perceived differently? Given that tenured professors are increasingly in the minority, in religious studies as well as in the humanities more generally, it is, I believe, a moral obligation for the tenured professoriate to support adjunct instructors in their public engagements and to protect them if they have written controversial research. Indeed, by the nature of their work, adjunct professors are more likely to be more engaged in the public sphere, and they should be understood as great resources for others thinking through these important questions.

Relatedly, given the new demographics of the humanities, it should not be a foregone conclusion that a scholar's place of employment is with an academic institution. If one is with an NGO or think tank, then the commitment to research as a way of making the world a better place is more clearly front and center. At an NGO, a scholar's publics are already multiple, and the scholar would more regularly reflect on the connection between research and the mission statement of the organization. While the mission itself might be different, many of the same dynamics would apply to scholars working at a for-profit institution, such as a company or a consulting firm.

THEORIES OF RELIGION, THEORIES OF THE PUBLIC SPHERE

Each institution discussed above also has a different understanding of its own publics. Is the small college in which one works "the town's college" and therefore focused on key local relationships? Is the seminary in which one works known to be more progressive or conservative than others in its sphere? Is the Roman Catholic university in which one teaches a veteran or a newcomer to its individual scholars having differences with the Vatican? Was the university in which one does one's research built with a legacy of slave labor from the surrounding counties in the preceding century? Does the city in which I teach have a large immigrant population, and from where? The answer to each of these questions will determine the kinds of publics that might be interlocutors for oneself or one's department.

Scholars of religion need now to take the time to learn what those publics are. Indeed, they have a unique perspective from which to embark on such a reflection, multiply positioned as scholars are. Moreover, many of these institutions themselves are in a multiple bind; as discussed above, they claim academic freedom as a secular perspective and yet have multiple constituencies to which they are being asked to answer. The neighboring communities and donors who fund chairs, in the case of Oberoi and Schwartz, are one kind of constituency. There are the critics, both near and far, who are invested in a cultural religious identity and life-script, such as the Catholic community in Detroit and throughout the USA in the Schaberg case; the Native communities throughout North America in the Gill case; or the neighboring and global Hindu and Ismaili communities in the Kripal and Kassam cases, respectively.

Most importantly, one might also think about the global environments in which universities themselves create departments and help them to thrive. Our case studies suggest this. In the late 1980s and early '90s, while multiculturalism emerged as a cultural force and the internet emerged as a media force, universities themselves were becoming globally elite places. The number of international students was on the rise, and the larger rhetoric of "globalism" was evolving into a key feature in many departments. University centers were being set up to discuss just this phenomenon. As global trade, markets, and cultures and transnational hermeneutics began to emerge, the American university in particular appeared a mecca for many in the less privileged parts of the globe. This led to an increasing internationalization of the faculty and the student body. But it also led to a keen sense of disparity in academic production. Thus, in a scathing sociology of knowledge from the southern hemisphere, A. Suresh Canagarajah's *A Geopolitics of Academic Writing* outlines how difficult it is for a scholar in urban Sri Lanka to apply for a Fulbright, as distinct from the experience of someone in a small college in the United States.[11]

In each of these case studies, as mentioned earlier, the university was understood as a place of privilege, and at times unreflective privilege that had no sense of the effects of the knowledge it was producing. This rhetoric was most pronounced in the case of Kripal, but it was also there in a different way in the Schaberg case. Indeed, Schaberg's theory of religion was based on feminist resistance from within a Catholic university. One does not want to assume cause and effect here, but the point remains clear that her Roman Catholic surroundings probably spurred her on to unmask as much as she possibly could other, more doctrinally correct forms of scholarship coming out of other Catholic universities. Not only might scholars look at the development of religion departments in this historical way, but they might also look at the institutional history of their own contexts and how that affects their writing about religion today. They might examine their own normative assumptions about how universities should work in the world and in relationship to their publics. These publics will be key to what, how, and why scholars write about the religious communities they do.

The same considerations might apply to public spaces and public spheres. No theory of religion can be adequate without a concomitant theory of the public sphere in which such religion can and should be discussed. One group working in the 1990s made attempts to create such a theory of the public sphere, what O. S. Guinness calls a "public philosophy."[12] Responding to controversies in the '90s about religion in the public schools (an eruptive space if there ever was one), he helped author the Williamsburg Charter. The charter was what he called a principled agreement involving chartered pluralism and, in the words of his fellow writer and activist Charles Haynes, "a vision of religious liberty in public life that, across the deep religious differences of a pluralistic society, guarantees and sustains religious liberty for all by forging a substantive agreement or freely chosen compact, that are the three R's of religious liberty: rights, responsibilities, and respect." The Williamsburg Charter was "born out of the fact that, when religious consensus in our diverse nation is not possible, agreement on civic principle is not only possible but urgently needed."[13]

The charter was also born out of the fact of multiple publics interacting. As Guinness explains it, the charter does not assume a monolithic sacred public square, where a single religion dominates, nor a naked public square, where religion is disallowed. Rather, it assumes a civil public square, where different faiths are freely allowed to enter, observing the three R's of rights, responsibilities, and respect.[14] Its principles were highly effective in resolving differences involving religion in public schools in several counties across the nation.

In such a charter there are risks of recreating the very same kind of liberal pluralism many scholars have outlined as problematic, an issue I will discuss below. But in some cases, academic versions of the Williamsburg Charter might, in effect, move from the (perhaps necessary) eruptive public spaces and create public spheres. Such spheres would involve awareness and analysis of the complex contours of the space between the religious community and academic and other institutions. It would involve a set of principles, simple in statement but complex in implementation. This analysis would look different in every situation, as every religion department has its own unique history and relationship to the towns, cities, and religious communities around it, and to national and international communities with which it interacts.

In other cases, such a charter might be ineffective. As we have seen, critics of the ideologies of liberal pluralism have argued that pluralism can be unconsciously exclusive, never truly living up to its claimed ideals. For some critics, it can be patronizingly inclusive, assuming a mainstream to which tolerated "others" must adapt. For still others, pluralism is insufficiently resistant to dominant ideologies and sweeps structural imbalances of social, economic, and historical power under a pseudo-harmonious rug. For all these reasons, some critics of scholarly practice may choose *not* to move from the eruptive public space but prefer to dwell there instead. In this they would be choosing what Chantal Mouffe has called "agonistic democracy" rather than the rationalist, deliberative democracy of Habermas. Agonistic democracy assumes that collective identifications and passions have a place in public argument.[15]

In addition, some scholars may choose to allow the eruptive public spaces simply to exist in a parallel universe and will not respond to critiques, given their own commitments to issues of academic freedom, or the work of exposing power imbalances within religious traditions themselves. I would argue, however, that in all cases, whether responsive or not, whether choosing to dwell in the eruptive public spaces or trying to move into public spheres, writers must develop a theory of scholars and publics that motivate and inform them.

An analysis in this vein would also foster a further awareness of multiple publics. In the current moment, many scholars still assume a single public rather than the multiple publics that actually can and do constitute their readerships. Such a public could be CNN, the church basement, the mosque, the Hindu temple, or the courthouse. But a scholar's assumption of a single public does determine whether and how he or she becomes engaged in the walls beyond the university. We saw that dynamic in Tazim Kassam's realization that her Ismaili readership would not be uniformly positive but multiple and polarized. We saw it in Kripal's account of how the gay, the straight, the secular, and the Hindu communities in India had different responses to *Kāli's Child* depending upon how they interpreted the relationship between sexuality and history. We saw it in Oberoi's understanding of himself as a Sikh in the Delhi riots, and later as a Sikh in the diaspora, and the radically different reading publics that such communities constituted. All of these competing transnational publics with various allegiances to various states made for an eruptive public space—an eruptive public sphere, indeed, in which the subject of "religion" was defined depending upon the actors involved and less on a given set of rules.

All of these ideas about scholars and publics presume that the humanities can and should be a form of civic agency in a vibrant democracy. Some have argued for this in the world of art, where, whether top down or bottom up, the work of public arts assumes that we are all cultural agents.[16] More and more are arguing for it in the work of the humanities more broadly.[17] As discussed in the introduction, because humanistic scholars of religion exist in the in-between of artifice and truth, the humanities' potential ability to navigate publics should be developed, engaged, and featured as part of this vibrancy. Leela Prasad has argued for this forcefully in her proposal that a failure of public life is one where negotiations are based on intellectual transactions, not on navigations of common democratic experience.[18]

What is more, we have learned from these case studies that the eruptive nature of the space is partly determined by whether statements are made by the participants for the general public rather than directed at a particular party. We also know that such spaces are partly shaped by whether, following Bohman, there is an anticipation of an answer back. In the Gill, Kripal, Schwartz, and Oberoi cases, there was a sense that statements on either side were not made for a general public, nor in anticipation of an answer back. Thus, the public space was eruptive for a while at its outset but then could not transition into a genuine public sphere where participants could follow agreed-upon rules and have a sense that others would answer back. Intriguingly, as of the writing of this book, a public sphere may emerge on the Ginans, in that Kassam has continued to publish in this arena. This may occur in the Schaberg case, too. Although Schaberg is no longer with us, the question of feminist scholarship and the Catholic Church hierarchy has been raised in a number of other places since her work first appeared. Intriguingly, the two scholars who stayed in their fields and continued to publish on similar topics also were able to forge a longer-lasting public conversation.

Yet in many of these cases, the public spaces intersected for a while in a single conversation and then diverted into parallel public spaces—even competing spaces or rivals in representation of a religious tradition. This was certainly true in each of the South Asian diaspora cases. Other actors in public spaces that emerged simply stopped trying to follow or negotiate common rules of engagement or to translate their views into the sphere of their interlocutors. This was true of Gill, Oberoi, Schwartz, and Kripal, whose leavetaking took various forms—either from the subfield (Gill, Kripal, and Oberoi) or from the academy altogether (Schwartz). These differing responses are a powerful instantiation of Albert O. Hirsch's thesis that people alienated by a work situation can have two possible responses: to exit, or to voice their complaint—even at times confrontationally.[19] These differing responses also have implications for the eruptive public spaces and public spheres more generally. We have seen above what can emerge and what can disappear as a result of the nature of the public space that controversy produces.

While I hope this book is a modest start to counteract the dearth of information, we still have very little actual data about how public spaces emerge, whether eruptive or not. The material covered in this book is an attempt to ground historically what some of the theories about the public sphere have been conjecturing, and to test those assumptions about what such publics actually are and how they behave. Following Fraser's focus on parity and complexity within a public sphere, we have learned from these case studies that controversial public spaces erupt when there is an imbalance in the relationship between institutions, the historical parity of dialogical partners, the perceived parity of dialogical partners, and the community's understanding of religion as a cultural resource. All of these factors contribute to the quality of the public space. The eruptive nature of the space is determined in part by whether the dialogue is in part understood to "right a power balance" or "correct a cultural misperception." It is also determined by the willingness of the scholar and the community members to remain in that public space and by their sense of the productivity of the debate. Most eruptive public spaces do not and cannot last, and they may not translate immediately into the kind of rule-governed sphere of which James Bohman has written.

It perhaps goes without saying that the publication of most scholarly books on religion do not erupt in scandalous controversy where moral entrepreneurs of various kinds take advantage of the situation to create normative discourse. Insofar as we comment on such controversies, we all do engage as moral entrepreneurs of one kind or another. Even as readerships are changing, most scholarly discourse carries on without the glare of the public eye.

But when scholars find themselves in eruptive public spaces, how might they "cross and dwell" in such moments? In the end, any scholar who might argue for and about religion in public (and in my view, this would include *any* scholar who publishes) should understand the nature of the public space he or she is entering. However, it is worth emphasizing that a basic exploration and understanding of the nature of one's various publics *before even beginning to write* will go a long way toward the effectiveness of scholarly discourse in the world. If scholars are to cross and to dwell, even momentarily, within different publics, as wise fools have done in literature and in history, they need to orient themselves accordingly. Whether empathizers or critics, re-presenters or explainers—and there can and should be room for all of these approaches—scholars need to grow wiser about their academic environments, the publics they might engage, the public spaces they might create, and the eruptions potentially contained therein.

One reader asked if I might conclude this book with a hopeful answer to the dilemmas I have outlined in these pages. My hopeful answer is in the call to sustained reflection with which we all should engage, living as we do on the fragile edges, fragile centers, and fragile in-betweens of multiple publics and multiple patrons. I see a great deal of hope in requiring all graduate programs in religion—and even undergraduate programs—to think about audiences and readerships in a systematic way: Who are my publics, who is included and who is excluded, and how do I make the best argument for the stance I ultimately take on the public role of the scholar of religion? The larger, more important point here is that the new dynamics of readership and eruptive public spaces have become part of our scholarly lives, and no matter how many vibrant centers focusing on religion and public life we create, in our educational practice we are not preparing our students for that reality.

A theory of public spaces as part of the study of religion should include required readings in theories of the public sphere. They may or may not be the work of the theorists whom I have engaged in this book. A theory of public spaces may also begin with a series of questions, with no predetermined answers—questions that can be asked from a wide range of methodological commitments. Reflection about the public sphere is important for the most secular of critics or the most sympathetic interpreters of a religious tradition, and anyone else existing between the two ends of that spectrum.

I began this chapter with a call to a kind of foolish wisdom, as scholars are increasingly asked to participate in a more eruptive public space. As a beginning of that wisdom, here are the questions a scholar might now want to ask as part of the necessary reflection on his or her work.

- In the continuum between criticism and empathy, where do I stand, and why?
- In the continuum between re-presenting and explaining, where do I stand, and why?
- What is my understanding of a scholar's role in the public sphere?
- What is my understanding of the public role of my institution in producing knowledge?
- What is my institution's understanding of its own public role?
- What is my institution's view of those who write for a public audience?
- What is the tradition of indigenous scholarship in the tradition about which I am writing, and how has it connected to university scholarship in the past?
- Should my work be accessible to others outside the academic world, or available first and foremost to specialists?
- What is my understanding of my readerships? Do I know the nature of the divisions within the communities that I am writing for and about, such that questions about authority, either my own or that of others, could emerge in the interpretation of my work?
- What is my understanding of my ethical obligation, if any, to the communities that I study after I have read their texts or interviewed their members?
- What is the history of vulnerability of the community about which I am writing?
- What is my assessment of that history of vulnerability? Given that assessment, what are my obligations?
- What is that community's record of engagement in the public space? Is it an eruptive public space or a public sphere, with rules of engagement?
- What is my institution's record of engagement in the public space? Is it an eruptive public space or a public sphere, with rules of engagement?
- If I choose to depart from indigenous claims, am I willing to engage with scholars who object to that departure? If so, how will I do so and upon what grounds? If not, how will I disengage and upon what grounds?
- How do I think that public sphere should be constituted in moments of controversy?
- Are there rules of engagement that I expect to be followed? If so, what are they, and why? If not, what are my expectations of myself and my interlocutors?

These questions might grow to become part of scholarly research and teaching, publishing, and curriculum building. They are, moreover, a living document, to which any and all in the "big tent" that is the study of religion should add.

The hope is also in the fact that perhaps the scholarly world is coming to a collective awareness of what and who is missing in its deliberations. We will come to different conclusions about how to respond to that awareness. In the words of Habermas's critic Max Pensky, we will express such an awareness on rare occasions and "in a language strange and broken, and therefore beautiful."[20] Our languages—scholarly and otherwise—in new public landscapes are indeed strange and broken. Yet, perhaps, in their striving, they contain a certain kind of beauty.

Epilogue

One might wonder whether the cases discussed in these pages were aberrations in an otherwise clear progression of liberalization that Mircea Eliade and W. C. Smith, each in his different way, argued for. Might they be simply a stumble (in the earliest sense of the word "scandal") on the otherwise ongoing path toward some common cultural knowledge?

I think not. The years following these cases in the 1990s continued to be rife with controversies between scholars and their publics, each with dynamics of their own, and to be studied on their own in further work. The larger contexts of religious controversies do provide important backdrops; as the early twenty-first century unfolded in the aftermath of 9/11, we saw an America increasingly affected by global controversy: the rise of arguments about the status of Israel; the increase of Islamic extremism; the conservative turn in the Catholic Church under Pope Benedict XVI; the growing concern of Hindu groups about the appropriation of their symbols by a commercially driven public; a progressively robust discourse in the many forms of identity politics; and an increase in public acts of violence against religious minorities, just to name a few.[1]

While theological and religious controversies occurring in the early twenty-first century are too numerous to name here, below are some involving scholars and their reading publics. Each situation involves different politics and different approaches to the study of religion. The scholarly works, the community's concerns, and the state's involvement in each of them are different. Individual readers may find themselves siding with community critics or scholars depending upon their views and the dynamics of the case study.

In the early twenty-first century, further cases involving community protest about misrepresentation of Native American symbols became part of scholarly discourse in the study of Native American religions. Some of these are contained in Michael Brown's *Who Owns Native Culture?*[2] In the case of the representation of female symbols, and the continuing criticism of perspectives such as Gill's, further examples can be found in books of essays such as Inéz Hernández-Avila's *Reading Native American Women: Critical and Creative Representations.*[3] Tracy Leavelle has traced the way that many Native groups, in disputes over land rights with the US government, must use categories that fit into the state's understanding of what is religious. In a dynamic similar to that discussed in chapter 5, Native groups must mobilize the idea of religion to gain authenticity in the eyes of US law and culture.[4]

In the Sikh case, many controversies occurred in India, but some also affected scholars working in North America. For example, Pashaura Singh was given the Sikh chair at UC Riverside in 2008, and many Sikh protests ensued about his work on the history of the Guru Granth, one of the major texts in the formation of the Sikh religion. Other debates around historical scholarship focusing on the work of Gurinder Singh Mann and W. H. McLeod also occurred but did not involve Amritsar's Shiromani Gurdwara Parbandhak Committee (Supreme Gurdwara Management Committee), the official theological and political body.[5]

In the Ismaili case, few publications since *Songs of Wisdom and Circles of Dance* have engaged public controversy. However, the larger question of Islam is another story. After 9/11, North American scholars whose books were deemed hostile to Wahhabism were banned in Arab countries and Malaysia. One compelling example is Amina Wadud's work on reading the Qur'an from a woman's perspective. Stephen Schwartz's work on Saudi "fundamentalism" and its role in terrorism is another. John Esposito's more general work on Islam (published in 2002 and again in 2011) and works by the law professor Khaled Abou El Fadl were banned even in Egypt and Riyadh.[6] After the Arab Spring, some governments have been sensitive to works that have been perceived as engaging "liberal" Islam. American scholars' books have been banned at the Riyadh and Cairo international book fairs. In 2009, Omid Safi wrote *Memories of Muhammad*, and the Malay Interior Ministry banned it, along with eleven other books by Shiite scholars, as a threat to public order and morality.[7] In a less formal vein, Qatari authorities forbade Sumathi Ramaswamy's book on M. F. Husain, *Barefoot across the Nation*, to be imported due to its inclusion of Husain's paintings, which depicted women's bodies.

In the Roman Catholic context, in 2007 the feminist theologian Elizabeth Johnson at Fordham University came into conflict with the Roman Catholic hierarchies for a feminist theology in *Quest for the Living God*.[8] The work was deemed in conflict with Catholic doctrine, and pantheistic in its depiction of the relationship between the three members of the trinity and its approach to the metaphorical understanding of the names of God. In addition, Johnson's quest for alternative Christian sources was a fundamental part of her method, as it was for Schaberg, and skirted the limits of theological discourse acceptable to the authorities. The non-Catholic Christian context was not addressed in this book, but it is important to mention that there were and are local controversies that made the national scene in the 1990s and beyond, such as that of David Frankfurter at the College of Charleston.[9]

In the Jewish world, Joel Kovel at Bard College, Marc Ellis at Baylor University, and Norman Finkelstein at DePaul University were all embroiled in controversies concerning their views on Israel.[10] The controversies involved a critique of twenty-first century Zionism (Kovel), a theory of twentieth-century Holocaust history and the State of Israel (Finkelstein), and a Jewish liberation theology focused on the Israeli treatment of the Palestinians (Ellis).

And in the Hindu world, scholars such as Sarah Caldwell and Paul Courtright were criticized in the early 2000s for their overly sexual rendering of Hindu traditions. Scholars and libraries who helped James Laine compose *Shivaji: Hindu King in Islamic India* were violently taken to task by a group protesting Laine's assessment of the king's lineage. Throughout the first two decades of the twenty-first century, a number of Hindu activists have protested what they perceive as the recolonization of Hindu studies by Western academic methods, including the secularization of Sanskrit or the use of secular methods that, in their view, produce inaccurate understandings and public representations of Hinduism. A Delhi-based group, Shiksha Bachao Andolan Samiti, filed a lawsuit demanding that Wendy Doniger's book *The Hindus: An Alternative History* be withdrawn from publication by Penguin India; Penguin India complied, resulting in an international counterprotest.[11] A. K. Ramanujan's essay "Three Hundred Ramayanas" and Paula Richman's work on the different kinds of Ramayanas in South Asian cultures have been attacked for undermining the sanctity of the epic tradition.[12] Francis X. Clooney's works have been condemned for comparing Hindu and Catholic traditions as a disguised form of evangelizing.[13]

There are many controversies and volumes that have not been named here; these citations are aimed to give readers an entryway into a much more voluminous literature. Perhaps a small subfield might emerge where the dynamics of controversy and analysis of the public spaces and spheres might become a new scholarly goal in the study of religion. If, as I suggested throughout this book, scholars take theories of the university and theories of the public sphere seriously as they pursue their work in the study of religion, this subfield would seem a strong desideratum.

The larger, more important point here is that the new dynamics of readership and eruptive public spaces have become part of our scholarly lives. It might be well to focus on some questions for scholars as they enter the field or reassess their own relationship to their subjects of study. As noted in chapter 11, a theory of public spaces and public spheres may well begin with a series of questions, with no predetermined answers—questions that can be asked from a wide range of methodological commitments. Reflection about public spaces, public spheres, and the local, national, and international moments for engagement—or the refusal of engagement—is important. Such reflection might help students at all levels: scholars, administrators, interested secular citizens, or members of religious communities. Further, it might thrive as part of the intellectual lives of the most secular of critics or the most committed of confessional fellow travelers in the study of religion, and anyone else existing between the two ends of that spectrum. It could better reveal, and perhaps color in, the multiple entanglements we have been encountering all along.

ACKNOWLEDGMENTS

I am grateful to countless fellow travelers who care about these issues and have lived them, including many of the voices described in this book. I also owe thanks to the universities, colleges, and other venues who have hosted lectures or sponsored short-term fellowships based on the chapters in this book: the Departments of Religion at the American University in Cairo, the University of Texas at Austin, and the University of Wisconsin–Madison; the Center for Humanistic Inquiry, the Seminar on Religion and Conflict (2006–11), and the Graduate Seminar in Religion in the Graduate Division of Religion, Emory University; the Committee on Religion and Modernity, the Seminar on Religion and Public Life, and the Kenan Center for Ethics at Duke University; the Presidential Panel Committee of the American Historical Society; the Association for Asian Studies; and the American Society for the Study of Religion. I have received support from the Center for Humanistic Inquiry, Emory University, and the Council of Independent Colleges for exploration of the ideas in this book.

People with whom I have had influential conversations about these issues over the years vary widely across the scholarly spectrum in their disciplinary perspectives and methodological approaches. Some may not even remember the conversations. This is not a list of like-minded people. Many of them are deeply opposed to each other on key issues in the study of religion, in the humanities, and the constitution of the public square. That is a good thing. They are Srinivas Aravamudan, Luke Bretherton, Jonathan Brockopp, David Chidester, Brad Clough, Paul Courtright, David Damrosch, Wendy Doniger, Laurent Dubois, Astrid Eckert, Timothy Fitzgerald, Joyce Flueckiger, David Frankfurter, Balu Gangadharan,

Rosemarie Garland-Thomson, Sander Gilman, Shalom Goldman, Ron Grimes, Leslie Harris, John S. Hawley, Sanjay Iyer, Ivan Karp, Pam Klassen, Cory Kratz, Ruby Lal, Susannah Laramee Kidd, Bruce Lawrence, Rosemary Magee, Barbara McGraw, Kevin Moore, Ebrahim Moosa, Jairam Ramesh, Velcheru Narayana Rao, Christian Novetzke, Martha Nussbaum, Erik Owens, Gyan Pandey, Eboo Patel, Michael Perry, Leela Prasad, Arshia Sattar, David Scobey, Winni Sullivan, Tom Tweed, Luke Whitmore, and Alan Wolfe.

For the superb editing help of David Gregory and J. T. Price, I am most grateful. I cannot begin to describe the virtues of my editor, the deeply insightful, unfailingly rigorous, faithfully compassionate, and superhumanly patient Alan Thomas.

NOTES

INTRODUCTION

1. This was the controversy over the reissue of Paul Courtright's book *Ganesha* at Emory University. I leave the introductory description of the moment somewhat generic to draw the reader in, and because this dynamic has now been part of the lives of many different scholars and communities in the study of religion.

2. Talal Asad, Wendy Brown, Judith Butler, and Saba Mahmood, *Is Critique Secular? Blasphemy, Injury, and Free Speech* (New York: Fordham University Press, 2009).

3. Craig Calhoun, Mark Juergensmeyer, and Jonathan VanAntwerpen, eds., *Rethinking Secularism* (New York: Oxford University Press, 2011). It is an excellent assessment of the problems with the term "secular" in contemporary discourse, both in the academy and beyond.

4. Among the many works of his that shape these critical readings of Habermas, the principals are focused on dialogue, the public sphere, and religion: *Theory of Communicative Action*, vol. 1, *Reason and the Rationalization of Society*, and vol. 2, *Lifeworld and System: A Critique of Functionalist Reason*, trans. Thomas A. McCarthy (Boston: Beacon Press; 1981); *The Structural Transformation of the Public Sphere: An Inquiry into a Category of Bourgeois Society*, tr. Thomas Burger and Frederick Lawrence (Cambridge, MA: MIT Press, 1989); and Habermas's essay on religion, "Religion in the Public Sphere," *European Journal of Philosophy* 14, no. 1 (2006): 1–25.

5. Claire Potter and Renee Romano, eds., *Doing Recent History: On Privacy, Copyright, Video Games, Institutional Review Boards, Activist Scholarship, and History That Talks Back* (Athens: University of Georgia Press, 2012).

6. Robert Greene II, "The Urgency of 1990s History," Society for U.S. Intellectual History blog, June 25, 2017, https://s-usih.org/2017/06/the-urgency-of-1990s-history/ (accessed July 9, 2018).

7. See Craig Calhoun, Eduardo Mendieta, and Jonathan VanAntwerpen, "Editors' Introduction," in *Habermas and Religion* (Cambridge, UK: Polity Press, 2013), 3–4.

8. These approaches seem to me equally powerful as a way of thinking about recent intellectual history and as a way of challenging traditional liberal theories.

9. María Herrera Lima, "The Anxiety of Contingency: Religion in a Secular Age," in Calhoun, Mendieta, and VanAntwerpen, *Habermas and Religion*, 51.

10. Thomas McCarthy, "The Burdens of Modernized Faith and Postmetaphysical Reason in Habermas's 'Unfinished Project of Enlightenment,'" in Calhoun, Mendieta, and VanAntwerpen, *Habermas and Religion*, 116.

11. Herrera Lima, "Anxiety," 61.

12. Jane Schaberg, *The Illegitimacy of Jesus: A Feminist Theological Interpretation of the Infancy Narratives* (San Francisco: Harper & Row, 1987), 118.

CHAPTER ONE

1. See Christian Wiese and Andreas Gotzmann, eds., *Modern Judaism and Historical Consciousness: Identities, Encounters, Perspectives* (Leiden: E. J. Brill, 2007); and Leora Batnitzky, *How Judaism Became a Religion: An Introduction to Modern Jewish Thought* (Princeton: Princeton University Press, 2011).

2. See my bibliography in "Defining Hinduism," in *Oxford Bibliographies*, http://www.oxfordbibliographies.com/view/document/obo-9780195399318/obo-9780195399318-0015.xml (accessed July 25, 2018).

3. See, among many other examples, the essays in Donald S. Lopez Jr., ed., *Curators of the Buddha: The Study of Buddhism under Colonialism* (Chicago and London: University of Chicago Press, 1995), as well as Peter Bishop, *Dreams of Power: Tibetan Buddhism and the Western Imagination* (London: Athlone Press, 1993); Anne Blackburn, *Buddhist Learning and Textual Practice in Eighteenth-Century Lankan Monastic Culture* (Princeton: Princeton University Press, 2001); and on science, Donald S. Lopez Jr., *Buddhism and Science: A Guide for the Perplexed* (Chicago: University of Chicago Press, 2008).

4. Talal Asad, "The Construction of Religion as an Anthropological Category," in Asad, *Genealogies of Religion: Disciplines of Reason and Power in Christianity and Islam* (Baltimore: Johns Hopkins University Press, 1993), 27–54. See, for example, Shahab Ahmed's *What Is Islam? The Importance of Being Islamic* (Princeton: Princeton University Press, 2015). In the equally voluminous literature on various constructions of the idea of Christianity, Molly Worthen's *Apostles of Reason: The Crisis of Authority in American Evangelicalism* (New York: Oxford University Press, 2014) stands out. It is a study of the institutional construction of the culture wars between religious conservatives and secular liberals, and the ways in which late twentieth-century evangelicals use methodologies of secularism itself.

5. Daniel Dubuisson, *The Western Construction of Religion* (Baltimore: Johns Hopkins University Press, 2003); Brent Nongbri, *Before Religion: A History of a Modern Concept* (New Haven: Yale University Press, 2013).

6. Timothy Fitzgerald, *The Ideology of Religious Studies* (Oxford: Oxford University Press, 2003). For a thorough assessment of this debate, see Kevin Schilbrack, "The Social Construction of 'Religion' and Its Limits: A Critical Reading of Timothy Fitzgerald," *Method and Theory in the Study of Religion* 24 (2012): 97–117.

7. Tomoko Masuzawa, *The Invention of World Religions; or, How European Universalism Was Preserved in the Language of Pluralism* (Chicago: University of Chi-

cago Press, 2005). D. G. Hart, writing in a very different field, argues something similar for the United States. As he sees it, in the study of religion in its earliest phase (1870–1925), the hope was that it could be a scientific and nonsectarian form of "enlightened" Christianity. From the mid-1960s onward, the study of religion became an essential part of liberal democracy and a key contribution to public life. However, for Hart, the study of religion now lacks a stable foundation because of its inability to make a case for itself absent a Protestant claim to coherence. Hart, *The University Gets Religion: Religious Studies in American Higher Education* (Baltimore: Johns Hopkins University Press, 1999). See also Barry Hankins's review, *Journal of Church and State* 42, no. 3 (Summer 2000): 593–95.

8. Winnifred Sullivan, "We Are All Religious Now, Again," *Social Research* 76, no. 4 (Winter 2009): 1181–98; also see her "Religion Naturalized: The New Establishment," in *After Pluralism: Reimagining Religious Engagements*, ed. Courtney Bender and Pamela Klassen (New York: Columbia University Press, 2010), 82–97.

9. Courtney Bender, *The New Metaphysicals: Spirituality and the American Religious Imagination* (Chicago: University of Chicago Press, 2010).

10. Russ McCutcheon, *The Discipline of Religion: Structure, Meaning, Rhetoric* (New York: Routledge, 2003), i. McCutcheon cites the work of Robert Shepard, whose socio-rhetorical analysis of the religion departments at Harvard and Chicago suggests that these departments thrived because they took on the very advocacy language that they rejected from the Christian theology. Similar to Masuzawa's thinking, McCutcheon states that while Shepard's study is valuable, it does not go far enough in engaging with the social, political, and economic forces that create such departments:

> Although these various historic periods are hardly identical, in all three cases the public discourse on religion played a significant role in political life—significant enough in the instance from the sixteenth century to necessitate seeing battles over religious doctrine as if they were the primary or even exclusive motive force in history (e.g., what we commonly call the Wars of Religion or contemporary scholars who study the Reformation and church history as if they were purely doctrinal affairs). I am suggesting that it was not a coincidence that the contest over who policed the rhetoric of religion took place in early twentieth-century America, that comparative religion as a science was contemporaneous with the height of European colonialism, and that the realignment of political power we today call the Reformation took place on the eve of the nation-state's birth. Although I am not suggesting a strict cause/effect relationship, I am suggesting that the discourse on religion provided some of the necessary conditions for such socio-political changes.

See his *The Discipline of Religion: Structure, Meaning, Rhetoric* (New York and London: Routledge, 2003), 42. McCutcheon is arguing that when religion becomes part of public discourse, there are a number of ways we can and should study such religious rhetoric beyond its own internal logic.

11. Ibid., 103.

12. Sheila Davaney and José Ignacio Cabezón, eds., *Identity and the Politics of Scholarship in the Study of Religion* (New York: Routledge, 2004).

13. See *Authentic Fakes: Religion and American Popular Culture* (Berkeley: University of California Press, 2005); for his work in African religions, *Savage Systems: Colonialism and Comparative Religion in Southern Africa* (Charlottesville: University Press of Virginia, 1996); and more recently, *Empire of Religion: Imperialism and Comparative Religion* (Chicago: University of Chicago Press, 2013). John Strijdom, "'Colonialism' and 'Material Culture' in David Chidester's *Oeuvre*," *Religion and Theology* 23, nos. 3-4 (2016): 386-402, provides an excellent overview.

14. Gary Laderman, *Sacred Matters: Celebrity Worship, Sexual Ecstasies, the Living Dead, and Other Signs of Religious Life in the United States* (New York: New Press, 2010).

15. Robert Orsi, "Snakes Alive: Religious Studies between Heaven and Earth," in Orsi, *Between Heaven and Earth: The Religious Worlds People Make and the Scholars Who Study Them* (Princeton: Princeton University Press, 2007), 177-204.

16. Ibid., 202.

17. Stephen Prothero, "Belief Unbracketed: A Case for the Religion Scholar to Reveal More of Where He or She Is Coming From," *Harvard Divinity Bulletin* 32, no. 2 (Winter/Spring 2004): 16-18.

18. Bender and Klassen, *After Pluralism*, 11-12.

19. See John Dewey's formulation of "things in their complex entanglements", and the enlightening discussion by Bender in *The New Metaphysics*, 5-7. Also see Nathan Schneider's interview of Bender in *The Immanent Frame*, June 21, 2010, https://tif.ssrc.org/2010/06/01/spirituality-entangled/ (accessed July 29, 2018). Dewey's original idea is based in a pragmatic epistemology, whereby the relationship between the knower and the known in its constantly changing, mutually modifying form was called "an entangled relation." John Dewey and Arthur Bentley, *Knowing and the Known* (1949), vol. 16 of *John Dewey: The Later Works, 1952-1953*, edited by Jo Ann Boydston (Carbondale and Edwardsville: Southern Illinois University Press, 1989).

20. As stated in the introduction, there are many aspects of the real-world entanglements that deserve further study beyond the beginning sketches of this book: institutional contexts and histories, personal experiences, and autobiographies, just to name a few.

21. Interview by Craig Martin, *Bulletin for the Study of Religion* blog, http://bulletin.equinoxpub.com/2015/11/genealogies-of-religion-twenty-years-on-an-interview-with-talal-asad/ (accessed July 15, 2018).

22. Excellent assessments of these traditions of thought can be found in Nick Crossley and John Michael Roberts, *After Habermas: New Perspectives on the Public Sphere* (Oxford: Blackwell, 2004); and Kate Nash, ed., *Transnationalizing the Public Sphere* (Cambridge, UK, and Malden, MA: Polity Press, 2014). Most importantly, I draw from the thinking of Herrera Lima, Pensky, McCarthy, Calhoun, and Butler in these most recent works: Craig Calhoun, Eduardo Mendieta, and Jonathan Van Antwerpen, eds., *Habermas and Religion* (Cambridge, UK: Polity Press, 2013); and Eduardo Mendieta and Jonathan Van Antwerpen, eds., *The Power of Religion in the Public Sphere* (New York: Columbia University Press, 2011).

23. Talal Asad, Wendy Brown, Judith Butler, and Saba Mahmood, *Is Critique Secular? Blasphemy, Injury, and Free Speech* (New York: Fordham University Press, 2009).

24. José Casanova, "Exploring the Postsecular: Three Meanings of 'the Secular' and Their Possible Transcendence," in Calhoun, Mendieta, and VanAntwerpen, *Habermas and Religion*, 27–48; Calhoun, Mendieta, and VanAntwerpen, "Editors' Introduction," in ibid., 5.

25. Thomas Tweed, *Crossing and Dwelling* (Cambridge, MA: Harvard University Press, 2008), 54.

26. Ibid., 152.

27. Jonathan Harmon and James W. Boettcher, eds., "Religion and the Public Sphere," special issue, *Philosophy & Social Criticism* 35, nos. 1–2 (2009).

28. Wendy Steiner, *The Scandal of Pleasure* (Chicago: University of Chicago Press, 1995), 123.

29. But in all this blooming confusion, in the late twentieth century, the secular study of religion was alive and kicking. If we define the secular study of religion by the number of undergraduates enrolled in religion courses, or by the number of PhDs in the field, there was a marked increase in the late 1990s and early 2000s in both areas. At the turn of the century, religious studies accounted for 1/20th of the majors in the country and offered 38 percent of the courses in any given semester's curriculum. In doctoral programs, whereas a very low percentage of departments offered courses in non-Christian traditions three decades ago, 59 percent offer courses in Buddhism, 49 percent offer courses in Hinduism, and 49 percent offer courses in Islam. Even more intriguingly, such tradition-specific courses in religions other than Christianity are on the whole 20 percent more frequently offered at public and private, nonsectarian universities and colleges than they are at Catholic and Protestant institutions. If such courses define the secular study of religion, religious studies grew in this period. "Religion and Theology Programs Census," *Religious Studies News*, Fall 2001, https://www.aarweb.org/sites/default/files/pdfs/Programs_Services/Survey_Data/Undergraduate/RSNAARCensus1.pdf (accessed March 12, 2019), ii. Now these statistics could be evidence, perhaps, of a certain kind of decadence—the kind of intellectual society that thrives on decay, the last efflorescence of an organism. Or, given the recent declines in the number of humanities majors overall, the study of religion might resemble James, one of the main characters in Elizabeth McCracken's fine first novel, *The Giant's House* (1996). James is an adolescent boy who grows a foot each year and quietly knows that because of his gargantuan growth, he is going to die soon. Perhaps, as a relatively new field, the study of religion is in that kind of adolescent overdrive that can lead to death. Or perhaps many of the early twenty-first-century trends in higher enrollment in religion classes could simply be due to the aftereffects of 9/11 and the vague public sense that people do very extreme things for ostensibly religious reasons.

30. It is therefore enlightening to turn to the anthropology of scandal—the context of the cases before us in this book. Max Gluckman's early paper on the Makah people

of the Northwestern Plateau gives us some important ways with which to begin think-ing ("Papers in Honor of Melville J. Herskovits: Gossip and Scandal," *Current Anthro-pology* 4, no. 3 [June 1963]: 307–16]. As he writes, citing Elizabeth Colson, "specific and restricted gossip within a group makes it different from other groups, both like and unlike." The gossip and scandal that are so biting in Makah life unite them into a group outside of general American society. And since this gossip and scandal involve the criticism and assessment of people against traditional values of Makah society, they maintain the tribe as Indians against whites and as Makah against other Indians: "To be a Makah, you must be able to join in the gossip, and to be fully a Makah you must be able to scandalize skillfully." Moreover, in Makah society, the biting gossip is used to maintain the principle of equality of all members. The group is too small to sustain any division of status within itself. Some old traditions and present ambitions drive individuals to assert themselves. They establish Makah superiority through the weapon of scandal, which in practice keeps them equal. Scandalizing is one of the principal means by which the group's separateness is expressed, though it is also the principal manner in which internal struggles are fought.

31. While the Makah case is particularly helpful in thinking about scandals and identity politics, Gluckman's perspectives on scandalizing can only tell us some things about group formation. There is a larger pattern to scandal studied by some sociolo-gists that may also be useful. As Gary Fine writes, "Scandal seems to appear suddenly, from the ether, a chance occurrence that moral entrepreneurs seize for their own ends": "Scandal, Social Conditions, and the Creation of Public Attention: Fatty Ar-buckle and the 'Problem of Hollywood,'" *Social Problems* 44, no. 3 (August 1997): 297.

32. Ibid.

33. Following Smelser, Fine takes up a less well known approach to scandal by examining how the structures and organizational maps of institutions permit or dampen collective action. Neil J. Smelser, *Theory of Collective Behavior* (New York: Free Press, 1962) and "Some Personal Thoughts on the Pursuit of Sociological Prob-lems," *Sociological Inquiry* 39 (1969): 155–67.

34. Jerry M. Lewis, "Comedy and Deviance: The Fatty Arbuckle Case," in *Mar-ginal Conventions: Popular Culture, Mass Media and Social Deviance*, ed. Clinton R. Sanders (Bowling Green, OH: Bowling Green State University Popular Press, 1990), 18–28.

35. Clark McPhail, *The Myth of the Madding Crowd* (New York: Aldine, 1991).

36. While Fine's work is focused on Hollywood and the case of Fatty Arbuckle, whose alleged violence against a young woman caused her death and led to an ex-posé of the wayward ways of 1920s Hollywood, the parallels between Hollywood and the academy are certainly present.

37. Alexander C. Kafka, "Sokal Squared," *Chronicle of Higher Education*, Oc-tober 3, 2018, https://www.chronicle.com/article/Sokal-Squared-Is-Huge/244714 (accessed October 5, 2018).

38. Ron Robin, *Scandals and Scoundrels: Seven Cases That Shook the Academy* (Berkeley: University of California Press, 2004), ix.

39. Ibid., x.

40. Robin writes in his introduction about previous controversies, such as that of the Sisson documents, where well-known academics pronounced "authentic" a set of fraudulent documents purporting to connect Bolshevik and German operations in World War I. He remarks that these ended nonviolently and mildly: the offenders were censored, and the profession's integrity was defended. And then the controversy disappeared from view. Ibid., 3–4.

41. We might think of the dilemma in terms of Michael Walzer's historical study of four categories of religious tolerance: resignation, indifference, curiosity, and enthusiasm. Walzer is interested in the broader categories of cultural elaboration, voluntary associations, and religious differences, and since many of our cases flow in between these designations, his work is helpful to us here. Most of the authors discussed in this book would fall into the category of curious or enthusiastic tolerators, or perhaps, in certain cases, indifferent tolerators, under the banner of historical objectivity or phenomenological epoche. And yet they find themselves in the paradox whereby the reciprocal tolerance of their readers cannot be guaranteed. Michael Walzer, "The Politics of Difference: Statehood and Toleration in a Multicultural World," *Ratio Juris* 10, no. 2 (June 1997): 165–76.

42. Ibid., 172.

43. Robin, *Scandals and Scoundrels*, 6.

44. Robin's focus is on the fields of history and anthropology—two foci that will be relevant to us in this book as well. He ranges from the unmasking of Margaret Mead to the debunking of the Tasaday in anthropology, and from the challenging of Joseph Ellis's persona as a Vietnam war veteran to the critique of Michael Bellesiles's use of evidence for the absence of a gun culture in the United States. In thinking about the meaning of these scandals, Robin posits, I think rightly, that the scandal serves to open up fissures that it may not be able to close—about fields poised between textual analysis and science, the public obligations of anthropology, and the role of the media in dictating the academic agenda. Ibid., 221.

45. Ibid., 223–24, 227.

46. Ibid., 32, 23.

47. Gilbert Ryle introduced this concept in a 1968 essay, where he writes that "to wink is to try to signal to someone in particular, without the cognisance of others, a definite message according to an already understood code." See "The Thinking of Thoughts: What Is 'Le Penseur' Doing?" in Ryle, *Collected Essays, 1929–1968* (London: Routledge, 2009), 494–510. Clifford Geertz made the concept famous in his essay "Thick Description," which makes a case that the best ethnography involves describing everyday reality, the motivations and intentions of speakers, and the ways in which those thoughts and actions are understood by the rest of the community. Attention to such detail renders our descriptions thick, and not thin. See "Thick Description: Toward an Interpretive Theory of Culture," in Geertz, *The Interpretation of Cultures: Selected Essays* (New York: Basic Books, 1973), 3–30. In a way, *Who Owns Religion?* asks a version of Ryle's question—"What are *our* Penseurs

doing in the study of religion?"—and follows Alessandro Duranti's compelling questions about the relationship between intent and effect in his *The Anthropology of Intentions: Language in a World of Others* (Cambridge: Cambridge University Press, 2015).

48. We might point to a salient example from film, when Robert Mitchum became involved in a scandal right at the end of the period when Ingrid Bergman was having a child out of wedlock. Mitchum survived because he was already understood to be the "bad boy" onscreen, whereas Bergman had a kind of wholesomeness in her roles that rendered her more vulnerable to scandal. In starker, more gendered terms, a man could be excused, but a woman could not. See James Damico, "Ingrid from Lorraine to Stromboli: Analyzing the Public's Perception of a Film Star," in *Star Texts: Image and Performance in Film and Television*, ed. Jeremy Butler (Detroit: Wayne State University Press, 1991), 240–54.

49. See Sumathi Ramaswamy, ed., *Barefoot across the Nation: Maqbool Fida Husain and the Idea of India* (New York: Routledge, 2011).

50. René Girard, *I See Satan Fall like Lightning* (Maryknoll, NY: Orbis, 2001); see particularly "Scandal Must Come," 7–18, 16 quoted.

51. Ibid., 16.

52. Ibid., 17.

53. Like Girard, Jordan approaches scandal as a disputed question that oddly enough can break open into truth-telling. More often than not, however, the disputed question breaks instead into scandal, and the subsequent "reform" of an institution, both of which, in Jordan's view, cover up the truth of the lived relationship. When discussing Bernardino's sermons against homosexuality, Jordan shows how Bernardino's admission of "sodomite" clerics surrounds the whole subject with scandal—a scandal that silences more disruptive truth, both about who the sodomite really isn't and about what institutions really are. Mark Jordan, *Telling Truths in Church: Scandal, Flesh, and Christian Speech* (Boston: Beacon Press, 2003).

54. Ibid., 47ff.

55. The scandals of Robert Clive and Warren Hastings were examples of the misconduct of the British Empire, but in the end, these controversies, especially that of Hastings, served to strengthen the empire. For Nicholas Dirks, in the case of these wayward entrepreneurs, the reform was conducted precisely so that the venality and corruption attached to their particular interests could be transformed into national interests. Scandal is, in Dirks's view, constitutive for empire, in which it is used as a cover to investigate what emerged as the normal and legitimate enterprise of empire. Scandals were a blot on the moral justifications of imperial activity and needed to be expunged from the record. In the aftermath of Hastings's trial, the attention "shifted" from colonizer to colonized. The locus for scandal moved from slavery, the custom of the colonizer, to the customs of the colonized, particularly *sati*, or the practice of self-immolation of widows on their husband's funeral pyre. See Dirks, *Scandal of Empire: India and the Creation of Imperial Britain* (Cambridge, MA: Belknap Press of Harvard University Press, 2008).

56. Steven M. Wasserstrom, *Religion after Religion: Gershom Scholem, Mircea Eliade, and Henry Corbin at Eranos* (Princeton: Princeton University Press, 1999), 101–2.

57. Ibid., 103, quoting Cynthia Ozick, "The Fourth Sparrow: The Magical Reach of Gershon Scholem," in her *Art and Ardor* (New York: E. P. Dutton, 1893), 178.

58. Ibid.

59. Mircea Eliade, *Shamanism: Archaic Techniques of Ecstasy*, trans. Willard R. Trask (New York: Bollingen Foundation, 1964), 511.

60. Wasserstrom, *Religion*, 106n46.

61. Wasserstrom's idea may be related to the gnosis that Jeffrey Kripal also writes of in *The Serpent and the Gift*. It is the gnosis in which historians of religion frequently participate, which he defines as a "form of intuitive, visionary, or mystical knowledge that privileges the primacy of personal experience and the depths of the self traditionally in order to acquire some form of liberation or salvation from a world seen as corrupt or fallen." Kripal, *The Serpent's Gift* (Chicago: University of Chicago Press, 2007), 4. The positionality of these two scholars is in real contrast, however: Wasserstrom writes of this as a form of cultural critique; Kripal writes of it experientially and more positively.

62. Ibid., 106–7.

CHAPTER TWO

1. Nancy Fraser, "Rethinking the Public Sphere" *Social Text* 25/26 (1990): 56–80.

2. Oskar Negt and Alexander Kluge, *Public Sphere and Experience: Toward an Analysis of the Bourgeois and Proletarian Public Sphere*, trans. Peter Labanyi (Minneapolis: University of Minnesota Press, 1993).

3. Ibid., 125.

4. John Rawls, "The Idea of the Public Revisited," *University of Chicago Law Review* 64 (1997): 765–807, rpt. in *The Idea of the Public Sphere: A Reader*, ed. Jostein Gripsrud et al. (Lanham, MD: Lexington Books, 2010), 222.

5. Ibid., 223.

6. William Connolly, *The Ethos of Pluralization* (Minneapolis: University of Minnesota Press), 1995.

7. Nancy Fraser, *Unruly Practices: Power, Discourse, and Gender in Contemporary Social Theory* (Minneapolis: University of Minnesota Press and Polity Press, 1989).

8. Nancy Fraser, *Redistribution or Recognition? A Political-Philosophical Exchange* (London: Verso, 2003); see also her *Scales of Justice: Reimagining Political Space in a Globalizing World* (Cambridge: Polity Press, 2008). As well, see her succinct statement of these principles in Nancy Fraser, "Rethinking the Public Sphere: A Contribution to the Critique of Actually Existing Democracy," *Social Text* 25/26 (1990): 56–80, rpt. in *The Idea of the Public Sphere: A Reader*, ed. Jostein Gripsrud et al. (Lanham, MD: Lexington Books, 2010), 127–48.

9. Fraser, "Rethinking," 141–42.

10. Ibid., 145.

11. Nancy Fraser, "Transnationalizing the Public Sphere: On the Legitimacy and Efficacy of Public Opinion in a Post-Westphalian World," in *Transnationalizing the Public Sphere*, ed. Kate Nash (Cambridge, UK, and Malden, MA: Polity Press, 2014), 8–42.

12. Kate Nash, "Toward Transnational Democratization?" in Nash, *Transnationalizing the Public Sphere*, 65.

13. Ibid.

14. Michael Walzer, "The Politics of Difference: Statehood and Toleration in a Multicultural World," *Ratio Juris* 10, no. 2 (June 1997): 165–76.

15. See María Herrera Lima, "The Anxiety of Contingency: Religion in a Secular Age," in Calhoun, Mendieta, and VanAntwerpen, *Habermas and Religion*, 54–55.

16. Thomas McCarthy, "The Burdens of Modernized Faith and Postmetaphysical Reason in Habermas's 'Unfinished Project of Enlightenment,'" in Calhoun, Mendieta, and VanAntwerpen, *Habermas and Religion*, 128; Calhoun, Mendieta, and VanAntwerpen, "Editors' Introduction," in ibid., 13.

17. Following Pensky, one imperfect form of translation into the public sphere is to bring to attention a sense of "what, not just who" is missing. Max Pensky, "Solidarity with the Past and the Work of Translation: Reflections on Memory Politics and the Post-secular," in Calhoun, Mendieta, and VanAntwerpen, *Habermas and Religion*, 301–21; Calhoun, Mendieta, and VanAntwerpen, "Editors' Introduction," 20.

18. McCarthy, "The Burdens of Modernized Faith," 116.

19. See J. M. Bernstein, "Forgetting Isaac: Faith and the Philosophical Impossibility of a Postsecular Society," in Calhoun, Mendieta, and VanAntwerpen, *Habermas and Religion*, 154–78; and Calhoun, Mendieta, and VanAntwerpen, "Editors' Introduction," 14.

20. See James Bohman, "A Postsecular Global Order? The Pluralism of Forms of Life and Communicative Freedom," in Calhoun, Mendieta, and VanAntwerpen, *Habermas and Religion*, 179–202; Calhoun, Mendieta, and VanAntwerpen, "Editors' Introduction," 16.

21. Talal Asad, "Freedom of Speech and Religious Limitation," in *Rethinking Secularism*, ed. Craig Calhoun, Mark Juergensmeyer, and Jonathan VanAntwerpen (New York: Oxford University Press), 288.

22. As Arnold Davidson puts it in an essay on historiography and the uses of evidence, "There is no formalizable set of rules that tells us how to decipher historical evidence . . . , but there are truly great historical works whose power partly resides in the ability of a historian to read the evidence, to show us how to enter into the codes of evidence in order to see what the evidence is, what it shows us about the phenomena we are interested in, what the phenomena are." See Davidson, "Carlo Ginzburg and the Renewal of Historiography," in *Questions of Evidence: Proof, Practice, and Persuasion across the Disciplines*, ed. James Chandler, Arnold I. Davidson, and Harry Hartounian (Chicago: University of Chicago Press, 1994), 314.

23. "Our Mission," National Council on Public History http://www.ncph.org (accessed August 31, 2016).

24. Ludmilla Jordanova, *History in Practice* (London: Arnold Publishers, 2000), 155.

25. V. N. Narayana Rao, personal communication, November 21, 2003.

26. Roger Friedland, "Money, Sex, and God: The Erotic Logic of Religious Nationalism," *Sociological Theory* 203 (2002): 381–425. See also Sikata Banerjee, *Make Me a Man! Masculinity, Hinduism, and Nationalism in India* (Albany: State University of New York Press, 2005).

27. Kirk A. Bingaman, *Freud and Faith: Living in the Tension* (Albany: State University of New York Press, 2003), 143.

28. Rogers Brubaker, "Religion and Nationalism: Four Approaches," *Nations and Nationalism* 18, no. 1 (2012): 19. See also Mark Juergensmeyer, *The New Cold War? Religious Nationalism Confronts the Secular State* (Berkeley: University of California Press, 1993).

29. Laurent Gayer, "The Globalization of Identity Politics: The Sikh Experience," May 2002, Centres d'Etudes et Recherches Internationales, https://www.science spo.fr/ceri/sites/sciencespo.fr.ceri/files/artlg_0.pdf, (accessed March 19, 2019), 36.

30. The theme of biblical hermeneutics in colonial and postcolonial contexts is also quite relevant in this present postcolonial global environment. Frequently, comparisons between the protestations of a minority community about the interpretation of their scripture and those of Christians about the Bible are seen as odious and condescending. Members of the minority communities often take scholars to be saying that "biblical hermeneutics went through it all, and it is now being reenacted with nonbiblical traditions of the formerly colonized, who, after all, have their scriptures, too." This is not what scholars usually mean when they make these comparisons; as the Schwartz case makes clear, biblical hermeneutics has never entirely freed itself from controversy. Moreover, hermeneutic scandals existed in all of the nonbiblical traditions long before the colonizing West started to describe them. The comparison between biblical scandals and present-day postcolonial ones is instructive and useful for serious thinkers about these issues because, as discussed earlier in this chapter, the question of secularity and the claims of secular study now stand front and center for all traditions, and at closer range than ever before.

31. Brian Axel's *The Nation's Tortured Body* (Durham: Duke University Press, 2001) also discusses this issue of the Sikh diaspora community being created through the internet; also see Rohit Chopra's forthcoming work on Indian internet nationalism in *History and Theory*.

CHAPTER THREE

1. Charles Taylor, "The Politics of Recognition," in *Multiculturalism: Examining the Politics of Recognition*, ed. Amy Gutmann (Princeton: Princeton University Press, 1994), 5.

2. James Beckford, *Religion and Advanced Industrial Society* (London: Unwin Hyman, 1989), 170–72.

3. David Morley and Kevin Robins, *Spaces of Identity: Global Media, Electronic Landscapes and Cultural Boundaries* (London and New York: Routledge, 1995) 44.

4. Frederick S. Lane, *The Decency Wars: The Campaign to Cleanse American Culture* (Amherst, NY: Prometheus Books, 2006), 160–68.

5. Ibid., 182–93.

6. Lane's argument in *Decency Wars* is that this combination led to a warped public discourse and gave a disproportionate amount of attention and legitimacy to religious conservatives' concerns in the 1980s, in the 1990s, and now in the twenty-first century.

7. Lane attacked the Christian right's role in the culture wars as being dangerous because of the idea that followers of Christian evangelical religion wished to impose their values, through the formation of public policy, on everyone else. He writes, "The decision of what to believe and which deity to embrace is an intensely personal decision, one in which government should have little interest and an even smaller role." Lane goes on, "Faith and religious values have an important role to play in American society, but not in the formation of its laws or the administration of its government." As a counterpoint to this trend, Lane argues for an expansion of the definition of "decency," making public education our next major intellectual project, and fostering a true marketplace of ideas in which the power of the FCC is minimized. Ibid., 289.

8. I am particularly persuaded by Barbara A. McGraw's description of the two-tiered public forum, and her distinction between the civic public forum, which involves both rights and responsibilities in the legal realm, and the conscientious public forum, which is the forum for persuasion and voluntary acceptance. See *Rediscovering America's Sacred Ground: Public Religion and Pursuit of the Good in Pluralistic America* (Albany: State University of New York Press, 2003), 17.

9. K. Anthony Appiah, *The Ethics of Identity* (Princeton: Princeton University Press, 2005), 162; Appiah, "Multiculturalism," in *Multiculturalism and the Politics of Recognition*, ed. Amy Gutmann (Princeton: Princeton University Press, 1994), 149–64.

10. Appiah, *The Ethics of Identity*, 163.

11. Linda Alcoff, *Visible Identities: Race, Gender, and the Self* (New York: Oxford University Press, 2006), 80.

12. See, for example, Lance Bennett and Robert Entman, eds. *Mediated Politics: Communication in the Future of Democracy* (Cambridge: Cambridge University Press, 2001); Lance Bennett and Alexandra Segerberg, eds., *The Logic of Connective Action: Digital Media and the Personalization of Contentious Politics* (Cambridge: Cambridge University Press, 2013); James Bohman, "Expanding Dialogue: the Internet, the Public Sphere, and Prospects for Transnational Democracy," in *The Idea of the Public Sphere: A Reader*, ed. Jostein Gripsrud, Hallvard Moe, Anders Molander, and Graham Murdock (Lanham, MD: Lexington Books, 2010), 247–69, also published in *After Habermas: New Perspectives on the Public Sphere*, ed. John Michael Roberts and Nick Crossley (Oxford: Blackwell, 2004), 131–56; Jean Camp and Y. T. Chien, "The Internet as Public Space: Concepts, Issues and Implications in Public Policy," *ACM SIGCAS Computers and Society* 30, no. 3 (September 2000): 13–19.

13. Bohman, "Expanding Dialogue," 249–50.

14. Ibid., 251.

15. Ibid. Bohman and others are clear that corporate or governmental control over the internet is a real issue in how this new set of public spheres might get redefined.

16. Anastasia Karaflogka, "Religious Discourse and Cyberspace," *Religion* 32, no. 4 (October 2002): 279–91. See also her *E-religion: A Critical Appraisal of Religious Discourse on the World Wide Web* (New York: Routledge, 2014), 162.

17. Nicole Stenger, "The Mind Is a Leaking Rainbow," in Michael Benedikt, *Cyberspace: First Steps* (Cambridge, MA, and London: MIT Press, 1991), 48–57, quoting Paul Virilio ("instants"), Eliade, and Lance Strate ("eternal presence"). See also Virilio, "Speed and Information: Cyberspace Alarm!" *CTheory*, article A030, August 27, 1995, http://www.ctheory.net/articles.aspx?id=72 (accessed March 12, 2019); and Strate, "Cybertime," in *Communication and Cyberspace: Social Interaction in an Electronic Environment*, ed. Ronald L. Jacobson and Stephanie Gibson (Cresskill, NJ: Hampton Press, 2003), 370–81.

18. Manuel Castells, *The Information Age: Economy, Society, and Culture*, vol. 1, *The Rise of the Network Society* (Oxford: Blackwell, 1996), 433.

19. Lev Manovich, *The Language of New Media* (Cambridge, MA: MIT Press, 2001), 76–77.

20. Rob Shields, "Hypertext Links: The Ethic of the Index and Its Space-Time Effects," in *The World Wide Web and Contemporary Cultural Theory*, ed. Andrew Herman and Thomas Swiss (New York and London: Routledge, 2000), 150.

21. Karaflogka, *E-religion*, 163.

22. See also Brenda Brasher, *Give Me That Online Religion* (New Brunswick, NJ: Rutgers University Press, 2004), esp. "A Taste of Forever: Cyberspace as Sacred Time," 48–67.

23. Ibid., 46–50, 23 (quoted).

24. Uma Narayan, *Dislocating Cultures: Identities, Traditions, and Third World Feminism* (New York: Routledge: 1997), 13–16. While Narayan uses "third world," the term appropriate to that time, many scholars have since replaced the term with "Global South."

25. Ibid., 126.

26. Ibid., 129.

27. Ibid., 136.

28. Also see Rajesh Rai and Chitra Sankaran, "Religion and South Asian Diaspora," *South Asian Diaspora* 3, no. 2 (March 2011): 5–13.

29. Narayan, *Dislocating Cultures*, 143.

30. Philip E. Devine, *Human Diversity and the Culture Wars: A Philosophical Perspective on Contemporary Cultural Conflict* (New York: Praeger, 1996), 57.

31. Rico Lie, *Spaces of Intercultural Communication: An Interdisciplinary Introduction to Communication, Culture, and Globalizing/Localizing Identities*, IAMCR book series (New York: Hampton Press, 2003).

32. For the locus classicus of this idea, also written during our period, see Kimberlé Crenshaw, "Demarginalizing the Intersection of Race and Sex: A Black Feminist

Critique of Antidiscrimination Doctrine, Feminist Theory and Antiracist Politics," *University of Chicago Legal Forum* 1989, no. 1, 139–67. More recently, also see Deborah Orr et al., eds., *Feminist Politics: Identity, Difference, and Agency* (Lanham, MD: Rowman & Littlefield, 2007).

33. Amartya Sen, *Identity and Violence: The Illusion of Destiny* (New York: W. W. Norton, 2006), 18ff.

CHAPTER FOUR

1. W. C. Smith, *The Meaning and End of Religion* (Minneapolis, MN: Fortress Press, 1991), 43.

2. W. C. Smith, *The Modernisation of a Traditional Society* (Bombay: Asia Publishing House, 1965), 2–3.

3. W. C. Smith, *Pakistan as an Islamic State* (Lahore: Kashmiri Bazar, 1951), 103.

4. W. C. Smith, *Islam in Modern History* (Princeton: Princeton University Press, 1959), 300.

5. Ibid., 301.

6. W. C. Smith, *The Faith of Other Men* (Boston: Dutton Adult, 1963); the seven lectures in the series were broadcast in 1962.

7. W. C. Smith, review of *The Middle East: Its Religion and Culture*, by Edward J. Jurji. *Canadian Journal of Theology* 4, no. 1 (1959): 69.

8. W. C. Smith, "Director's Address," *Harvard Divinity School Newsletter*, September 1964, 10–16, 12 quoted.

9. W. C. Smith, "Orientalism and Truth," public lecture in honor of T. Cuyler Young, 1969, Harvard Divinity School Faculty Writings File, bMS 13001/Smith, W. C.: Writings of Wilfred Cantwell Smith.

10. W. C. Smith, "The Theology of Religions: Participation as a Possible Concept for a Theology of the Religious History of Mankind," paper submitted for discussion to the Annual Meeting of the American Theological Society, New York, January 1969, Harvard Divinity School Faculty Writings File, bMS 13001/Smith, W. C., box 2, 18.

11. Ibid., 18, 20.

12. Ibid., 32.

13. W. C. Smith, "Secularity and the History of Religion," in *The Spirit and Power of Christian Secularity*, ed. Albert Schlitzer (South Bend, IN: University of Notre Dame Press, 1969), 50.

14. Ibid.

15. W. C. Smith, "Faith as a Universal Human Quality," Bea Lecture, Woodstock College, New York City, March 18, 1971, Harvard Divinity School Faculty Writings File, bMS 13001/Smith, W. C., box 2, 25.

16. Smith, "Secularity and the History of Religion," 54.

17. W. C. Smith, memo to Krister Stendahl, private correspondence, CSWR archives, 1975.

18. Smith, *The Modernisation of a Traditional Society*, 24.

19. Ibid., 35.

20. Ibid.

21. Ibid., 40.

22. Ibid.

23. Ibid., 42.

24. W. C. Smith, "The Place of Oriental Studies in a Western University," *Diogenes* 4, no. 16 (Winter 1956): 105.

25. Ibid., 109.

26. W. C. Smith, *The Role of Asian Studies in the American University*, plenary address, New York State Conference for Asian Studies, Colgate University, October 11, 1975 (Hamilton, NY: Fund for the Study of the Great Religions of the World, Colgate University, 1976), 7. In this lecture, Smith also renounces the "modernization" theory of the twentieth century—describing it, at its worst, as cruel.

27. W. C. Smith, "1983 Presidential Address: The Modern West in the History of Religion," *Journal of the American Academy of Religion* 52, no. 1 (March 1984): 17.

28. Relatedly, in this and other lectures, W. C. Smith resists the idea that any theology should "belong" to a particular religion without engagement with other religious traditions.

29. W. C. Smith, memorandum to D. S. Kothari, August 27, 1965, W. C. Smith Papers, Oviatt Library, California State University, Northridge, 16.

30. Ibid, 19.

31. Ibid., 20.

32. Ibid., 21.

33. Ibid., 22.

34. W. C. Smith, *Modern Culture from a Comparative Perspective*, ed. John W. Burbidge (Albany: State University of New York Press, 1997), 94.

35. Ibid.

36. Ibid.

37. Ibid., 95–96.

38. Ibid., 97.

39. Jonathan Herman, "Who Cares if the Qur'an is the Word of God? W. C. Smith's Charge to the Aspiring Public intellectual," in *The Legacy of Wilfred Cantwell Smith*, ed. Ellen Bradshaw Aitken and Arvind Sharma (Albany: State University of New York Press, 2017), 126.

40. Moshe Idel, "The Camouflaged Sacred in Mircea Eliade's Self Perception, Literature, and Scholarship," in *Hermeneutics, Politics, and the History of Religions*, ed. Christian K. Wedemeyer and Wendy Doniger (New York: Oxford University Press, 2010), 160; Mircea Handoca, *Mircea Eliade: Contributii bibliografice* (Bucharest: Romanian Relief Literary Society, 1980).

41. By Bryan Rennie: "An Encounter with Eliade" and "The Life and Works of Mircea Eliade," in *Encounters with Mircea Eliade*, ed. Mihaela Gligor and Mac Linscott Ricketts (Cluj-Napoca: Casa Cărţii de Ştiinţă, 2005), 199–202, 203–16; "Mircea Eliade: A Secular Mystic in the History of Religions?" *Origini: Journal of Cultural*

286 NOTES TO PAGES 98–101

Studies 3/4 (2003): 42–54; "Mircea Eliade: 'Secular Mysticism' and the History of Religions," *Religion* 38, no. 4 (2008): 328–37. By Mac Linscott Ricketts: *Mircea Eliade: The Romanian Roots, 1907–1945*, vol. 1 (New York: Columbia University Press, 1988); "Fate in the *Forbidden Forest*," *Dialogue* 8 (1982): 101–19; "On Reading Eliade's Stories as Myths for Moderns," paper presented at the Midwestern Modern Language Association, Cincinnati, Ohio, 1982; translation of Eliade's novel *The Forbidden Forest* (Notre Dame, IN: University of Notre Dame Press, 1978); "The United States' Response to Eliade's Fiction," in *Changing Religious Worlds: The Meaning and End of Mercea Eliade*, ed. Bryan Rennie (Albany: State University of New York Press, 2001), 79–94.

42. See the excellent essays in Christian Wedemeyer and Wendy Doniger, eds., *Hermeneutics, Politics, and the History of Religions: The Contested Legacies of Joachim Wach and Mircea Eliade* (Oxford: Oxford University Press, 2010); Joseph Frank, *Responses to Modernity: Essays in The Politics of Culture* (New York: Fordham University Press, 2012), especially the chapter "Eliade, Cioran, Ionescu: The Treason of the Intellectuals," 136–56; Bruce Lincoln, *Theorizing Myth: Scholarship, Ideology, and Narrative* (Chicago: University of Chicago Press, 1999), in particular "From the Second World War to the Present (and Possibly a Little Beyond)," 141–58. See also Marta Petreu, *An Infamous Past: E. M. Cioran and the Rise of Fascism in Romania*, trans. Bogdan Aldea (Chicago: Ivan R. Dee, 2005); Adriana Berger, "Mircea Eliade: Romanian Fascism and the History of Religions in the United States," in *Tainted Greatness: Antisemitism and Cultural Heroes*, ed. Nancy Harrowitz (Philadelphia: Temple University Press, 1994) 51–74; Norman Manea, "Happy Guilt: Mircea Eliade, Fascism, and the Unhappy Fate of Romania," *New Republic*, August 5, 1991, 27–36; "The Incompatibilities," *New Republic*, April 20, 1998, 32–37.

43. Mac Linscott Ricketts, translator's preface to Mircea Eliade, *Autobiography*, vol. 2 (Chicago: University of Chicago Press, 1988), xiii.

44. Mircea Eliade, *Autobiography*, vol. 1 (Chicago: University of Chicago Press, 1981), 138.

45. Ibid. 1:224.

46. Ibid.

47. Ibid. 1:226.

48. Ibid. 1:236–37.

49. Ibid.

50. Ibid. 1:282.

51. Ibid. 1:291.

52. Mircea Eliade, *Autobiography* (Chicago: University of Chicago Press, 1988), 2:73.

53. Ibid. 2:114.

54. See, for example, his discussions of the receptions of his translations in ibid. 2:168, 171, 174.

55. Ibid. 2:148.

56. Ibid. 2:168.

57. Ibid. 2:114.

58. Ibid. 2:125.

59. Mircea Eliade, "Critics Corner," *Theology Today* 24, no. 3 (1967): 385.

60. Mircea Eliade, "History of Religions and a New Humanism: The history of religious meanings must always be regarded as forming part of the history of the human spirit," *Criterion* 1, no. 2 (Summer 1962): 9.

61. Ibid., 9.

62. Ibid., 9–10.

63. Ibid., 8–9.

64. Delia O'Hara, "Mircea Eliade: Some Last Thoughts . . . ," interview, *Chicago*, June 1986, 151.

65. Eliade, "Europe, Asia, America, Corespondenta," Corespondenta A-H, 112 (Idel's translation from the original), quoted in Moshe Idel, "The Camouflaged Sacred in Mircea Eliade's Self-Perception, Literature, and Scholarship," in Wedemeyer and Doniger, *Hermeneutics, Politics, and the History of Religions*, 186.

66. Mac Linscott Ricketts. *Mircea Eliade: The Romanian Roots, 1907–1945*, vol. 1 (New York: Columbia University Press, 1988), 464.

67. Idel, "Camouflaged Sacred," 188ff.

68. Eliade, *Autobiography*, 2:258.

69. Ibid.

70. Ibid., 70–76.

71. Anne Mocko, "Tracing the Red Thread: Anti-Communist Themes in the Work of Mircea Eliade," in Wedemeyer and Doniger, *Hermeneutics, Politics, and the History of Religions*, 293.

72. Ibid., 299.

73. O'Hara, "Mircea Eliade," 179.

74. Ibid., 180.

75. Steven M. Wasserstrom, *Religion after Religion: Gershom Scholem, Mircea Eliade, and Henry Corbin at Eranos* (Princeton: Princeton University Press, 1999), 241.

76. Ibid., 242.

77. Ibid.

78. Ibid., 235.

79. Mircea Eliade, "Cultural Fashions and the History of Religions," in *The History of Religions: Essays on the Problem of Understanding*, ed. Joseph M. Kitagawa (Chicago: University of Chicago Press, 1967), 21.

80. Ibid., 22.

81. Ibid.

82. Ibid., 31.

83. Ibid., 32.

84. Mircea Eliade, "The Occult and the Modern World," in Eliade, *Occultism, Witchcraft, and Cultural Fashions: Essays in Comparative Religion* (Chicago: University of Chicago Press, 1976), 47–68.

85. Ibid., 63.

86. Ibid., 65.

87. Ibid., 67.

88. Idel, "The Camouflaged Sacred," 166.

89. Mircea Eliade and Mac Linscott Ricketts, *The Portugal Journal* (Albany: State University of New York Press, 2010), 1.293, quoted in Idel, "The Camouflaged Sacred," 166.

90. Idel, "The Camouflaged Sacred," 166.

91. Ibid., 178, quoting Eliade, *Santierul, Proza*, 364. For similar sentiments, see also *The Portugal Journal* 1.293; and N. J. Girardot and Mac Linscott Ricketts, eds., *Imagination and Meaning: The Scholarly and Literary Worlds of Mircea Eliade* (New York: Seabury Press, 1982), 114–16.

92. Idel, "The Camouflaged Sacred," 151.

93. Ibid., 150.

94. Ibid.

95. Ibid.

96. Matei Calinescu, "Eliade and Ionesco in the Post–World War II Years: Questions of Identity in Exile," in Wedemeyer and Doniger, *Hermeneutics, Politics, and the History of Religions*, 109.

97. Ibid.

98. O'Hara, "Mircea Eliade," 177.

99. Christian K. Wedemeyer, "Introduction I: Two Scholars, a 'School,' and a Conference," in Wedemeyer and Doniger, *Hermeneutics, Politics, and the History of Religions*, xxi.

CHAPTER FIVE

1. Olof Pettersson, *Mother Earth: An Analysis of the Mother Earth Concepts according to Albrecht Dieterich*, Scripta Minora, Regiae Societas Humanorum Litterum Lindensis, 1965–66:3 (Lund: CWK Gleerup, 1967), 7–15. See also the historical method of J. Z. Smith in "When the Bough Breaks," *History of Religions* 12 (1973): 342–71.

2. Sam D. Gill, *Mother Earth: An American Story* (Chicago: University of Chicago Press, 1987), 29.

3. Ibid., 28–29.

4. Ibid., 43.

5. Cayuse chieftains Stachas and Young Chief, the Nez Perce known as Lawyer, and a Yakima chief called Ohwi, all in 1885; an unidentified Cayuse leader in 1871; Joseph of the Nez Perce in 1876.

6. Gill, *Mother Earth*, 63.

7. Ibid., 86.

8. Ibid., 100.

9. Åke Hultkrantz, *The Religions of the American Indians* (Berkeley: University of California Press, 1979), originally published as *De amerikanska indianernas religioner*, 1967; Hultkrantz, *Belief and Worship in Native North America* (Syracuse,

NY: Syracuse University Press, 1981); Hultkrantz, "The Religion of the Goddess in North America," in *The Book of the Goddess Past and Present: An Introduction to Her Religion*, ed. Carl Olson (New York: Crossroad, 1983), 202–16.

10. Ibid., 111, 120–21.

11. Ibid., 157.

12. Howard L. Harrod, review of *Mother Earth: An American Story* and *Native American Religious Action: A Performance Approach to Religion*, by Sam D. Gill, *Journal of Religion* 68, no. 4 (October 1988): 625.

13. Bruce Forbes, review of *Mother Earth: An American Story*, by Sam D. Gill, *Journal of American History* 75, no. 3 (1988): 884.

14. Christopher Vecsey, review of *Mother Earth: An American Story* and *Native American Religious Action: A Performance Approach to Religion*, by Sam D. Gill, *American Indian Quarterly* 12, no. 3 (Summer 1988): 255.

15. Ibid., 256.

16. Åke Hultkrantz, "Mother Earth: An American Story," review of *Mother Earth: An American Story*, by Sam D. Gill, *Ethnohistory* 37, no. 1 (Winter 1990): 73–74.

17. Sam D. Gill, "The Academic Study of Religion," in "Settled Issues and Neglected Questions in the Study of Religion," special issue, *Journal of the American Academy of Religion* 62, no. 4 (Winter 1994): 973.

18. Ibid., 967.

19. Ibid., 972.

20. Christopher Jocks, "Response: American Indian Religious Traditions and the Academic Study of Religion: A Response to Sam Gill," *Journal of the American Academy of Religion* 65, no. 1 (Spring 1997): 172.

21. Ibid., 173, 175.

22. Lee Irwin, "Response: American Indian Religious Traditions and the Academic Study of Religion," *Journal of the American Academy of Religion* 66, no. 4 (Winter 1998): 888.

23. Ibid., 890.

24. M. Annette Jaimes and George Noriega, "History in the Making: How Academia Manufactures the 'Truth' about Native American Traditions," *Bloomsbury Review* 4, no. 5 (1988): 25. See also Charles L. Briggs, "The Politics of Discursive Authority in Research on the 'Invention of Tradition,'" in "Resisting Identities," special issue, *Cultural Anthropology* 11, no. 4 (November 1996): 437.

25. Briggs, "The Politics of Discursive Authority," 436.

26. Eric Hobsbawm and Terence Ranger, eds., *The Invention of Tradition* (Cambridge: Cambridge University Press, 1983).

27. Ward Churchill, "Sam Gill's *Mother Earth*: Colonialism, Genocide and the Expropriation of Indigenous Spiritual Tradition in Contemporary Academia," *American Indian Culture and Research Journal* 12, no. 3 (1988): 49–68.

28. Barbara Alice Mann, "Where Are Your Women? Missing in Action," in *Unlearning the Language of Conquest: Scholars Expose Anti-Indianism in America*, ed. Don Trent Jacobs (Austin: University of Texas Press, 2006), 120–34.

290 NOTES TO PAGES 131–148

29. Elizabeth Cook-Lynn, "Who Gets to Tell the Stories?" *Wicazo Sa Review* 9, no. 1 (Spring 1993): 60–64.

30. Ibid., 60.

31. Ward Churchill, "The New Racism: A Critique of James A. Clifton's 'The Invented Indian,'" *Wicazo Sa Review* 7, no. 1 (Spring 1991): 58; also see the chapter of the same name in his *Fantasies of the Master Race: Literature, Cinema, and the Colonization of the American Indian* (San Francisco: New Light Books, 1998), 121–36, 122.

32. Vine Deloria Jr., "Comfortable Fictions and the Struggle for Turf," *American Indian Quarterly* 16, no. 3 (Summer 1992): 401.

33. Ibid., 403, 410.

34. Ronald L. Grimes, "This May Be a Feud, but It Is Not a War: An Electronic, Interdisciplinary Dialogue on Teaching Native Religions," in "To Hear the Eagles Cry: Contemporary Themes in Native American Spirituality," special issue, *American Indian Quarterly* 20, no. 3 (Summer–Autumn 1996): 440.

35. Ibid., 441.

36. Ibid., 6.

37. Ibid., 433.

38. Ibid., 439.

39. Ibid., 445–46.

40. Ibid., 443.

41. Ibid., 447.

42. Michael F. Brown, *Who Owns Native Culture?* (Cambridge, MA: Harvard University Press, 2003).

43. Sam Gill, "The Academic Study of Religion," in "Settled Issues and Neglected Questions in the Study of Religion," special issue, *Journal of the American Academy of Religion* 62, no. 4 (Winter 1994): 971.

44. Ibid., 971–72.

45. http://puffin.creighton.edu/lakota/teaching.html, 11; see also the inclusion of Speights's ideas in Grimes, "This May Be a Feud."

CHAPTER SIX

1. Harjot Oberoi, *The Construction of Religious Boundaries: Culture, Identity, and Diversity in the Sikh Tradition* (Chicago: University of Chicago Press, 1994), 29.

2. Ibid., 34–35.

3. Ibid., 88.

4. Ibid., 89.

5. Ibid., 136.

6. Ibid., 201.

7. Ibid., 202.

8. Ibid., 254.

9. Ibid., 255–56.

10. Ibid., 302.

11. Ibid., 377.

12. Ibid., 417.

13. Edward Said, *Orientalism* (New York: Vintage Books, 1979); Ron Inden, *Imagining India* (Bloomington: Indiana University Press, 1990); Bernard Cohn, *Colonialism and Its Forms of Knowledge: The British in India* (Princeton: Princeton University Press, 1996); Dipesh Chakrabarty, *Provincializing Europe: Postcolonial Thought and Historical Difference* (Princeton: Princeton University Press, 2007). See, for example, Purnima Dhavan's mention of Oberoi alongside these other authors in her review of *Gurus and Their Followers: New Religious Reform Movements in Colonial India*, ed. Antony Copley, *Journal of Asian Studies* 61, no. 2 (May 2002): 745–46.

14. See his article in Martin E. Marty and R. Scott Appleby, eds., *Fundamentalisms and the State: Remaking Polities, Economies, and Militance* (Chicago: University of Chicago Press, 1993): 256–88; and Clyde Wilcox's review in *Review of Religious Research* 36, no. 4 (June 1995): 396–97.

15. M. S. S. Pandian, "Culture and Consciousness: Historiography as Politics," *Social Scientist* 18, nos. 8–9 (August–September 1990): 85–93.

16. Harjot Oberoi, "The Worship of Pir Sakhi Sarvar: Illness, Healing and Popular Culture in the Punjab," *Studies in History* 3 (February 1987): 30; see his discussion of this larger issue of pirs and Sikhism in *Construction of Religious Boundaries*, 85–89.

17. Ibid., 30.

18. J. E. Llewellyn, review of *The Construction of Religious Boundaries: Culture, Identity, and Diversity in the Sikh Tradition*, by Harjot Oberoi, *Journal of Religion* 77, no. 1 (January 1997): 182–83.

19. Meeta Mehrotra, review of *The Construction of Religious Boundaries: Culture, Identity, and Diversity in the Sikh Tradition*, by Harjot Oberoi, *Review of Religious Research* 37, no. 3 (March 1996): 281–82.

20. Nikky-Guninder Kaur Singh, review of *The Construction of Religious Boundaries: Culture, Identity, and Diversity in the Sikh Tradition*, by Harjot Oberoi, *Journal of Asian Studies* 55, no. 3 (August 1996): 760–62.

21. W. H. McLeod, review of *The Construction of Religious Boundaries: Culture, Identity, and Diversity in the Sikh Tradition*, by Harjot Oberoi, *Pacific Affairs* 67, no. 4 (Winter 1994): 615.

22. Daniel Gold, review of *The Construction of Religious Boundaries: Culture Identity and Diversity in the Sikh Tradition*, by Harjot Oberoi, *Journal of the American Oriental Society* 116, no. 3 (July–September 1996): 586–87.

23. Ibid., 587.

24. J. S. Grewal, *Historical Perspectives on Sikh Identity* (Patiala, India: Panjabi University Press, 1997) and *Contesting Interpretations of the Sikh Tradition* (New Delhi: Manohar, 1998); Pashaura Singh and N. Gerald Barrier, eds., *The Transmission of Sikh Heritage in the Diaspora* (New Delhi: Manohar, 1996), *Sikh Identity: Continuity and Change* (New Delhi: Manohar, 1999), and *Sikhism and History* (New Delhi: Oxford University Press, 2004).

25. Max Arthur MacAuliffe, *The Sikh Religion: Its Gurus, Sacred Writings, and Authors*, vol. 1 (London: Forgotten Books, 2015), 296.

292 NOTES TO PAGES 153–172

26. Gurdev Singh, ed., *Perspectives on the Sikh Tradition* (Chandigarh: Siddharth Publications for Academy of Sikh Religion & Culture, Patiala, 1986). Daljeet Singh, Jaljit Singh, and Kharak Singh, discussed immediately below, are included in this volume.

27. W. H. McLeod, *The Evolution of the Sikh Community: Five Essays* (New York: Oxford University Press, 1975), 466.

28. J. S. Grewal, *Contesting Interpretations of the Sikh Tradition* (New Delhi: Manohar, 1998), 227, 234.

29. Pashaura Singh, review of *Contesting Interpretations of the Sikh Tradition* and *Historical Perspectives on Sikh Identity*, by J. S. Grewal, *Journal of the American Oriental Society* 120, no. 3 (July–September 2000): 466.

30. Grewal, *Contesting Interpretations of the Sikh Tradition*, 16.

31. J. S. Grewal, *Historical Perspectives on Sikh Identity* (Patiala, India: Panjabi University, 1997), 14.

32. Daljeet Singh, cited in Grewal, *Historical Perspectives on Sikh Identity*, 466.

33. Gurdarshan Singh Dhillon, review of *Contesting Interpretations of the Sikh Tradition* and *Historical Perspectives on Sikh Identity*, https://sikhcentre.wordpress .com/2009/11/06/review-of-j-s-grewals-contesting-interpretations/; also cited by by J. S. Grewal, *Historical Perspectives on Sikh Identity*, 466, 468.

34. Harjot Oberoi, "What Has a Whale Got to Do with It? A Tale of Pogroms and Biblical Allegories," in *Sikh Religion, Culture and Ethnicity*, ed. Christopher Shackle, Arvind-Pal Singh Mandair, and Gurharpal Singh (New York: Routledge, 2013), 199.

35. Ibid.

36. Ibid., 201.

37. Jasbir Singh Mann, Surinder Singh Sodhi, and Gurbaksh Singh Gill, eds., *Invasion of Religious Boundaries: A Critique of Harjot Oberoi's Work* (Vancouver, BC: Canadian Sikh Study & Teaching Society, 1995), http://www.globalsikhstudies.net /pdf/invasion%20of%20relious.pdf (accessed July 10, 2016).

38. Talal Asad, "Multiculturalism and British Identity in the Wake of the Rushdie Affair," *Politics and Society* 18, no. 4 (1990): 455–80.

39. See Heinz Scheifinger, "Om-line Hinduism: World Wide Gods on the Web," *Australian Religion Studies Review* 23/3 (2010): 329–30.

40. Oberoi, "What Has a Whale Got To Do with It?", 200.

41. Ibid., 202.

CHAPTER SEVEN

1. Henry Corbin, *Cyclical Time and Ismaili Gnosis* (London: Kegan Paul International, 1983); and Wladimir Ivanow, "The Importance of Studying Ismailism," *Ilm* 1, no. 3 (March 1976) 8–9, 20; *Ismaili Tradition concerning the Rise of the Fatimids* (London and New York, Oxford University Press, 1942); *Ismaili Literature: A Bibliographical Survey* (Tehran: Tehran University Press, 1963).

2. See the historical discussion in Tazim R. Kassam, *Songs of Wisdom and Circles of Dance: Hymns of the Satpanth Ismā'īlī Muslim Saint, Pīr Shams* (Albany: State University of New York Press, 1995), 7–15.

3. Ibid., 1.

4. Ibid., 36ff, 122.

5. Ibid., 108–9.

6. Ibid., 108–14, 153–61.

7. Kinga Markus, review of *Songs of Wisdom and Circles of Dance: Hymns of the Satpanth Ismā'īlī Muslim Saint, Pīr Shams*, by Tazim R. Kassam, *Asian Folklore Studies* 55, no. 2 (January 1996): 386.

8. Zawahir Moir, review of *Songs of Wisdom and Circles of Dance: Hymns of the Satpanth Ismā'īlī Muslim Saint, Pīr Shams*, by Tazim R. Kassam, *Bulletin of the School of Oriental and African Studies* 60, no. 2 (1997): 387–88.

9. Ali S. Asani, review of *Songs of Wisdom and Circles of Dance: Hymns by the Satpanth Ismā'īlī Muslim Saint, Pīr Shams*, by Tazim R. Kassam, *Journal of the American Oriental Society* 119, no. 2 (1999): 327.

10. Ali S. Asani, *The Harvard Collection of Ismaili Literature in Indic Languages: A Descriptive Catalog and Finding Aid* (Boston: G. K. Hall, 1992).

11. Tazim R. Kassam, "Balancing Acts: Negotiating the Ethics of Scholarship and Identity," in *Identity Politics of Scholarship in the Study of Religion*, ed. José Ignacio Cabezón and Sheila Greeve Davaney (New York: Routledge, 2004), 134–35.

12. Ibid., 150.

13. Ibid., 135.

14. Ibid., 133.

15. Ibid., 142.

16. Ibid., 144.

17. Ibid., 146.

18. Ibid., 149. See, for another example, "The Insider/Outsider Problem," February 20, 2012, http://www.religiousstudiesproject.com/podcast/podcast-george -chryssides-on-the-insideroutsider-problem/.

19. Ibid., 157.

20. See Max Pensky, "Solidarity," in *Habermas and Religion*, ed. Craig Calhoun, Eduardo Mendieta, and Jonathan VanAntwerpen (Cambridge, UK: Polity Press, 2013), 304, for a compelling formulation of this idea.

21. Tazim Kassam and Françoise Mallison, eds., *Ginans: Texts and Contexts. Essays on Ismaili Hymns from South Asia in Honor of Zawahir Moir* (New Delhi: Matrix, 2007).

22. Kassam, "Balancing Acts," 157.

CHAPTER EIGHT

1. Jane Schaberg, *The Illegitimacy of Jesus: A Feminist Theological Interpretation of the Infancy Narratives*, 2nd ed. (San Francisco: Harper & Row, 1987); Sheffield: UK Sheffield Academic Press, 1995), 34. Citations refer to Sheffield Academic edition.

2. Ibid., 32–33.

3. Ibid., 38–39.

4. Ibid., 94–100.

5. Ibid., 139, 41.

6. Ibid., 144.

7. Ibid., 164–65.

8. Ibid., 178.

9. Ibid., 194.

10. Ibid., 199; Jane Schaberg, "Feminism Lashes Back: Responses to the Backlash," *Bibliocon* 3 (1998): 45–52.

11. Mary H. Schertz, review of *The Illegitimacy of Jesus: A Feminist [Theological] Interpretation of the Infancy Narratives*, by Jane Schaberg, *Journal of the American Academy of Religion* 60, no. 2 (Summer 1992): 358–61.

12. Janice Capel Anderson, review of *The Illegitimacy of Jesus: A Feminist Theological Interpretation of the Infancy Narratives*, by Jane Schaberg, *Journal of Religion* 69, no. 2 (April 1989): 238–39.

13. Ibid., 239.

14. David T. Landry, "Narrative Logic in the Annunciation to Mary," *Journal of Biblical Literature* 114, no. 1 (1995): 65–79, 65 quoted.

15. Raymond E. Brown, *The Birth of the Messiah: A Commentary on the Infancy Narratives in Matthew and Luke* (New York: Doubleday, 1977), 307.

16. Landry, "Narrative Logic," 69–70.

17. Ibid., 70–71; Schaberg, *The Illegitimacy of Jesus*, 87–88.

18. Landry, "Narrative Logic," 75–76; Schaberg, *The Illegitimacy of Jesus*, 87, 226n35.

19. Alice Bach, "Homepage," *Bibliocon* 1 (1997): 2.

20. Schaberg, "Feminism Lashes Back," 46.

21. Ibid.

22. "Reinterpreting the Bible," *Detroit Free Press*, Sunday, February 14, 1993, 1F, 6F.

23. Ibid.; also see "From Our Readers," *Detroit Free Press*, February 2, 1993, 6A, which both defends feminist scholarship and condemns her writings as contrary to Roman Catholic teachings and disrespectful of the figure of Mary.

24. Schaberg, "Feminism Lashes Back," 47.

25. Ibid., 48.

26. Ibid., 49.

27. Ibid., 47.

28. Ibid.

29. Ibid., 48.

30. Ibid.

31. Ibid., 49.

32. Annette Kolodny, "Paying the Price of Antifeminist Intellectual Harassment," in V. Clark et al, eds. *Antifeminism in the Academy*, ed. V. Clark et al. (New York: Routledge, 1996), 28.

33. Schaberg, "Feminism Lashes Back," 47.

34. Frank Reilly, "Jane Schaberg, Raymond E. Brown, and the Problem of the Illegitimacy of Jesus," *Journal of Feminist Studies in Religion* 21, no. 1 (Spring, 2005):

58, citing Raymond E. Brown, *The Critical Meaning of the Bible* (New York: Paulist, 1981), 41; Schaberg, *Illegitimacy of Jesus*, 14–19.

CHAPTER NINE

1. Howard Eilberg-Schwartz, *God's Phallus: And Other Problems for Men and Monotheism* (Boston: Beacon Press, 1994), 163.

2. Esther Fuchs, review of *God's Phallus: And Other Problems for Men and Monotheism*, by Howard Eilberg-Schwartz, *Journal of the American Academy of Religion* 65, no. 1 (Spring 1997): 199–201.

3. Stanley N. Rosenbaum, review of *God's Phallus: And Other Problems for Men and Monotheism*, by Howard Eilberg-Schwartz, *AJS Review* 21, no. 1 (1996): 164–66, 166 quoted.

4. Bernhard Lang, review of *The Savage in Judaism: An Anthropology of Israelite Religion and Ancient Judaism*, by Howard Eilberg-Schwartz, *Journal for the Scientific Study of Religion* 39, no. 1 (June 1992): 148–50.

5. Don C. Benjamin, review of *The Savage in Judaism: An Anthropology of Israelite Religion and Ancient Judaism*, by Howard Eilberg-Schwartz, *Biblical Archaeologist* 56, no. 1 (March 1993): 49–50.

6. Gillian Feeley-Harnik, review of *The Savage in Judaism: An Anthropology of Israelite Religion and Ancient Judaism*, by Howard Eilberg-Schwartz, *American Anthropologist*, n.s., 94, no. 3 (September 1992): 719–20.

7. Gary Anderson, review of *The Savage in Judaism: An Anthropology of Israelite Religion and Ancient Judaism*, by Howard Eilberg-Schwartz, *Journal of Religion* 72, no. 3 (July 1992): 465–67.

8. Jonathan Boyarin, "Savage Escapes from Anthropology Department, Captures Jewish Studies Professor," *Anthropological Quarterly* 65, no. 4 (October 1992): 195–99.

9. Ayala Gabriel, review of *The Savage in Judaism: An Anthropology of Israelite Religion and Ancient Judaism*, by Howard Eilberg Schwartz, *Journal of the American Academy of Religion* 60, no. 1 (Spring 1992): 153–58. See also S. C. Reif, review of *The Savage in Judaism: An Anthropology of Israelite Religion and Ancient Judaism*, by Howard Eilberg-Schwartz, *Vetus Testamentum* 43, no. 2 (April 1993): 281–82.

10. Raphael Patai, review of *The Savage in Judaism: An Anthropology of Israelite Religion and Ancient Judaism*, by Howard Eilberg-Schwartz, *AJS Review* 17, no. 1 (Spring 1992): 91–93, quoting Eilberg-Schwartz, *The Savage in Judaism*, 28.

11. Michael Fishbane, review of *The Savage in Judaism: An Anthropology of Israelite Religion and Ancient Judaism*, by Howard Eilberg-Schwartz, *History of Religions* 32, no. 3 (February 1993): 306–8.

12. Murray L. Wax, review of *The Savage in Judaism: An Anthropology of Israelite Religion and Ancient Judaism*, by Howard Eilberg-Schwartz, *Journal for the Scientific Study of Religion* 30, no. 3 (September 1991): 328–29.

13. Howard Eilberg-Schwartz, "Comment on JSSR's Book Review of 'The Savage in Judaism,'" *Journal for the Scientific Study of Religion* 31, no. 2 (1992): 224–25.

14. See the account in Jonathan Mahler, "Howard's End: Why a Leading Jewish Studies Scholar Gave up his Academic Career," *Lingua Franca*, March 1997, 51–57.

15. Ibid., 4.

16. Howard Schwartz, "From Seminary to Silicon Valley," unpublished manuscript, 120–21.

17. Ibid., 122–23.

18. Ibid., 133.

19. Ibid.

20. Ibid., 153.

21. Ibid.

22. Ibid., 167. Schwartz later elaborates on this idea: "I have to confess that I have struggled with this issue of soul myself in the software industry. When I was a professor, I felt that work was a calling. My soul and work were aligned. I found meaning in educating. But as I transitioned into Silicon Valley, I lost that alignment. Though I did work that many people would have happily done and may have found soul in, my work did not satisfy my passion. Though I like the people I work with and find the technology interesting, the problem of growing a business just doesn't engage my passion." Ibid., 179.

23. Ibid., 168.

24. Ibid., 174. Schwartz expands, "It is well known across the software industry that companies 'oversell' their software. Overselling is a polite word for misleading and at times outright lying to customers about the capabilities of the software. Enterprise software is a complex system that ties together multiple business processes and other business systems. It often takes months and even years to deploy properly. And a sales cycle with a new customer can take six months to a year or more. For this reason, software companies are selling capabilities that are often not even in their products yet and may not even be on the product roadmap. Often companies are promising capabilities well ahead of development. And often they know that those promised capabilities may never be delivered."

25. Schwartz writes of his parents: "They had constructed themselves as ethnic Jews and had developed little in the way of a spiritual identity. They were part of the generation that had separated ethnicity and religiousness, seeing their Jewish identity primarily in culture, foods, jokes, and later in identification with Israel. I was part of a new generation that did not grow up with Anti-Semitism, who identified the need for a spiritual sensibility. And though I tried, I could not find those needs in Jewish community and tradition." Ibid., 189.

26. Ibid., 190.

CHAPTER TEN

1. Jeffrey Kripal, "Mystical Homoeroticism, Reductionism, and the Reality of Censorship: A Response to Gerald James Larson," *Journal of the American Academy of Religion* 66, no. 3 (Autumn 1998): 627–35, 632 quoted.

2. Jeffrey Kripal, *Kālī's Child: The Mystical and the Erotic in the Life and Teachings of Ramakrishna* (Chicago: University of Chicago Press, 1995), 5.

3. Ibid., 23.

4. Gananath Obeyesekere, *Medusa's Hair: An Essay on Personal Symbols and Religious Experience* (Chicago: University of Chicago Press, 1981).

5. Kripal, *Kālī's Child*, 324.

6. Brian Hatcher, "Kali's Problem Child: Another Look at Jeffrey Kripal's Study of Sri Ramakrishna," *International Journal of Hindu Studies* 3, no. 2 (August 1999), 171.

7. Jeanne Openshaw, review of *Kālī's Child*, by Jeffrey Kripal, *Times Higher Education Supplement*, December 15, 1995, 22.

8. André Padoux, review of *Kālī's Child*, by Jeffrey Kripal, *Archives de Sciences Sociales des Religions* 94 (April–June 1996): 85–86.

9. Laurie Patton, review of *Kālī's Child*, by Jeffrey Kripal, *Journal of the History of Sexuality* 7.2 (October, 1996): 278–9.

10. Malcolm McLean, review of *Kālī's Child*, by Jeffrey Kripal, *South Asia: Journal of South Asian Studies*, n.s., 19, no. 1 (June 1996): 116–17.

11. Glen Hayes, review of *Kālī's Child*, by Jeffrey Kripal, *Religious Studies Review* 23, no. 1 (1997): 95–96; David Haberman, review of *Kālī's Child*, by Jeffrey Kripal, *Journal of Asian Studies* 56, no. 2 (1997): 531–52; Carl Olson, review of *Kālī's Child*, by Jeffrey Kripal, *International Journal of Hindu Studies* 1, no. 1 (1997): 201–2.

12. Carl Olson, "Vivekananda and Ramakrishna Face to Face: An Essay on the Alterity of a Saint," *International Journal of Hindu Studies* 2.1 (1998): 51.

13. William Parsons, "Psychoanalysis and Mysticism: The Case of Ramakrishna," *Religious Studies Review* 23, no. 4 (1997): 355–61.

14. Narasingha Sil, "The Question of Ramakrishna's Homosexuality," *Statesman*, January 31, 1997.

15. "Now Let It Rest," *Statesman*, February 18, 1997, 10.

16. Swami Atmajnanananda, "Scandals, Cover-ups, and Other Imagined Occurrences in the Life of Ramakrishna: An Examination of Jeffrey Kripal's *Kālī's Child*," *International Journal of Hindu Studies* 1–2 (August 1997): 401.

17. Gerald Larson, "Polymorphic Sexuality, Homoeroticism, and the Study of Religion," *Journal of the American Academy of Religion* 65, no. 3 (1997): 664.

18. Jeffrey Kripal, "Mystical Homoeroticism, Reductionism, and the Reality of Censorship: A Response to Gerald James Larson," *Journal of the American Academy of Religion* 66.3 (Autumn 1998): 627–35.

19. Ibid., 632.

20. Kripal, *Kālī's Child*, 2nd ed., xiv, xxii.

21. Hugh Urban, review of *Kālī's Child*, by Jeffrey Kripal, *Journal of Religion* 78, no. 2 (April 1998): 319.

22. Steven F. Walker, review of *Kālī's Child*, by Jeffrey Kripal, *Religion* 28, no. 2 (1998): 209–11.

23. William Radice, review of *Kālī's Child*, by Jeffrey Kripal, *Bulletin of the School of Oriental and African Studies* 61, no. 1 (1998): 160–61.

24. John S. Hawley, review of *Kālī's Child*, by Jeffrey Kripal, *History of Religions* 37, no. 4 (1998): 401–4.

25. Hatcher, "Kali's Problem Child," 75–76.

26. Jeffrey Kripal, "Secret Talk: Sexual Identity and the Politics of Scholarship in the Study of Hindu Tantrism," *Harvard Divinity Bulletin* 29, no. 4 (Winter 2000–2001): 14–17; and "Textuality, Sexuality, and the Future of the Past: A Response to Swami Tyagananda," *Evam: Forum on Indian Representations* 1, nos. 1–2 (2002): 191–205.

27. Jeffrey Kripal, *Roads of Excess, Palaces of Wisdom: Eroticism and Reflexivity in the Study of Mysticism* (Chicago: University of Chicago Press, 2001), 201.

28. Ibid., 200.

29. See Kripal, "Mystical Homoeroticism, Reductionism, and the Reality of Censorship," 632.

30. James Clifford, *On the Edges of Anthropology: Interviews* (Chicago: Prickly Paradigm, 2003); James Clifford and George Marcus, eds., *Writing Culture: The Poetics and Politics of Ethnography* (Berkeley: University of California Press, 1986); Lila Abu-Lughod, "Can There Be a Feminist Ethnography?" *Women and Performance: A Journal of Feminist Theory* 5, no. 1 (1990): 7–27; Katie Cannon, *Katie's Canon: Womanism and the Soul of the Black Community* (New York: Continuum, 1995).

31. Swami Tyagananda and Pravrajika Vrajaprana, *Interpreting Ramakrishna: Kālī's Child Revisited* (Delhi: Motilal Banarsidass, 2010), xiii.

32. Tyagananda and Vrajaprana, *Interpreting Ramakrishna*, 186.

33. Kripal, *Kālī's Child*, 2nd ed., xxiii–xxiv.

34. Hatcher, "Kali's Problem Child," 167.

35. Tyagananda and Vrajaprana, *Interpreting Ramakrishna*, 204.

36. Hawley, review of *Kālī's Child*, 404.

37. Tyagananda amd Vrajaprana, *Interpreting Ramakrishna*, 212–18, 358.

38. Rajiv Malhotra, "Wendy's Child Syndrome," Sulekha, 2002, http://rajivmalhotra .com/library/articles/risa-lila-1-wendys-child-syndrome/ (accessed October 31, 2016).

39. K. Anthony Appiah, *The Ethics of Identity* (Princeton: Princeton University Press, 2005), 24.

CHAPTER ELEVEN

1. Craig Calhoun, Eduardo Mendieta, and Jonathan VanAntwerpen, "Editors' Introduction," in *Habermas and Religion* (Cambridge, UK: Polity Press, 2013), 16; see also James Bohman, "A Postsecular Global Order? The Pluralism of Forms of Life and Communicative Freedom," in ibid., 180.

2. One reader worried about this metaphor, saying that the last thing the embattled study of religion needed was to be misinterpreted as foolish. I am here taking the risk that readers will be sharp and nuanced enough in their reading that the many layers of meaning in this image will be generative.

3. Robert Hillis Goldsmith, *Wise Fools in Shakespeare* (East Lansing: Michigan State University Press, 1955), 48.

4. As quoted in Lee Siegel, *Laughing Matters* (1987), 287; see also F. B. J. Kuiper, *Varuṇa and Vidūṣaka: On the Origin of the Sanskrit Drama* (Amsterdam: North-Holland, 1979); G. K. Bhat, *The Vidushaka* (Ahmedabad: New Order Book Co.,

1959); and J. T. Parikh, *The Vidushaka: Theory and Practice* (Surat: Chunilal Gandhi Vidyabhavan, 1953). Also see Keith N. Jefferds, "Vidūṣaka versus Fool: A Functional Analysis," *Journal of South Asian Literature* 16 (1981): 61–73.

5. One excellent example of a historical treatment of the changing nature of a public is Christian Novetzke's *The Quotidian Revolution: Vernacularization, Religion, and the Premodern Public Sphere in India* (New York: Columbia University Press, 2016). There, Novetzke depicts how the emergence of a vernacular Marathi literature in Maharashtra, India, allowed for the emergence of a new public sphere that could encompass debates about social inequality and other forms of difference. This was possible particularly because the debates and performative traditions surrounding them were conducted in the idiom of everyday life. This account of the changing nature of scholarship, readership, and expression in religious communities is the kind of historical work we might introduce into the study of religion.

6. Wendy Steiner, *The Scandal of Pleasure* (Chicago: University of Chicago Press, 1995), 123.

7. David Damrosch, *We Scholars: Changing the Culture of the University* (Cambridge, MA: Harvard University Press, 1995), 211. David Scobey, in his life work of Imagining America, has put in a program of public scholarship to create just these kinds of engagements, as well as proposals for structures to support them. See https://imaginingamerica.org (accessed August 2, 2018).

8. James F. Keenan, SJ, *University Ethics: How Colleges Can Build and Benefit from a Culture of Ethics* (Lanham, MD: Rowman & Littlefield, 2015).

9. Jon Roberts and James Turner, *The Sacred and the Secular University* (Princeton: Princeton Unversity Press, 2000).

10. Talal Asad, "Freedom of Speech and Religious Limitations," in Calhoun, Juergensmeyer, and VanAntwerpen, *Rethinking Secularism.*

11. A. Suresh Canagarajah, *A Geopolitics of Academic Writing* (Pittsburgh: University of Pittsburgh Press, 2002).

12. Os Guinness, "A World Safe for Diversity: Religious Liberty and the Rebuilding of the Public Philosophy," in *Religion in American Public Life: Living with Our Deepest Differences*, ed. Azizah Y. al-Hibri, Jean Bethke Elshtain, and Charles C. Haynes (New York: W. W. Norton, 2001), 139.

13. Charles Haynes, "From Battle Ground to Common Ground: Religion in the Public Square of 21st Century America," in ibid., 108.

14. Guinness, "A World Safe for Diversity," 149.

15. Chantal Mouffe, "Deliberative Democracy or Agonistic Pluralism," December 2000, https://www.ihs.ac.at/publications/pol/pw_72.pdf.

16. Doris Summer, *The Work of Art in the World: Civic Agency and Public Humanities* (Durham: Duke University Press, 2014).

17. Martha C. Nussbaum, *Not for Profit: Why Democracy Needs the Humanities* (Princeton: Princeton University Press, 2010); Michael Bérubé and Jennifer Ruth, *The Humanities, Higher Education, and Academic Freedom: Three Necessary Arguments* (New York: Palgrave MacMillan, 2015).

18. Leela Prasad, "Co-being, a Praxis of the Public: Lessons from Hindu Devotional (Bhakti) Narrative, Arendt, and Gandhi," *Journal of the American Academy of Religion* 85, no. 1 (March 2017): 199–223. In his *Learning in the Plural: Essays on the Humanities and Public Life* (East Lansing: Michigan State University Press, 2014), xix, David Cooper remarks that the cultural disciplines have been cut off from "meaningful participation in democractic renewal, education for citizenship, and public problem solving." If scholars of religion understood themselves to be more connected to those processes, there could be a great revival of humanistic thinking in the public square.

19. Albert O. Hirsch, *Exit, Voice and Loyalty: Responses to Decline in Firms, Organizations, and States* (Cambridge, MA: Harvard University Press, 1970).

20. Max Pensky, "Solidarity," in Calhoun, Mendieta, and VanAntwerpen, *Habermas and Religion*, 321. This awareness may be part of what some recent theorists mean when they argue for decolonizing academia.

EPILOGUE

1. John D. Carlson and Erik C. Owens, eds., *The Sacred and The Sovereign: Religion and International Politics* (Washington, DC: Georgetown University Press, 2003) sets the stage for these geopolitical shifts in the first decade of the twenty-first century and their implications for the study and public understanding of religion, in North America and beyond. See also Wade Clark Roof, ed., *Americans and Religions in the Twenty-First Century* (Thousand Oaks, CA: Sage Publications, 1998); and Gerson Moreno-Riaño, ed., *Tolerance in the Twenty-First Century: Prospects and Challenges* (Lanham, MD: Lexington Books, 2006).

2. Michael Brown, *Who Owns Native Culture?* (Cambridge, MA: Harvard University Press, 2003).

3. Inéz Hernández-Avila, *Reading Native American Women: Critical/Creative Representations* (New York: AltaMira Press, 2005).

4. Tracy Leavelle, "The Perils of Pluralism: Colonization and Decolonization in American Indian Religious History," in *After Pluralism: Reimagining Religious Engagement*, ed. Courtney Bender and Pamela Klassen (New York: Columbia University Press, 2010), 156–78. This argument is in some ways similar to that of Sam Gill's; however, it is placed within the framework of what forms of rhetoric are available and convincing in colonial and postcolonial contexts, rather than focusing on the idea that a particular religious figure such as Mother Earth is less robust than has been claimed.

5. Pashaura Singh, *The Guru Granth Sahib: Canon, Meaning and Authority* (New Delhi: Oxford University Press, 2000); see Girja Kumar's *The Book on Trial: Fundamentalism and Censorship in India* (Delhi: Har Anand Publications, 1997), 351–74; Amarjeet Singh Grewal, Pashaura Singh as well as Piar Singh were engaged by Sikh theological authorities surrounding their claims about the history of the Guru Granth; so, too, was Giana Gurdit Singh in the later 2000s. Also in the '00s, G. S. Afghana wrote controversial works around the authorship of the Dasam Granth,

and Jathedar Joginder Singh was engaged in a controversy around the life of Guru Hargobind, the sixth guru. I am grateful to Gurinder Singh Mann, personal communication, for this information.

6. I am grateful to Bruce Lawrence for a sober assessment of the situation in the early 2000s and beyond. See Amina Wadud, *Qur'an and Woman: Rereading the Sacred Text from a Woman's Perspective* (New York: Oxford University Press, 1999); Stephen Schwartz, *The Two Faces of Islam: Saudi Fundamentalism and Its Role in Terrorism* (New York: Anchor Books, 2003); John Esposito, *What Everyone Needs to Know about Islam* (New York: Oxford University Press, 2002; 2nd ed., 2011). On Khaled Abou El Fadl, see Monika Jung-Mounib, "God Does Not Have an Equal Partner," 2005, http://en.qantara.de/content/khaled-abou-el-fadl-god-does-not-have-an-equal-partner (accessed November 15, 2106).

7. Omid Safi, *Memories of Muhammad: Why the Prophet Matters* (New York: Harper Collins, 2009); "Home Ministry Bans Publication of 12 Books." *Star*, February 4, 2014, https://www.thestar.com.my/news/nation/2014/02/04/home-ministry-bans-publication-of-12-books (accessed April 23, 2019).

8. Elizabeth Johnson, *Quest for the Living God: Mapping Frontiers in the Theology of God* (New York: Continuum Press, 2007).

9. In that controversy, students at the college complained to a local Episcopalian youth minister about the representation of Jesus in the classrooms of the Religion Department, as well as anti-Christian bias by Frankfurter and others in the department. Another religion professor, Donald Schley, complained that his position was not continued and Frankfurter was hired instead because of anti-Christian bias, particularly against those with degrees from schools with confessional backgrounds. Schley sued the college in 1992, claiming he was denied a job because he was a devout Christian. The case was resolved in 1995, when a federal magistrate ruled that there was no bias in the hiring of Frankfurter over Schley. See Skip Johnson, "Sermon Slams Professor for Corrupting Bible Students," *Charleston* (SC) *Post-Courier*, May 11, 1991; Carolyn Mooney, "Judge Finds No Anti-Christian Bias in Tenure Case," *Chronicle of Higher Education* 41, no. 23 (February 17, 1995): A18.

10. Norman Finkelstein, *Beyond Chutzpah: On the Misuse of Anti-Semitism and the Abuse of History*, updated ed. (Berkeley: University of California Press, 2008); M. H. Ellis, *Toward a Jewish Theology of Liberation: The Challenge of the 21st Century* (Maryknoll, NY: Orbis Books, 1987; rpt. with a new preface by Julia Neuberger, Canterbury, UK: SCM Press, 2002); M. H. Ellis, *Israel and Palestine—Out of the Ashes: The Search for Jewish Identity in the Twenty-First Century* (London: Pluto Press, 2002); Joel Kovel, *Overcoming Zionism: Creating a Single Democratic State in Israel/Palestine* (London: Pluto Press, 2007).

11. Sarah Caldwell, *Oh Terrifying Mother: Sexuality, Violence, and the Worship of the Goddess Kali* (New York and London: Oxford University Press, 1999); Paul Courtright, *Ganesha: Lord of Obstacles* (New York and London: Oxford University Press, 1985); James Laine, *Shivaji: Hindu King in Islamic India* (New York: Oxford University Press, 2003); Wendy Doniger, *The Hindus: An Alternative History* (New York: Oxford University Press, 2009). Also see Brian K. Pennington, "The Unseen

Hand of an Underappreciated Law: The Doniger Affair and Its Aftermath," *Journal of the American Academy of Religion* 84, no. 2 (June 2016): 323–36. Barbara McGraw's "The Doniger Affair: Censorship, Self-Censorship, and the Role of the Academy in the Public Understanding of Religion" addresses the "place between" the academy and the community in the controversy: https://www.aarweb.org/about/in-the -public-interest-the-doniger-affair (accessed September 12, 2018). The early book in this critical trend was Krishnan Ramaswamy, Antonio de Nicolas, and Aditi Baner-jee, eds., *Invading the Sacred: An Analysis of Hinduism Studies in America* (Kolkata: Rupa, 2007).

12. A. K. Ramanujan, "Three Hundred Rāmāyaṇas: Five Examples and Three Thoughts on Translation," in *Many Rāmāyaṇas: The Diversity of a Narrative Tradition in South Asia*, ed. Paula Richman (Berkeley: University of California Press, 1991), 22–49; Mukul Kesavan, "Three Hundred Ramayanas—Delhi University and the Purging of Ramanujan," *Telegraph*, October 27, 2011; Ajoy Mahaprastha, "The Rule of Unreason," *Frontline: India's National Magazine*, November 5–18, 2011, https:// frontline.thehindu.com/static/html/fl2823/stories/20111118282312500.htm (accessed August 3, 2018).

13. See Nandagopal R. Menon, "Virtual Assaults," *Frontline: India's National Magazine*, February 11–24, 2006, https://frontline.thehindu.com/static/html/fl2303/stories /20060224002009600.htm (accessed July 12, 2018).

BIBLIOGRAPHY

Abou El Fadl, Khaled. "God Does Not Have an Equal Partner." *Qantara.de.* http://
en.qantara.de/content/khaled-abou-el-fadl-god-does-not-have-an-equal
-partner. Accessed November 15, 2016.

Abu-Lughod, Lila. "Can There Be a Feminist Ethnography?" *Women and Performance: A Journal of Feminist Theory* 5, no. 1 (1990): 7–27.

Ahmed, Shahab. *What Is Islam? The Importance of Being Islamic.* Princeton: Princeton University Press, 2015.

Albanese, Catherine L. Review of *Sacred Words: A Study of Navajo Religion and
Prayer*, by Sam D. Gill. *Journal of the American Academy of Religion* 50, no. 4
(December 1982): 627.

Alcoff, Linda Martín. *Visible Identities: Race, Gender, and the Self.* New York: Oxford University Press, 2006.

Al-Hibri, Azizah Y., Jean Bethke Elshtain, and Charles C. Haynes, eds. *Religion
in American Public Life: Living with Our Deepest Differences.* New York: W. W.
Norton, 2001.

Almagor, Raphael Cohen. *Speech, Media and Ethics: The Limits of Free Expression.*
New York: Palgrave, 2005.

Andersen, Margaret L., and Patricia Hill Collins, eds. *Race, Class, and Gender.* 6th ed.
Belmont, CA: Thomson Wadsworth, 2007.

Anderson, Gary. Review of *The Savage in Judaism: An Anthropology of Israelite
Religion and Ancient Judaism*, by Howard Eilberg-Schwartz. *Journal of Religion*
72, no. 3 (July 1992): 465–467.

Anderson, Janice Capel. Review of *The Illegitimacy of Jesus: A Feminist Theological
Interpretation of the Infancy Narratives*, by Jane Schaberg. *Journal of Religion* 69,
no. 2 (April 1989): 238–39.

Appiah, Kwame Anthony. "Multiculturalism." In Gutmann, *Multiculturalism: Examining the Politics of Recognition*, 149–64.

———. *The Ethics of Identity.* Princeton: Princeton University Press, 2005.

———. "What's So Special about Religious Disputes?" Paper presented at the Berkley Center for Religion, Peace, and World Affairs, Georgetown University, Washington, DC, September 12, 2006.

Asad, Talal. "The Construction of Religion as an Anthropological Category." In Asad, *Genealogies of Religion: Disciplines of Reason and Power in Christianity and Islam*, 27–54. Baltimore: Johns Hopkins University Press, 1993.

———. *Formations of the Secular: Christianity, Islam, Modernity*. Stanford, CA: Stanford University Press, 2003.

———. "Freedom of Speech and Religious Limitations." In Calhoun, Juergensmeyer, and VanAntwerpen, *Rethinking Secularism*, 282–98.

———. "Multiculturalism and British Identity in the Wake of the Rushdie Affair." *Politics and Society* 18, no. 4 (1990): 455–80.

Asad, Talal, Wendy Brown, Judith Butler, and Saba Mahmood. *Is Critique Secular? Blasphemy, Injury, and Free Speech*. New York: Fordham University Press, 2009.

Asani, Ali. S. *The Harvard Collection of Ismaili Literature in Indic Languages: A Descriptive Catalog and Finding Aid*. Boston: G. K. Hall, 1992.

———. Review of *Songs of Wisdom and Circles of Dance: An 'Anthology of Hymns by the Satpanth Ismāʿīlī Muslim Sait, Pīr Shams*, by Tazim R. Kassam. *Journal of the American Oriental Society* 119, no. 2 (1999): 327–28.

Axel, Brian. *The Nation's Tortured Body*. Durham, NC: Duke University Press, 2001.

Baber, H. E. *The Multicultural Mystique: The Liberal Case against Diversity*. Amherst, NY: Prometheus Books, 2008.

Babin, Pierre, and Angela Ann Zukowski. *The Gospel in Cyberspace: Nurturing Faith in the Internet Age*. Chicago: Loyola Press, 2002.

Bach, Alice. "Homepage." *Bibliocon* 1 (1997): 2–10.

Balagangadhara, S. N. "India and Her Traditions: A Reply to Jeffrey Kripal." Sulekha Blogs, September 20, 2002, http://www.sulekha.com/blogs/blogdisplay .aspx?cid=4501. Accessed August 20, 2016.

Banerjee, Sikata. *Make Me a Man! Masculinity, Hinduism, and Nationalism in India*. Albany: State University of New York Press, 2005.

Barrier, N. Gerald, and Pashaura Singh, eds. *Sikh Identity: Continuity and Change*. New Delhi: Manohar, 1999.

Barry, Brian. *Culture and Equality: An Egalitarian Critique of Multiculturalism*. Cambridge, MA: Harvard University Press, 2001.

Batnitzky, Leora. *How Judaism Became a Religion: An Introduction to Modern Jewish Thought*. Princeton: Princeton University Press, 2011.

Beckford, James. *Religion and Advanced Industrial Society*. London: Unwin Hyman, 1989.

Bender, Courtney. *The New Metaphysicals: Spirituality and the American Religious Imagination*. Chicago: University of Chicago Press, 2010.

Bender, Courtney, and Pamela Klassen, eds. *After Pluralism: Reimagining Religious Engagements*. New York: Columbia University Press, 2010.

Benjamin, Don C. Review of *The Savage in Judaism: An Anthropology of Israelite*

Religion and Ancient Judaism, by Howard Eilberg-Schwartz. *Biblical Archaeologist* 56, no. 1 (March 1993): 49–50.

Bennett, Lance, and Robert Entman, eds. *Mediated Politics: Communication in the Future of Democracy*. Cambridge: Cambridge University Press, 2001.

Bennett, Lance, and Alexandra Segerberg, eds. *The Logic of Connective Action: Digital Media and the Personalization of Contentious Politics*. Cambridge: Cambridge University Press, 2013.

Berger, Adriana. "Mircea Eliade: Romanian Fascism and the History of Religions in the United States." In *Tainted Greatness: Antisemitism and Cultural Heroes*, edited by Nancy Harrowitz, 51–74. Philadelphia: Temple University Press, 1994.

Bernstein, J. M. "Forgetting Isaac: Faith and the Philosophical Impossibility of a Postsecular Society." In Calhoun, Mendieta, and VanAntwerpen, *Habermas and Religion*, 154–78.

Bérubé, Michael, and Ruth, Jennifer. *The Humanities, Higher Education, and Academic Freedom: Three Necessary Arguments*. New York: Palgrave MacMillan, 2015.

Bhambra, Gurminder K., and Victoria Margree. "Identity Politics and the Need for a 'Tomorrow.'" *Economic and Political Weekly* 45, no. 15 (April 10–16, 2010): 59–66.

Bingaman, Kirk A. *Freud and Faith: Living in the Tension*. Albany: State University of New York Press, 2003.

Bishop, Peter. *Dreams of Power: Tibetan Buddhism and the Western Imagination*. London: Athlone Press, 1993.

Blackburn, Anne. *Buddhist Learning and Textual Practice in Eighteenth-Century Lankan Monastic Culture*. Princeton: Princeton University Press, 2001.

Bohman, James. "Expanding Dialogue: The Internet, the Public Sphere, and Prospects for Transnational Democracy." In Gripsrud, Moe, Molander, and Murdock, *The Idea of the Public Sphere: A Reader*, 247–69. Lanham, MD: Lexington Books, 2010.

———. "A Postsecular Global Order? The Pluralism of Forms of Life and Communicative Freedom." In Calhoun, Mendieta, and VanAntwerpen, *Habermas and Religion*, 179–202.

Boyarin, Jonathan. "Savage Escapes from Anthropology Department, Captures Jewish Studies Professor." *Anthropological Quarterly* 65, no. 4 (October 1992): 195–99.

Brasher, Brenda E. *Give Me That Online Religion*. New Brunswick, NJ: Rutgers University Press, 2004.

Briggs, Charles L. "The Politics of Discursive Authority in Research on the 'Invention of Tradition.'" In "Resisting Identities," special issue, *Cultural Anthropology* 11, no. 4 (November 1996): 435–69.

Brown, Michael F. *Who Owns Native Culture?* Cambridge, MA: Harvard University Press, 2003.

Brown, Raymond E. *The Birth of the Messiah: A Commentary on the Infancy Narratives in Matthew and Luke*. New York: Doubleday, 1977.

———. *The Critical Meaning of the Bible*. New York: Paulist, 1981.

Brown, Wendy. Introduction to *Is Critique Secular? Blasphemy, Injury, and Free Speech*, by Talal Asad, Judith Butler, and Saba Mahmood. New York: Fordham University Press, 2013.

Brubaker, Rogers. "Religion and Nationalism: Four Approaches." *Nations and Nationalism* 18, no. 1 (2012): 2–20.

Buckley, Jorunn Jacobsen, and Thomas Buckley. "Response: Anthropology, History of Religions, and a Cognitive Approach to Religious Phenomena." *Journal of the American Academy of Religion* 63, no. 2 (Summer 1995): 343–52.

Cabezón, José Ignacio. "Identity and the Work of the Scholar of Religion." In Cabezón and Davaney, *Identity and the Politics of Scholarship in the Study of Religion*, 43–59.

Cabezón, José Ignacio, and Sheila Greeve Davaney, eds. *Identity and the Politics of Scholarship in the Study of Religion*. New York: Routledge, 2004.

Caldwell, Sarah. *Oh Terrifying Mother: Sexuality, Violence and the Worship of the Goddess Kali*. New York and London: Oxford University Press, 1999.

Calhoun, Craig, ed. *Habermas and the Public Sphere*. Cambridge, MA: MIT Press, 1993.

Calhoun, Craig, Mark Juergensmeyer, and Jonathan VanAntwerpen, eds. *Rethinking Secularism*. New York: Oxford University Press, 2011.

Calhoun, Craig, Eduardo Mendieta, and Jonathan VanAntwerpen, eds. *Habermas and Religion*. Cambridge, UK: Polity Press, 2013.

Calinescu, Matei. "Eliade and Ionesco in the Post–World War II Years: Questions of Identity in Exile." In Wedemeyer and Doniger, *Hermeneutics, Politics, and the History of Religions*, 103–32. Oxford: Oxford University Press, 2010.

Camp, Jean, and Y. T. Chien. "The Internet as Public Space: Concepts, Issues and Implications in Public Policy." *ACM SIGCAS Computers and Society* 30, no. 3 (September 2000): 13–19.

Campbell, Heidi. *Exploring Religious Community Online: We Are One in the Network*. New York: Peter Lang, 2010.

Canagarajah, A. Suresh. *A Geopolitics of Academic Writing*. Pittsburgh: University of Pittsburgh Press, 2002.

Cannon, Katie. *Katie's Canon: Womanism and the Soul of the Black Community*. New York: Continuum, 1995.

Carlson, John D., and Erik C. Owens, eds. *The Sacred and The Sovereign: Religion and International Politics*. Washington, DC: Georgetown University Press, 2003.

Casanova, José. "Exploring the Postsecular: Three Meanings of 'the Secular' and Their Possible Transcendence." In Calhoun, Mendieta and VanAntwerpen, *Habermas and Religion*, 27–48.

Castells, Manuel. *The Information Age: Economy, Society, and Culture*, vol. 1, *The Rise of the Network Society*. Oxford: Blackwell, 1996.

Chakrabarty, Dipesh. *Provincializing Europe: Postcolonial Thought and Historical Difference*. Princeton: Princeton University Press, 2007.

Chidester, David. *Authentic Fakes: Religion and American Popular Culture*. Berkeley: University of California Press, 2005.

———. *Empire of Religion: Imperialism and Comparative Religion*. Chicago: University of Chicago Press, 2013.

———. *Savage Systems: Colonialism and Comparative Religion in Southern Africa*. Charlottesville: University Press of Virginia, 1996.

Chopra, Rohit. *Technology and Nationalism in India: Cultural Negotiations from Colonialism to Cyberspace*. New York: Cambria Press, 2008.

Chryssides, George, and Christopher R. Cotter. "The Insider/Outsider Problem." Religious Studies Project podcast, February 20, 2012. http://www.religious studiesproject.com/podcast/podcast-george-chryssides-on-the-insideroutsider -problem/.

Churchill, Ward. "The New Racism: A Critique of James A. Clifton's 'The Invented Indian.'" *Wicazo Sa Review* 7, no. 1 (Spring 1991): 51–59.

———. "Sam Gill's *Mother Earth*: Colonialism, Genocide and the Expropriation of Indigenous Spiritual Tradition in Contemporary Academia." *American Indian Culture and Research Journal* 12, no. 3 (1988): 49–68.

Clifford, James. *On the Edges of Anthropology: Interviews*. Chicago: Prickly Paradigm, 2003.

Clifford, James, and George Marcus, eds. *Writing Culture: The Poetics and Politics of Ethnography*. Berkeley: University of California Press, 1986.

Cohn, Bernard. *Colonialism and Its Forms of Knowledge: The British in India*. Princeton: Princeton University Press, 1996.

Connolly, William. *The Ethos of Pluralization*. Minneapolis: University of Minnesota Press, 1995.

Cook-Lynn, Elizabeth. "Who Gets to Tell the Stories?" *Wicazo Sa Review* 9, no. 1 (Spring 1993): 60–64.

Cooper, David. *Learning in the Plural: Essays on the Humanities and Public Life*. East Lansing: Michigan State University Press, 2014.

Corbin, Henry. *Cyclical Time and Ismaili Gnosis*. London: Kegan Paul International, 1983.

Courtright, Paul. *Ganesha: Lord of Obstacles*. New York and London: Oxford University Press, 1985.

Crenshaw, Kimberlé. "Demarginalizing the Intersection of Race and Sex: A Black Feminist Critique of Antidiscrimination Doctrine, Feminist Theory and Antiracist Politics." *University of Chicago Legal Forum* 1989, no. 1, 139–67.

Crossette, Barbara. "Indian Starts a Campaign against Cash for Militants." *New York Times*, August 18, 2002.

Crossley, Nick, and John Michael Roberts, eds. *After Habermas: New Perspectives on the Public Sphere*. Oxford: Blackwell, 2004.

Dalrymple, William. "India: The War over History." *New York Review of Books*, April 7, 2005.

Damico, James. "Ingrid from Lorraine to Stromboli: Analyzing the Public's Perception of a Film Star." In *Star Texts: Image and Performance in Film and Television*, edited by Jeremy Butler, 240–54. Detroit: Wayne State University Press, 1991.

Damrosch, David. *We Scholars: Changing the Culture of the University*. Cambridge, MA: Harvard University Press, 1995.

Davaney, Sheila Greeve. "Between Identity and Footnotes." In Cabezón and Davaney, *Identity and the Politics of Scholarship in the Study of Religion*, 25–41.

Davidson, Arnold I. "Carlo Ginzburg and the Renewal of Historiography." In *Questions of Evidence: Proof, Practice, and Persuasion across the Disciplines*, edited by James Chandler, Arnold I. Davidson, and Harry Hartounian, 304–20. Chicago: University of Chicago Press, 1994.

Dawson, Lorne L., and Douglas E. Cowan, eds. *Religion Online: Finding Faith on the Internet*. New York: Routledge, 2004.

Deloria, Vine, Jr. "Comfortable Fictions and the Struggle for Turf." *American Indian Quarterly* 16, no. 3 (Summer 1992): 397–410.

Devine, Philip E. *Human Diversity and the Culture Wars: A Philosophical Perspective on Contemporary Cultural Conflict*. New York: Praeger, 1996.

Dewey, John, and Arthur Bentley. *Knowing and the Known*. 1949. Vol. 16 of *John Dewey: The Later Works, 1925–1953*, edited by Jo Ann Boydston. Carbondale and Edwardsville: Southern Illinois University Press, 1989.

Dhavan, Purnima. Review of *Gurus and Their Followers: New Religious Reform Movements in Colonial India*, edited by Antony Copley. *Journal of Asian Studies* 61, no. 2 (2002): 745–46.

Dhillon, Gurdarshan Singh. Review of *Contesting Interpretations of the Sikh Tradition and Historical Perspectives on Sikh Identity*, by J. S. Grewal. https://sikhcentre.wordpress.com/2009/11/06/review-of-j-s-grewals-contesting-interpretations/. Accessed November 10, 2016.

Dietrich, Richard S. Review of *The Illegitimacy of Jesus: A Feminist Interpretation of the Infancy Narratives*, by Jane Schaberg. *Interpretation: A Journal of Bible and Theology* 43, no. 2 (April 1989): 208.

Dirks, Nicholas. *Scandal of Empire: India and the Creation of Imperial Britain*. Cambridge, MA: Belknap Press of Harvard University Press, 2008.

Doniger, Wendy. *The Hindus: An Alternative History*. New York and London: Oxford University Press, 2009.

Dubuisson, Daniel. *The Western Construction of Religion*. Baltimore: Johns Hopkins University Press, 2003.

Ebersole, Gary L. Review of *Storytracking: Texts, Stories, and Histories in Central Australia*, by Sam D. Gill. *Journal of Religion* 79, no. 4 (October 1999): 706–708.

Eck, Diana L. "Religious Studies—The Academic and Moral Challenge: Personal Reflections on the Legacy of Wilfred Cantwell Smith." In *The Legacy of Wilfred Cantwell Smith*, edited by Ellen Bradshaw Aitken and Arvind Sharma, 21–35. Albany: State University of New York Press, 2017.

Eilberg-Schwartz, Howard. "Campus Debate Leaves Us No Middle Ground." *Golden Gater*, April 27, 1995.

———. "Comment on JSSR's Book Review of 'The Savage in Judaism.'" *Journal for the Scientific Study of Religion* 31, no. 2 (1992): 224–25.

———. *God's Phallus: And Other Problems for Men and Monotheism*. Boston: Farrar, Straus & Giroux, 1994.

———. *The Savage in Judaism: An Anthropology of Israelite Religion and Ancient Judaism*. Bloomington: Indiana University Press, 1990.

Eliade, Mircea. *Autobiography*. 2 vols. Chicago: University of Chicago Press, 1981–88.

———. "Critics Corner." *Theology Today* 24, no. 3 (1967): 385.

———. "Cultural Fashions and the History of Religions." In *The History of Religions: Essays on the Problem of Understanding*, edited by Joseph M. Kitagawa, 21–38. Chicago: University of Chicago Press, 1967.

———. *The Forbidden Forest*. Translated by Mac Linscott Ricketts. Notre Dame, IN: University of Notre Dame Press, 1978.

———. "History of Religions and a New Humanism: The History of Religious Meanings Must Always Be Regarded as Forming Part of the History of the Human Spirit." *Criterion* 1, no. 2 (Summer 1962): 8–11.

———. "A New Humanism." In Eliade, *The Quest*, 1–11. Chicago: University of Chicago Press, 1969; Midway Reprint, 1984.

———. "The Occult and the Modern World." In Eliade, *Occultism, Witchcraft, and Cultural Fashions: Essays in Comparative Religion*, 47–68. Chicago: University of Chicago Press, 1976.

———. *Shamanism: Archaic Techniques of Ecstasy*. Translated by Willard R. Trask. New York: Bollingen Foundation, 1964.

———. *Symbolism, the Sacred, and the Arts*. Edited by Diane Apostolos-Cappadona. New York: Crossroad, 1986.

Eliade, Mircea, and Mac Linscott Ricketts. *The Portugal Journal*. Albany: State University of New York Press, 2010.

Ellis, M. H. *Israel and Palestine—Out of the Ashes: The Search for Jewish Identity in the Twenty-First Century*. London: Pluto Press, 2002.

———. *Toward a Jewish Theology of Liberation: The Challenge of the 21st Century*. Maryknoll, NY: Orbis Books, 1987. Rpt. with a new preface by Julia Neuberger. Canterbury, UK: SCM Press, 2002.

Esposito, John. *What Everyone Needs to Know about Islam*. Oxford: Oxford University Press, 2011.

Eversole, Finley. "Foundation for the Arts, Religion and Culture." *Theology Today* 24, no. 3 (October 1967): 383–85.

Feeley-Harnik, Gillian. Review of *The Savage in Judaism: An Anthropology of Israelite Religion and Ancient Judaism*, by Howard Eilberg-Schwartz. *American Anthropologist*, n.s., 94, no. 3 (September 1992): 719–20.

Fine, Gary Alan. "Scandal, Social Conditions, and the Creation of Public Attention: Fatty Arbuckle and the 'Problem of Hollywood.'" *Social Problems* 44, no. 3 (August 1997): 297–323.

Fineman, Martha. "The Vulnerable Subject: Anchoring Equality in the Human Condition." *Yale Journal of Law and Feminism* 20, no. 1 (2008): 1–23.

Fink, John. Editorial. *Chicago*, June 1986, 4.

Finkelstein, Norman. *Beyond Chutzpah: On the Misuse of Anti-Semitism and the Abuse of History*. Updated ed. Berkeley: University of California Press, 2008.

Fishbane, Michael. Review of *The Savage in Judaism: An Anthropology of Israelite Religion and Ancient Judaism*, by Howard Eilberg-Schwartz. *History of Religions* 32, no. 3 (February 1993): 306–8.

Fitzgerald, Timothy. *The Ideology of Religious Studies*. Oxford: Oxford University Press, 2003.

Forbes, Bruce. Review of *Mother Earth: An American Story*, by Sam D. Gill. *Journal of American History* 75, no. 3 (1988): 884.

Frank, Joseph. *Responses to Modernity: Essays in the Politics of Culture*. New York: Fordham University Press, 2012.

Fraser, Nancy. *Redistribution or Recognition? A Political-Philosophical Exchange*. London: Verso, 2003.

———. "Rethinking the Public Sphere." *Social Text* 25/26 (1990): 56–80.

———. *Scales of Justice: Reimagining Political Space in a Globalizing World*. Cambridge: Polity Press, 2008.

———. "Transnationalizing the Public Sphere: On The Legitimacy and Efficacy of Public Opinion in a Post-Westphalian World." In Nash, *Transnationalizing the Public Sphere*, 8–42.

———. *Unruly Practices: Power, Discourse, and Gender in Contemporary Social Theory*. Minneapolis: University of Minnesota Press and Polity Press, 1989.

Friedland, Roger. "Money, Sex, and God: The Erotic Logic of Religious Nationalism." *Sociological Theory* 203 (2002): 381–425.

"From Our Readers." *Detroit Free Press*, February 2, 1993, 6A.

Fuchs, Esther. Review of *God's Phallus: And Other Problems for Men and Monotheism*, by Howard Eilberg-Schwartz. *Journal of the American Academy of Religion* 65, no. 1 (Spring 1997): 199–201.

Gabriel, Ayala. Review of *The Savage in Judaism: An Anthropology of Israelite Religion and Ancient Judaism*, by Howard Eilberg-Schwartz. *Journal of the American Academy of Religion* 60, no. 1 (Spring 1992): 153–58.

Gayer, Laurent. "The Globalization of Identity Politics: The Sikh Experience." May 2002. Centres d'Etudes et Recherches Internationales, https://www.sciencespo.fr/ceri/sites/sciencespo.fr.ceri/files/artlg_0.pdf, (accessed March 19, 2019)

Geertz, Clifford. "Thick Description: Toward an Interpretive Theory of Culture." In Geertz, *The Interpretation of Cultures: Selected Essays*, 3–30. New York: Basic Books, 1973.

Geller, Jay. "*En Jeu*: Lincoln Logs or Pick-Up Sticks." *Method & Theory in the Study of Religion* 17 (2005): 18–26.

Getty, Mary Ann. Review of *The Illegitimacy of Jesus: A Feminist Theological Interpretation of the Infancy Narratives*, by Jane Schaberg. *Horizons* 16, no. 2 (Fall 1989): 377–78.

Gill, Sam D. "The Academic Study of Religion." In "Settled Issues and Neglected Questions in the Study of Religion," special issue, *Journal of the American Academy of Religion* 62, no. 4 (Winter 1994): 965–75.

———. *Mother Earth: An American Story*. Chicago: University of Chicago Press, 1987.

———. "No Place to Stand: Jonathan Z. Smith as *Homo Ludens*, the Academic Study of Religion *Sub Specie Ludi*." *Journal of the American Academy of Religion* 66, no. 2 (Summer 1998): 283–312.

Girard, René. *I See Satan Fall like Lightning*. Maryknoll, NY: Orbis, 2001.

Girardot, N. J., and Mac Linscott Ricketts, eds. *Imagination and Meaning: The Scholarly and Literary Worlds of Mircea Eliade*. New York: Seabury Press, 1982.

Global Sikh Studies. http://globalsikhstudies.net/. Accessed October 31, 2016.

Gluckman, Max. "Papers in Honor of Melville J. Herskovits: Gossip and Scandal." *Current Anthropology* 4, no. 3 (June 1963): 307–16.

Gold, Daniel. *Aesthetics and Analysis in Writing on Religion: Modern Fascinations*. Berkeley: University of California Press, 2003.

———. Review of *The Construction of Religious Boundaries: Culture, Identity, and Diversity in the Sikh Tradition*, by Harjot Oberoi. *Journal of the American Oriental Society* 116, no. 3 (July–September 1996): 586–87.

Goldsmith, Robert Hillis. *Wise Fools in Shakespeare*. East Lansing: Michigan State University Press, 1955.

Goodstein, Laurie. "Pagans Sue on Emblem for Graves." *New York Times*, September 30, 2006.

Greene, Robert II. "The Urgency of 1990s History." Society for U.S. Intellectual History blog, June 25, 2017. https://s-usih.org/2017/06/the-urgency-of-1990s-history/. Accessed July 9, 2018.

Grewal, J. S. *Contesting Interpretations of the Sikh Tradition*. New Delhi: Manohar, 1998.

———. *Historical Perspectives on Sikh Identity*. Patiala, India: Panjabi University, 1997.

Griffiths, Paul J. "Religion and the Agony of the University." Paper presented at the conference "Studying and Teaching Religion in the Secular University: The End of a Discipline?" at the Humanities Institute of the University of Illinois, Chicago, January 30, 2003.

Grim, John A. "Cultural Identity, Authenticity, and Community Survival: The Politics of Recognition in the Study of Native American Religions." In "To Hear the Eagles Cry: Contemporary Themes in Native American Spirituality," special issue, *American Indian Quarterly* 20, no. 3 (Summer–Autumn 1996): 353–76.

Grimes, Ron. "Teaching Native American Religions." Discussion forum. Posted May 6, 1993. http://puffin.creighton.edu/lakota/teaching.htm. Accessed June 6, 2016.

———. "This May Be a Feud, but It Is Not a War: An Electronic, Interdisciplinary Dialogue on Teaching Native Religions." In "To Hear the Eagles Cry: Contemporary Themes in Native American Spirituality," special issue, *American Indian Quarterly* 20, no. 3 (Summer–Autumn 1996): 433–50.

Gripsrud, Jostein, Hallvard Moe, Anders Molander, and Graham Murdock, eds. *The Idea of the Public Sphere: A Reader*. Lanham, MD: Lexington Books, 2010.

Guinness, Os. "A World Safe for Diversity: Religious Liberty and the Rebuilding of the Public Philosophy." In al-Hibri, Elshtain, and Hays, *Religion in American Public Life: Living with Our Deepest Differences*, 137–52.

Gutmann, Amy. Introduction to Gutmann, *Multiculturalism: Examining the Politics of Recognition*, 3–24.

———, ed. *Multiculturalism: Examining the Politics of Recognition*. Princeton: Princeton University Press, 1994.

Haberman, David. Review of *Kālī's Child*, by Jeffrey Kripal. *Journal of Asian Studies* 56, no. 2 (1997): 531–52.

Habermas, Jürgen. "Religion in the Public Sphere." *European Journal of Philosophy* 14, no. 1 (2006): 1–25.

———. *The Structural Transformation of the Public Sphere: An Inquiry into a Category of Bourgeois Society*. Translated by Thomas Burger and Frederick Lawrence. Cambridge, MA: MIT Press, 1989.

———. *Theory of Communicative Action*, vol. 1, *Reason and the Rationalization of Society*, and vol. 2, *Lifeworld and System: A Critique of Functionalist Reason*. Translated by Thomas A. McCarthy. Boston: Beacon Press; 1981.

Handoca, Mircea. *Mircea Eliade: Contributii bibliografice*. Bucharest: Romanian Relief Literary Society, 1980.

Hankins, Barry. Review of *The University Gets Religion: Religious Studies in American Higher Education*, by D. G. Hart. *Journal of Church and State* 42, no. 3 (Summer 2000): 593–95.

Hardgrave, Robert L., Jr. "An Early Portrayal of the Sikhs: Two 18th Century Etchings by Baltazard Solvyns." *International Journal of Punjab Studies* 3 (1996): 213–27.

Harmon, Jonathan, and James W. Boettcher, eds. "Religion and the Public Sphere," special issue, *Philosophy & Social Criticism* 35, nos. 1–2 (2009).

Harrod, Howard L. Review of *Mother Earth: An American Story* and *Native American Religious Action: A Performance Approach to Religion*, by Sam D. Gill. *Journal of Religion* 68, no. 4 (October 1988): 625–626.

Hart, D. G. *The University Gets Religion: Religious Studies in American Higher Education*. Baltimore: Johns Hopkins University Press, 1999.

Hatcher, Brian. "Kali's Problem Child: Another Look at Jeffrey Kripal's Study of Sri Ramakrishna." *International Journal of Hindu Studies* 3, no. 2 (August 1999): 165–82.

Hawley, John Stratton. "The Damage of Separation: Krishna's Loves and Kali's Child." *Journal of the American Academy of Religion* 72, no. 2 (June 2004): 369–93.

———. "Defamation/Anti-Defamation: Hindus in Dialogue with the Western Academy." Paper presented at the annual meeting of the American Academy of Religion, Denver, Colorado, November 17, 2001.

———. Review of *Kālī's Child*, by Jeffrey Kripal. *History of Religions* 37, no. 4 (1998): 401–4.

Hayes, Glen. Review of *Kālī's Child*, by Jeffrey Kripal. *Religious Studies Review* 23, no. 1 (1997): 95–96.

Haynes, Charles. "From Battle Ground to Common Ground: Religion in the Public Square of 21st Century America." In al-Hibri, Elshtain, and Haynes, *Religion in American Public Life: Living with Our Deepest Differences*, 96–136.

Hearon, Holly. Review of *The Resurrection of Mary Magdalene: Legends, Apocrypha, and the Christian Testament*, by Jane Schaberg. *Review of Biblical Literature*, November 18, 2002, 513–16.

Herman, Jonathan. "Who Cares if the Qur'an is the Word of God? W. C. Smith's Charge to the Aspiring Public intellectual." In *The Legacy of Wilfred Cantwell Smith*, edited by Ellen Bradshaw Aitken and Arvind Sharma, 117–34. Albany: State University of New York Press, 2017.

Hernández-Avila, Inéz. *Reading Native American Women: Critical/Creative Representations*. New York: AltaMira Press, 2005.

Herrera Lima, Maria. "The Anxiety of Contingency: Religion in a Secular Age." In Calhoun, Mendieta, and VanAntwerpen, *Habermas and Religion*, 49–71.

Hirsch, Albert O. *Exit, Voice and Loyalty: Responses to Decline in Firms, Organizations, and States*. Cambridge, MA: Harvard University Press, 1970.

Hobsbawm, Eric, and Terence Ranger, eds. *The Invention of Tradition*. Cambridge: Cambridge University Press, 1983.

Højsgaard, Morten T., and Margit Warburg, eds. *Religion and Cyberspace*. London: Routledge, 2005.

"Home Ministry Bans Publication of 12 Books." *Star*, February 4, 2014. https://www.thestar.com.my/news/nation/2014/02/04/home-ministry-bans-publication-of-12-books. Accessed April 23, 2019.

Hultkrantz, Åke . *Belief and Worship in Native North America*. Syracuse, NY: Syracuse University Press, 1981.

———. Review of *Mother Earth: An American Story*, by Sam D. Gill. *Ethnohistory* 37, no. 1 (Winter 1990): 73–74.

———. "The Religion of the Goddess in North America," in *The Book of the Goddess Past and Present: An Introduction to Her Religion*, edited by Carl Olson, 202–16. New York: Crossroad, 1983.

———. *The Religions of the American Indians*. Berkeley: University of California Press, 1979. Originally published as *De amerikanska indianernas religioner*, 1967.

Idel, Moshe. "The Camouflaged Sacred in Mircea Eliade's Self-Perception, Literature, and Scholarship." In Wedemeyer and Doniger, *Hermeneutics, Politics, and the History of Religions*, 159–96. New York: Oxford University Press, 2010.

Inden, Ron. *Imagining India*. Bloomington: Indiana University Press, 1990.

India Culture. "Propaganda, Mutilation of Hindu History, Faith, Culture & Civilization." http://indiaculture.net/talk/messages/65/1039.html?1121024928. Accessed July 27, 2005.

Indra, Sinha. *The Great Book of Tantra*. South Paris, ME: Park Street Press, 1993.

Irwin, Lee. "Response: American Indian Religious Traditions and the Academic Study of Religion." *Journal of the American Academy of Religion* 66, no. 4 (Winter 1998): 887–92.

Iser, Wolfgang. "The Interplay between Creation and Interpretation." *New Literary History* 15, no. 2 (Winter 1984): 387–95.

Ivanow, Wladimir. "The Importance of Studying Ismailism." *Ilm* 1, no. 3 (March 1976): 8–20.

———. *Ismaili Literature: A Bibliographical Survey.* Tehran: Tehran University Press, 1963.

———. *Ismaili Tradition concerning the Rise of the Fatimids.* London and New York: Oxford University Press, 1942.

Jaimes, M. Annette, and George Noriega. "History in the Making: How Academia Manufactures the 'Truth' about Native American Traditions." *Bloomsbury Review* 4, no. 5 (1988): 24–26.

Jefferds, Keith N. "Vidūṣaka versus Fool: A Functional Analysis." *Journal of South Asian Literature* 16 (1981): 61–73.

Jocks, Christopher. "Response: American Indian Religious Traditions and the Academic Study of Religion: A Response to Sam Gill." *Journal of the American Academy of Religion* 65, no. 1 (Spring 1997): 169–76.

———. Review of *Weaving Ourselves into the Land: Charles Godfrey Leland, "Indians," and the Study of Native American Religions*, by Thomas C. Parkhill. *History of Religions* 39, no. 1 (August 1999): 90–93.

Johnson, Elizabeth. *Quest for the Living God: Mapping Frontiers in the Theology of God.* New York: Continuum Press, 2007.

Johnson, Skip. "Sermon Slams Professor for Corrupting Bible Students." *Charleston* (SC) *Post-Courier*, May 11, 1991.

Jordan, Mark D. *Telling Truths in Church: Scandal, Flesh, and Christian Speech.* Boston: Beacon Press, 2003.

Jordanova, Ludmilla. *History in Practice.* London: Arnold Publishers, 2000.

Juergensmeyer, Mark. *The New Cold War? Religious Nationalism Confronts the Secular State.* Berkeley: University of California Press, 1993.

———. *Religious Nationalism Confronts the Secular State.* Delhi: Oxford University Press, 1993.

Kafka, Alexander C. "Sokal Squared." *Chronicle of Higher Education*, October 3, 2018. https://www.chronicle.com/article/Sokal-Squared-Is-Huge/244714. Accessed October 5, 2018.

Karaflogka, Anastasia. *E-religion: A Critical Appraisal of Religious Discourse on the World Wide Web.* New York: Routledge, 2014.

———. "Religious Discourse and Cyberspace." *Religion* 32, no. 4 (October 2002): 279–91.

Kassam, Tazim R. "Balancing Acts: Negotiating the Ethics of Scholarship and Identity." In Cabezón and Davaney, *Identity and the Politics of Scholarship in the Study of Religion*, 133–62. New York: Routledge, 2004.

———. "Representing Islam: A Critique of Language and Reality." Paper presented at "Perspectives in Islamic Studies" Conference, Institute of Ismaili Studies, London, United Kingdom, August 22–24, 1998.

———. *Songs of Wisdom and Circles of Dance: Hymns of the Satpanth Ismāʿīlī Muslim Saint, Pīr Shams*. Albany, NY: State University of New York Press, 1995.

Kassam, Tazim R., and Françoise Mallison, eds. *Ginans: Texts and Contexts. Essays on Ismaili Hymns from South Asia in Honor of Zawahir Moir*. New Delhi: Primus Books, 2010; originally published 2007.

Katakam, Anupama, and Nandagopal R. Menon. "Politics of a Ban." *Frontline*, February 11–24, 2006. http://www.flonnet.com/fl2303/stories/20060224002609300.htm. Accessed February 23, 2006.

Keenan, James F., SJ. *University Ethics: How Colleges Can Build and Benefit from a Culture of Ethics*. Lanham, MD: Rowman and Littlefield, 2015.

Kesavan, Mukul. "Three Hundred Ramayanas—Delhi University and the Purging of Ramanujan." *Telegraph*, October 27, 2011.

Kidwell, Clara Sue. Review of *Native American Religious Action: A Performance Approach to Religion*, by Sam D. Gill. *American Indian Culture and Research Journal* 11, no. 2 (1987): 97–99.

Kohn, Eric. "A Filmmaker's 'Blues' Prompts Traditionalists to See Red." *Forward*, May 29, 2008.

Kolodny, Annette. *Failing the Future: A Dean Looks at Higher Education in the Twenty-First Century*. Durham: Duke University Press, 2000.

———. "Paying the Price of Antifeminist Intellectual Hrrassment." In *Antifeminism in the Academy*, edited by V. Clark et al., 3–34. New York: Routledge, 1996).

Kovel, Joel. *Overcoming Zionism: Creating a Single Democratic State in Israel/Palestine*. London: Pluto Press, 2007.

Kripal, Jeffrey J. "Comparative Mystics: Scholars as Gnostic Diplomats." *Common Knowledge* 10, no. 3 (2004): 485–517.

———. "Inside-Out, Outside-In: Existential Place and Academic Practice in the Study of North American Guru-Traditions." Paper presented at "Transformative Practices: An Esalen Invitational Conference," Esalen Center for Theory & Research, Big Sur, California, November 28–December 2, 1999.

———. *Kālī's Child: The Mystical and the Erotic in the Life and Teachings of Ramakrishna*. Chicago: University of Chicago Press, 1995.

———. *Kālī's Child: The Mystical and the Erotic in the Life and Teachings of Ramakrishna*. 2nd ed. Chicago: University of Chicago Press, 1998.

———. "Mystical Homoeroticism, Reductionism, and the Reality of Censorship: A Response to Gerald James Larson." *Journal of the American Academy of Religion* 66, no. 3 (Autumn 1998): 627–35.

———. "Psychoanalysis and Hinduism: Re-membering a Presence of Mythological Proportions." In *Religion and Psychology: Mapping the Terrain—Contemporary Dialogues, Future Prospects*, edited by Diane Jonte-Pace and William B. Parsons, 255–79. New York: Routledge, 2000.

———. "Revealing, Concealing and Becoming the Secret: Some Personal Reflections on the Reception of *Kālī's Child*." Paper presented at the University of Pennsylvania, Philadelphia, September 12, 1997.

———. *Roads of Excess, Palaces of Wisdom: Eroticism and Reflexivity in the Study of Mysticism*. Chicago: University of Chicago Press, 2001.

———. "Secret Talk: Sexual Identity and the Politics of Scholarship in the Study of Hindu Tantrism." *Harvard Divinity Bulletin* 29, no.4 (Winter 2000–2001): 14–17.

———. *The Serpent's Gift*. Chicago: University of Chicago Press, 2007.

———. "Teaching the Hindu Tantra with Freud: Transgression as Critical Theory and Mystical Technique." In *Teaching Freud*, edited by Diane Jonte-Pace, 213–37. New York: Oxford University Press, 2003.

———. "Textuality, Sexuality, and the Future of the Past: A Response to Swami Tyagananda." *Evam: Forum on Indian Representations* 1, nos. 1–2 (2002): 191–205.

Kuiper, F. B. J. *Varuṇa and Vidūṣaka: On the Origin of the Sanskrit Drama*. Amsterdam: North-Holland, 1979.

Kukathas, Chandran. "Cultural Toleration." In *Ethnicity and Group Rights*, edited by Will Kymlicka and Ian Shapiro, 69–104. New York: New York University Press, 1997.

Kumar, Girja. *The Book on Trial: Fundamentalism and Censorship in India*. Delhi: Har Anand Publications, 1997.

Laderman, Gary. *Sacred Matters: Celebrity Worship, Sexual Ecstasies, the Living Dead, and Other Signs of Religious Life in the United States*. New York: New Press, 2010.

Lafferty, Theodore T. "A Scandal in Philosophy, or How to Make Philosophy Interesting." *International Journal of Ethics* 43, no. 4 (1933): 439–43.

Laine, James. *Shivaji: Hindu King in Islamic India*. New York: Oxford University Press, 2003.

Landry, David T. "Narrative Logic in the Annunciation to Mary." *Journal of Biblical Literature* 114, no. 1 (1995): 65–79.

Lane, Frederick S. *The Decency Wars: The Campaign to Cleanse American Culture*. Amherst, NY: Prometheus Books, 2006.

Lang, Bernhard. Review of *God's Phallus: And Other Problems for Men and Monotheism*, by Howard Eilberg-Schwartz. *Numen* 39, no. 1 (June 1992): 148–50.

Larson, Gerald. "Polymorphic Sexuality, Homoeroticism, and the Study of Religion." *Journal of the American Academy of Religion* 65, no. 3 (1997): 655–65.

Lawson, E. Thomas. Review of *Beyond the Primitive: The Religions of Nonliterate Peoples*, by Sam D. Gill. *Journal of the American Academy of Religion* 51, no. 3 (September 1983): 531.

Leavelle, Tracy. "The Perils of Pluralism: Colonization and Decolonization in American Indian Religious History." In Bender and Klassen, *After Pluralism*, 156–78.

Lewis, Jerry M. "Comedy and Deviance: The Fatty Arbuckle Case." In *Marginal Conventions: Popular Culture, Mass Media and Social Deviance*, edited by Clinton R. Sanders, 18–28. Bowling Green, OH: Bowling Green State University Popular Press, 1990.

Lie, Rico. *Spaces of Intercultural Communication: An Interdisciplinary Introduction to Communication, Culture and Globalizing/Localizing Identities*. IAMCR book series. New York: Hampton Press, 2003.

Lincoln, Bruce. *Theorizing Myth: Scholarship, Ideology, and Narrative*. Chicago: University of Chicago Press, 1999.

Llewellyn, J. E. Review of *The Construction of Religious Boundaries: Culture, Identity, and Diversity in the Sikh Tradition*, by Harjot Oberoi. *Journal of Religion* 77, no. 1 (January 1997): 182–183.

Lopez, Donald S. *Buddhism and Science: A Guide for the Perplexed*. Chicago: University of Chicago Press, 2008.

———, ed. *Curators of the Buddha: The Study of Buddhism under Colonialism*. Chicago, London: University of Chicago Press, 1995.

MacAuliffe, Max Arthur. *The Sikh Religion: Its Gurus, Sacred Writings, and Authors*. Vol. 1. London: Forgotten Books, 2015.

MacFarquhar, Neil. "At Harvard, Students' Muslim Traditions Are a Topic of Debate." *New York Times*, March 21, 2008.

Mahaprastha, Ajoy. "The Rule of Unreason." *Frontline: India's National Magazine*, November 5–18, 2011. https://frontline.thehindu.com/static/html/fl2823/stories/20111118282312500.htm. Accessed August 3, 2018.

Mahler, Jonathan. "Howard's End: Why a Leading Jewish Studies Scholar Gave Up His Academic Career." *Lingua Franca*, March 1997, 51–57.

Malhotra, Rajiv. "Wendy's Child Syndrome." Sulekha, 2002. http://rajivmalhotra.com/library/articles/risa-lila-1-wendys-child-syndrome/. Accessed October 31, 2016.

Manea, Norman. "Happy Guilt: Mircea Eliade, Fascism, and the Unhappy Fate of Romania." *New Republic*, August 5, 1991, 27–36.

———. "The Incompatibilities." *New Republic*, April 20, 1998, 32–37.

Mann, Barbara Alice. "Where Are Your Women? Missing in Action." In *Unlearning the Language of Conquest: Scholars Expose Anti-Indianism in America*, edited by Don Trent Jacobs, 120–34. Austin, TX: University of Texas Press, 2006.

Mann, Jasbir Singh, Surinder Singh Sodhi, and Gurbakhsh Singh Gill, eds. *Invasion of Religious Boundaries: A Critique of Harjot Oberoi's Work*. Vancouver, BC: Canadian Sikh Study & Teaching Society, 1995. http://www.globalsikhstudies.net/pdf/invasion%20of%20relious.pdf. Accessed July 10, 2016.

Manovich, Lev. *The Language of New Media*. Cambridge, MA: MIT Press, 2001.

Markus, Kinga. Review of *Songs of Wisdom and Circles of Dance: Hymns of the Satpanth Ismāʿīlī Muslim Saint, Pīr Shams*, by Tazim R. Kassam. *Asian Folklore Studies* 55, no. 2 (1996): 386–88. http://ismaili.net/Source/0940b.html. Accessed August 1, 2016.

Martin, Craig. "Genealogies of Religion, Twenty Years On: An Interview with Talal Asad." *Bulletin for the Study of Religion* blog, November 25, 2015. http://bulletin.equinoxpub.com/2015/11/genealogies-of-religion-twenty-years-on-an-interview-with-talal-asad/. Accessed July 15, 2018.

Masuzawa, Tomoko. *The Invention of World Religions; or, How European Universalism Was Preserved in the Language of Pluralism*. Chicago: University of Chicago Press, 2005.

McCarthy, Thomas. "The Burdens of Modernized Faith and Postmetaphysical Reason in Habermas's 'Unfinished Project of Enlightenment.'" In Calhoun, Mendieta, and VanAntwerpen, *Habermas and Religion*, 115–31.

McCracken, Elizabeth. *The Giant's House*. New York: Dial Press, 1996.

McCutcheon, Russell T. "The Category 'Religion' in Recent Publications: A Critical Survey." *Numen* 42, no. 3 (October 1995): 284–309.

———. *Critics Not Caretakers: Redescribing the Public Study of Religion*. Albany: State University of New York Press, 2001.

———. *The Discipline of Religion: Structure, Meaning, Rhetoric*. New York: Routledge, 2003.

———. "'It's a Lie. There's No Truth in It! It's a Sin!' On the Limits of the Humanistic Study of Religion and the Costs of Saving Others from Themselves." Working paper, Department of Religious Studies, University of Alabama, Tuscaloosa, 2006.

———. *Manufacturing Religion: The Discourse on Sui Generis Religion and the Politics of Nostalgia*. New York: Oxford University Press, 1997.

McGraw, Barbara A. "The Doniger Affair: Censorship, Self-Censorship, and the Role of the Academy in the Public Understanding of Religion." American Academy of Religion. https://www.aarweb.org/about/in-the-public-interest-the-doniger-affair. Accessed September 12, 2018.

———. *Rediscovering America's Sacred Ground: Public Religion and Pursuit of the Good in Pluralistic America*. Albany: State University of New York Press, 2003.

McLean, Adrienne L. "The Cinderella Princess and the Instrument of Evil: Surveying the Limits of Female Transgression in Two Postwar Hollywood Scandals." *Cinema Journal* 34, no. 3 (Spring 1995): 36–56.

McLean, Malcolm. Review of *Kālī's Child*, by Jeffrey Kripal. *South Asia: Journal of South Asian Studies*, n.s., 19, no. 1 (June 1996): 116–17.

McLeod, W. H. *The Evolution of the Sikh Community: Five Essays*. New York: Oxford University Press, 1975.

———. Review of *The Construction of Religious Boundaries: Culture, Identity, and Diversity in the Sikh Tradition*, by Harjot Oberoi. *Pacific Affairs* 67, no. 4 (Winter 1994): 615.

McPhail, Clark. *The Myth of the Madding Crowd*. New York: Aldine, 1991.

Mehrotra, Meeta. Review of *The Construction of Religious Boundaries: Culture, Identity, and Diversity in the Sikh Tradition*, by Harjot Oberoi. *Review of Religious Research* 37, no. 3 (March 1996): 281–82.

Mendieta, Eduardo, and Jonathan VanAntwerpen, eds. *The Power of Religion in the Public Sphere*. New York: Columbia University Press, 2011.

Menon, Nandagopal R., "Virtual Assaults." *Frontline: India's National Magazine*, February 11–24, 2006. https://frontline.thehindu.com/static/html/fl2303/stories/20060224002009600.htm. Accessed July 12, 2018.

Mocko, Anne. "Tracing the Red Thread: Anti-Communist Themes in the Work of Mircea Eliade." In Wedemeyer and Doniger, *Hermeneutics, Politics, and the History of Religions*, 285–306. Oxford: Oxford University Press, 2010.

Moir, Zawahir. Review of *Songs of Wisdom and Circles of Dance: Hymns of the Satpanth Ismāʿīlī Muslim Saint, Pīr Shams*, by Tazim R. Kassam. *Bulletin of the School of Oriental and African Studies* 60, no. 2 (1997): 387–88.

Montgomery, Meredith H. "One-Year-Old Program Diversifies Curriculum." *Golden Gater*, May 18, 1995.

Mooney, Carolyn. "Judge Finds No Anti-Christian Bias in Tenure Case." *Chronicle of Higher Education* 41, no. 23 (February 17, 1995): A18.

Mooney, James. *The Ghost-Dance Religion and the Sioux Outbreak of 1890*. Lincoln: University of Nebraska Press, 1991.

Moreno-Riaño, Gerson, ed. *Tolerance in the Twenty-First Century: Prospects and Challenges*. Lanham, MD: Lexington Books, 2006.

Morley, David, and Kevin Robins. *Spaces of Identity: Global Media, Electronic Landscapes and Culture Boundaries*. London and New York: Routledge, 1995.

Morrison, Kenneth K. Review of *Native American Religious Action: A Performance Approach to Religion*, by Sam D. Gill. *Journal of the American Academy of Religion* 61, no. 1 (Spring 1993): 142–144.

Mouffe, Chantal. "Deliberative Democracy or Agonistic Pluralism." December 2000. https://www.ihs.ac.at/publications/pol/pw_72.pdf.

Narayan, Uma. *Dislocating Cultures: Identities, Traditions, and Third World Feminism*. New York: Routledge, 1997.

Nash, Kate. "Toward Transnational Democratization?" In Nash, *Transnationalizing the Public Sphere*, 60–79.

———, ed. *Transationalizing the Public Sphere*. Cambridge, UK, and Malden, MA: Polity Press, 2014.

Negt, Oskar, and Alexander Kluge. *Public Sphere and Experience: Toward an Analysis of the Bourgeois and Proloterian Public Sphere*. Translated by Peter Labanyi. Minneapolis: University of Minnesota Press, 1993.

Neki, J. S. "Studies in Sikhism: A Report on Recent Conferences Abroad." http://www.maboli.com/seva/sikh_review?1994/august_94/REPORT.htm. Accessed July 3, 2016.

Nomani, Asra Q. "You Still Can't Write about Muhammad." *Wall Street Journal*, August 6, 2008. http://online.wsj.com/article/SB121797979078815073.html. Accessed August 21, 2008.

Nongbri, Brent. *Before Religion: A History of a Modern Concept*. New Haven: Yale University Press, 2013.

Novetzke, Christian. *The Quotidian Revolution: Vernacularization, Religion, and the Premodern Public Sphere in India*. New York: Columbia University Press, 2016.

"Now Let It Rest." *Statesman*, February 18, 1997, 10.

Nussbaum, Martha C. *The Clash Within: Democracy, Violence, and India's Future*. Cambridge, MA: Harvard University Press, 2007.

———. *Not for Profit: Why Democracy Needs the Humanities*. Princeton: Princeton University Press, 2010.

Oberoi, Harjot. *The Construction of Religious Boundaries: Culture, Identity, and Diversity in the Sikh Tradition*. Chicago: University of Chicago Press, 1994.

———. "Sikh Fundamentalism: Translating History into Theory." In *Fundamentalisms and the State: Remaking Polities, Economies, and Militance*, edited by Martin E. Marty and R. Scott Appleby, 256–88. Chicago: University of Chicago Press, 1993.

———. "What Has a Whale Got to Do with It? A Tale of Pogroms and Biblical Allegories." In *Sikh Religion, Culture and Ethnicity*, edited by Christopher Shackle, Gurharpal Singh, and Arvind-pal Singh Mandair. New York: Routledge, 2013.

———. "The Worship of Pir Sakhi Sarvar: Illness, Healing and Popular Culture in the Punjab." *Studies in History* 3 (February 1987): 29–55.

Obeyesekere, Gananath. *Medusa's Hair: An Essay on Personal Symbols and Religious Experience*. Chicago: University of Chicago Press, 1981.

O'Hara, Delia. "Mircea Eliade: Some Last Thoughts about Our Relationship with Our Gods, Finding the Sacred in the Profane, and the Value of Crisis in Our Lives, from a World-Renowned Historian of Religions." Interview. *Chicago*, June 1986, 147–51, 177–80.

Olson, Carl. Review of *Kālī's Child*, by Jeffrey Kripal. *International Journal of Hindu Studies* 1, no. 1 (1997): 201–2.

———. "Vivekananda and Ramakrishna Face to Face: An Essay on the Alterity of a Saint." *International Journal of Hindu Studies* 2, no. 1 (1998): 43–66.

Openshaw, Jeanne. Review of *Kālī's Child*, by Jeffrey Kripal. *Times Higher Education Supplement*, December 15, 1995.

Orr, Deborah, Dianna Taylor, Eileen Kahl, Kathleen Earle, Christa Rainwater, and Linda López McAlister, eds. *Feminist Politics: Identity, Difference, and Agency*. Lanham, MD: Rowman & Littlefield, 2007.

Orsi, Robert. "Snakes Alive: Religious Studies between Heaven and Earth." In Orsi, *Between Heaven and Earth: The Religious Worlds People Make and the Scholars Who Study Them*, 177–204. Princeton: Princeton University Press, 2007.

Osiek, Carolyn. "Silent Night." Review of *The Illegitimacy of Jesus: A Feminist Theological Interpretation of the Infancy Narratives*, by Jane Schaberg. *CrossCurrents: The Journal of the Association for Religion and Intellectual Life* 38, no. 3 (1988): 360–61.

"Our Mission." National Council on Public History. http://www.ncph.org. Accessed August 31, 2016.

"Outline for Discussion Leaders." Supplement to "The Muslim World," special issue, *Current Affairs* 10, no. 4 (February 1956).

Padoux, André. Review of *Kālī's Child*, by Jeffrey Kripal. *Archives de sciences sociales des religions* 94 (April–June 1996): 85–86.

Pandian, M. S. S. "Culture and Consciousness: Historiography as Politics." *Social Scientist* 18, nos. 8–9 (August–September 1990): 85–93.

Parikh, J. T. *The Vidushaka: Theory and Practice*. Surat: Chunilal Gandhi Vidyabhavan, 1953.

Parsons, William. "Psychoanalysis and Mysticism: The Case of Ramakrishna." *Religious Studies Review* 23, no. 4 (1997): 355–61.

Patai, Raphael. Review of *The Savage in Judaism: An Anthropology of Israelite Religion and Ancient Judaism*, by Howard Eilberg-Schwartz. *AJS Review* 17, no. 1 (Spring 1992): 91–93.

Patton, Laurie. Review of *Kālī's Child*, by Jeffrey Kripal. *Journal of the History of Sexuality* 7, no. 2 (October 1996): 278–79.

Pensky, Max. "Solidarity with the Past and the Work of Translation: Reflections on Memory Politics and the Post-secular." In Calhoun, Mendieta, and VanAntwerpen, *Habermas and Religion*, 301–21.

Perkins, Pheme. Review of *The Resurrection of Mary Magdalene: Legends, Apocrypha, and the Christian Testament*, by Jane Schaberg. *Theology Today* 60, no. 1 (April 2003): 134.

Perry, Michael J. *Religious Faith and Liberal Democracy*. Cambridge: Cambridge University Press, 2003.

Petreu, Marta. *An Infamous Past: E. M. Cioran and the Rise of Fascism in Romania*. Translated by Bogdan Aldea. Chicago: Ivan R. Dee, 2005.

Pettersson, Olof. *Mother Earth: An Analysis of the Mother Earth Concepts according to Albrecht Dieterich*. Scripta Minora, Regiae Societas Humanorum Litterum Lindensis, 1965–66:3. Lund: CWK Gleerup, 1967.

Pontifical Biblical Commission. "The Interpretation of the Bible in the Church." http://www.bible-researcher.com/catholic-interpretation.html. Accessed October 31, 2016.

Potter, Claire, and Renee Romano, eds. *Doing Recent History: On Privacy, Copyright, Video Games, Institutional Review Boards, Activist Scholarship, and History That Talks Back*. Athens: University of Georgia Press, 2012.

Prasad, Leela. "Co-being, a Praxis of the Public: Lessons from Hindu Devotional (Bhakti) Narrative, Arendt, and Gandhi." *Journal of the American Academy of Religion* 85, no. 1 (March 2017): 199–223.

Prothero, Stephen. "Belief Unbracketed: A Case for the Religion Scholar to Reveal More of Where He or She Is Coming From." *Harvard Divinity Bulletin* 32, no. 2 (Winter/Spring 2004): 16–18.

Radice, William. Review of *Kālī's Child*, by Jeffrey Kripal. *Bulletin of the School of Oriental and African Studies* 61, no. 1 (1998): 160–61.

Rai, Rajesh, and Chitra Sankaran. "Religion and South Asian Diaspora." *South Asian Diaspora* 3, no. 2 (March 2011): 5–13.

Ramanujan, A. K. "Three Hundred Rāmāyaṇas: Five Examples and Three Thoughts on Translation." In *Many Rāmāyaṇas: The Diversity of a Narrative Tradition in South Asia*, edited by Paula Richman, 22–49. Berkeley: University of California Press, 1991.

Ramaswamy, Krishnan, Antonio de Nicolas, and Aditi Banerjee, eds. *Invading the Sacred: An Analysis of Hinduism Studies in America*. Kolkata: Rupa, 2007.

Ramaswamy, Sumathi, ed. *Barefoot across the Nation: Maqbool Fida Husain and the Idea of India*. New York: Routledge, 2011.

Rawls, John. "The Idea of the Public Revisited." In Gripsrud, Moe, Molander, and Murdock, *The Idea of the Public Sphere: A Reader*, 205–34. Originally published in *University of Chicago Law Review* 64 (1997): 765–807.

Reid, Barbara E. Review of *The Illegitimacy of Jesus: A Feminist Theological Interpretation of the Infancy Narratives*, by Jane Schaberg. *Catholic Biblical Quarterly* 52, no. 2 (1992): 364–65.

Reif, S. C. Review of *The Savage in Judaism: An Anthropology of Israelite Religion and Ancient Judaism*, by Howard Eilberg-Schwartz. *Vetus Testamentum* 43, no. 2 (April 1993): 281–82.

Reilly, Frank. "Jane Schaberg, Raymond E. Brown, and the Problem of the Illegitimacy of Jesus." *Journal of Feminist Studies in Religion* 21, no. 1 (Spring 2005): 57–80.

"Reinterpreting the Bible." *Detroit Free Press*, Sunday, February 14, 1993, 1F, 6F.

"Religion and Theology Programs Census." *Religious Studies News*, Fall 2001. https://www.aarweb.org/programs-services/aar-undergraduate-survey-2000. Accessed March 12, 2019.

Rennie, Bryan. "An Encounter with Eliade." In *Encounters with Mircea Eliade*, edited by Mihaela Gligor and Mac Linscott Ricketts, 199–202. Cluj-Napoca: Casa Cărţii de Ştiinţă, 2005.

———. "The Life and Works of Mircea Eliade." In *Encounters with Mircea Eliade*, edited by Mihaela Gligor and Mac Linscott Ricketts, 203–16. Cluj-Napoca: Casa Cărţii de Ştiinţă, 2005.

———. "Mircea Eliade: A Secular Mystic in the History of Religions?" *Origini: Journal of Cultural Studies* 3/4 (2003): 42–54.

———. "Mircea Eliade: 'Secular Mysticism' and the History of Religions." *Religion* 38, no. /4 (2008): 328–337.

"Response." *Harvard Divinity School Newsletter*, September 1964.

Ricketts, Mac Linscott. "Fate in the *Forbidden Forest*." *Dialogue* 8 (1982): 101–19.

———. *Mircea Eliade: Romanian Roots, 1907–1945*, vol. 1. New York: Columbia University Press, 1988.

———. "On Reading Eliade's Stories as Myths for Moderns." Paper presented at the Midwestern Modern Language Association, Cincinnati, Ohio, 1982.

———. "The United States' Response to Eliade's Fiction." In *Changing Religious Worlds: The Meaning and End of Mircea Eliade*, edited by Bryan Rennie, 79–94. Albany: State University of New York Press, 2001.

Robin, Ron. *Scandals and Scoundrels: Seven Cases That Shook the Academy*. Berkeley: University of California Press, 2004.

Roberts, Jon, and James Turner. *The Sacred and the Secular University*. Princeton: Princeton Unversity Press, 2000.

Rockefeller, Steven C. "Comment." In Gutmann, *Multiculturalism: Examining the Politics of Recognition*, 87–98.

Roof, Wade Clark, ed. *Americans and Religions in the Twenty-First Century*. Thousand Oaks, CA: Sage Publications, 1998.

Rosenbaum, Stanley N. Review of *God's Phallus: And Other Problems for Men and Monotheism*, by Howard Eilberg-Schwartz. *AJS Review* 21, no. 1 (1996): 164–66.

Ross-Bryant, Lynn. "The Land in American Religious Experience." *Journal of the American Academy of Religion* 58, no. 3 (Autumn 1990): 333–55.

Roth, Philip. *I Married a Communist*. New York: Vintage, 1998.

Rozehnal, Robert. Review of *Progressive Muslims: On Justice, Gender, and Pluralism*, by Omid Safi. *Future Islam*, November 11, 2004. http://www.futureislam.com/20041101/reviews/rob-rozehnal/Progressive%20Muslims-Review-prn.htm. Accessed August 15, 2016.

Rushdie, Salman. *Shame*. New York: Picador, 1984.

Ryle, Gilbert. "The Thinking of Thoughts: What Is 'Le Penseur' Doing?" 1968. In Ryle, *Collected Essays, 1929–1968*, 494–510. London: Routledge, 2009.

Safi, Omid. *Memories of Muhammad: Why the Prophet Matters*. New York: HarperCollins, 2009.

Said, Edward. *Orientalism*. New York: Vintage Books, 1979.

Schaberg, Jane. "Feminism Lashes Back: Responses to the Backlash." *Bibliocon* 3 (1998): 45–52.

———. "Feminist Interpretations of the Infancy Narrative of Matthew." *Journal of Feminist Studies in Religion* 13, no. 1 (1997): 35–62.

———. *The Illegitimacy of Jesus: A Feminist Theological Interpretation of the Infancy Narratives*. San Francisco: Harper & Row, 1987.

———. *The Resurrection of Mary Magdalene: Legends, Apocrypha, and the Christian Testament*. New York: Continuum, 2004.

Schaberg, Jane, and Melanie Johnson-Debaufre. *Mary Magdalene Understood*. New York: Continuum, 2006.

Scheifinger, Heinz. "Om-line Hinduism: World Wide Gods on the Web." *Australian Religion Studies Review* 23, no. 3 (2010): 325–45.

Schertz, Mary H. Review of *The Illegitimacy of Jesus: A Feminist [Theological] Interpretation of the Infancy Narratives*, by Jane Schaberg. *Journal of the American Academy of Religion* 60, no. 2 (Summer 1992): 358–61.

Schilbrack, Kevin. "The Social Construction of 'Religion' and Its Limits: A Critical Reading of Timothy Fitzgerald." *Method and Theory in the Study of Religion* 24 (2012): 97–117.

Schneider, Nathan. "Spirituality, Entangled: An Interview with Courtney Bender." *Immanent Frame*, June 21, 2010, https://tif.ssrc.org/2010/06/01/spirituality-entangled/. Accessed July 29, 2018.

Schwartz, Howard. "From Seminary to Silicon Valley." Unpublished MS in author's possession.

Schwartz, Stephen. *The Two Faces of Islam: Saudi Fundamentalism and Its Role in Terrorism*. New York: Anchor Books, 2003.

Sen, Amartya. *Identity and Violence: The Illusion of Destiny*. New York: W. W. Norton, 2006.

Sheehan, Bernard W. Review of *Mother Earth: An American Story*, by Sam D. Gill. *Journal of the American Academy of Religion* 56, no. 3 (Autumn 1988): 574–76.

Shields, Rob. "Hypertext Links: The Ethic of the Index and Its Space-Time Effects." In *The World Wide Web and Contemporary Cultural Theory*, edited by Andrew Herman and Thomas Swiss, 145–55. New York and London: Routledge, 2000.

Shorter, David. "Defining the Canon: A Response to Arnal and Gill's 'Approaches to the Study of Religion.'" *Method & Theory in the Study of Religion* 11 (1999): 401–7.

Siegel, Lee. *Laughing Matters: Comic Tradition in India*. Chicago: University of Chicago Press, 1987.

Sil, Narasingha. "The Question of Ramakrishna's Homosexuality." *Statesman*, January 31, 1997.

Singh, Gurdev, ed. *Perspectives on the Sikh Tradition*. Chandigarh: Siddharth Publications for Academy of Sikh Religion & Culture, Patiala, 1986.

Singh, Kharak. "The Punjab Problem and Fundamentalism." *SikhSpectrum.com Monthly*, December 2002.

Singh, Nikky-Guninder Kaur. Review of *The Construction of Religious Boundaries: Culture, Identity, and Diversity in the Sikh Tradition*, by Harjot Oberoi. *Journal of Asian Studies* 55, no. 3 (August 1996): 760–62.

Singh, Pashaura. *The Guru Granth Sahib: Canon, Meaning and Authority*. New Delhi: Oxford University Press, 2000.

———. Review of *Contesting Interpretations of the Sikh Tradition and Historical Perspectives on Sikh Identity*, by J. S. Grewal. *Journal of the American Oriental Society* 120, no. 3 (July–September 2000): 465–68.

———. *Sikhism and History*. Edited by Pashaura Singh and N. Gerald Barrier. New Delhi: Oxford University Press, 2004.

Singh, Pashaura, and N. Gerald Barrier, eds. *The Transmission of Sikh Heritage in the Diaspora*. New Delhi: Manohar, 1996.

———, eds. *Sikh Identity: Continuity and Change*. New Delhi: Manohar, 1999.

Smelser, Neil J. "Some Personal Thoughts on the Pursuit of Sociological Problems." *Sociological Inquiry* 39 (1969): 155–67.

———. *Theory of Collective Behavior*. New York: Free Press, 1962.

Smith, J. Z. "When the Bough Breaks." *History of Religions* 12 (1973): 342–71.

Smith, Wilfred Cantwell. "1983 Presidential Address: The Modern West in the History of Religion." *Journal of the American Academy of Religion* 52, no. 1 (March 1984): 3–18.

———. "Anti-Islamic Bias Shows." *Toronto Globe and Mail*, July 5, 1995.

———. "As Harris Sees It." *Toronto Globe and Mail*, November 27, 1995.

———. "The Christian and the Religions of Asia." Sermon presented at the Sunday morning service at the Canadian Institute of Public Affairs/Canadian Broadcasting Commission Conference, Geneva Park, Lake Couchiching, Ontario, August 9, 1959. Harvard Divinity School Faculty Writings File, bMS 13001/ Smith, W. C., box 1.

———. "The Comparative Study of Religion: Reflections on the Possibility and

Purpose of a Religious Science." Harvard Divinity School Faculty Writings File, bMS 13001/Smith, W. C., box 1.

———. "Faith and Belief: As Seen by a Comparative Religionist." Public lecture at the University of Toronto, January 9, 1968. Harvard Divinity School Faculty Writings File, bMS 13001/Smith, W. C., box 1.

———. "Faith as a Universal Human Quality." Bea Lecture, Woodstock College, New York City, March 18, 1971. Harvard Divinity School Faculty Writings File, bMS 13001/Smith, W. C., box 2.

———. *The Faith of Other Men*. Boston: Dutton Adult, 1963.

———. *Islam in Modern History*. Princeton: Princeton University Press, 1957.

———. Letter to Krister Stendahl, October 7, 1972. W. C. Smith Papers, Oviatt Library, California State University, Northridge.

———. *The Meaning and End of Religion*. Minneapolis, MN: Fortress Press, 1991.

———. Memorandum to D. S. Kothari, August 27, 1965. W. C. Smith Papers, Oviatt Library, California State University, Northridge.

———. *Modern Culture from a Comparative Perspective*. Edited by John W. Burbidge. Albany: State University of New York Press, 1997.

———. *Modernisation of a Traditional Society*. Bombay: Asia Publishing House, 1965.

———. "The Muslim World." *Current Affairs* 10, no. 4 (February 1956): 4–26.

———. *On Understanding Islam*. New York: New American Library of World Literature, 1963.

———. "Orientalism and Truth." Public lecture in honor of T. Cuyler Young, Harvard Divinity School Faculty Writings File, bMS 13001/Smith, W. C., box 2.

———. *Pakistan as an Islamic State*. Lahore: Kashmiri Bazar, 1951.

———. "The Place of Oriental Studies in a Western University." *Diogenes* 4, no. 16 (Winter 1956): 104–11.

———. *On Understanding Islam*, by Wilfred Cantwell Smith. New York: New American Library of World Literature, 1963.

———. "Religious Atheism? Early Buddhist and Recent American." Charles Strong Memorial Lecture, Australia, July 1966. Harvard Divinity School Faculty Writings File, bMS 13001/Smith, W. C., box 1.

———. Review of *The Middle East: Its Religion and Culture*, by Edward J. Jurji. *Canadian Journal of Theology* 4, no. 1 (1959): 68–69.

———. *The Role of Asian Studies in the American University*. Hamilton, NY: Fund for the Study of the Great Religions of the World, Colgate University, 1976. Published after being presented as the plenary address at the New York State Conference for Asian Studies, Colgate University, October 11, 1975.

———. "Secularity and the History of Religion." In *The Spirit and Power of Christian Secularity*, edited by Albert Schlitzer, 33–57. South Bend, IN: University of Notre Dame Press, 1969.

———. "The Teaching of Religion: Academic Rigour, and Personal Involvement." Paper presented to the Canadian Society for the Study of Religion, Carleton

University, Ottawa, Canada, June 12, 1967. Harvard Divinity School Faculty Writings File, bMS 13001/Smith, W. C., box 1.

———. "The Theology of Religions: Participation as a Possible Concept for a Theology of the Religious History of Mankind." Paper submitted for discussion to the Annual Meeting of the American Theological Society, New York, January 1969. Harvard Divinity School Faculty Writings File, bMS 13001/Smith, W. C., box 2.

Sommer, Doris. *The Work of Art in the World: Civic Agency and Public Humanities.* Durham: Duke University Press (2014).

Steiner, Wendy. *The Scandal of Pleasure.* Chicago: University of Chicago Press, 1995.

Stenger, Nicole. "The Mind Is a Leaking Rainbow." In *Cyberspace: First Steps*, edited by Michael Benedikt, 48–57. Cambridge, MA: MIT Press, 1991.

Strate, Lance. "Cybertime." In *Communication and Cyberspace: Social Interaction in an Electronic Environment*, edited by Ronald L. Jacobson and Stephanie Gibson, 370–81. Cresskill, NJ: Hampton Press, 2003.

Strijdom, John. "'Colonialism' and 'Material Culture' in David Chidester's *Oeuvre*." *Religion and Theology* 23, nos. 3–4 (2016): 386–402.

Sullivan, Winnifred. "Religion Naturalized: The New Establishment." In Bender and Klassen, *After Pluralism: Reimagining Religious Engagement*, 82–97.

———. "We Are All Religious Now, Again." *Social Research* 76, no. 4 (2009): 1181–98.

Summer, Doris. *The Work of Art in the World: Civic Agency and Public Humanities.* Durham: Duke University Press, 2014.

Swami Atmajnanananda. "Scandals, Cover-ups, and Other Imagined Occurrences in the Life of Ramakrishna: An Examination of Jeffrey Kripal's *Kālī's Child*." *International Journal of Hindu Studies* 1–2 (August 1997): 401–20.

Swami Tyagananda and Pravrajika Vrajaprana. *Interpreting Ramakrishna: Kālī's Child Revisited.* Delhi: Motilal Banarsidass, 2010.

Taylor, Charles. "The Politics of Recognition." In Gutmann, *Multiculturalism and the Politics of Recognition*, 25–74.

Tweed, Thomas. *Crossing and Dwelling.* Cambridge, MA: Harvard University Press, 2008.

Urban, Hugh. Review of *Kālī's Child*, by Jeffrey Kripal. *Journal of Religion* 78, no. 2 (April 1998): 319.

Vecsey, Christopher. Review of *Mother Earth: An American Story* and *Native American Religious Action: A Performance Approach to Religion*, by Sam D. Gill. *American Indian Quarterly* 12, no. 3 (Summer 1988): 254–56.

Virilio, Paul. "Speed and Information: Cyberspace Alarm!" *CTheory*, August 27, 1995. http://www.ctheory.net/articles.aspx?id=72. Accessed October 31, 2016.

———. *Speed and Politics: An Essay on Dromology.* Translated by Mark Polizzotti. New York: Semiotext(e), 1986.

Wadud, Amina. *Qur'an and Woman: Rereading the Sacred Text from a Woman's Perspective.* New York: Oxford University Press, 1999.

Walker, Steven F. Review of *Kālī's Child* by Jeffrey Kripal. *Religion* 28, no. 2 (1998): 209–11.

Walker, Theodore, Jr. "The 'Mother Earth' Concept in Native America." Discussion forum. Last modified March 24, 1997. http://faculty.smu.edu/twalker/mother4 .htm. Accessed October 10, 2016.

Walzer, Michael. "The Politics of Difference: Statehood and Toleration in a Multicultural World." *Ratio Juris* 10, no. 2 (June 1997): 165–76.

———. "Response to Kukathas." In *Ethnicity and Group Rights*, edited by Will Kymlicka and Ian Shapiro, 105–11. New York: NYU Press, 1997.

———. *Thinking Politically: Essays in Political Theory*. Edited by David Miller. New Haven: Yale University Press, 2007.

Wasserstrom, Steven M. *Religion after Religion: Gershom Scholem, Mircea Eliade, and Henry Corbin at Eranos*. Princeton: Princeton University Press, 1999.

Wax, Murray L. Review of *The Savage in Judaism: An Anthropology of Israelite Religion and Ancient Judaism*, by Howard Eilberg-Schwartz. *Journal for the Scientific Study of Religion* 30, no. 3 (September 1991): 328–29.

Weaver, Jace, ed. *Defending Mother Earth: Native American Perspective on Environmental Justice*. Maryknoll, NY: Orbis Books, 1996.

Wedemeyer, Christian K., and Wendy Doniger, eds. *Hermeneutics, Politics, and the History of Religions: The Contested Legacies of Joachim Wach and Mircea Eliade*. Oxford: Oxford University Press, 2010.

Weinstein, Natalie. "SFSU Dean: Near Eastern Studies Could Ease Tensions." *J. Weekly*, July 21, 1995. http://www.jweekly.com/article/full/1311/sfsu-dean -near-eastern-studies-could-ease-tensions/. Accessed June 4, 2006.

Wiener, Jon. *Historians in Trouble: Plagiarism, Fraud, and Politics in the Ivory Tower*. New York: New Press, 2005.

Wiese, Christian, and Andreas Gotzmann, eds. *Modern Judaism and Historical Consciousness: Identities, Encounters, Perspectives*. Leiden: E. J. Brill, 2007.

Wilcox, Clyde. "Remaking Politics." Review of *Fundamentalisms and the State: Remaking Politics, Economies, and Militance*, by Martin E. Marty and R. Scott Appleby. *Review of Religious Research* 36, no. 4 (June 1995): 396–97.

Wilson, Robin. "A Scholar's Conclusion about Mary Stirs Ire." *Chronicle of Higher Education*, October 6, 1993.

Worthen, Molly. *Apostles of Reason: The Crisis of Authority in American Evangelicalism*. New York: Oxford University Press, 2014.

Zaleski, Jeff. *The Soul of Cyberspace: How New Technology Is Changing Our Spiritual Lives*. New York: Harper Edge, 1997.

Zombietime. "Mohammed Image Archive: The Jyllands-Posten Cartoons." http:// www.zombietime.com/mohammed_image_archive/jyllands-posten_cartoons/. Accessed November 1, 2016.

INDEX

Abu-Lughod, Lila, 241
Alcoff, Linda, 73
Anderson, Gary, 205
Anderson, Janice, 191
Appiah, Kwame Anthony, 11, 71–73, 141–42, 164, 180–81, 198–99, 240
Asad, Talal, 4, 21, 25, 47, 60, 157, 253, 259
Asani, Ali, 175
Axel, Brian, 281n31

Barrier, Gerald N., 152
Bender, Courtney, 22, 24, 274n19
Benjamin, Walter, 45
Bingaman, Kirk, 28
Bohman, James, 4, 8, 59, 74–76, 259–60, 283n15
Boyarin, Jonathan, 206, 220, 260
Brasher, Brenda, 78
Briggs, Charles, 130
Brown, Michael, 140, 266
Brown, Wendy, 4
Brubaker, Rogers, 64–65

Cabezon, Jose, 23
Caldwell, Sarah, 267
Calinescu, Matei, 114
Canagarajah, A. Suresh, 256
Cannon, Katie, 233
Chakrabarty, Dipesh, 149
Chidester, David, 22–23, 251
Churchill, Ward, 12, 130–32, 137

Cohn, Bernard, 149, 201
Connolly, William, 52
controversy, 1, 3–7, 10, 14, 21–29, 130, 142, 143, 52–54, 156, 164, 165–66, 169, 175–76, 179, 181, 193, 198–99, 208, 218–20, 230–34, 236, 241, 249–50, 260, 262, 265–66, 268; idea of, 33–34, 47, 52, 55–56, 36; in 1990s, 74, 79, 122
Corbin, Henri, 44–45, 107, 131, 171
Courtright, Paul, 131, 267, 69
Crenshaw, Kimberlé, 283n32

Damrosch, David, 249
Davaney, Sheila, 23
Deloria, Vine, 12, 132–38
Dewey, John, 274n19
Dhillon, Gurdashan, Singh, 155, 159
Dirks, Nicholas, 55–56, 278n55
Doniger, Wendy, 115, 232, 267, 301–2n11
drama: classical, 16, 44, 246–47; Native American, 122; political, 26, 44–47, 245
Dubuisson, Daniel, 21
Durham, 74

Eliade, Mircea, 11, 44–46, 77, 85–86, 97–118, 124, 166, 200, 241, 265; Eliadean perspective, 142, 182, 221
Ellis, Joseph, 36
Ellis, M. H., 267
Esposito, John, 266

Feeley-Harnik, Gillian, 205
feminism: and biblical criticism, 185, 191, 193–94, 199, 207; and study of religion, 27, 53, 181, 196–97, 201, 256, 259, 267, 283n32, 294n23
Fine, Gary, 34, 55, 276n33
Finkelstein, Norman, 267
Fishbane, Michael, 207
Fitzgerald, Timothy, 21–22
fool, as metaphor in study of religion, 16, 25, 27, 44, 64, 246–49, 253
Forbes, Bruce, 126
Fraser, Nancy, 8, 22, 49, 52, 57, 59, 73, 75, 85, 126–27, 129, 143, 166, 171, 183, 185, 221, 235, 279n8
Fraserian idea of public sphere, 52–54, 66–67, 245, 260
Friedland, Roger, 64
Fuchs, Esther, 204

Gabriel, Ayala, 206–7, 220
Gayer, Laurent, 65, 239
Gill, Samuel, 12, 55, 62, 78, 121, 129–51, 153, 160, 66, 171–73, 189, 213, 226, 236, 247–48, 260, 264, 267–68
Girard, Rene, 42, 278n53
Gluckman, Max, 275–76n30
Gold, Daniel, 151–52
Goldsmith, Robert, 246
Greene, Robert, 7
Grewal, J. S., 152–55
Grimes, Ron, 78, 133–139, 142, 221
Guinness, Os, 257

Haberman, David, 227
Habermas, Jürgen, 4, 7–8, 16, 26, 28, 49–61, 87, 258, 263; Habermasian idea of public sphere, 10, 24, 57–59, 71, 84, 140, 180, 185, 198, 218, 239, 245
Handoca, Mircea, 97
Harrod, Howard, 126
Hart, D. G., 273n7
Hatcher, Brian, 226, 231, 236
Hawley, John Stratton, 231, 236
Hayes, Glen, 227
Haynes, Charles, 257
Herman, Jonathan, 97

Hernandez-Avila, Inez, 266
Herrera Lima, Maria, 8, 57, 59
Hirsch, Albert, 260
Hobsbawm, Eric, 130
Hultkrantz, Åke, 124, 127

Idel, Moshe, 97, 104
Inden, Ron, 149
internet, 3, 6, 10–11, 14, 15, 36, 38, 51, 54; as alternative world, 213–16, 221; as public space, 74–76, 78; readerships in, 6, 49; and religion, 78, 84, 118, 133–39, 159–61, 175, 236–38, 241, 247, 249; rise of, 51, 67, 70, 256
Irwin, Lee, 127, 129
Ivanow, Wladimir, 171, 175

Jaimes, Annette, 129–30, 132
Jocks, Christopher, 127–29
Johnson, Elizabeth, 267
Jordan, Mark, 43–44, 278n53
Jordanova, Ludmilla, 63

Karaflogka, Anastasia, 76–77
Kassam, Tazin, 13, 55, 62, 79–81, 163–64, 166, 169–84, 239, 240, 252, 256, 258–59
Kolodny, Annette 197
Kovel, Joel 267
Kripal, Jeffrey, 14–15, 33, 55, 62, 65, 78–79, 81, 159, 164, 201–2, 204, 218, 220, 222, 223–41, 252, 256, 258–60, 279n61

Laderman, Gary, 23
Laine, James, 267
Landry, David, 191–93
Lane, Frederick, 69, 282nn6–7
Lang, Bernhard, 205
Larson, Gerald, 229
Leavelle, Tracy, 266
liberal arts, 6, 199, 253
liberalism, in study of religion, 2–3, 8, 10–11, 21, 32, 37, 51, 53, 86, 96–97, 114–17, 132, 218, 241, 257–58, 266
liberal paradox, 2, 16, 22, 24, 32, 37, 117, 221–22, 241, 248
Lie, Rico, 83

life-script,11, 71–73, 164, 180–81, 199,
    219, 240, 256; definition, 71–72
Llewellyn, J. E., 150

MacAuliffe, Max Arthur, 152
Mahaprastha, Ajoy
Mahler, Jonathan, 220
Mann, Barbara Alice, 131
Mann, Gurinder Singh, 158, 266
Mann, Jasper Singh, 159
Markus, Kinga, 174
Marxism, 50, 87–88, 92, 105–6, 110, 116,
    149, 210
Masuzawa, Tomoko, 21, 24
McCarthy, Thomas, 16, 65
McCracken, Elizabeth, 275n29
McCutcheon, Russell, 22–23, 128, 250–
    51, 273n10
McGraw, Barbara, 282n8
McLean, Malcolm, 227
McCleod, W. H., 151–54, 157–58, 266
Mehrotra, Meeta, 150
Mocko, Anne, 105–6
Moir, Zawahir, 174–75
Mooney, James, 123
Morley, David, 69
Mouffe, Chantal, 258
multiculturalism: and politics of recogni-
    tion, 3, 6, 10–11, 49, 65, 67–68, 78, 82,
    94, 155, 157, 165, 178, 181, 220, 256;
    theory of, 8, 55, 67–68

Narayan, Uma, 79–82, 142, 164, 182, 240
Nash, Kate, 56
Negt, Oskar, 50
Nongbri, Brent, 21

Oberoi, Harjot, 12–13, 15, 55, 70, 87–89,
    153–74, 185, 188–90, 203, 209, 221,
    226–27, 230, 244, 246–48, 260, 266–68
Obeyesekere, Gananath, 225
Olson, Carl, 227–28
Openshaw, Jeanne, 226
Orsi, Robert, 23–24

Padoux, André, 227
Pandian, M. S. S., 149–50,

Parsons, William, 227–28
Patai, Raphael, 207
Pensky, Max, 59, 218, 263, 280n17
Pettersson, Olof, 121
postcoloniality: and biblical herme-
    neutics, 199, 229; and controversies
    in the study of religion, 44, 78–79;
    and Hindu identity, 240, 245, 248;
    and Ismaili identity, 183; and Native
    American identity, 140; and publics
    spheres and spaces, 64–67, 78, 84; and
    Sikh identity, 158, 165–66; theory of,
    79–82, 281n30, 300n1, 300nn4–5
Potter, Claire, 5
Prasad, Leela, 259
Prothero, Stephen, 24
public sphere: and internet, 74–76;
    and multiculturalism, 69, 82; and
    1990s, 69–71; in study of religion,
    3–9, 10–12, 15–16, 24, 51–52, 57–59,
    60–61, 63, 73, 86, 88, 97–98, 100, 103,
    108, 115–18, 122, 126–27, 129, 132,
    142–43, 145, 150, 154, 165–66, 169,
    171, 175, 177, 181, 183, 185, 193, 196,
    200–201, 209, 211, 213, 220–21, 228–
    30, 234–36, 238, 241, 245–46, 248, 250,
    255–62; theory of, 4, 7–8, 11, 26–27,
    32, 37, 49–51, 52–55, 56–57, 62, 67,
    255–62
public space, eruptive: definition of, 60,
    62; and history, 61–63; and internet,
    74–76; and postcoloniality, 64–66; and
    sexuality, 63–64; in study of religion,
    9–11, 15–16, 26–28, 36–37, 49, 66–68,
    74–76, 82–86, 97, 118, 121, 141–43,
    166, 183, 198–99, 210, 221, 234, 236,
    241, 245–46, 248, 252, 257–62, 268

Radice, William, 231, 235
Ramaswamy, Sumathi, 266
Rawls, John, 51–53, 57, 70
religion, study of, 12, 19–21, 29–34, 36,
    39; and feminism, 198; and institu-
    tions, 250–54; and Ismaili traditions,
    177; and Judaism, 207–8, 213; and
    Native American traditions, 120–28,
    141–42, 150, 158, 177; and political

religion, study of (*cont.*)
   drama, 44–47; and public spaces, 255–63; and public sphere, 50, 77, 85–86, 102; and scandal, 2, 4, 9, 15, 39–47, 50, 55, 63, 85, 186, 190, 204, 208, 218, 230, 245, 247–48, 254, 260; and Sikhism, 150, 158, 177
Rennie, Bryan, 98
Reilly, Frank, 199
Ricketts, Mac Linscott, 98
Robin, Ron, 36–38, 277n40, 277n44
Rosenbaum, Stanley, 204, 208
Ross-Bryant, Lynn
Roth, Philip, 34
Rushdie, Salman, 13, 32, 97, 157, 169, 176
Ryle, Gilbert, 277n47

Safi, Omid, 266
Said, Edward, 157
secularism: idea of, 4, 6, 8–9, 29–31, 57–60, 61, 64, 71, 74, 87, 95, 245, 250; and study of religion, 3–4, 21, 64, 66, 82, 95–96, 108–9, 116–17, 129, 149, 153, 156, 163, 165–66, 180, 193, 198–99, 216, 218, 221, 235, 239, 241, 251–53, 261, 267–68
scandal, idea of, 10–12, 14, 19, 21, 23, 23–39, 55–56, 66, 134
Schwartz, Howard (Eilberg), 14–15, 62, 73, 78–79, 82, 64–65, 182, 201–22, 240, 245, 252, 256, 259–60, 266, 281n30, 296nn22–25
Scholem, Gershom, 44–45, 107, 179, 187
Schaberg, Jane, 13–14, 62, 78–79, 82, 157, 163, 181, 183, 185–200, 202, 219, 252, 256, 259, 267
Schertz, Mary H., 191
Schwartz, Stephen, 266
Sen, Amartya, 83

Sil, Narasingha, 227–28, 231
Singh, Gurdev, 153
Singh, Kharak, 153, 159
Singh, Nikky-Guninder Kaur, 155
Singh, Pashaura, 152, 154, 158, 266
Smelser, Neil J., 276n33
Smith, W.C., 11, 85, 86–97, 98, 101–2, 112, 115–16, 143, 166, 183, 200, 221, 241, 265, 285nn26–28
Steiner, Wendy, 32, 248
Swami Atmajnanananda, 228–30
Swami Tyagananda, 233, 235–36, 238

Taylor, Charles, 8, 57, 67–68, 178
Tweed, Thomas, 9, 27–28, 118, 246, 251

university: and communities, 16, 35, 41, 62–63, 86; and Eliade, 98, 112–14; and Ismaili identity, 177, 182; and Hindu identity, 237–38, 267; history of, 21, 44; and Jewish identity, 209–11, 213, 218–19, 267; and Native American identity, 143, 266; and publics, 39, 51, 55–56, 66; and Roman Catholica iden-tity, 185, 195–200, 267; and scholars of religion, 261–62; and Sikh identity, 145–46, 155–56, 158–59, 165–67, 241; and W. C. Smith, 92–96; and study of religion, 2, 4, 16, 246, 250–58, 268
Urban, Hugh, 227, 230, 235

Vecsey, Christopher, 126

Wadud, Amina, 266
Walker, Steven F., 231
Walzer, Michael, 37, 277n41
Wasserstrom, Steven, 44–47, 107, 279n61
Wax, Murray, 207–8, 220
Wedemeyer, Christian K., 115